HOW BRITAIN WON THE WAR OF 1812

The Royal Navy's Blockades of the United States,
1812 – 1815

HOW BRITAIN WON THE WAR OF 1812

The Royal Navy's Blockades of the United States, 1812 – 1815

Brian Arthur

THE BOYDELL PRESS

First published 2011
The Boydell Press, Woodbridge

ISBN 978 1 84383 665 0

The Boydell Press is an imprint of Boydell & Brewer Ltd
PO Box 9, Woodbridge, Suffolk IP12 3DF, UK
and of Boydell & Brewer Inc.
668 Mount Hope Ave, Rochester, NY 14620, USA
website: www.boydellandbrewer.com

A catalogue record for this book is available
from the British Library

The publisher has no responsibility for the continued existence or accuracy of URLs for
external or third-party internet websites referred to in this book, and does not
guarantee that any content on such websites is, or will remain, accurate or appropriate.

Papers used by Boydell & Brewer Ltd are natural, recyclable products
made from wood grown in sustainable forests

Designed and typeset by Tina Ranft, Woodbridge, Suffolk
Printed and bound in the United States of America

For Jacqueline

CONTENTS

LIST OF ILLUSTRATIONS

FIGURES

COVER

'A Naval Brig Pursuing another Brig', by Thomas Butterworth (1768–1842)
© Bridgeman Art Library: REA197505

MAPS

Maps reproduced by kind permission of Nicola Lidgett

LIST OF TABLES

ACKNOWLEDGEMENTS

My sincere thanks are due to my editor Peter Sowden, of Boydell and Brewer, and to my erstwhile PhD supervisors, Professor Sarah Palmer, Director of the Greenwich Maritime Institute, and Professor Roger Knight. I am grateful to Professor Andrew Lambert of King's College London for his encouragement throughout, and for writing the Foreword. I would also like to thank Dr Ned Wilmott and Dr Clive Wilkinson for their early suggestions and enthusiasm, and Dr Peter LeFevre for several useful discussions. Thanks must go too to my friend Chris Ware for his encouragement from the outset, including the long-term loan of essential and often valuable books, and for reading a draft.

I am particularly grateful to Faye Kert, who kindly sent me from Canada a copy of her list of British prizes sent into Halifax, Nova Scotia, during the war, now in her *Prize and Prejudice: Privateering and Naval Prize in Atlantic Canada in the War of 1812*, published in 1997. Her adapted findings, shorn of the activities of privateers, helped to measure the efficiency of the Royal Navy's blockades of the United States.

Nicola Lidgett provided the maps, while Reginald Stafford-Smith, 'former naval person', friend and neighbour, read several drafts with his relentless eye for detail; I am grateful to both, and to the staff of the Dreadnought Library of the University of Greenwich and the Caird Library of the National Maritime Museum in London. My thanks are also due to the librarians of the Institute of Historical Research in London, The National Archives at Kew, the British Library at both Euston and Colindale and the London School of Economics. I was especially impressed by the helpful staff of the Brynmor Jones Library of the University of Hull, who were at the time of my research there wrestling with the consequences of a serious flood, and of the Huntington Library in San Marino, California, who were in the throes of rehousing their entire collection.

I am grateful to Charles Consolvo, former student of the Greenwich Maritime Institute at the University of Greenwich, and his Admiral Sir John Chambers-White Bursary for its funding of an important week's work in the National Library of Scotland in Edinburgh. I am indebted also to Dr Julian Gwyn for sharing his knowledge of New World resources.

The opportunity to see vital American primary sources, both manuscript and printed, was made possible with the help of Dr Nigel Rigby, Head of Research, and Janet Norton at the National Maritime Museum in London, and with the award of the Caird North America Research Fellowship, which so generously provided the travel, subsistence and accommodation funds for a three-month research visit to the United States. This work could not have been completed without access to the extensive Brown and Ives Archive, correspondence held in the John Carter Brown Library in Providence, Rhode Island. I was particularly grateful to Mrs Sylvia Brown, a member of the Brown family of Providence and London, who took time from her own research to point me in the right direction, and to Director Dr Ted Widmer and the staff, as well as the international group of other Research Fellows.

My wife and I remain grateful for the generous hospitality of the people we met in Providence, RI, especially that of Rick and Roxanne Sasse, for much transport, including sailing from Newport into Buzzard's Bay, and some unforgettable meals. My thanks are due also to the staff of the Rockerfeller and John Hay libraries in Providence, and especially to Philip Weimerskirk, keeper of Special Collections in Providence Public Library, for his help and flexible closing times, and to the staff of the New York Historical Society, Washington's Library of Congress, the US Coast Guard Academy Library in New London, Connecticut, and the Research Library of the Whaling Museum in New Bedford, Massachusetts. Such help and hospitality made the War of 1812 seem even more regrettable. Needless to say, any mistakes made in interpreting the information gathered are my own.

My family have borne my obsession with stoicism and patient forbearance, and I am indebted to them for this. Most of all, however, my thanks are due to my wife, without whose support and encouragement none of this would have been possible.

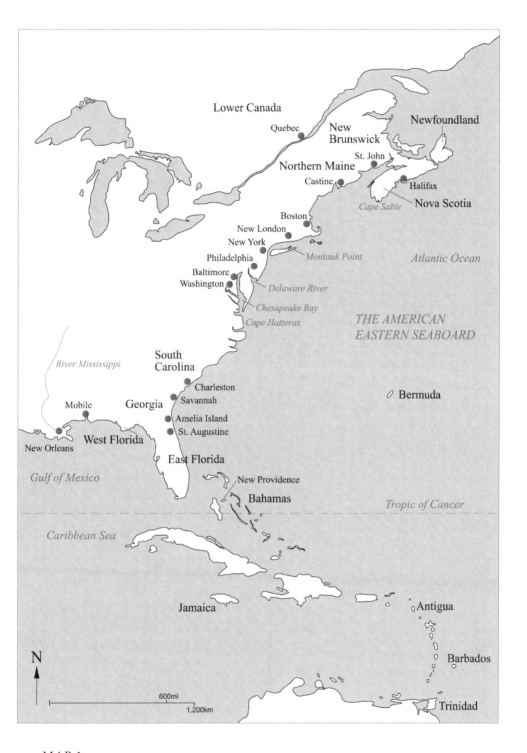

MAP 1.
The American Eastern Seaboard, Gulf of Mexico and Caribbean Sea

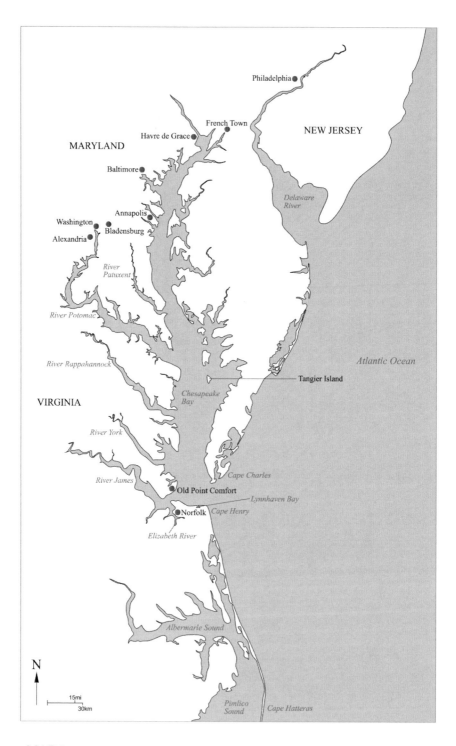

MAP 2.
Chesapeake Bay and the Delaware River

ABBREVIATIONS

AC	*Annals of Congress*
ASP: C	American State Papers: IX, Claims
ASP: C&N	American State Papers: IV, Commerce and Navigation, 2 vols
ASP: F	American State Papers: III, Finance, 5 vols
ASP: FR	American State Papers: I, Foreign Relations, 6 vols
ASP: NA	American State Papers: VI, Naval Affairs
ASP: M	American State Papers: X, Miscellaneous
BJL	Brynmor Jones Library
BL	British Library
BL C	British Library Newspaper Collection, Colindale, London
FCO	Foreign and Commonwealth Office Library, London
GP	Gallatin Papers. Correspondence of Albert Gallatin, held in New York Historical Society, New York
IHR	Institute of Historical Research, University of London
JCBL	John Carter Brown Library, Providence, Rhode Island
JHL	John Hay Library, Providence, Rhode Island
LBK/2	Correspondence between Admiral Sir John Borlase Warren, and Lord Melville, held in Caird Library, National Maritime Museum, Greenwich, London
LC	Library of Congress, Washington DC
NC	*Naval Chronicle*, vols 28–33
NLS	Correspondence of Vice Admiral Sir Alexander Cochrane, held in National Library of Scotland, Edinburgh
NMM	National Maritime Museum, Greenwich, London, Caird Library
NYHS	New York Historical Society, New York
ODNB	*The Oxford Dictionary of National Biography*
TNA	The National Archives, Kew, Surrey

NOTE ON US DOLLAR/POUND STERLING CONVERSION RATES, 1803–1815

An exchange rate agreed between the British and American governments on 16 September 1803 of $4.44 to the pound sterling seems to have remained relatively stable between 1812 and 1815, and has been used throughout.

Source: Foreign Secretary Lord Hawksberry to Anthony Merry, British Minister at Washington, 16 September 1803, in B. Mayo, ed., *Instructions to British Ministers to the United States 1791–1812*, 3 vols, Washington DC, Annual Report of the American History Association, 1936, vol. III, p. 200.

All quotations retain the original spelling and punctuation.

FOREWORD

Andrew Lambert, Laughton Professor of Naval History in the Department of War Studies, King's College, London

AFTER TWO CENTURIES of almost complete neglect British historians have finally turned their attention to the Anglo-American War of 1812, the 'other' war that raged alongside the later stage of the Great War against Napoleonic France. While little more than a distracting, annoying side-show for the British, the American war threatened the security of Canada, a large imperial territory with important timber and shipbuilding resources, the economic livelihood of the West Indian colonies, and the balance of power on the North American continent. In order to defeat the American invasion of Canada Britain needed a strategy that would be cheap, effective and successful.

In this essential book Brian Arthur shifts the historical focus away from the obvious military highlights – the land war in Canada, heroic naval combat on the broad Atlantic, the destruction of Washington DC and the defence of New Orleans – to the subtler basis of British strategy. He demonstrates that the key offensive asset in the British armoury was economic warfare, conducted by naval blockades and prize courts. This was the classic strategy of seapower, and it reflected long experience. The lessons of the American Revolutionary War had been clear enough: Britain could not defeat America while it was heavily engaged in an existential war with other major powers. Many British decision-makers had experience of the earlier conflict – some, like Admiral Sir Alexander Cochrane, had lost a brother.

In 1812 British economic warfare policy, fine-tuned by twenty years of near-continuous war against Revolutionary and Napoleonic France, was truly formidable. Statesmen, admirals, captains and judges understood the issues; most had known nothing but war all their adult lives; and most were thoroughly professional. Indeed, the ostensible cause of war, restraints on maritime trade and the impressment of seafarers, were essential to the success of economic war against France. Little wonder the British Government refused to compromise on impressment, merely extending the blockade war to America once the Madison administration had rejected British attempts to restore peace. The British did so, as Brian Arthur shows, well aware of the weaknesses, sectional tensions and stresses within the American body politic, democracy, a free press and frequent visitors ensuring a ready flow of intelligence across the Atlantic. War had been likely since 1807, so no one was unduly surprised, or short of a solution.

More significantly, as this book demonstrates, the United States Government invaded Canada without the fiscal means to wage war beyond a year, or at most two. By contrast, the British fiscal system, based on domestic taxes, secure loans and expanding trade, enabled the state to fight for decades, having blocked the initial American offensive. Once the British blockade began American federal revenues, almost entirely drawn from import duties, dried up, along with inter-state trade. All this had been predicted by Albert Gallatin (Secretary of the US Treasury 1801–14), but his warnings had been ignored by President Madison and the land-hungry 'War-Hawk' Congress that voted for conflict. By mid-1814 the United States was fast running out of money and credit. The capture of Washington DC prompted a run on the major domestic banks, much of the capital fled to Canada and the year ended in national bankruptcy – in November the United States Government defaulted on interest payments and loans. British economic warfare cut the sinews of American military power and forced Washington to make peace. In the end America was fortunate to get out of the war on the terms that were available in October 1812.

British victory was moderated by wider concerns to cut expenditure after twenty-two years of total war, to stabilise Europe at the Congress of Vienna and to resume trade with a major economic partner. America was a vital cog in the international trading system that propelled the British economy. Furthermore, the British had no interest in reversing the judgment of 1782: this was no 'Second War of Independence' – after all, America invaded British territory, not the other way round. Although the two economies had been closely connected the British were able to find alternative sources of supply and new markets for their exports. For the United States the position was very different. Jefferson's Embargo Act had already demonstrated the catastrophic effects of trying to influence British behaviour, and forewarned London of the likely consequences of war.

Intelligent, targeted economic warfare enabled Britain to fight the United States to a standstill with a fraction of its armed forces, without compromising the total war effort against Napoleonic France. After 1815 the strategic and economic relationship between the two powers reflected the lessons of the war and growing structural divergence. After a brief efflorescence the American maritime sector steadily declined in absolute and relative terms. As new lands were added the nation became continental, focused on the internal frontier. As a result the United States Government spent a fortune fortifying every port city on the entire coast from Maine to the Mississippi, and improving inland communications: it did not challenge the Royal Navy's dominance of the Atlantic and the Western Hemisphere. In consequence any resumption of hostilities in the next seventy years would have resulted in a British economic blockade. Without the military resources to defend Canada, and heavily involved in the politics of Europe and Asia, Britain had to rely on the proven economic weapon. Without an overwhelming military force British crisis diplomacy had to make its point with a degree of subtlety. In 1833 they sent Admiral Sir George Cockburn, with his Flag in HMS *President*, to head the North American Station: combining the man who burnt the White House with the greatest British prize of the war made the point. In the next crisis the British Government dispatched Alexander Baring, scion of a great banking house that held a large part of the American national debt, to discuss the frontier of Maine. If the symbols of British power were warships, the sinews were, as ever, economic. In each Anglo-American crisis a compromise settlement was found, despite deeply antagonistic views, because the commercial and territorial benefits of a highly unlikely victory for either side would have been outweighed by the inevitable damage to trade, while providing unwelcome opportunities for other powers to interfere. In essence the *status quo ante bellum* agreed in 1814 at the Treaty of Ghent was the most likely outcome of any renewed struggle. Little wonder America was careful not to challenge the few British vital interests in the Western Hemisphere, while Britain did not stand in the way of American expansion against third parties. So potent was the lesson that in 1861 the Federal Government adopted British economic blockade practice to crush the Confederacy. The lessons of 1812 conditioned Anglo-American relations right down to 1914, when President Woodrow Wilson decided that challenging British economic war strategy risked aligning America with Germany, the new European hegemon. In two world wars America waged economic war with well-honed British tools, the critical element in allied victory.

By shifting the academic focus from battle and glory to the slow grinding wheels of economic attrition Brian Arthur has refreshed the literature on the War of 1812 just in time for the bicentenary. There will be few more significant contributions to the discussion.

PREFACE

THIS BOOK STUDIES PART OF BRITAIN'S early-nineteeth-century supremacy at sea and the Royal Navy's use of maritime blockades and convoys as economic warfare against a United States republic not yet thirty years old. It is not a general history of the War of 1812; rather, it briefly traces the evolution of both offensive and defensive economic warfare at sea, and then examines Britain's aggressive use of commercial and naval blockades, and the protective use of merchant convoys, during it. This strategy had evolved during a succession of wars, and was to prove particularly successful when used by Britain in the Anglo-American war of 1812–15 – the so-called 'War of 1812'. This was, in effect, part of Britain's long-term war with France, declared by the French Revolutionary government in February 1793 and continued by Napoleon until his downfall. Apart from a brief respite during the Peace of Amiens, between March 1802 and May 1803, it was to last until the autumn of 1815, when Napoleon was finally and permanently exiled on St Helena.

During Britain's war with France French military successes in Continental Europe could be contained only by British seapower. Britain possessed not only the world's largest merchant fleet but also the Royal Navy, the world's strongest maritime fighting force. Britain's maritime commercial blockade of France had isolated her colonies, dislocated her overseas trade and seriously damaged the French economy, while the Royal Navy's blockades of French ports had prevented the amalgamation of France's Brest and Toulon fleets, making the invasion of Britain impracticable and the military reinforcement of French colonies extremely difficult.

But the exercise of British seapower against the French increasingly resulted in conflict with neutral maritime countries, including the United States. The American merchant fleet had expanded rapidly since 1800 to become the second largest in the world, and threatened to replace blockaded French trading vessels. American naval forces had also gained confidence in a successful, although undeclared, sea war with France between 1798 and 1800. Britain's 'impressment' – the enforced recovery of apparently renegade British seamen from American merchant vessels – increased the tension already generated by the Royal Navy's practice of stopping neutral vessels at sea and searching for what Britain defined as 'contraband', otherwise bound for France. These difficulties, unresolved by diplomacy, eventually led to a war which some Americans thought could lead to a United States occupation of Canada and an end to British maritime supremacy in North America. In the long run, such American war aims took insufficient account of British maritime blockades.

Congress and President James Madison had declared war on Britain in June 1812. On land American hopes were not realised. In 1812 Canadian militia and British regular troops were to defeat American invasions of Canada at Detroit, Niagara and beside Lake Champlain. At sea, after several early disappointments, a series of victories in single-combat against Royal Naval vessels in 1812 raised American morale. By the summer of 1814, with Napoleon temporarily dealt with in Europe, the British captured Washington and Alexandria, although by the end of the year the Americans had successfully defended both Baltimore and New Orleans. American naval successes on the Lakes, and a lack of British decisiveness, made a British invasion of the United States from the North unrealistic. But, especially since the spring of 1813, the British blockades had stifled both domestic and overseas American trade and had penned in much of the United States Navy, which was unable as a result to prevent the financial and economic consequences of the British commercial blockade of the United States.

The American Atlantic seaboard provides the best evidence of the effectiveness of the Royal Navy's wartime blockades of the United States. Most densely populated, it provided most of the United States' tax revenue, and it was from the wealthy farmers, merchants and bankers of the Atlantic ports and their hinterland that the Madison administration would increasingly need to borrow to finance the war. The British maritime commercial blockade of Chesapeake Bay and the Delaware River was ordered as soon as November 1812, but even after March 1813, when it was widened to include the Mississippi delta, that of the Atlantic seaboard remained crucial. It now also included New York, the biggest single source of American customs revenue.

In an attempt to widen the political differences between New England and the rest of the Union, the Royal Navy's commercial blockade initially excluded New England's busy and prosperous ports, where many merchants and shippers had long been vehemently opposed to the prospect of war with the United States' major trading partner. Their opposition remained outspoken even after the war began, despite its benefiting them financially. Only after late April 1814 was the British maritime commercial blockade extended to New England, in order to prevent the use of its ports by neutral merchant vessels adding to American customs revenues.

Trustworthy evidence of British commercial blockade in the Caribbean is harder to come by, and documentary records less readily available. Contemporary newspapers, and sometimes secondary sources, are often less reliable. Nevertheless, the totals of American vessels captured in the Caribbean and the Gulf of Mexico and taken into such British Caribbean ports as Antigua and Jamaica were later provided to Parliament by the port's Vice-Admiralty Courts and included in final figures published at the end of the war.

The profit-seeking activities of British, Canadian and American privateers, which generally concentrated on smaller prizes and were often not fully reported to their respective governments, are not recounted here. The official totals of all privateer's captures are, however, included in the final comparisons of British and American prize-taking.

The role of the relatively small United States Navy is fully recognised, and the impact of its successes, both at sea and on the Lakes, considered, as are the severe difficulties imposed on it by the British *naval* blockade, which increasingly confined it to port. This incarceration increasingly gave the British unhindered access to the American shoreline, and made possible intrusive and damaging amphibious operations. These included the British capture of Washington in August 1814, with its profound fiscal and financial implications. At the same time the lack of an American maritime supremacy on the St Lawrence made the United States' ambitions for the occupation of Canada wholly unrealistic, despite a tactical American naval victory on Lake Erie in September 1814.

The practical problems of maritime blockades, both naval and commercial, are also reviewed, along with the extent to which solutions could be found. The long-standing question of the relative importance of British commercial blockades and the self-imposed legislative American 'restrictive system' – Congressional trade restrictions intended to curb British activities at sea – is also addressed. The effects of Madison's embargoes of American foreign trade on the American economy are compared with the impact of the Royal Navy's commercial blockades.

The legality of Britain's methods of war at sea is studied, and the legitimacy of American grievances considered. The contemporary British and American economies and their respective governments are compared, and their systems of taxation and borrowing are reviewed. The vulnerability of the developing United States to British economic warfare, and its social, economic and political consequences, are each discussed. The increasingly severe economic and political predicament in which the Madison administration found itself as the British blockades were both tightened and extended is comprehensively studied, as is the ending of the war with the Treaty of Ghent, signed on Christmas Eve 1814, and the long-term significance of the settlement. The frequently heard view that the war was probably unnecessary, and certainly unimportant, will be vigorously challenged. Until now, the degree of success of the British maritime blockades of the United States in the War of 1812 has been seriously under-estimated.

INTRODUCTION

[T]he noiseless, steady, exhausting pressure with which sea power acts [was] cutting off the resources of the enemy while maintaining its own, supporting war in scenes in which it does not itself appear or appears only in the background, and striking blows only at rare intervals.[1]

CAREFUL STUDY OF THE WAR OF 1812 between Britain and the United States began almost as soon as conflict ended in February 1815. Described then in America as a 'second war of independence', the war remains both important and controversial. From the outset, each study tended to concentrate on particular aspects of the war. In 1817 William James, a British lawyer-turned-historian, was meticulous in refuting some of the more extravagant contemporary American naval claims in his *Full and Correct Account of the Chief Naval Occurrences of the Late War.*[2] Since then, almost every separate action has been minutely dissected and its naval and military significance analysed at length.

Alfred Mahan's *Sea Power in its Relations to the War of 1812*, published in Boston in 1905, also dealt in detail with the war's early single-ship actions, which caught the public imagination then and since.[3] Mahan's description and evaluation of British maritime blockades against the United States was part of his argument in favour of 'a naval force adequate to the protection of our commerce'.[4] He attributed the bankruptcy of New England merchants to British maritime blockade, but stopped short of admitting the eventual insolvency of the American government. He quoted a 'distinguished naval officer' who noted the 'stagnation' of 'both foreign and domestic commerce' and who endorsed the exaggerated claim that American coastal trade had been 'entirely annihilated', together causing the merchants' inability to continue funding the war. These were, he wrote, 'the cause of that *impending* bankruptcy with which the Government was *at one time threatened*'.[5] With less than complete candour, Mahan then reverted to his theme: the need for a large American fleet.

Also in 1905, Theodore Roosevelt's chapter on the naval war of 1812 in

Clowes' *History of the Royal Navy* forcefully advocated the United States' 'possession of a great fighting navy'.[6] Citing Henry Adams' examples, Roosevelt noted that 'the unceasing pressure of the British fleet' on America's 'extended seaboard' had 'created the wildest inequalities in the prices of commodities in different parts of the county'.[7] Roosevelt conceded that, 'throughout the last year of the war, the blockade was so vigorous that the shipping rotted at the wharves of the seaports and grass grew in the business quarters of the trading towns'. He did not, however, discuss the impact of the loss of American foreign trade on tax revenues and government borrowing or the Madison administration's resultant bankruptcy and abandonment of its original war aims.[8]

In 1969, Reginald Horsman's *War of 1812* briefly discussed in the course of a general history of the war how its American financing was 'essentially unsound'. Citing an authority on Gallatin, the American Secretary of the Treasury in 1812, and Henry Adams' history of Madison's administration, Horsman outlined the outcome of each successive attempt of the United States government to borrow sufficient funds to continue the war.[9] Like Adams, he conceded that, when the last attempt failed, 'the country was bankrupt', and that, by 1814, the government was unable to pay the interest on its debts. Horsman, however, attributed the American government's financial difficulties to the lack of preparedness among New England's Federalist minority to lend the proceeds of their continued trade, which was initially increased by their deliberate exclusion from Britain's initial maritime blockades. In doing so, Horsman provided an incomplete and unjust explanation, which, although coming closest to the connection between British blockades and American financial collapse, left much unexplained, which the present study will rectify.

By 1983, J. C. A. Stagg justifiably felt that 'Certainly, the [American] Treasury was increasingly embarrassed by the lack of funds to finance the war, but the reasons for this were broadly political in nature, and not really the fault of the department itself'.[10] He did not go on to attribute the erosion of tax revenue, the dislocation of the economy and the government's eventual inability to borrow further to the loss of American foreign trade through British maritime blockade. Of the final Ghent peace treaty, Stagg conceded that 'the time of making it [was] more fortunate than the peace itself'.[11]

In 2006, Ian Toll traced the need for the American Navy's eponymous *Six Frigates* without reflecting on the impact of their inability to leave port at will or, more importantly, on the fiscal and financial consequences of their failure to lift the British commercial blockade of the United States until the peace.[12] Jon Latimer's *1812: War with America* of 2007 discusses the role of British 'raids and blockades' in hindering the American war effort and in diverting American attention from the land war over the possession of Canada, as well as in confining to harbour much of the American navy, but again without dwelling long, or in detail, on the fiscal and financial consequences of the Royal Navy's blockades.[13]

Recent studies include Wade Dudley's attempt to quantify the relative efficiencies of Britain's maritime blockades in a 'comparative analysis' of those against France in the periods 1793–1802 and 1803–1814, and of the United States between 1812 and 1815.[14] Valid quantification of the effectiveness of blockades so geographically dissimilar is almost certainly impossible when important factors apply to only one of the two locations of the blockades. The British blockade of Brest, conducted by vessels released in turn for repair and resupply to Torbay or Plymouth, has to be compared with the initial blockade of the Chesapeake and Delaware, and eventually all of the 2,000-mile American eastern seaboard, by vessels repairable only by the limited facilities of Halifax, Nova Scotia, or Bermuda, or by recrossing the Atlantic.

Inevitable contact with the American shore involved a greater risk of desertion than rarer landings in France, and imposed an unavoidable constraint on British inshore operations against the United States, applicable only there. Apparently objective 'scores' attributed by Dudley to the consequences of each blockade purport to measure their effectiveness, although attempted quantification of the 'public outrage' induced by each blockade must surely be largely subjective. The assertion that London's increased marine insurance rates indicate a significant risk to British overseas trade from American warships, including privateers, is apparently contradicted by Rodger's finding that, generally, rates were 'no higher between 1812 and 1814 than they had been between 1810 and 1811'.[15] Dudley's conclusion that the British blockades of the United States were comparatively unsuccessful neither appraises their consequences nor bears close examination.

In 1991, Nicholas Tracy's *Attack on Maritime Trade* appeared to agree with President Madison's legalistic argument that, since some American vessels successfully evaded the British blockading squadrons, the blockades themselves were ineffective and therefore illegal, and should be discontinued.[16] But no complete blockade of the entire American coastline, 'close' or 'distant', was ever either feasible or contemplated. If, however, the British naval blockade could contain enough of the United States' navy to prevent not only any lifting of the Royal Navy's commercial blockade until the peace but also American interference with British landings almost anywhere on the enemy coast then, by any standards, it was efficient enough. If the British commercial blockade was efficient enough to exploit the vulnerability of the import-dependent American tax-gathering system and expose the irrationality of lending further to a government unable to pay its present debts, then comparison with other blockades is unnecessary. If the blockades combined to dislocate the American agrarian, commercial, fiscal, financial and, therefore, political infrastructures, such as to make peace necessary for national survival, they had performed their task. Whether or not this was the case will be investigated by what follows.

It would appear that the results of the long-term imposition on the United States of British maritime blockades, both commercial and naval, have not been sufficiently discussed, and that, therefore, their possible effectiveness has been seriously under-estimated. The issue of whether or not the application of Britain's sea and naval power to its new enemy was successful while its war against

Napoleonic France continued deserves further attention. The purpose of this book is, therefore, to investigate the link between the British maritime blockades of the United States, their fiscal, financial, economic and political consequences, and the subsequent preparedness of the American administration to end the war of 1812 on terms significantly favourable to Britain in the long run: a task not before undertaken at sufficient depth.

Chapter 1 explains the theory and practice of maritime economic warfare in the form of offensive blockades and defensive convoys, both crucial manifestations of British seapower. It outlines the evolution of maritime economic warfare and the use of blockade in a succession of British wars, with its implied conflict with neutrals including, by the early nineteenth century, an emergent United States. Following on from this, Chapter 2 discusses the legal and practical constraints on the nineteenth-century use of economic warfare and the potential solutions then available.

The real interdependence of the economies of Britain and the United States after American independence, and the implications of their respective stages of economic, fiscal and financial development, are discussed in Chapter 3. This chapter detects the vulnerability of the American agrarian economy, particularly in terms of the contemporary administration's dependence on foreign trade for raising revenue and borrowing funds, and especially when in conflict with the world's greatest exponent of maritime economic warfare. The economic, fiscal and financial infrastructures of the two economies and their suitability for a long war are compared.

Chapter 4 traces the development of Britain's economic warfare against the United States in the North Atlantic and the Caribbean under Admiral Sir John Borlase Warren, from his assumption of command in August 1812 until his replacement in April 1814. The implementation of maritime economic warfare by his successor, Vice-Admiral Sir Alexander Cochrane, from April 1814 until the end of the war in February 1815, by which time hostilities had also reached the Gulf of Mexico and the Pacific, is the subject of Chapter 5. Subsequently, Chapters 6 and 7 examine in turn the respective effectiveness of Britain's economic warfare against America under Warren's and Cochrane's leadership, tracing in each case the implications for the economy and administration of the United States and its capacity to continue the war.

Empirical evidence of the effects of the progressive application of the commercial blockade of the United States is presented in Chapter 7, which examines changes in the prices of commodities such as sugar and of the American government's securities, such as Treasury notes.[17] A comparison of changes in commodity and security prices, linked to the chronology of major political and maritime events, will serve to measure the relative effects of embargo and blockade, a recurrent and difficult problem in assessing the significance of British economic warfare in North America. An objective assessment of the effectiveness of Britain's economic warfare against the United States is the aim of the Conclusion.

The extent to which Britain's seapower – the use of a merchant fleet of more than two million tons – was able to continue to support Britain's overseas trade, including its vital commerce with British North America and the West Indies during the war with the United States, forms part of the enquiry. This book investigates how far British trade protection allowed the export of significant quantities of Britain's manufacturing output, clearly crucial to Britain's continued ability to finance its war efforts, and the maintenance of international communication, on which Britain's predominant financial position partly depended. It will also attempt to resolve the question of whether British naval power, with the compulsory convoying of merchantmen, succeeded in allowing the importation not only of crucial raw materials but also of colonial produce, then processed into important re-exports.

Whether or not the Royal Navy could at the same time destroy or capture sufficient American merchant vessels to make a significant impact on the United States' vital customs duties, the American administration's largest single source of tax revenue and its ability to finance the war, is therefore crucial. Whether or not the British commercial blockade could sufficiently deplete the private incomes from which savings might be lent to the American government, or so far lower employment as to erode the Republican Party's electoral strength, will also be addressed. It will investigate whether prolonged and widespread British dislocation of American trade could interfere sufficiently with the United States' money supply, and the everyday value of currency in both government and private transactions, to erode the user's trust in the current administration, or even in the federal structure of American political Union. It will also ask how far the inflation apparently caused by commercial blockade would reduce American financial support for the war, already seen by some, especially in New England, as an ill-advised method of addressing concerns over the United States' relations with Britain.

In short, this book will argue that the effectiveness of British maritime strategies – both defensive convoy protection and particularly the aggressive commercial and naval blockades – contributed enormously through their fiscal and economic impact to the production of a satisfactory conclusion to the War of 1812 for Britain. The Royal Navy in North America between 1812 and 1815 provided an early example of remarkably successful economic warfare.

In 1992 Colin Gray argued that 'To date, no hostile *guerre de course* – [war on commerce] – in modern history has succeeded in shaping the track, let alone dictating the outcome, of war *for a sea power*.'[18] In a book making no mention of the War of 1812 he omitted to point out that it was precisely because the United States did not possess a navy capable of preventing British maritime blockade between 1812 and 1815 that, together, naval and commercial blockade both affected the course and dictated the outcome of the War of 1812.

CHAPTER 1

CONVOYS AND BLOCKADES: THE EVOLUTION OF MARITIME ECONOMIC WARFARE

Fleets employed to cover a coast, are not only precarious in their
exertions, which depend much upon winds, but are miserably
confined as to all the effects of naval war. Those effects are only felt
when our fleets can keep the sea to protect our commerce and
annoy that of our enemies, as well as to defend our distant
possessions, and to cover descents and continued incursions.
(Wm Eden, MP, Commissioner for Conciliation with America, 1778–9)[1]

BY THE EARLY NINETEENTH CENTURY maritime blockade was the
offensive arm of economic warfare, used against an enemy in conjunction with
the convoy protection of a nation's own overseas trade. The term 'offensive
blockade' was used to describe the interception of an enemy's merchant,
transport or naval vessels, usually on their entering or leaving harbour. Defensive
economic warfare involved the gathering of merchant vessels to sail as convoys
under the armed protection of as many warships as could be spared. Belligerents
with sufficient naval means were increasingly expected to impose a policy of
'stop and search' on all vessels found in specified areas, and those carrying goods
'interdicted' by proclamation as 'contraband' were at best turned back or,
otherwise, detained. Crews and cargoes thought likely to benefit an enemy were
either subject to an enforced sale or, subject to law, confiscated. At the beginning
of each European war legislation was needed to legitimise what otherwise would
have constituted piracy, a practice almost universally condemned but nonetheless
still carried out in some parts of the world. As each war began the British
Parliament passed Prize Acts under which a High Court of Admiralty could
declare vessels found breaching blockades to be legally 'prizes of war'.

Vessels engaged in offensive naval or commercial blockade would often have
been well placed to take other measures, such as the interception of an opponent's
diplomatic communications or personnel, thus perhaps gaining foresight of an
enemy's intentions or gathering useful intelligence about the effectiveness of their

government's own measures. In time, an effective blockade might leave an enemy both economically and diplomatically isolated, potentially deprived of military, financial, logistical, diplomatic or moral support. The psychological pressure of such isolation might eventually increase an enemy's willingness to negotiate.

A maritime power could impose a commercial blockade of an enemy's ports to hinder their trade. A naval or 'military' blockade could reduce, if not preclude, their ability to send out warships to lift a commercial blockade or dispatch transports with troops to fight elsewhere. Overseas communication could be delayed or prevented. Used together by a belligerent with sufficient maritime resources, such blockades, in the long run, were likely to prove effective. For neutrals, however, they were at best inconvenient and costly and at worst a breach of their maritime sovereignty – and, as such, deeply resented. Traditionally, neutrals should have been given sufficient prior notice by proclamation in an official publication, in Britain's case the *London Gazette*, to allow neutral vessels to avoid confrontation. According to what was sometimes referred to as the 'Law of Nations', maritime blockades were to be conducted throughout by a naval force large enough for it to be uninterrupted and evenly applied to all those whose interests might be damaged thereby; the employment of an insufficiently strong or intermittent blockading force would lead to accusations of its being an illegal 'paper blockade', said to contravene the putative 'Law of Nations'. The legitimacy of such a body of law, however, was not universally agreed.

In practice, blockading squadrons would routinely be expected to perform several roles at once, with perhaps different degrees of importance. A naval blockade would aim for the incarceration of an enemy's warships in harbour, so that, ideally, they would take no further part in the war. A maritime commercial blockade would seek to deprive an enemy not only of the physical resources and economic benefits of imports but also of the profits from the export of a domestic surplus or processed re-exports, and therefore the revenue from the taxation of overseas trade, such as shipping registration and enrolment fees, lighthouse dues or the customs duties on imports. Governments frequently placed duties on the importation of essentials such as salt or luxuries such as wine. The demand for such goods was often price and income-inelastic and such taxes were therefore reliable and cheap to administer but vulnerable to foreign interference. By prolonged and widespread interference with an enemy's overseas trade maritime powers could thus realistically expect to inflict, comparatively cheaply, sufficiently serious economic damage on an enemy to impair their ability to continue a war.

In such wars at sea 'public' warships were often supplemented by 'privateers' – armed and often heavily manned privately owned warships primarily intended to make shared profits by capturing enemy merchant vessels, although they sometimes also carried cargoes. Their hostile actions were legitimised by government-issued 'letters of marque'.[2] They commonly complemented the activities of state-owned warships provided by governments or, nominally in Britain's case, the Crown. Privateers are, generally, outside the scope of this work. Royal Naval prizes sent into Halifax, Nova Scotia, between 1812 and 1815 are shown as Appendix A, Table 1. In measuring the effectiveness of the Royal Navy's economic warfare in terms of its blockades of the United States all prizes of privateers have been excluded from this list and from calculations based on the totals. Fay Kert's comparison of British prize tonnages taken into Halifax after capture by privateer and Royal Naval vessels throughout the war shows that privateers appear to have concentrated on taking smaller enemy vessels.[3] In 1813, for example, privateers took an almost 6% greater share of the total tonnage of vessels under 100 tons than did the Royal Navy, but only 7.7% of the Royal Navy's capture of vessels over 200 tons. In 1814 and 1815 all enemy vessels of over 200 tons were taken by Royal Naval vessels, rather than privateers.

The priority for privateers was profit-making, their tactical decisions being based on expediency, even risk avoidance, rather than the strategic aims of their national government, beyond its definition of 'enemy' and 'neutral'. Those who operated privateers were less accountable than naval officers commanding warships, and links with government policy more likely to be found in official correspondence than in the largely unrecorded views of those simply seeking profit. Since this book's focus is the effectiveness of the traditional British government policy of economic warfare, especially blockade, it will thus concentrate on the activities of the British Royal Navy and those of the 'public' warships of the United States Navy, and the commercial vessels of both countries. It will attempt to measure the economic, fiscal, financial and political effects of Britain's blockades of the United States as the major part of the economic warfare waged by the Royal Navy between 1812 and 1815.

VICE-ADMIRALTY COURTS: THE PROCESS OF LAW

Captured vessels were usually sent under a prize crew into a port of the captor's country, in either homeland or colony, to be 'libelled' and brought before a specialist court to be tried. For British prizes, this would be in one of thirty Vice-Admiralty Courts established in such ports around the world. The prize would normally be brought under the jurisdiction of the Court nearest to the point of capture. Judges expert in maritime law would hear evidence and legal argument before deciding whether or not a vessel should be 'condemned' as in breach of a properly constituted blockade. Such a vessel, and probably its cargo, would be liable to confiscation and subsequent sale, or if found to be within its rights when captured, restored to its legitimate owners. The legal process was inevitably lengthy and expensive.

Eventually, the net proceeds of sale at auction were shared on a sliding scale based on seniority and responsibility. According to scales revised in 1808, captains would receive two-eighths of the prize money, less a third paid to directing flag officers. Naval lieutenants, masters, physicians, and captains of marines would share another eighth. Midshipmen and senior petty officers such as gunners, bosuns and carpenters would receive shares of a further eighth. The remaining half of the prize money was divided between petty officers and ratings. This distribution system successfully motivated blockading operations until 1815.[4]

Once condemned, particularly when new, vessels taken as prizes could legally be taken into the blockading force, often as tenders to larger vessels, useful for entering harbours and penetrating estuaries. Less properly, captured cargoes were sometimes immediately confiscated at sea and diverted to the captor's own use. Other prizes were burned, or even blown up, to avoid the captor's need to allocate a prize crew, with the consequent risks of under-manning. Often unpopular with crews deprived of prize-money, such tactics nevertheless effectively reduced the cost and inconvenience of maritime blockade. Governments often paid 'head money' to captors as an incentive for the capture of enemy crew members, who were often highly and expensively trained seamen, thus further reducing the opponent's ability to continue fighting.

Captured enemy vessels and cargoes were not infrequently, although often illegally, released on payment of a cash ransom paid in specie – money in precious metal form. Such vessels could complete the interrupted voyage, but might be captured again on a subsequent voyage, adding further to the illicit rewards of maritime blockade. Conversely, blockading vessels would often intercept and recapture vessels of the same nationality as themselves or their allies, releasing their crews from often lengthy captivity and making prisoners of the enemy's prize crew.

CLOSE AND DISTANT BLOCKADE

Close blockade could be conducted 'inshore', defined as being within sight of land. Especially when long enemy coastlines were to be blockaded, small, shallow-draught vessels could more easily avoid natural obstacles and could prove useful in penetrating estuaries and inlets. Light, handy vessels could intercept coastal shipping and fishing vessels, interrupt communications and gather intelligence by observing activity in enemy harbours, reporting to heavier forces further offshore, which could be summoned to prevent enemy attempts to enter or leave port. Distant blockade, conducted by larger vessels better able to withstand heavier seas, possibly remaining beyond the horizon, could cover a wider stretch of enemy coastline, and perhaps several ports. Their sometimes unseen but continual presence could exert psychological pressure on those blockaded. In good visibility, patrolling squadrons of far separated vessels, signalling to each other with flags by day and lights by night, could detect enemy activity within distances of up to thirty miles. By 1812, such blockades had been used by Britain since January 1793, often with great effect against both Revolutionary and Napoleonic France, and being broken by the Peace of Amiens for only 14 months between March 1802 and May 1803.

CONVOYS AND BLOCKADES: THE EVOLUTION OF MARITIME ECONOMIC WARFARE

The use of maritime blockade, however, had long been controversial. The denial of free passage at sea to enemies or commercial rivals had been practised in medieval Europe by those maritime powers able to enforce claims of sovereignty over neighbouring and quite distant seas. Venice enforced its ownership of the Adriatic, Denmark and Sweden disputed control of the Baltic until agreeing to share it in 1622, while the English claimed sovereignty of the 'British Seas' from the coasts of Norway to those of Spain. Formalised maritime rights were initially based on accumulated decisions taken by states around the Mediterranean known as the 'Consolato del Mare' – the Consulate of the Sea – first published in 1494, and long widely accepted.[5]

However, in 1604, the Dutch jurist Hugo Grotius applied international and 'natural' law – as distinct from traditional or ecclesiastical rulings – to maritime prize-taking, and, in 1633, republished *De Mari Libero*, which argued that the seas were free for common use, a principle welcomed by neutrals.[6] English writers, however, including John Sheldon and John Boroughs, re-asserted the national right to exclusive control of defined areas of sea. Sir John Boroughs' *The Sovereignty of the British Seas Proved by Records* was written in 1633, but was not published until 1651. It was followed by Charles Malloy's *Treatise of Affairs Maritime and of Commerce*, first published in 1676 and regularly reprinted to become 'the standard English language interpretation of international maritime law'. Malloy's *Treatise* is described as 'one of the most extreme legal arguments for England's sovereignty of the sea, which he claimed extended from Cape Finisterre to Van Staten in Norway'.[7] This body of legal opinion, especially where it concerned the maritime rights of neutrals, was to become significant on both sides of the Atlantic.

Maritime blockade played a practical part in English politics between 1649 and 1653 when used in eradicating resistance to the Commonwealth by containing a small royalist naval force under Prince Rupert. Successively blockaded in a number of ports, the royalist force was eventually disbanded in 1653. And only after the English republic's navy blockaded the port of Dunkirk in 1652 did it obtain the diplomatic recognition of France.[8] Maritime blockade could thus be diplomatically powerful.

It was during the first Anglo-Dutch war of 1652–4 that maritime economic warfare developed characteristics later to become familiar in North American waters, however. Competing Dutch merchantmen were obliged to pass through the North Sea and English Channel, where they were vulnerable to attacks from English warships. The Dutch countered this *de facto* commercial blockade by attacking English warships with their own, and by convoying their merchantmen with some success. Contact between the rival warships led to successive fleet actions, but Dutch commerce was temporarily disrupted. Although Dutch seaborne trade was to recover quickly after the Treaty of Westminster ended the war in 1654, a workable English strategy of commercial blockade had thus been developed,[9] and Britain had established the basics of its offensive and defensive maritime economic warfare. Any of the enemy's trade was contraband, and the defence of Britain's trade was a naval responsibility, to be implemented respectively by commercial blockade, protected by complementary naval blockade, and by the convoy protection of merchant vessels, principles to be further developed in a succession of future wars.

English blockade of the Spanish coast was less successfully attempted during Cromwell's war with Spain, although some New World silver was seized in the Canaries, reducing Spanish capacity to finance war elsewhere. A blockade of Dutch commerce in the Channel was resumed in a second Anglo-Dutch war of 1665–7, together with the destruction, north of Texel in 1666, of 150 Dutch merchant vessels estimated to be worth the equivalent of over a million pounds.[10] During the following year, however, English trade suffered Dutch harassment and the Royal Navy defeat on the Medway.[11] A third Anglo-Dutch war began in 1672, again partly aimed at curtailing Dutch maritime trade, having first disposed of the Dutch fleet in battle. In 1673, after indecisive preliminaries, an attempt to blockade the Dutch coast and impound a Dutch East India Company convoy failed. Another Treaty of Westminster in 1674 ended this less successful attempt at commercial blockade, an activity which, if properly financed – as Charles II's had not been – remained potentially viable and effective.[12] Furthermore, the apparent right of belligerents under international law to attack merchant vessels and limit the trading activities of neutral shipping in wartime was claimed in 1697, after a neutral Swedish fleet carrying war supplies through the Channel to France was captured by the Royal Navy.[13]

During the War of Spanish Succession (1709–13) the Tories advocated direct maritime attacks on enemy trade as an alternative to a Continental policy which implied a standing army, to which they were opposed, and on which a strong central government relied, as in Cromwell's time. Although 'corn was contraband', the corollary of naval blockade was still limited by practicalities. 'Naval developments, particularly in the field of hygiene and supply, had not yet reached a point where close and continuous blockade of enemy bases, which in the new circumstances was bound to be an important strategic requirement, was practicable.'[14] During the eighteenth century this lack of logistical support was to become less of a limiting factor in the employment of maritime blockades and their significance as a strategy. Royal dockyards were steadily developed in Britain throughout the century. Furthermore, 'Throughout the eighteenth century, in spite of government procrastination in providing proper facilities, the superiority of the navy's victualling service afforded significant operational advantages.' Among these advantages was the feasibility of maritime commercial blockade.[15] The prospect of prolonged maritime blockade in North America, however, would not become practicable until further port facilities were created in Nova Scotia and Bermuda, facilitated by the accelerating growth of Britain's economic and financial strength.

During England's war with France between 1744 and 1748 Admiral Martin had twelve ships with which 'to annoy the enemy's ships and commerce' to be found on the French trading routes south-west of Ushant.[16] With France the enemy, more ready access to the Atlantic was required than that offered by the ports of south-eastern England, and Britain's western harbours and dockyard facilities became strategically invaluable. The workforce of the Royal Dockyard at Plymouth 'doubled in size between 1739 and 1748, overtaking that at

Woolwich', and continued to grow thereafter, promoted by real fears of French invasion between 1744 and 1759 together with the increasing need to defend distant colonies.[17] Subsequently the availability of repair and revictualling facilities in western England acted as a 'force multiplier', making the Royal Navy's close blockade of the French a practical proposition.

The use of maritime economic warfare in the eighteenth century inevitably affected neutrals. In wartime, they could potentially replace a belligerent's carrying trade, interdicted by their enemy's commercial blockade, even if such trade was forbidden to them by protective legislation in peacetime. Britain sought to clarify its own position by a doctrine known as 'the Rule of 1756', which maintained that trade closed to neutrals in peacetime could not be conducted in wartime, thereby profitably nullifying a British blockade. According to this 'rule', trade between enemy colonies and their home ports was forbidden to neutrals. As the volume and range of seaborne trade increased, this British position was to become increasingly important.

Maritime economic warfare was employed by Britain against France during the course of the Seven Years War. On 19 February 1757 Walter Titley, the English Minister at Copenhagen, wrote to Robert D'Arcy, Earl of Holdernesse, Secretary of State for the Northern Department, that 'the only way to prevent' French 'Superiority over us ... is to drain the French of Men & Money by a War upon the Continent, while England cuts off the chief sources of their Wealth by destroying their Trade & Navigation'. It should be done 'By this Method, & this only ... as Her Finances (tho' Great) are certainly not sufficient to carry on a successful War on both Elements at once'. He added, however, that Holdernesse knew best 'how far this Scheme may be practicable; and whether England, on whom the weight of the whole Machine must repose, is able to support it'.[18] Maritime blockade was again considered practicable, and the necessary Prize Act passed.

The continuous blockade of the Brittany coast by the ships of Admiral Sir Edward Hawke was made possible by relieving ships in rotation for refitting and resupply in south-west England. Having escaped the blockade in a gale, the French took refuge in Quiberon Bay, but were caught and decisively beaten there by Hawke on 20 November 1759. French invasion of Britain having been averted, the blockade thereafter decimated French seaborne trade and prevented the reinforcement of overseas colonies. Pondicherry, in French-held India, was captured in January 1761 after naval blockade since the previous spring. Similarly, blockades contributed to successes in relieving Gibraltar and on the St Lawrence.[19] The blockade of the French coast during 1759 interrupted coastal shipping so effectively that their Atlantic dockyards were deprived of timber, seamen and supplies, the ports of trade and the French government of revenue.[20] During the Seven Years War the Royal Navy captured, including those taken in 1755, 959 enemy vessels, of which almost 83% were condemned as lawful prize.[21] Maritime blockade had been proved practicable.

BLOCKADE AND THE WAR OF AMERICAN INDEPENDENCE

Discussion of the potential of both naval and commercial maritime blockades became urgently topical with the outbreak of rebellion in Britain's American Colonies during the 1770s, culminating in the War of American Independence. Before the fighting began in earnest the British Secretary at War, Lord Barrington, had considered blockade especially appropriate when considering the transport and communication difficulties imposed by great distances. In December 1774 he wrote:

> A conquest by land is unnecessary when the country can be
> reduced first to distress, and then to obedience, by our Marine
> totally interrupting all commerce and fishery and even seizing all
> the ships in the ports with very little expense and bloodshed.[22]

A memorandum apparently written in July 1775 by Rear-Admiral Sir Hugh Palliser, British commander in North America until 1774, estimated that a minimum of fifty vessels would be needed on the coasts of America 'to annoy the rebellious provinces'. Crucially, these should 'attend the operations of the army' as well as convoy, blockade and 'cruising' duties. Palliser thought that 'A less number of ships … will be insufficient', and that more would be needed if rebellion spread beyond New England. In the event, Rear-Admiral Thomas Graves was to have only twenty-seven, excluding three surveying ships.[23] By December 1777 the Earl of Sandwich, First Lord of the Admiralty, wrote to Prime Minister Lord North that 'Lord Howe has had this year about 90 ships of all sorts', and that 'with a force properly stationed' in America 'could have made it very difficult for the Americans to receive their supplies, carry on their trade, and fit out privateers to annoy the trade of Great Britain. The contrary has been the case'.[24]

Conventionally, Kennedy argues that 'the Royal Navy could control the eastern seaboard and river estuaries; but further west the rebels could act with impunity'.[25] But, as much then as later, the bulk of accumulated wealth to pay for imports was concentrated in the Colonial coastal and estuarial towns. While at least initially self-sufficient in food, until the end of 1777 nine-tenths of the rebel's manufactured weapons, ammunition and gunpowder, as well as textiles and footwear, would have to be imported from France into these eastern ports,[26] and foreign reinforcements would always have to be brought by sea. Therefore, even a Royal Navy as greatly in need of modernisation and expansion as that in 1775–6 could have made a more useful contribution in the crucial early stages of this American war by applying economic warfare. Freed of its priority to protect army transports and supplies, the Royal Navy could have been concentrating primarily on depriving its opponents of French manufactures. Rodger argues that blockade 'would rather encourage than suppress rebellion'.[27] It may, however, have proved economically effective. A promised end to blockades, together with fiscal, political and commercial concessions from London, could well have brought the rebellion to an earlier negotiated settlement.

Admittedly, without expansion, Britain's North America squadrons would have struggled to cope with the number of Colonial ports, harbours and undeveloped creeks. Equally, as Rodger points out, such blockades would inevitably have had to include the Caribbean, since the prevailing clockwise Atlantic winds and currents meant that European ships customarily dropped down to around latitude 15 degrees North to cross the ocean, passing close to the French, Dutch and Danish West Indies and the Bahamas. British searching of neutral ships for contraband would have risked widening the war.

Nonetheless, especially at the outset, a 'more effective use might have been made of an unchallenged supremacy at sea'.[28] By Glete's calculations, Britain's naval strength in 1775 exceeded that of either France or Spain, both in total and in their respective numbers of battleships and cruisers. The navies of France and Spain combined, however, had six more battleships than Britain in 1775, and twelve more by 1780. While the number of British battleships remained static at 117 between 1775 and 1780, the French fleet of battleships grew from 59 to 70, an increase approaching 20%; and the total number of French warships grew by 38%, compared with Britain's 26%. Over the same period, the number of British cruisers increased from 82 to 111, while the cruisers of France and Spain combined rose from 65 to 92, a bigger increase than Britain's. However, the number of Britain's 'small ships' more than doubled in the same time, from 28 to 58.[29] These may have been precisely the weapons most suitable for both blockade and convoy protection in Britain's American war.

Earlier explanations as to why 'the British fleet could have imposed a total ban on American ports but, instead, … rode at anchor in New York harbour' have been modified.[30] Syrett argues that, although British blockade of the American eastern seaboard was feasible, the Royal Navy's cooperation in amphibious military operations against Charleston, New York and Philadelphia was given priority at the outset, precluding effective blockade.[31] Priorities would change later in this war, and in Britain's later wars in North America.

Buel notes that, until the end of 1777, Admiral Richard Howe put his naval resources at the disposal of his brother Sir William, commander of the British land forces.[32] The British need to deal American armies a decisive blow before foreign intervention became conclusive gave land campaigns precedence over maritime blockade, which was, at best, a slow and cumulative process. Later Parliamentary prohibition of this ancillary naval role allowed the British maritime blockades of 1782 to be made sufficiently effective in disrupting coastal shipping for the Continental economy to be damaged by inflation. Difficulties in raising revenue by taxing commerce also damaged the American Confederation's cause.[33] Belatedly effective maritime blockade came too late, however, to prevent the loss of the American Colonies to Britain in 1783, but valuable experience of successful blockade of the American eastern seaboard nonetheless remained among those who had conducted it. Moreover, the development of the Royal Navy's western bases continued. The workforce at Plymouth's Royal Dockyard increased by more than 70% between 1711 and

1782, moving it from fifth to first place in terms of the size of its skilled dockyard labour.[34]

In 1780, British maritime blockade had been sufficiently effective to provoke opposition in northern Europe. Russia, Denmark and Sweden, combined as a League of Armed Neutrality, threatened war if the Royal Navy continued to interfere with neutral vessels, declaring that 'a blockade would be recognised only … where it constituted literally a physical barrier to entry into a neutral port'.[35] The coalition, and its threat, dissolved for the time being, however, in 1781. The legal position countries adopted tended to reflect their naval potential.

THE ROYAL NAVY'S BLOCKADE OF FRANCE, 1793–1812

When France declared war on Britain on 1 February 1793 Parliament enacted the necessary Prize Acts in 1793 and 1798 to facilitate Britain's use of its maritime blockade strategy.[36] The main purposes of the Royal Navy's blockades had been to prevent the combination of France's Brest and Toulon fleets and the invasion of Britain, as well as to deprive France of its unhindered access to world trade. There had been no Brest fleet at Trafalgar.[37] The blockades had made the sea-transport of French troops extremely difficult, precluding any large-scale or successful invasion of Britain and Ireland, so that British blockade could be aimed, primarily, at the economic isolation of France.

After 1800 Earl St Vincent had revived the use of close blockade of the French in the Channel.[38] The effectiveness of the British blockade meant that neither the naval protection of French colonies nor the dispatch of reinforcements to colonial garrisons proved possible. As a result, France had been deprived of all its overseas possessions, with their raw materials, tropical produce and protected markets for manufactures. This policy had been recommended to Parliament by Henry Dundas, later Lord Melville, First Lord of the Admiralty, in March 1801.[39] The loss of colonial markets had reduced French manufactured exports, thereby stimulating demand for British manufactured goods. Although not precisely quantified at the time, the blockades had reduced French customs receipts by four-fifths between 1807 and 1809.[40] The Royal Navy's blockades of France had preserved British political autonomy and heavily damaged the French economy.[41]

According to French sources, the British maritime blockade of France had quickly proved successful. As early as 1797 the head of the French Bureau of Commerce had written:

> The former sources of our prosperity are either lost or dried up.
> Our agricultural, manufacturing and industrial power is almost
> extinct … The maritime war paralyses our distant navigation and
> even diminishes considerably that of our coasts; so that a great
> number of French ships remain inactive, and perhaps decaying in
> our ports.[42]

As well as in daily newspapers of varying quality and allegiance, details of the

Royal Navy's blockading activities were discussed in such specialised periodicals as the *Naval Chronicle*, published in London since 1799. British reports were often reproduced in contemporary American publications, particularly in New England. The public in both Britain and the United States were therefore familiar with the maritime commercial and naval blockades of Britain's enemies. In Britain, blockade was evidently supported, both by influential newspaper editors and office-holders alike.

As a result, however, the controversies surrounding the use of maritime commercial blockade were again sharpened by other trading nations, largely focussed on the definition of contraband and the treatment of neutrals found to be carrying it. Britain's specific difficulties with the United States centred on American wartime trade with France and the shipment of French colonial produce. Precisely what constituted enemy property, liable to confiscation or diversion, had long been contentious. Weapons and ammunition seemed unambiguous and the confiscation of specie not unexpected, but the inclusion of foodstuffs, clothing, footwear, timber and building materials, for example, which could be for either military or civilian use, were debatable.

A lack of clarity either in the orders of policy-makers or among those charged with implementing them may have contributed to what in retrospect looks like the loss of a valuable opportunity for effective economic warfare earlier in Britain's war with France. Although in an Atlantic action on the 'Glorious First of June' in 1794 Admiral Lord Howe captured six French ships of the line, while a seventh sank, the valuable convoy of 116 merchantmen which they had been protecting, laden with much-needed American wheat, was allowed to reach Brest unharmed. An opportunity for gaining military and political advantage by fostering hardship and unrest among the civilian population of France had apparently been lost, when more than British public jubilation might have been achieved.[43]

Sustained maritime blockades became an ever more practical proposition as repair and victualling facilities were further developed in a greater number of harbours in Britain and abroad.[44] British governments were both politically prepared and economically able to allocate the necessary funds, victuals and naval and manpower resources to prolonged blockades. As O'Brien demonstrates, a relatively wide tax-base and sound financial institutions made heavy taxation and enormous long-term government borrowing feasible.[45] Occasional alarms apart, Britain's fiduciary paper currency and monetary mechanisms were reliable. Administrative facilities, with accumulated skills and experience and a comparative absence of corruption, made logistical support systems possible. Britain's wealth from a developing science-based agriculture, internal transport, advanced work-force specialisation, world-wide trade and increasing industrialisation underpinned a national capacity to support campaigns of maritime blockade.

Furthermore, Britain's blockade of an enemy's trade coincided with a desire to protect the market for its own carrying trade. Britain's merchant fleet was the world's largest, importing raw materials and supporting an imperative need for outlets for its increasing surplus output of manufactured goods and re-exports. Britain's total registered shipping first exceeded 2 million tons in 1804. By 1804–6 Britain's seaborne trade imported over 40% of its food and enabled its textile manufacturers to export almost 60% of their output. Between 1772 and 1804 Britain's total imports grew by 50.3% and total exports by 111.44%. War with France had so far failed to cause significant damage to British trade: between 1792 and 1804 alone, British imports increased by almost 49% and total exports by 50.4%. Complementing the protective use of convoys, made compulsory in 1793, stringently so after 1803, Britain could use naval blockade to confine to port those enemy vessels which might otherwise have attacked its merchant vessels engaged in such trade all over the world, on which its prosperity, and therefore its ability to continue fighting, ultimately depended.[46]

THE PROBLEM OF NEUTRALS

Britain's maritime blockade of France inevitably involved contact with neutral merchant vessels of various nationalities and gave rise to irreconcilable interpretations of maritime law. By December 1800, the French contrived a revival of the concept of 'Armed Neutrality' among the countries of northern Europe, including Denmark, Russia and Sweden, as a means of countering the British blockade. The Danish fleet was seen in Britain as the most capable of enforcing French requirements in the Baltic. Diplomacy having failed, on 2 April 1801 the Royal Navy destroyed the Danish fleet at anchor off Copenhagen, significantly weakening a European threat to the effectiveness of the British commercial blockade of France.

The elimination of French trade with their overseas possessions made an important contribution towards Britain's avoidance of defeat and the securing of the sound British economy essential to hopes of eventual victory. While inflicting serious economic damage on France, Britain's economy could benefit, remaining sufficiently viable to subsidise Prussia and Holland, paying out a further £35m to allies in the period 1810–15.[47] The great danger for a belligerent power investing in the maritime blockade of an enemy with overseas trade and possessions, however, was that the enemy's displaced merchant fleet would simply be replaced by that of a neutral eager to profit from the vacancy. The American merchant marine expanded rapidly after 1800, exceeding a million tons by 1807.[48] If French merchantmen were to be replaced by American vessels, the expensive commercial blockade of both French homeland and colonies would be nullified. On renewal of war with France, prize law as interpreted in England ruled that the 'goods of an enemy on board the ship of a neutral might be taken, while the goods of a neutral on board the ship of an enemy should be restored'.[49] Britain thus insisted that French cargoes on American ships were liable to seizure, but Americans argued that any such cargo, unless obvious contraband, was immune from confiscation or diversion. 'Free ships', they argued, made for 'free goods'. Controversy became sufficiently acrimonious for Sir Christopher Robinson's work reporting on 'the Cases argued and determined by Sir William Scott in the High Court of Admiralty', published in London in 1799, to be republished in 1800 in Philadelphia.[50]

It was now that Sir William Scott distinguished between naval blockade of immediate strategic importance and maritime commercial blockade. He wrote in 1800 that

> A blockade may be more or less rigorous, either for the single purpose of watching the military operations of the enemy, and preventing the egress of his fleet ... or on an extended scale, to cut off all access of neutral vessels to that interdicted place; which is strictly and properly a blockade, for the other is in truth no blockade at all, as far as neutrals are concerned.[51]

The first was later to prove effective and of great significance outside Brest, and both, used together, were to be decisive when employed by the Royal Navy in North America between 1812 and 1815.

From the outset Britain sought to enforce the Rule of 1756, thought to be applicable to American carriers replacing blockaded French merchant vessels. Initially Britain condoned breaches of its blockade by American vessels on 'discontinuous voyages', ostensibly importing goods from the French West Indies to the southern United States, unloading, but immediately reloading and re-exporting them to Europe. Shippers paid customs duties on the 'imports', which the American government customarily re-imbursed as 'drawback' – a rebate less administrative costs. This conciliatory policy, however, formalised by a British Admiralty Court decision involving the American vessel *Polly* in 1800, contributed to a marked increase in American shipping between the Caribbean and Europe, and American re-exports increased almost thirty times, from $1.8m in 1792 to $53.2m in 1805, causing concern to Britain's West India Committee – which represented sugar growers, merchants and shippers – as well as to the British government.[52]

An Admiralty Court ruling on the detained American vessel *Essex* in May 1805 then reversed a policy which had seemed to threaten the effectiveness of the British maritime blockade of France. Sir William Scott ruled that the routine American re-imbursement of customs duty as 'drawback' meant that such French colonial goods had not legally been imported into the United States, and were not therefore neutral American goods, but liable to British confiscation. Some Americans referred indignantly to their trade being as controlled by Britain as it had been before independence, and James Monroe, the American Minister in London, went so far as to demand financial compensation for lost trade from the British government.

However, after a brief flurry of detentions of American vessels by the Royal Navy, during which American insurance rates rose and shipper's profits fell, a newly elected British government under Grenville and Fox in effect reversed the *Essex* ruling. The 'Fox Blockade' of northern Europe, proclaimed in May 1806, was absolute only between the Seine and Ostend, and was taken by its lack of reference to American 're-exports' to imply that such discontinuous voyages could be resumed.[53] Monroe, however, although initially impressed by British pragmatism, began to assert that only American force would prevent such British interference in future.

THE CONTINENTAL SYSTEM AND ORDERS IN COUNCIL

Economic warfare between Britain and France escalated after January 1806, with France increasingly using her domination of other European countries to strike at British trade. In February 1806 the French procured the exclusion of British vessels from Prussian ports, adding to Britain's list of enemies. In November 1806, after Prussia had itself been defeated by the French, the Berlin Decree launched a Continental System designed to close all European ports to British vessels. In reply, in January 1807, the first of fourteen successive British Orders in Council extended the naval blockade of France, and eventually declared all ships trading in ports from which British vessels were excluded liable to capture. Spencer Perceval succinctly summarised the purpose of Britain's measures: 'The objects of the Orders in Council were not to destroy the trade of the Continent, but to force the Continent to trade with us.'[54]

A short-lived alliance between Britain, Russia and Prussia ended with the defeat of Russian and Prussian armies at Freidland. The resultant Treaty of Tilsit of July 1807 recruited Russian cooperation into the economic warfare against Britain, in which the Prussians were again included. In September 1807 the Royal Navy dissuaded Denmark from joining economic war against Britain only by a second bombardment of Copenhagen. Britain's fifth Order in Council, made on 11 November 1807, in effect forced trade in neutral vessels with French-dominated Europe to pass through British ports, with the transit fees paid adding to British revenues. In December 1807 Napoleon's Milan Decree sought to extend the Continental System by detaining neutral vessels, often American, which traded with Britain. It was further widened the following year by its inclusion of the ports of Spain and Portugal. Perhaps unsurprisingly, some in Britain saw the profitable expansion of neutral American maritime trade as an opportunistic and unprincipled exploitation of the British pre-occupation with an undemocratic European tyrant. Given Britain's earlier relationship with Americans, actual cooperation was probably too much to expect, but not, perhaps, the avoidance of active opposition. An attempt by the Americans to resist European interference in their neutral trade with economic pressure, by passing a Non-Importation Act in April 1806, greatly harmed Anglo-American relations.[55]

THE ISSUE OF IMPRESSMENT

Bad feeling between the governments of the United States and Britain was further aggravated by the impressment by the Royal Navy of apparently British seamen from American merchant vessels at sea. Desertion from the Royal Navy had long been a major problem, despite being a capital offence.[56] Therefore, the 'allegiance' of British seamen found on neutral vessels was, according to the Prince Regent, 'no optional duty which they can decline or resume at pleasure', but 'began with their birth and can only terminate with their existence'.[57] Nevertheless, higher wages, better conditions and a reduced risk of impressment so much encouraged the transfer of British merchant seamen that, by 1807, of 55,000 seamen engaged in American overseas trade, 'not less than 40% were British born'.[58] Their loss would be a serious economic handicap to American trade, and a Republican Congressman denounced their reclamation by the Royal Navy as an 'odious and tyrannic practice'.[59]

Accounts of the number of allegedly British seamen impressed from American vessels varied. Hezekiah Niles, a Baltimore journalist, estimated that by 1812 6,257 seamen, mostly American, had been impressed into the Royal Navy.[60] After the war, the British lawyer-turned-historian William James cited a Boston newspaper's account of a Congressional speech to reduce the number, at least to his own satisfaction, to 156.[61] Perhaps more credibly, William Dudley's 'conservative estimate' of 9,991 American seamen impressed between 1796 and 1 January 1812 'compensates for duplication of names'.[62] The British Foreign Office did investigate some authenticated mistakes, although repatriations appear to have been few.[63]

Some Royal Naval officers reclaimed apparently British seamen whenever opportunity arose, their decisions complicated by the 'similarity of language and manners', the availability of false naturalisation papers, and the American need for trained seamen.[64] The British search for deserters, however, had political implications when the examination of coastal vessels involved the violation of American territorial waters and even the exchange of gunfire between British and American warships. When, in June 1807, deserters from the British squadron off Chesapeake Bay joined American vessels, including USS *Chesapeake*, then leaving for sea, HMS *Leopard* was ordered to retrieve them. When the *Chesapeake*'s captain had refused permission to board *Leopard* opened fire, killing three Americans. Three of the four men taken from the *Chesapeake* were found to be American and released; the fourth, a British subject, was hanged.

News of the incident, on reaching Washington, strengthened President Thomas Jefferson's determination that an Anglo-American treaty 'of amity commerce and navigation', which had been signed on 31 December 1806, should not be submitted for Senate approval.[65] The Monroe–Pinkney treaty settled all outstanding trade issues, but attempts to agree on clauses defining legitimate impressment failed and, despite the allocation of extra time, the treaty was never ratified. In March 1807 a return to Tory government in Britain hardened attitudes and meant that Foreign Secretary Canning would not agree to any renegotiation. War was probably averted by the Admiralty's recall of the North America station's commander, Vice-Admiral George Berkeley, being seen as tacit agreement that British impressment policy could not include the stopping of neutral warships. Britain was eventually to offer financial compensation, but not before Jefferson, in July 1807, excluded British warships from all American waters.

A TRADITION OF BRITISH BLOCKADE

On the morning of 6 August 1807 an editorial in London's *Morning Post* expressed exasperation with American maritime, commercial and foreign policy and volunteered its opinion that 'Three weeks of blockade of the Delaware and Boston Harbour would make our presumptuous rivals repent of their puerile public conduct.'[66] That any section of British public opinion should recommend so unambiguously the blockade of a transatlantic partner-turned-rival while Britain was still engaged in a prolonged war with France measured the breakdown of a markedly interdependent commercial relationship.

However, from the outset, independent Americans were aware of their vulnerability to British maritime economic warfare. Perhaps partly as a result, Secretary of the Treasury Gallatin wrote from Washington to President Jefferson on 25 July 1807 that

> All those places which deserve the name of towns, & which, by the shipping they contain, or as deposits of produce & merchandise, offer a temptation of plunder or destruction, ought to have at least a battery to protect them against attack by a single frigate or other small force.[67]

Specifically, he thought that 'the practicality of preventing an enemy from keeping possession of the Chesapeake by <u>anything short of a superior naval force</u>' should be 'inquired into'. He realised, however, that the United States could not deploy such a force since, earlier in the year, Jefferson had made it clear that he preferred gunboats, suitable only for sheltered waters, and in February Congress had ordered an additional two hundred.[68]

Gallatin thought that the risk to

> Charleston ... next to New York, the greatest deposit of domestic produce in wartime, may be greater still ... the Potomac may be easily defended. But, an active enemy might land at Annapolis, march to the city, and re-embark before the militia could be collected to repel him ... <u>Washington</u> will be an object, in order to destroy the ships & naval stores, but particularly as a stroke which would give the enemy reputation & attach disgrace to the United States.[69]

Gallatin next raised the possibility of an American pre-emptive strike, timed for 'this autumn' or 'this winter': that is, of 1807.

> But, as long as the British hold Halifax they will be able, by the superiority of their naval force, to <u>blockade</u> during the greater part of the year, all our principal seaports, and particularly New York, including the Sound, Philadelphia, the Chesapeake and Charleston. If we take it, the difficulty to refit and obtain refreshment will greatly diminish that evil, and enable us to draw some advantage from our small navy on our own coast.[70]

Gallatin's intention seems to have been the permanent occupation of at least part of Canada, rather than temporarily as a bargaining-chip in any future negotiation over British naval encroachments into American territorial waters or about impressment. The Americans would surely have realised that, having once captured Halifax, any future withdrawal from it could result in an immediate resumption of the British practice to which they had previously objected.

Gallatin next discussed war finance. Gross customs revenue for 1806 had been $14.6m and, given American neutrality, was likely to exceed $15m in 1807.[71] Gallatin estimated that these 'present imposts' would be reduced by war to about $8m. This could be rectified by 'additional duties and taxes' of $2.5m, income from government land sales worth $0.5m and the call for a loan of $7m, a total of a further $10m, making available, if the loan call was successful, about $18m.[72] He then moved on to practicalities. 'As for transports on the coast of Maine for [attacks on] New Brunswick and Nova Scotia, the embargo by Congress will give enough to us': that is, the envisaged legislative ban on American overseas trade would make available sufficient merchant ships to transport troops to the Maritime Provinces.[73] In the event, Jefferson's embargo was not to be put into effect until December 1807.[74] A swift American attack on Britain's lightly held Halifax naval base, while Britain was heavily engaged in its war with France, might just conceivably have resulted in a precipitate peace based on *uti possidetis*, each signatory keeping what it held when the fighting stopped. Influential though Gallatin may have been, Jefferson evidently had not thought so.

JEFFERSON'S EMBARGO

In December 1807 Jefferson made an attempt to impose on Britain a fundamental change of policy by the use of economic sanctions in the form of an embargo on all American seaborne trade with Britain. He had intended cutting off the American export of crucial raw materials such as cotton and the importation of British manufactured goods. In the event, Jefferson's embargo was to cause greater economic harm to the United States than to its intended victim, and caused irreparable damage to his political career and subsequent reputation; he left office in March 1809, according to one British historian, 'a beaten man'.[75] British vessels nevertheless remained excluded from American waters, and trade with Britain forbidden by a Non-Intercourse Act.[76]

Both Jefferson and James Madison, his Secretary of State, believed that American trade restrictions would force both European belligerents to respect 'neutral rights', although the far greater extent of Anglo-American trade meant that Britain would be more affected than France. Despite Jefferson's experience, having succeeded to the presidency in 1809 Madison signed Macon's No. 2 Bill on 1 May 1810, which offered resumed trade to whichever European power repealed its restrictions on neutral trade. Napoleon's deceptive Cadore Letter to the American Minister in Paris, apparently dated 5 August 1810, made it look as if France had done so, thereby ensuring that after 2 February 1811 American trade restrictions applied solely to Britain.[77]

Furthermore, in an effort to monitor British vessels and to reduce impressment from coastal shipping United States warships increasingly patrolled the American eastern seaboard. On 16 May 1811 the American heavy frigate *President* was sent from Annapolis to investigate reports of both British and French warships stopping American vessels offshore. In darkness, gunfire was exchanged between the *President* and the British sloop *Little Belt* and, as a result, the smaller vessel was badly damaged, nine British seamen were killed and twenty-three others were wounded. Diplomatic relations between Britain and the United States were further strained. The incident was apparently triggered by American opposition to impressment rather than interference with neutral American trade,[78] but if, as Tracy argues, the incident was seen by contemporary Americans as 'a sign of the growing tendency in the United States to resist British exercise of maritime commercial control, even if it put the republic in the balance on the side of the Buonapartist Empire', then, at least until the defeat of Napoleon, further Anglo-American conflict was, if not inevitable, then extremely likely.[79]

MADISON'S ADDRESSES TO CONGRESS

By 5 November 1811 Madison was complaining in his Presidential Message to Congress that 'our coasts and the mouths of our harbours have again witnessed scenes, not less derogatory to the dearest of our natural rights, than vexatious to the regular course of our trade. Among the occurrences produced by British ships of war hovering on our coasts', he specifically mentioned the *Little Belt* incident, 'rendered unavoidable' by the British sloop having fired first on the heavy frigate, 'being therefore alone chargeable with the blood unfortunately shed in maintaining the honour of the American flag'.[80] Britain's Orders in Council and opposition to American designs on the Spanish territories in West and East Florida were added to Madison's catalogue of complaints, making war between a neutral engaged in trade and a belligerent imposing maritime blockade on a third party seem ever more likely. Madison then announced that American 'gunboats have, in particular harbours, been ordered into use. The ships of war before in commission, with the addition of a frigate, have been chiefly employed as a cruising guard to the rights of our coast.' '[T]he British Cabinet', he concluded, 'perseveres ... in the execution, brought home to the threshold of our territory, of measures which ... have the character, as well as the effect, of war on our lawful commerce.'[81]

On 1 June 1812 Madison again addressed Congress, complaining that British efforts to prevent neutral American carriers nullifying the blockade of France meant that 'British cruisers have also been ... violating the rights and peace of our Coasts. They hover over and harass our entering and departing Commerce ... and have wantonly spilt American blood within the sanctuary of our territorial jurisdiction.'[82] He ignored the violation of territorial jurisdiction involved in the United States' annexation of Spanish West Florida in October 1810, which had led to Britain's reinforcement of its North America squadron, and left unmentioned the current American designs on East Florida.[83] He also accused 'British traders and garrisons' with arming and inciting the 'Indians' 'connecting their hostility with that influence' in explaining renewed warfare on America's north-west frontiers. Alternative explanations for the possession of British muskets by the indigenous tribes were not explored, although it was not apparently until November 1812, with the war already begun, that the British government was to supplement the same 'articles which were sent out last year with the Addition of 2000 Light Musquets adapted for the use of the Indian tribes'.[84]

Madison did not mention that the Republican 'War Hawks', including the Speaker of the House, Henry Clay, argued that renewed hostility with north-west frontier 'Indians' would provide the pretext for the United States' invasion of Canada. This, they thought, could be completed before Britain could respond with sufficient strength, particularly once Quebec and the naval base at Halifax, Nova Scotia, had been seized.[85] Jefferson told Madison that the occupation of Quebec in 1812 and Halifax in 1813 would allow 'the final expulsion of England from the American continent'.[86] While still at war with France, and with Baltic supplies vulnerable, Britain could not afford to abandon Canadian bases or supplies of timber, naval stores and provisions.[87]

John Morier, Britain's chargé d'affaires in Washington, had long suspected the Madison administration of 'eager Subserviency to France' and, in January 1811, reported as much to the Foreign Office in London.[88] Twelve days later he described a letter written to the American Secretary of State Robert Smith as 'a pretty plain declaration that the French government & that of the US, regarding Britain as their common enemy, are united in pursuing certain measures against her', describing Smith as having 'displayed evident Symptoms of a Fear of Displeasing the French'.[89]

THE DECLARATION OF WAR

On 10 April 1812 Foreign Secretary Castlereagh reminded Augustus Foster, the British Minister in Washington, of the likely origins of the war. Since the Americans

> co-operated with France by prohibiting, in concurrence with her, the
> importation of British produce and manufactures into the Ports of
> America ... and continue to exclude British Commerce and British
> Ships of War from her Ports, while they are open to those of the enemy,
> it is then clear that we are at issue with America upon principles which,
> upon the part of this Govt. you are not at liberty to compromise.[90]

Castlereagh, nevertheless, thought that war was not yet inevitable:

> It is more probable that the near aspect [that] the question has now
> assumed may awaken them to the ****** folly of attempting either
> to force or intimidate Gr. Br., & that alarmed at the danger seen to
> themselves of the former attempt and the hopelessness of the latter,
> they may see an opportunity of receding without disgrace.[91]

Far from seeking any such opportunity, Madison referred the question to the House Foreign Relations Committee, which supported a declaration of war. The House of Representatives voted for war, but the Senate delayed its approval, although eventually agreed. Ironically, as the House of Commons considered the revocation of the Orders in Council as far as America was concerned, on 18 June 1812 the United States declared war on Britain.[92]

A week before war was declared, the First Lord of the Admiralty, Robert Dundas, Lord Melville, wrote to Admiral Lord Keith:

> The American Government are proceeding [at] great lengths in the way of provocation, with a view probably to local objects & to produce irritation against this Country ... undoubtedly such dangerous conduct may involve us in a quarrel.

Local British diplomats and naval and military commanders, he thought, 'seem to be using their utmost endeavour to guard against such an extremity; but it may be beyond their power to avert'.[93] He was soon to be proved right.

The possible use of maritime economic warfare and blockade was seldom far from either public minds or those of British decision-makers. The strategy had seemed equally applicable to the Mediterranean as to America when, earlier in the year, the Foreign Office had instructed the Admiralty to 'institute a strict and rigorous Blockade of the Islands of Corfu, Trano & Paxo & their several Dependencies on the Coast of Albania'.[94] It would now seem that just such a policy would need to be applied to the United States.

Unsurprisingly, therefore, when in June 1812 mutual Anglo-American irritation culminated in an American declaration of war the British Admiralty was in due course instructed to implement just such a policy of naval and commercial blockades of the United States. By 21 November 1812, after a fruitless British attempt to restore peace, the Secretary of State for War, Lord Bathurst, had ordered a precisely similar blockade of the American Atlantic seaboard to start 'forthwith' with, specifically, 'a strict and rigorous Blockade of the Ports and Harbors of the Bay of the Chesapeake and of the River Delaware'.[95] By 27 November the Admiralty had relayed the order to its Commander-in-Chief of the 'United Command' of the West Indies and North America, Admiral Sir John Borlase Warren; and on 26 December 1812 their Lordships reinforced the order with a further letter calling for 'a complete and vigorous Blockade'.[96]

The outbreak of war with the United States hardened attitudes and suspended much further debate in Britain on the legality of maritime blockade. British public opinion largely reflected the government's determination that Britain could

> never acknowledge any blockade to be illegal which has been duly notified, and is supplied by an adequate force, merely upon the ground of its extent, or because the ports or coasts blockaded are not at the same time invested by land.[97]

Therefore, by the spring of 1813, despite Britain's preoccupation with the ongoing war against Napoleon, the Royal Navy began its maritime blockades of the United States in earnest. From the outset, however, in the event of the States bordering on British North America seceding from the Union, their trade with Britain 'shall not be interrupted', but 'allowed to be carried on without molestation'.[98]

Both before and after the American declaration of war Melville received a great deal of unsought advice, some potentially useful.[99] One letter of January 1813, from Admiral Sir Henry Stanhope, a veteran of the War of American Independence, was better informed than most.[100] He recommended a survey of the warships laid up 'in ordinary' and selection of the best to be cut down as 58-gunned 'razees' (see p. 32). He realised that British attacks on 'Sea Port Towns' would, for the present, be 'unavailable and disastrous without such a Land Force as the Circumstances of the Country could not perhaps readily admit'. He would, however, 'effectually blockade them by such a well connected Chain of commanding Force as They should not be able to oppose, composed of small Squadrons under the Command of active and intelligent officers'. Knowing from personal experience that 'the Coast of America in its vast Extent, has innumerable small Harbours and Inlets as well for Trade as for the building and equipping of Armed vessels', he recommended 'keeping them in perpetual Alarm' by using Marines for feint and genuine attacks on coastal targets before 'the speediest Reembarkation'. Over the remaining two years of war, much of this advice was to be followed with great effect.

CHAPTER 2

WAR AT A DISTANCE:
CONSTRAINTS AND SOLUTIONS

I think the fact is that the Admiralty have merely humbugged Sir J
… They have equally tricked him in withdrawing reinforcements
and most shamefully neglected the squadron in the West Indies,
and on this Coast. What the devil they intend is hard to divine, bur
certain it is to say that our navy will be disgraced and our trade
ultimately ruined unless very speedy addition is made to every
division in these seas. (George Hulbert, Flag Secretary and Prize
Agent to Admiral Sir John Warren, to his brother John Hulbert,
2 January 1813)[1]

IF THE ROYAL NAVY WAS TO IMPOSE the hardships of economic warfare
on the enemy, its new war would generally have to be fought across the Atlantic.
There, its main North America base at Halifax, Nova Scotia, was almost 2,500
miles from London or Liverpool and over 600 miles from New York, the United
States' major port and commercial centre. As shown by Map 1, it would need
bases at St John's, Newfoundland, and St John, New Brunswick, to contribute to
the defence of Canada. It would also have to use its base in Bermuda, itself 650
miles from the nearest American mainland at Cape Hatteras, North Carolina.
This, however, was 700 miles from New York and 1,000 from Savannah, Georgia.
Prevailing winds, currents and trade routes all meant that vessels from Europe
would frequently approach North America from the Caribbean, and the West
Indies would therefore be involved in Britain's war with the United States. Bases
in Jamaica, the Bahamas and Antigua in the Leeward Islands would also be
needed.

It would take the first Commander-in-Chief of a new United Command of
North America and the West Indies, Admiral Sir John Borlase Warren, six and
a half weeks to reach his post from Portsmouth, typically encountering contrary
winds and autumnal gales.[2] On arrival, he would be responsible for British naval
and diplomatic affairs over an American eastern seaboard of over 2,000 miles,

without taking into account major estuaries and innumerable creeks and inlets or the circumference of many major islands such as Long Island, off New York.

Geographically, therefore, Warren's responsibilities would range from Newfoundland and New Brunswick, at latitude 48 degrees north, to include the entire American eastern seaboard to the Mississippi estuaries, Mobile and New Orleans, and extend across the Caribbean to the Leeward Islands at latitude 12 degrees north. Even during Britain's engagement in a world-wide war against the French Empire, this vast area represented an intimidating responsibility and, for all but the most able and energetic, an intellectual burden and psychological constraint on decision-making. Decisions regarding one area would affect others, often far distant and beyond reach, in ways difficult to predict. Although, at fifty-nine, Warren was far from being the oldest serving naval Commander-in-Chief, it might well have been a daunting prospect for him, and, even after receiving some urgently needed reinforcements, Warren reminded the First Lord of the Admiralty in late December 1813 that 'The Extent of this Coast however is [so] immense; that to shut up all ports would require Twice my Numbers.'[3]

Delays in communication over such distances would present a major problem both before and throughout the war. Dispatches from the American coast might occasionally reach Liverpool or Plymouth in as little as twenty-four days, but still needed express overland transport to London before governmental decisions were possible. Any initial advantage gained by rapid eastward transit would be offset by the six-week westward voyage with any reply.[4] Within the North American theatre written communications, often necessarily duplicated to safeguard against loss or delay, could take weeks to reach those expected to implement them. Such delays would have to be allowed for in the transmission of political instructions relayed by the Admiralty in London to the commander-in-chief, and in his tactical orders to subordinates.

Before the American declaration of war, Foreign Secretary Castlereagh's instructions to the Lords Commissioners of the Admiralty on 9 May 1812 ponderously attempted to cover every eventuality 'in consideration of the length of time that must necessarily elapse between any hostile measures on the part of the United States and any orders which the commanders of His M[ajest]y's Ships & Vessels upon their coasts could receive from your Lordships'. British commanders in North America were to have 'Instructions & Authority to repel any hostile aggression', but were 'at the same time to take especial care that they commit no Act of Aggression'. If warlike American intentions were 'certified to them' by documentary evidence they were to 'pursue such measures either offensive or defensive as may be most effective for annoying the Enemy' and 'protecting the Trade of His M[ajest]y's Subjects'. Castlereagh reiterated to their Lordships that they must 'strictly command and enjoin the Commanders … to exercise all possible forbearance'.[5] This constraint so impressed itself on Vice-Admiral Herbert Sawyer, Commander in Chief North America at Halifax, that, even after HMS *Belvidera* had been attacked by USS *President* on 23 June, and lives lost on both sides, he was to release the three American prizes the *Belvidera* took as she made good her escape to Nova Scotia. When *Belvidera* reached Halifax on 27 June Sawyer had not received any official confirmation of war, and so remained cautiously averse to any risk of reprimand.

The lack of rapid transatlantic communication had itself contributed to the outbreak of the war. Britain's eventual acceptance of Napoleon's apparent renunciation of the French Berlin and Milan decrees, which had attempted the economic isolation of Britain, would lead to Parliament's revocation of Britain's retaliatory Orders in Council.[6] Two-thirds of Madison's catalogue of complaints against Britain to Congress on 1 June 1812 had been his denunciation of the Orders, and, in the absence of diplomatic progress, on 18 June 1812 the United States had declared war. Unknown to Congress, Parliament was to revoke the Orders as far as America was concerned on 23 June, to be effective from 1 August. The issue of Royal Naval impressment of Americans at sea remained unresolved, however, and subsequent British attempts at armistice were to come to nothing. Most of the American maritime trade that Britain would seek to disrupt was to be found on the United States' eastern coastline at some stage of the transaction and, therefore, for the British, this was to be a war fought at a distance.

When the United States declared war on Britain in June 1812 the Royal Navy was, from the outset, constrained by the number of vessels it could keep in North America. The fact was well recognised in Britain, with the war against France in its nineteenth year. Despite Britain's superior numbers of warships, demands were such that shortages became critical. On 17 June 1812 Admiral George Hope of the Board of Admiralty confided privately to Admiral Lord Keith that intelligence grew of a build-up of French warships at Aix Roads, causing such anxiety that a pre-emptive strike was contemplated. 'We are bringing forward frigates as fast as we can, but how it will be possible to keep up the system of Blockade [of France] as he increases his Force, is beyond my comprehension for it is totally impossible to increase our navy in that ratio.' Nevertheless, he added, 'America … at this moment is very doubtful & we must provide for whatever may happen there.'[7]

That Britain's Royal Navy was overstretched was also recognised by some in Congress. Recommending American naval expansion to the House in January 1812, Republican Representative Langdon Cheves rejected the argument that an American navy would inevitably be overwhelmed by the Royal Navy. A British fleet with 'the high sounding number of a thousand ships appals the mind', but was 'a great misconception' when subjected to 'an examination of its actual force and the numerous requisitions which are made upon it'.[8] Furthermore, in his speech opposing American naval expansion, fellow Republican Adam Seybert was mistaken in asserting that Halifax, Nova Scotia, and Bermuda could 'afford every facility to fit and repair' British vessels in North America. Therefore, he had wrongly argued that the twenty-nine British vessels in Halifax and Newfoundland specified in his copy of Steel's List for July 1811 alone constituted 'a force in itself very superior to that of all the vessels belonging to the American navy'.[9] In common with the Royal Navy's Caribbean bases, neither Halifax nor

Bermuda had dry-dock facilities, and in other respects, like the persistent shortage of skilled labour, Britain's naval bases in North America were far from ideal. Vessels needing major repair would have to return to Britain.[10]

A later list of the 'active sea-going material of the Royal navy, exclusive of harbour vessels and inefficient or non-fighting ships', compiled from earlier sources, reduced Britain's effective fleet still further. According to Clowes Britain had in 1811 a total of 657 vessels, of which 124 were ships of the line. By 1812 continued hard use had reduced these figures to 623 and 120 respectively.[11] In reply to Warren's persistent pleas for reinforcements the Admiralty insisted that by 10 February 1813 his 'United Command' had no fewer than 97 vessels, including 'Eleven Sail of the Line', 34 frigates, 38 sloops and 12 smaller craft, so generous a proportion as to be creating strain elsewhere. He had, the Admiralty insisted, a force 'much greater in proportion than the National Navy of the Enemy … would seem to warrant'. Therefore 'it may not be possible to maintain on the Coast of America for any length of time a force so disproportionate to the Enemy as that which, with a view of enabling you to strike some decisive blow, they have now placed under your orders'.[12] The American navy, however, was not conveniently concentrated so as to facilitate any immediate 'decisive blow', nor would blockade produce immediate results. The Admiralty's ill-considered criticism shows, at least, a confusion of objectives.

If, by then, Warren had indeed been sent 'about one seventh of all the Sea going Vessels in the British Navy', the Royal Navy would have had a total of 679 vessels.[13] In fact, not all of the vessels promised had arrived, and others were so unfit for use on arrival as to need immediate repair. On such an extended coastline, all those vessels available to him would not even allow Warren to place 'all of the Enemy's Ports in a state of close and permanent Blockade'.[14]

Furthermore, during the first six months of the war the number of vessels available for blockading or any other duties was to be depleted by a succession of unexpected British defeats in single ship actions. The defeat of HMS *Guerriere*, 38, by USS *Constitution*, 44, on 19 August 1812 had come before Warren's arrival in Halifax, and was not therefore due to his personal 'want of due precaution', but other 'naval Disasters' were to follow, and did indeed 'make a strong impression on the public mind', both then and since.[15] The loss of the *Macedonian* to the American heavy frigate *United States* followed on 25 October 1812. The defeat of HMS *Java*, also by the *Constitution*, although under a different commander, came on 29 December 1812. These major defeats were accompanied by those of smaller British vessels. On 14 August 1812 HMS *Alert*, 16, had surrendered to the American frigate *Essex*, 32, to be followed on 13 October by the schooner *Laura*, 10. The *Frolic*, 18, was taken by the *Wasp*, also of 18 guns, on 18 October and, although later recaptured, had been among those British vessels unavailable between August and December 1812.[16] Moreover, on 10 September 1813 an entire British squadron of six vessels was lost in a fleet action with nine American vessels on Lake Erie, a defeat which, in the event, the Americans proved unable to exploit fully.[17]

Nonetheless, these surrenders came as a profound shock to naval professionals, politicians, newspaper editors and the nation as a whole, many of whom had come to regard the Royal Navy as practically invincible. Complacency, a preference for paint and polish and in some cases an absence of regular gun-drill were each to contribute to a series of British vessels striking their colours to American opponents. At the resultant court-martial the loss of the *Peacock* to the USS *Hornet* on 24 February 1813 was attributed at least in part to a 'want of skill in directing the Fire, owing to an omission of the Practice of exercising the crew in the use of the Guns for the last three Years … '.[18] Warren ordered that 'times of exercising the Great Guns and small Arms be always entered in the Ships Log conformable to the General printed Instructions'.[19] The Admiralty later issued a circular order that the scouring of iron stanchions and ring bolts should be 'gradually discontinued' and replaced by 'exercise at Arms'.[20] The early defeats were to some extent redressed in British minds by the capture on 1 June 1813 of the American frigate *Chesapeake* by the British frigate *Shannon*, where gun-drill had long been exemplary. More importantly, however, these actions did not prevent the Royal Navy's now persistent application of an increasingly effective commercial blockade of the American population.

Less unexpectedly, navigational hazards also reduced the number of British vessels available on the North America and West Indies stations. The first casualty was the sloop *Emulous*, from the Halifax squadron, grounded and lost on Cape Sable on 2 August 1812 and soon to be followed by the loss of the schooner *Chub*. A more serious loss on 5 October 1812 was that of the sixth rate *Barbadoes*, 24, newly transferred to the Leeward Islands squadron and carrying £60,000 as the payroll for Halifax Dockyard.[21] Another significant loss was that of the frigate *Southampton*, 32, of the Jamaica squadron, which struck a Caribbean reef on 27 November 1812, together with *Vixen*, an American prize taken five days before.[22] On 5 December 1812 the brig *Plumper*, carrying £70,000 from Halifax to St John, New Brunswick, was lost off Point Lepreau.[23] For British blockading squadrons, and the American vessels attempting to evade them, shifting sandbars were to pose a navigational problem throughout the war.

THE NAVY ESTIMATES

In Britain, Parliament regularly made the necessary financial provision for warship building, manning the Royal Navy and repairing wear and tear. Annual estimates of the cost of Royal Naval operations across the world were debated and voted on. The 'ordinary estimate' for ships and dockyard facilities was fixed at £1.6m in 1811 and £1.4m in 1812. It was to exceed £1.7m for both 1813 and 1814 and approach £2.3m in 1815.[24] 'Extra' estimated expenditure, customarily intended to meet increased maintenance and add new ships, exceeded £2m in 1811, but was reduced to £1.7m in 1812. It was to rise by more than 66% in 1813 to more than £2.8m, and to remain above £2m for the following year.[25] The annual parliamentary vote for the number of seamen and marines was a financial formula which provided theoretically for 145,000 men in both 1811 and 1812.

Having fallen to 140,000 in 1813 this was to reach a total of 207,400 in 1814. In practice, these figures meant that around 130,000 men were financially allowed for between 1812 and 1814.[26]

Ultimately, financial constraints governed the logistical support for the war in North America as elsewhere, and determined the supplies of provisions and ordnance. The Navy Estimate fixed annually by the House of Commons had reached £19.8m in 1811, and despite having fallen slightly to £19.3m in 1812 was to reach a record £20m in 1813. It reverted to £19.3m for 1814. Clearly, Britain's economic strength and relative financial and fiscal efficiency was such that as well as the political will, the necessary finance, although customarily in arrears, was nevertheless available to fight the Americans as well as the French between 1812 and 1815.[27]

According to the Admiralty, on his arrival at Halifax on 26 September 1812 Warren's United Command was to be comprised of eighty-three named 'Ships in Sea Pay'. Some, however, were in urgent need of refurbishment or repair. Thirty-seven were based either at Halifax or Newfoundland, and the rest in the Caribbean.[28] Among them were the elderly 64-gunned *Africa*, launched as long before as 1781, and the obsolescent *Antelope*, 50. Eight frigates with between 38 and 32 guns were supplemented by twenty-five brigs and sloops with fewer than 20 guns, and by two receiving ships.

Later, in December 1812, Warren would revert to an earlier idea as a practical solution to his shortage of useful vessels. He suggested to the Admiralty, as others had before him, that six or seven elderly battleships due for refit should be cut down, or 'razed', from three decks to two, and from 74 guns to 58.[29] This would remove heavy, deteriorated upper-works, keeping the sturdy lower hull and leaving a fighting ship robust enough to match the relatively new American heavy frigates, nominally of 44 guns. Lighter than before, they might prove faster, and, with a reduced draught, could be more useful in the shallow water of harbours and estuaries. The razees *Goliath*, *Majestic* and *Saturn* were ready for use in North America by late 1813. Another cost-saving solution, first tried almost twenty years before, was to build several vessels from pitch pine, or deal, a cheaper, lighter wood than oak. Even with earlier and more frequent refits, these derisively termed 'fir-frigates' would prove neither durable nor very resistant to battle damage, but *Leander* and *Newcastle* would nevertheless be available by 1814.[30]

The Royal Navy in North America was opposed by a United States Navy of seventeen vessels, of which seven were frigates.[31] Three were heavy frigates, nominally of 44 guns but mounting more, the practice of most sailing navies. Sturdily constructed, with crucial parts of southern 'live' oak, they had proved resistant to damage and were usually fast enough to outsail potentially superior opposition, such as a British 74, in all but the heaviest seas. Three further frigates were rated at 36 guns, and a fourth at 32. Ten years of Republican opposition to naval expansion and economising on maintenance had, however, contributed to a deterioration in their condition. Two frigates, the *Boston* and the *New York*, were found to be beyond repair, and another, the *Adams*, was razeed into a 28-gun corvette.[32] Only eight other sloops and brigs, carrying between 18 and 12 guns, had been built since 1800, including the brig *Viper*, added as recently as 1810. Flotillas of gunboats intended to guard harbours and estuaries had been built, but had proved unusable beyond sheltered waters, and were unpopular and difficult to man. Seagoing traditions in American coastal regions meant that skill levels in the United States 'public' vessels were often very high, and morale had been raised by American naval successes against North African pirates and in the Quasi War against France between 1797 and 1801.[33] By December 1812, the United States Navy had lost to the Royal Navy nothing bigger than the *Wasp*, 18.[34]

Despite its comparatively small size, the United States Navy formed a significant constraint on both British strategic planning and tactical operations. It posed a potential threat to British seaborne trade, especially in the early stages of a maritime economic war, with voyages begun before its declaration still incomplete. British vessels used to convoy economically important merchant ships could not at the same time be used to blockade American ports, and those that stopped to deal with an American threat to a merchant convoy could not guard it against the possibility of attack by other American vessels, including privateers, as it sailed on. Even with relatively small numbers, American warships presented the British with a problem of priorities.

REPROVISIONING, REFIT AND REPAIR

Whatever the number of British warships available on the North American station, they would inevitably need continual reprovisioning, refit and repair, and their crews time to recover from the cumulative effects of illness and injury, especially after action or bad weather. Theoretically, only a third of the force available might be deployed at any one time since one-third might be under repair and another third in transit to or from its base. In practice, operational necessity and the expertise of specialist crew members such as sailmakers, riggers and carpenters would make it possible to postpone a return to port. Copper sheathing, routinely applied to the hulls of Royal Naval vessels since about 1779, offered protection against marine worms and weed growth, and had increased the time before hull-cleaning was necessary once more.[35] Nevertheless, in October 1813 Warren had reported to the Admiralty that one-fifth of his force was either on passage or needed refitting or heavy repair.[36]

An acute shortage of food and water might make return imperative, and occasionally this factor was a constraint on Britain's implementation of maritime economic warfare. One of the most serious potential limits to a strategy of blockade which, in order to be both legal and effective, required a continuous presence was the need of blockading crews for provisions. To a great extent, however, the basic supplies of food and drink for blockading squadrons was to be provided by the Victualling Board's provisioning service, which has been described as 'the most important triumph of eighteenth-century British naval administration', and which continued its work into the early years of the following century.[37] Failing or contrary winds might take a squadron off station, or prolong a passage to another, but generally the crew's needs for food and drink were reliably and efficiently catered for. The availability of basic foodstuffs allowed the Royal Navy in North America to remain 'on station, performing the tasks of seapower'.[38]

Provisioning agents in Halifax and Bermuda made local purchases to supplement supplies of preserved food sent out from Britain by contractors such as Andrew Belcher, responsible in 1813 for victualling the North America station.[39] Salt beef, salt pork, split peas, butter and cheese were sent out in casks, with bagged biscuit. 'Strong' beer and spirits, including rum, complemented or replaced often long-stored water, while fresh meat, milk and eggs might be supplied by livestock kept aboard. Provisions might be acquired by *ad hoc* arrangements made offshore, such as fishing over the side or the confiscation of an enemy cargo.

Shortages might be resolved with illicit American supplies bought or taken from the shore, from visiting boats or from those encountered at sea. Profit-seeking Americans had long been a handicap to the United States' war effort. Madison's second embargo attempted to reduce, if not eradicate, 'the palpable and criminal intercourse held with the enemy's forces blockading or invading the waters and shores of the United States'.[40] However, while in Massachusetts Bay in October 1813, Captain Hayes of the razee *Majestic* found that 'The Inhabitants of Province Town are disposed to be on friendly terms, and have promised to allow the ships to take water from their Wells and on reasonable terms will supply them with fish Fruit and Vegetables & also good firewood.' In return, Hayes provided 'a note to several Owners of Schooners going for a Cargo, stating the assistance afforded the *Majestic* and recommending their being permitted to pass.'[41] The Royal Navy's need for food and water therefore occasionally prevented the achievement of a completely impervious commercial blockade of the United States.

RECRUITMENT AND DESERTION

The recruitment and retention of sufficient manpower was a problem in both navies, especially limiting operations involving contact with the shore. Although better paid than British crews, American seamen transferred from the sea to gunboats or the Lakes, and, so deprived of their bounties or incentives, tended to desert or fail to re-enlist on completion of their agreed term. As the war progressed and British commercial blockade increased unemployment among American merchant seamen, the problem for the United States Navy might have been eased but for the dissatisfaction caused by lack of pay other than in Treasury notes subject to up to 25% discount.[42]

Between 1811 and 1813 29,405 men were press-ganged into the Royal Navy, but in the same period 27,300 deserted.[43] Recruitment and retention was so great a problem for the navy in Britain that even when ships were newly available crews were hard to find. On 4 June 1813 Melville wrote to Warren that 'Some of our Fir Frigates have been launched, and others are coming forward. The whole will probably be completed in the course of this year, but we have great Difficulty in procuring men for them.'[44] For the British, desertion was such a lasting concern that, soon after arriving in Halifax, Warren had issued a proclamation promising deserters leniency and encouraging British seamen in American service to return. It was something his predecessor had already tried, although with little success in either case. Warren went further, however, writing to ask Melville to suggest to the Prince Regent that a royal pardon of deserters would prove effective.[45]

The desertion problem may have been worsened by low morale caused partly by delays in the distribution of prize money. On 5 November 1812 Warren wrote to Melville that such delay caused

> a bad effect among the Seamen as the Contrast is too great for their
> feelings to observe the Americans as Capturing, Condemning
> Selling and Dividing the profits of the British ships [taken] & that
> not one of the enemy vessels brought in by their Exertions has as yet
> been bestowed upon them.[46]

After the early months of 1813, even unshared prizes, which formed the majority, took a year to settle.[47] Adjudication for the sixth of prizes shared between a number of captors took longer. As Warren's accounts were later to show, some disputes remained unresolved until long after the war, by which time some beneficiaries were untraceable, or possibly dead.[48] Especially when commanders sank or burned prizes in order to avoid delays and the need for sending away prize crews when already shorthanded, blockade duty became unprofitable and unpopular with both officers and men. A motive for remaining in naval service was gone, and blockade appeared to vacillate between tedium, danger and disappointment.[49]

The problem remained no less acute in 1814. In both January and February Niles' *Weekly Register*, a Baltimore periodical, mentioned the 'mass desertions' of British seamen from *Albion*, *Superb* and *Newcastle*.[50] This may not have been merely propaganda, since on 25 June 1814 Rear-Admiral George Cockburn was to write to Warren's successor, Vice-Admiral Alexander Cochrane, that, although blockade 'this last Month has cost the Enemy around us more than a Million of Dollars', desertion remained a problem, with 'Many instances of our Marines walking over to the Enemy'.[51] A 'significant number' of deserting British seamen evidently enlisted in the United States Navy or in American privateers, despite the risk of capital punishment if captured – or, at less hazard, in the American merchant service.[52]

It is often more or less explicitly suggested that a major constraint on the Royal Navy's use of maritime economic warfare in North America and the West Indies between 1812 and 1815 was the mediocre, or even poor, quality of some British naval personnel. Individual captains and lieutenants, such as Broke of the *Shannon*, are often praised for their competence and courage. Broke is rightly admired for his innovation and dedication to gun-drill, vindicated on 1 June 1813 by his swift defeat of the *Chesapeake*. Nonetheless, criticism was made of both Sawyer and Warren, and some of the seamen and marines they commanded, with the implication that twenty years of almost continuous war with France was by then involving some scraping of Britain's barrel of manpower.[53]

Warren himself, however, had been selected as commander-in-chief from a number of possibilities. Sir Alexander Cochrane, his eventual successor, had written to Lord Melville, First Lord of the Admiralty, in April 1812:

> Should the Embargo said to have taken place in America end in a
> War and there is a vacancy for that Command they have the offer of
> my services having a perfect knowledge of the Coast from my
> having served there in the American War and five years since while
> France aided the United States.

Having been Governor of Guadeloupe after contributing to its capture in 1810, he added,

> Should my services be required in the Western World either here or
> on the Coast of America I will be ready in twenty four hours notice
> to embark on board any ships that may be sent for me.[54]

Warren was nonetheless preferred, partly because of his diplomatic experience as plenipotentiary extraordinary to St Petersburg between 1802 and 1804, apparently thought likely to equip him for dealing with the potential armistice to which the British government hoped the Americans might agree on learning of the revocation of its Orders in Council, as far as they affected America. Furthermore, Warren's service record was impressive. As well as having dealt successfully with an earlier French threat to Ireland, Warren had expertise in precisely the sort of economic warfare now to be employed against America. Warren had earlier commanded one of the independent squadrons engaged in the blockade of France, which 'with the best young captains and a free hand to cruise' had in doing so 'won a large share of glory and prize money'. The effect of these squadrons 'on French coasting trade [had] reduced Brest by 1795 to near starvation'.[55]

Warren's success, however, had led, perhaps inevitably, to a reputation for acquisitiveness. By 1806 he seems to have made an enemy of a somewhat misanthropic Admiral of the Fleet, Earl St Vincent, who felt that 'Sir JW is a mere partisan, preferring prize money to the public good at all times'.[56] Earlier in the year he had accused Warren of duplicity and greed, writing that he would 'intrigue for a chief command … He wants money and will not be contented with the small pittance likely to be the lot of the puisne flag officer in this fleet.'[57] By November 1806 others shared a poor view of Warren, one writing that he was 'indefensible' and 'now good for nothing but fine weather & easy sailing & is no longer enough in earnest about the duties of his profession to go through them with credit to himself & advantage to the service'. The writer, Thomas Grenville, then First Lord of the Admiralty, added that he was 'very sorry for it'.[58] But, even if wholly deserved, Warren's reputation might seem to have made him well-suited for a war based on the capture of as much American commercial property at sea as possible and the destruction of strategically important infrastructure ashore.

On 17 June 1812 the 'Most Secret' letter of the Foreign Secretary, Lord Castlereagh, had told Warren that 'In a few days you will receive some formal Documents upon the Subject, with Instructions as to your Conduct towards the American Govt' in advance of his appointment to the 'United Command' on 3 August. At least initially, Warren clearly enjoyed not only the respect and confidence of Melville, the current First Lord, and the Admiralty's political representative in the Cabinet, but also that of Castlereagh, whom he met in early August 1812 to receive his instructions in person.[59]

However, success in maritime commercial blockade was necessarily a slow and cumulative process, and criticism of Warren's operational conduct was renewed in the tone and substance of First Secretary of the Admiralty Croker's letters, conveying their Lordship's disappointment at the lack of prompt success against the United States Navy. Croker commented on Warren's lack of 'judicious arrangement' of 'adequate' resources.[60] Many subsequent historians have taken their cue from these observations without making sufficient allowance for the complexity of the circumstances and the timescale in which Warren was expected to succeed. The self-interested machinations of the West India Committee were eventually to secure reseparation of the United Command and Warren's displacement by Cochrane just as the temporary end of the war in Europe eased Britain's shortage of vessels and manpower.

The prevalence of sickness amongst naval personnel at every level also limited British operations in North America. At Halifax, Vice-Admiral Sawyer did not long survive Warren's arrival; on 7 October 1812 Warren used Sawyer's poor health as the ostensible reason for suggesting his removal.[61] Warren's secretary and prize agent George Hulbert welcomed Sawyer's replacement as second-in-command by Rear-Admiral Sir George Cockburn. 'The change is favourable to Sir J and instead of an old woman he has got a devilish active fellow and just such as he wanted.'[62] By 3 March 1813 Cockburn's squadron was blockading the Chesapeake. Blockading operations there, however, were curtailed for 1813 as early as 6 September, when Warren was obliged to leave Lynnhaven Bay for Halifax 'as the men have been afflicted with a fever and ague sometimes prevalent in this Climate'. Warren's postscript added that he too had 'been unwell' but hoped that 'a few weeks in Nova Scotia will recover my health'.[63] The climates found in the various parts of Warren's 'United Command' may well have exacerbated the shortage of those available for duty. The problem of sickness was again experienced the following year when almost 44% of two battalions of Royal Marines raiding the Chesapeake in November 1814 were thought by Captain Barrie of the *Dragon* to be 'such poor things naturally and so very sick that I shall be able to do little with them'.[64]

Warren's shortages of vessels and manpower, especially at the initial stages of the war, were all the more severe when seen in relation to the wide range of responsibilities imposed upon him by the Cabinet, where naval views were represented by the First Lord, Viscount Melville. The 'pleasure' of the Prince Regent and Privy Council, agreed by the Cabinet and sent as instructions by the Foreign Secretary, Lord Castlereagh, to the Lords Commissioners of the

Admiralty, were duly transmitted as orders from Melville and the Board of Admiralty. Warren was made responsible for exploring the possibilities of an armistice 'as was [e]nunciated by Lord Castlereagh' in early August. Before sailing on 14 August Warren was supplied by the Foreign Office, via the Lords Commissioners of the Admiralty, with precise instructions and an agreed draft letter to Madison, or Secretary of State Monroe, 'should he find it suited to circumstances at the time of his arrival off the Coast'.[65]

On his arrival at Halifax Warren found that forty-six American vessels, over half of them full-rigged ships, had been detained before 17 September under the terms of the General Embargo on American shipping which the British government had applied on 31 July 'in any of the ports, harbours or roads within any part of his Majesty's domains'.[66] But Castlereagh's 'secret instructions' of 6 August, given to Warren before he left, were to 'make a proposition to the American government'. In the event of the Americans revoking their letters of marque, Warren was to suspend hostilities.[67] Since American prizes taken between May and 1 August were 'to be restored less costs', energetic pursuit of further American prizes was effectually constrained by the wait for an American answer, as well as by Warren's need to employ his limited resources to protect British merchant vessels from American privateers. While waiting, Warren noted that no revocation of American letters of marque appeared, and that privateers were still being equipped and manned.[68]

Warren sent his letter to Madison, via Secretary of State Monroe, on 30 September 1812, but did not receive Monroe's answer until 16 November.[69] Until receipt of Monroe's reply, full-scale implementation of the Royal Navy's commercial blockade had been greatly restrained by the British diplomatic effort, for which Warren had, in part, been selected. Whereas 110 American vessels had been detained in Halifax harbour or brought in for adjudication between the declaration of war on 18 June and Warren's armistice proposal of 30 September, only eight were captured during October and none at all in November, while Warren waited for an American reply. Only two were taken during December, while news spread that the Americans had, in effect, again chosen war.[70]

If, in November, a two-month delay in a British response was to be avoided, Warren had to make an appropriate decision on Monroe's reply. In the event, the American answer made any armistice conditional on a prior British abandonment of impressment. Deciding that this was unacceptable, Warren resumed the maritime blockade. Britain could not reasonably have been expected to concede any of its sovereign rights before negotiations began. Warren's naval initiative had been limited by political instructions which, while imposing heavy responsibilities, had left him ample scope for serious error.

'LICENCES WITHOUT NUMBER'

Similarly, Warren had to deal with the complexities of neutral vessels carrying 'Letters of Protection' against British detention, often called 'Commercial Licences for Trading with the Enemy'. These were issued, with varying degrees of propriety, to neutral shippers, including Americans, to export American flour and grain to British armies in Canada, the Iberian Peninsula, Gibraltar and the British West Indies, as well as to the civilian populations. By allowing neutral and even United States merchant vessels out of some American ports, and by permitting their eventual return, even if only in ballast, such licences were held by some to render all British blockades illegal, even when neutrals were warned by proclamation. Some Americans argued that 'by the maritime law, any blockade abrogated all licences to trade; if otherwise the blockade was to be deemed to be broken'.[71] Those boarded could claim vociferously that Britain could issue licences or proclaim blockades, but not both. In any case, licences seemed to Warren to have proliferated 'beyond all idea for Spain Gibr & the West Indies from the Americas', having been issued not only by Augustus Foster, the British Minister in Washington, but also from Halifax by Vice-Admiral Sawyer, by Andrew Allen, the former British Consul in Boston, and, from Britain, by the Home Secretary, Viscount Sidmouth. By October 1812 Warren had successfully sought Sawyer's replacement and Allen's conduct was being officially questioned.[72] By February 1813, Warren felt that it was 'impossible to Institute a Blockade of the Enemies Ports in the Face of Neutral Licences and protections without Number', a situation 'which required from the Admiralty clear and explicit Instructions to enable me to act with Effect'.[73]

Such licences were familiar to all concerned since, officially, an average of almost 10,000 a year had been issued between 1807 and 1811 alone, part of a total of 53,156 each valid for up to nine months.[74] A conciliatory British offer in May 1812 to share equally with American applicants the number of licences issued for trade with Europe had come to nothing. By the end of August 1812 another 500 had been issued. The number of licences encountered by British blockading squadrons had also been increased by convincing forgeries, openly on sale in American cities for up to $5,000, complicating the day-to-day decisions of boarding officers.[75] Such British difficulties in the early months of the war contributed to something approaching American complacency. On 11 September 1812 John Maybin, a Philadelphia commercial agent, wrote

> I believe with some of our Merchants the Confidence they have that the British Cruisers will not Molest them going to Lisbon and Cadiz – others have a Pas[s]port under the Authority from Admiral Sawyer & Mr Foster – for which I am told they pay one Dollar per Barrel.[76]

Warren's frustration is occasionally evident, possibly straining his relations with London. As late as August 1813 he complained to Melville that 'The swarm of Licences to Neutral Flags to the Eastern States renders the warships of no avail & is beyond an idea in consequence.'[77]

Vessels flying false colours also constrained British commercial blockade at sea, with potentially career-damaging reprimands awaiting junior officers guilty of creating misunderstandings with, for example, Russian, Swedish and Danish neutrals. 'If the war is to proceed', Warren wrote, 'it should be with activity against the South', which had sent 'to Sea Numbers of Ships under Spanish, Portuguese and of late obtained Swedish Colours from St Bartholemews: the property is thus covered … '.[78] If commercial blockade of the United States was to be effective, the problems posed by both unrestricted licences and the use of false colours would have to be resolved.

Warren himself felt a lack of unequivocal instructions and, on 7 October 1812, asked Melville for unambiguous orders. He seems to have felt particularly aggrieved after meeting a newly arrived American agent for prisoners of war, who

> enquired if I had been informed that Orders by the King and Council had been issued in England to permit all Ships with Supplies of Provisions to The Peninsula to pass free, which I answered in the negative having received no Instructions on that Head.[79]

Warren's inherently ambiguous orders were a major constraint on the operation of an impervious commercial blockade. By April 1814, however, the problems brought by licences had been largely resolved for his successor by the end of Wellington's need for American grain and flour, the reseparation of Warren's United Command and the extension of the British blockade to include the ports of New England.

THE DEMANDS OF CONVOY

Especially during the early stages of the war, the reconciliation of the simultaneous demands of both offensive and defensive maritime economic warfare in North America constituted a real constraint on each. By March 1813 *The Times* had castigated both government and Admiralty for the loss of 'Five hundred merchantmen and three frigates' to American warships.[80] From the outset, however, the Admiralty had revoked almost all existing licences to sail without convoy protection and given Warren 'positive direction that no Merchant Vessels should be permitted to sail without Convoy and that frequent and regular protection should be afforded between the different Ports' of Warren's command.[81] The West India Committee, a powerful pressure group representing growers, merchants and shippers, regularly reminded government and Admiralty that British merchant vessels would need protection in the Caribbean and during their voyages to and from Britain. As a result Melville wrote, in part reassuringly, to Warren from London that

> The clamour has been great here, though apparently unfounded, on your withdrawing a large portion of the West India force to the northward. The provision of sufficient convoys between Quebec & Halifax & the West Indies will not escape your attention.[82]

Other vessels trading between Canada and Britain would also have to be convoyed. The need to defend British trade from American attack was undeniable, but placed a strain on Warren's limited resources. By September 1813 earlier losses, vessels on 'numerous Blockades' and 'Others gone home with Convoys', had together produced 'the greatest Difficulty ... to answer these Several Demands of Service'. Warren would 'find it difficult to preserve & relieve the several Blockades and to guard the Islands & furnish the Convoys constantly Demanded & Ships'.[83]

Warren had little choice. He had been provided with an abstract of the 1798 Convoy Act, which it was 'their Lordships intention to enforce', and reminding him that 'no persons' were 'authorized to grant Licences to Sail without Convoy'. It specified severe penalties for masters leaving a convoy without permission.[84] For shippers, costly delay in assembling convoys was partly offset by reduced insurance premiums, but for Warren there were few advantages. One solution was to use vessels returning to Britain for repair, or to order vessels to complete a convoy duty before returning to patrol. Another was to allow escorts to leave a convoy just long enough to burn or sink a capture before rejoining the slower merchantmen. In December 1812 the *Shannon*, ordered to escort a convoy bound for Britain, was 'prowling about, half convoying and half cruizing and very angry at our want of success', hoping to 'dismiss our merchantmen in a week or ten days' and 'then stride about more freely'.[85]

The possibility of separate squadrons of American warships escaping simultaneously in order to join forces to lift the British blockade of a major American port formed another constraint on the allocation of Warren's blockading squadrons. Too great a concentration at one port might leave another blockading squadron vulnerable. In early June 1813 an anxious Melville wrote privately to Warren trusting that his 'Squadrons off New York and Boston will be on their guard against being caught between two fires by the junction of the Enemy from those Ports'. Melville hoped that he would soon 'learn that your most important object, the blockading [of] the Enemy's Ships of War in their Ports has been attained, as also the other objects of putting a total stop to their Trade and Annoyance of their Coast'.[86] The first was clearly vital in order to achieve the second and third objectives while unmolested by American warships, particularly any acting in concert. Warren's solution was to ensure, as far as possible, that at least one 74 and several frigates were stationed at each important port. Although a welcome change from equivocal instructions about vessels carrying licences or flying false neutral colours, without adequate reinforcements such exhortations would not help.

NAVAL HELP FROM THE FRENCH

The possibility of French intervention in this Anglo-American war, as in the last, took up time and effort in London as well as in North America. Although, theoretically, French warships blockaded in the Channel should not be able to cross the Atlantic, in unfavourable weather and visibility an escape would not be impossible. The need for maintaining the blockades of French ports also acted as a constraint since it meant that fewer British vessels were available for service against the United States. In October 1812 Warren had alerted Melville that

'There is a report in the U: States that bonaparte has pledged himself to Lend them 20 Sail of the Line a Division of which may be Shortly Expected.'[87]

A 'Secret & Confidential' letter from the Admiralty Office to Warren, dated 19 June 1813, again discussed concern that escaping 'French Squadrons from Brest or Rochfort' were 'not unlikely to appear off the North American coast'. Warren was further warned to 'prevent surprise of any of your blockading squadrons'. On the same day Admiral Lord Keith was ordered to instruct the senior officer of any relieving force to take under his command on arrival only enough of Warren's North American squadrons to enable him to match a potentially combined force of French and United States warships on the American eastern seaboard. He was to be reminded of the importance of the British blockading squadrons, and warned not to 'weaken or divert any blockading squadron off any of the Ports in which any American National Ship may be'.[88] Although unlikely, the prospect of French intervention was thus a constraint on British actions on both sides of the Atlantic. In the event, any hopes Madison might have entertained of French naval, military or financial help, were made unrealistic by the British maritime blockade of France.

Nevertheless, Melville's increasingly evident concern was at least in part a reflection of the domestic political climate in which he held office. Melville represented the Admiralty in Cabinet and in Parliament, where Warren's perceived lack of progress was subject to Opposition scrutiny and barbed comment. How their conduct of the American war was seen at home was a constant factor in the decision-making of both men. Warren particularly knew that, all the while, well-placed applicants were eager to supplant him.

The officers and men comprising the British blockade's boarding parties were clearly expected to conform not only to current legal constraints but also to the moral and social standards of their time, as shown by the note book of one young officer evidently expected to learn the comprehensive and strict regulations concerning maritime blockade. Those painstakingly written out by James Dunn aboard the frigate *Spartan* between 1811 and 1813 contained precise legal and practical 'Directions for examining Ships at Sea, and sending them for adjudication'. 'In the visitation & search of Neutral Vessels', for example, he 'must exercise as little hardship or personal vexation as possible and must detain Ships no longer than is necessary for a fair examination into the use, property & destination of the Ship's Cargo'.[89]

The rules were punctiliously applied. On 12 May 1813, for example, HMS *Hogue* took and burned the 366-ton American merchantman *Acteon* returning in ballast from Cadiz to Boston with a licence to export grain granted by the British Minister in Cadiz. Two years later the American owner claimed damages against Captain Thomas Capel of the *Hogue* in London's Admiralty Court. There, Sir William Scott, Lord Stowell, ruled that the owner had been 'unjustly deprived of his property' and awarded 'restitution with costs and damages' totalling £4,000, payable by Capel, who could make 'representation' to the British government for compensation if it thought his decision to burn *Acteon* acceptable.[90]

Proper conduct was also expected towards captured enemy personnel. Civilian passengers on vessels intercepted, especially women and children, would generally have expected courteous, even generous, treatment at the hands of the Royal Navy, and, according to contemporary American newspapers, both they and prisoners evidently received it on most occasions.[91] Seven rioting American seamen killed on 6 April 1815, while still held at Dartmoor prison in England, proved an unfortunate exception.[92]

Throughout 1813 British commanders at all levels spent much time concerned with shortages. In March 1813 Warren had been ordered to 'make Bermuda your permanent Station, it is the most centrical Spot within the Limit of your Station.'[93] But, although Bermuda offered refuge from the biting winter cold and persistent fogs of more northerly waters, such as Halifax between November and March, it suffered serious shortages. Warren had complained to Croker in February 1813 that 'There is not any Rope … left in the Stores of the Royal Yard nor any to be had in the Islands, the ships are in great want, and the Stores in Halifax being likewise drained I apprehend the highest inconvenience in refitting my squadron.'[94]

Periodic shortages of naval stores in both Halifax and Bermuda and the more permanent lack of such dockyard facilities as dry docks, and of such skilled workers as shipwrights, did nothing to ease Warren's anxiety over fulfilling the Admiralty's escalating demands. Although costly both to build and defend, 'Had a dry dock been built at Halifax, it would have changed the strategic balance, not only in the North Atlantic, but also in the West Indies.'[95]

Although for Warren provisioning was a permanent concern, his commanders also made local arrangements. On 1 May 1813 Hardy in *Ramillies*, stationed off Block Island, got 'plenty of water and stock from it and we also get our linen washed there. The inhabitants are very much alarmed … but as long as they supply us we shall be very civil to them.'[96] On 1 June 1813 Warren had returned to Bermuda 'with Ships being reduced in the article of Provisions to one week'.[97] Meanwhile, Capt Oliver of *Valiant*, responsible for keeping Decatur's squadron blockaded in New London, 'anchored off Gardiner's Island, from whence we could see the Enemy Ships in New London River &c … sent the *Acasta* to Fort-pondbay where she got wood and water with great ease also a few Cattle.'[98] By July, Warren was anxious that the Americans might 'fortify Old Point Comfort and prevent the Ships employed upon the Blockade watering or laying so High up in Lynhaven Bay (sic) as may be necessary for their protection in December and January.'[99]

WEATHER AND CLIMATE

The most consistently frustrating constraints on the Royal Navy's operation of economic warfare in North America were probably those posed by climate and the weather. Temperature inversion in warmer weather caused spring fogs and summer mists known as 'frets'. In June 1813 Warren had confessed that, despite a 74 and three frigates outside Boston, both *President* and *Congress* had escaped 'in a fog which is prevalent at this Season'.[100] Reduced visibility was common even in August. By late November 1813 'Gales of wind & fog which so frequently occurs on this coast' had caused stragglers to lose sight of convoy escorts, so becoming more vulnerable to risk of capture.[101] On 30 December 1813 Warren had to admit that 'on dark Nights with Strong Winds' several fast merchant ships had escaped to sea.[102] Such setbacks were likely to produce recriminations and to lower morale.

Winter weather conditions on the United States north-eastern seaboard often made watching a harbour such as Boston or New York so difficult as to make failure in blockading them all too likely, while making depreciation of both ships and crews both unavoidable and difficult to rectify. In February 1813 Warren had reminded the Admiralty that blizzards often rendered blockading Boston and Rhode Island extremely difficult between November and March.[103] Meanwhile, between Boston and Halifax, Broke had encountered strong north-easterly gales. The *Shannon's* crew had been issued with heavy worsted under-garments, together with mittens: necessary, but restricting, while handling frozen sails and rigging.[104]

Weather conditions created problems for British blockading squadrons even in summer, when fogs were frequent and persistent, and while prevailing westerly winds assisted attempts by determined American masters and commanders to evade patrols which, however diligent, could not be everywhere at once, and which spent much time and effort beating back towards the American coast.

On 12 November 1813 the weather then sought to compound Warren's problems when a wayward and unseasonal 'hurricane' struck as far north as Halifax, causing unpredictable devastation. The following day Warren reported that, although lasting only ninety minutes,

> the direful effects of it are beyond belief, and the damages
> sustained by the Men of war and Shipping are extremely great,
> between fifty and Sixty Sail of Ships were driven ashore, many of
> them bilged, and others carried so far above the high Water mark,
> as to prevent their being again got off ... The *San Domingo, La
> Hogue, Maidstone, Epervier, Fantome, Manly, Nemessis, Morgiana,
> Canso* were parted from their Anchors and put ashore, the whole
> are afloat except *Epervier* & *Manly*, & have not received material
> injury [although] *Maidstone* & *Fantome* must be hove down before
> they can leave the Port.[105]

Nymphe was among those seriously damaged, having 'lost her Bowsprit Foremast and Topmasts, [and] had the Starboard Quarter stove in'. Warren concluded that 'His Majestys Ships are materially crippled by this event' but that he would 'use every possible endeavour to have them repaired with every dispatch which the Strength of this Yard & their own means admit of'.[106] This meteorological setback was particularly unwelcome at this time since Warren was about to extend the British commercial blockade and, even before the unseasonal hurricane did such severe damage at Halifax, the constant demands of blockade and convoy duties, so often in adverse weather and difficult navigational conditions, had strained the North American dockyards' resources. All of them were running seriously short of materials and even of provisions.[107]

In April 1814 Lieutenant Napier in the frigate *Nymphe* wrote in his journal of 'damp penetrating fogs, constantly and alternately changing to rain'. Easterly onshore winds brought 'snow and sleet'. Poor visibility hindered contact with other blockading vessels and, especially at night, allowed blockaded vessels to escape. Here, too, 'hard frosts' made necessary thick winter clothing, reducing mobility. In June a three-day westerly gale drove patrolling vessels off station, as the prevailing wind so often did, threatening the continuity essential to blockade; it was followed in August by the start of the hurricane season.[108] The continual demands of blockade resulted in casualties even in relatively good weather, as in HMS *Marlborough* on 26 December 1812. The journal of ordinary seaman George Hodge on that day recorded 'A fresh breeze – a strange sail in sight. Fell from the for[e] top mast Matthew Donelson and was drownded'.[109] Donelson's loss underlines the relentless year-round cost of maritime blockade, naval or commercial, to the Royal Navy on the coasts of North America in the early nineteenth century.

By the summer of 1813 more than a dozen named vessels of the United States Navy had been blockaded, taken or destroyed by the Royal Navy's naval blockade, as distinct from its toll of American merchant vessels. Even by the spring of 1813 the growing number of losses suggested that while direct attack on British blockading squadrons, often including 74s, was probably impracticable, some form of American retaliation was necessary. On 3 March Congress had authorised the payment of a cash bounty to the successful designer of a submarine, or an underwater explosive device, such as a spar-mounted mine known as a 'torpedo'.[110] Worth up to 50% of the value of a British naval vessel destroyed, this reward drew the attention of such inventors as Elijah Mix and Robert Fulton, who each contacted Secretary of the Navy Jones.[111] Possibly as a result of a newspaper article written by Fulton on 4 March, the Admiralty advised Warren that 'your ships should take proper precautions against the torpedoes & submarine explosions with which I see you are threatened while at anchor in American Waters'.[112] Despite the warning, in June 1813 attempts to torpedo HMS *Plantagenet* in Chesapeake Bay almost succeeded, and the booby-trapped cargo of the American schooner *Eagle* exploded while being examined by a British boarding party, killing one lieutenant and ten seamen.[113] Thereafter, additional patrols were rowed round anchored British capital ships, especially at night, and captures brought in were kept at a distance from flagships until carefully searched after a deliberate delay.[114]

The Royal Navy's economic warfare in North America was evidently heavily constrained, especially in its early stages, by the conflicting demands of diplomacy, convoy and blockade, and by the number and severity of the practical problems involved. But, despite such constraints, it was, ultimately, to prove remarkably successful.

CHAPTER 3

FROM BUSINESS PARTNERS TO ENEMIES: BRITAIN AND THE UNITED STATES BEFORE 1812

[W]ith an extensive and fertile country, and a small population compared to the extent of our territory, we have annually a large surplus to export to foreign markets; … on the export of this surplus, which is cut off by war, depends in a great degree, the ability of the farmer to meet taxes. ('State of the Finances', John Eppes, Chairman of Ways and Means Committee, House of Representatives, 10 October 1814)[1]

THE TREATY OF PARIS, securing the independence of the United States from Britain in September 1783, had been preceded by a British Order in Council of 2 July that year, changing the terms under which Americans had traded as colonial Britons.[2] It was thought by some that Britain's major trading partners were about to become foreign trading rivals. John Holroyd, Lord Sheffield, argued in his influential pamphlet that to allow the Americans any trading advantages for which they no longer qualified could threaten Britain's long-term commercial and maritime supremacy.[3] Conversely, the West India Committee, lobbying Parliament on behalf of the plantation owners, shippers and merchants of the British West Indies, argued as early as April 1783 that permission for 'American ships as heretofore, freely to bring the produce of the dominions of the United States to the sugar colonies and to take back our produce in return is … essential'.[4]

Despite the debate, in fact, 'a single Atlantic economy' soon re-asserted itself,[5] an 'extensive flow of goods, ideas, skilled migrants and capital' again contributing to a great degree of economic interdependence between the United States and the United Kingdom.[6] Britain still shared, especially with the American eastern seaboard, both a common language and culture. Moreover, despite enormous potential and natural advantages, American economic development was initially hampered by shortages of both real and financial capital, difficult terrain and great distances. The high cost of overland transport offset all but local comparative advantage, and secondary industry remained largely domestic and small scale. The United States was therefore still heavily dependent on British credit and European imports for manufactures, including metal goods, pottery and textiles from Britain.

Nonetheless, especially after independence, American primary industries such as agriculture, forestry and fishing quickly produced exportable surpluses. Tertiary industries, including both coastal and trans-Atlantic shipping, developed to distribute imports and export agricultural surpluses. American vessels increasingly transported the colonial products of European countries. Commercial and financial centres grew on the American eastern seaboard, among them Boston, Philadelphia and Providence, Rhode Island. American population growth was rapid. A colonial population of about 2m in 1770 grew to around 3.9m by 1790, and to 5.3m by 1800, with an average annual increase of almost 3.6% for the previous ten years.[7] By 1810, the total population of the United States was about 7.2m, compared with approximately 17.9m for the United Kingdom.[8]

CONJOINED ECONOMIES

The population growth of the United States provided a vital market for British manufactured textiles by creating more demand than the small American textile industry could meet. British output expanded beyond domestic demand after a succession of technological innovations developed by entrepreneurs with access to financial capital. After 1793, when war closed European markets, Britain replaced them with New World outlets such that, by 1798, 60% of British textile manufactures went to North America and the Caribbean.[9] British cotton exports to North America alone grew from 37% of total cotton exports in the 1780s to 53% in the 1800s. British woollen exports to the United States over the same period also increased.[10]

Cotton played a crucial role in the early-nineteenth-century Atlantic economy for both Britain and the United States. As a bulky crop, the raw cotton grown in the southern United States was regularly shipped in large American vessels to Liverpool. As cotton manufacturing concentrated in Lancashire, external economies contributed to a British advantage in selling price so that, by 1805, manufactured cotton formed 42% of British exports.[11] Therefore, by the early years of the nineteenth century, Britain and the United States were not only major trading partners but were also mutually dependent as both source and market for the other's specialised output. American wheat, flour, rice, timber, tobacco and raw cotton found outlets in Britain, and as a largely agrarian economy and expanding market for manufactured and processed goods, the United States was crucially important to Britain's economic development. Each became the other's major customer and source of supply. Trading, financial and family links continued to develop between London, Liverpool and Manchester in Britain, and Baltimore, Savannah and New Orleans in the United States.

On both sides of the Atlantic many recognised the importance of this interdependence, and some sought to preserve it as political and diplomatic relationships deteriorated. After the war Republican Congressman Adam Seybert reflected that, between 1802 and 1804, American exports to Britain and its dependencies had averaged $23.7m annually, representing 34.6% of the total, almost twice those to France, the United States' next most important customer.[12] American imports from Britain and its dependencies between 1802 and 1804 averaged $35.7m a year, which Seybert calculated to be 47.4% of the total. It was almost three times the American imports from France (16.4%). Anglo-American trade between 1802 and 1804 showed an unfavourable balance for the United States of $12m, almost three times its next largest trade deficit of $4.4m with 'China and other native Asiatic parts'.[13]

Specifically, between 1806 and 1811, Britain had imported from America an annual average of 34.6m lbs of raw cotton. In 1811 alone British imports of raw cotton from the United States had reached 46.9m lbs, compared with an annual average for the years 1805–9 of 69.2m lbs imported into Britain from all parts of the world.[14] Seybert's figures suggest that at this time more than two-thirds of Britain's raw cotton imports usually came from the southern United States. Furthermore, Seybert noted, on aggregate between 1805 and 1811, the United States 'received annually, 20.1% of the manufactures and produce exported from Britain', even when excluding 'foreign and colonial produce'. During the same period the total value of British exports to the United States 'of every description', including foreign and colonial re-exports, averaged $36.5m a year.[15]

THE QUESTION OF ADVANTAGE AND CAUTIOUS ACCOUNTING

Seybert later argued that, in the years before 1812, Anglo-American trade had been at a marked advantage to Britain. He attempted to quantify Britain's comparative advantage by claiming that 'It is generally calculated that raw materials gain sevenfold by being manufactured.'[16] Similarly, 'In 1800, the merchandise exported from the United States to Great Britain was worth $74.23 per ton', whereas 'that imported from Great Britain was worth $240 per ton'.[17] Therefore, between 1795 and 1801, the average annual imbalance against the United States 'in favour of Great Britain, of $15.2m, was only $70,166 less than the apparent unfavourable balance produced by our trade with all parts of the world collectively taken'.[18] Of 1795–1801's aggregate imbalance of $106.1m, no less than $92.5m resulted from 'our trade with England and Scotland whence we chiefly import manufactured articles'.[19]

Between 1790 and 1815 American exports had totalled $847m, while 'foreign goods imported and not re-exported' reached $1,231m, producing an adverse balance of visible trade of $384m.[20] However, as Nettels showed, these figures did not present a complete or accurate picture of contemporary American trade. In colonial times the British Navigation Acts ensured that such exports were probably carried in British bottoms and insured in London. Perhaps as an accounting legacy, exports were still valued as their price in America before being sent abroad, and although the now foreign buyers would have to pay shipping and insurance costs as part of the total price paid, such costs were not added to United States export values. By 1807, however, 90% of the value of exports was carried in American vessels.[21] As the American merchant fleet expanded, the selling merchant was often at least part ship-owner. This was the case with the New England firm of Brown & Ives, affluent and influential importers and export merchants of Providence, Rhode Island, sole-owners of five vessels and part-owners of four more.[22] Shipping costs were, therefore, not always separately recorded in their overall profit and loss accounts, and although freight earnings and insurance premiums were, what would later be called 'invisible exports', they were not added to the 'prime cost'. Exports were being conservatively counted as 'free on board'.[23]

Imports, too, seemed to show that Anglo-American trade was very much to British advantage. By 1807 94% of the value of United States imports was also said to be brought in American vessels, despite almost half of the imports coming from Britain, which, with the world's largest merchant fleet, traditionally offered both shipping and marine insurance.[24] However, after 1790, the offices of marine insurance brokers were to be found in many American ports, including those of Campbell & Richie in Boston, sometimes used by Brown & Ives.[25] Many American merchant vessels carried 'supercargoes', trusted agents responsible for the profitable disposal of export cargoes and the arrangement of return cargoes. Prices of return cargoes from foreign ports during round trips may have included an insurance premium, but many insurance contracts for vessels, and both outward and return cargoes, would have been made in America at the outset. The sometimes unnecessary inclusion of all shipping costs and insurance premiums would therefore have increased the apparent value of American imports, but made comparison with contemporary export earnings even more invalid. Some imports were counted when taxed *ad valorem*, according to their value as 'prime cost', others at specific rates per weight. Still others were tax-free, and therefore practically ignored by record-keeping customs officials. Estimates of such tax-free imports have been a lasting cause of inaccuracy.

Contemporary overseas trade figures also excluded 'foreign exports' – that is, re-exports (imported and often processed natural products including spices, blended teas and coffee) – carried mostly to Europe and the West Indies. These were so extensive and valuable that between 1798 and 1800, and again between 1805 and 1808, they exceeded the value of 'domestic exports' sold abroad, such as timber, grain and, increasingly, flour.[26] Between 1803 and 1807 the United States' annual average adverse balance of trade was $19.8m.[27] According to Bogart, Nettels' authority, freights earned during this time by American shipping averaged $32m a year.[28] Given the accuracy of Bogart's estimate, Nettel's conclusion that 'Whatever the exact figures, it seems certain that freights and profits' from re-exports, when added to American 'domestic exports' 'gave the Union a profitable status in world commerce' is important.[29] In modern terms, although the United States had an adverse annual balance of visible trade with Britain overall, when 'invisible items' such as the earnings of American shipping were included it had a favourable balance of payments. This makes what was to follow seem all the more remarkable. An incomplete understanding of America's foreign trading position may well have motivated Madison's preparedness to risk maritime blockade by a declaration of war on Britain.

The apparent imbalance in Anglo-American trade, although based on an incomplete understanding of it, was often greatly resented. 'Such', wrote Seybert, 'have been our contributions for the advancement of the skill and industry of a nation which, for raw materials, is the most dependent on other countries'. Quoting the British member of parliament, banker, financier and pamphleteer Alexander Baring, Seybert concluded that 'Our tribute "paid, to a considerable extent, for the support of the fleets and armies" of Great Britain.'[30]

Britain's almost continuous war with France since 1793 in fact contributed considerably to American prosperity, although David Warden, 'Late Consul for the United States at Paris', exaggerated when claiming in 1819 that 'The state of European warfare from the year 1802 to 1812 gave to America almost all the carrying trade or freight of the commercial world, valued at 10% upon the capital.'[31] Nonetheless, the United States' merchant marine had certainly reached 1.1m tons by 1807 and, by then, 92.7% of the tonnage engaged in the United States' foreign trade was American.[32] Furthermore, Warden argued, 'The United States also gained 5% by exchange, so that the annual profit of commerce and navigation have been estimated at 15% upon the capital.'[33] More plentiful financial capital also meant that, by 1806, more cargoes were American-owned, leading Barnabas Bidwell to assert in Congress that 'We are no longer mere freighters for foreigners', but work 'on our own capital, and for our own account'.[34] However, an aggressively expanded United States merchant fleet increasingly encountered both competing British merchant vessels and the Royal Navy, intercepting neutrals while conducting its effective commercial blockade of France.

DIPLOMACY AND DEBATE

In 1794 it had looked as if the Jay Treaty would resolve the difficulties of Anglo-American trade by defining neutral rights in wartime.[35] During the following period of prosperity American visible exports almost trebled, from $33m in 1794 to $94.1m in 1801; after falling during a temporary European peace, they again peaked in 1807 at $108.3m.[36] But, from the outset, American access to trade with and between the British West Indies had been a bone of contention on both sides of the Atlantic. The American Senate had ratified the treaty only when Article XII, restricting American access, was suspended. Orthodox British mercantilists objected to it on principle as reducing the overall value of British trade.[37]

According to Article XII, either British or American vessels could import livestock, timber, grain and flour to the West Indies without any higher or additional duties becoming payable. American vessels could export 'any molasses, sugar, coffee, cocoa or cotton' from the West Indies, but only to the United States and certainly not to wartime European markets, on which American traders would have made most profit.[38] Subsequent American trade with the West Indies was to be the focus of much British resentment. Robert Banks Jenkinson, later Lord Hawkesbury and still later Lord Liverpool, wrote in January 1796 that 'Our West India Islands will never be safe if the subjects of the United States are allowed to have a free intercourse with them and import among other articles their democratic principles into those islands.'[39]

American trade to and from the West Indies had indeed grown rapidly, and in clear contravention of the restrictions of Article XII. As soon as 1805, James Stephen, a lawyer who had lived in St Kitt's until 1794, argued in an influential pamphlet that neutral American shipping of French colonial exports was simply *War in Disguise*.[40] He noted that, although in no position to fight Britain, the Americans were partly negating British war efforts by supporting the commerce of the French West Indies and by assisting French competition, undercutting the 'West India trade' of British planters and merchants. Stephen predicted that 'by the ruin of its commerce and its commercial revenue (infallible consequences of a war with this country)' the United States 'would have no resources for the great and extraordinary demands of maritime war, but very heavy interior taxation'. Referring to the Treasury Secretary's Report to Congress for 1801, Stephen noted that

> external commerce contributes more than nine-tenths of the whole revenue of the country; and that if this source of supply were cut off, ... there would be a deficit of $2,400,000 to be provided for, beyond the interest of the public debt, before any war fund could be raised.[41]

Joseph Marryat, writing in 1807, also greatly deplored any British trading concessions which 'ever led to new demands, as the history of all our negotiations with America has abundantly demonstrated'.[42] He added a note that, by 1807, 'General Smith of Baltimore, acknowledged in the senate of the United States, that the amount of West India produce annually re-exported, after supplying the home consumption of America, was twenty-eight millions of dollars, or nearly seven millions sterling'.[43] Increased American participation in the West Indian carrying trade clearly competed with British colonial shipping, which Marryat recognised as 'the nursery of seamen and naval power'.[44]

Alexander Baring, however, argued in 1808 that Britain's evident recession was caused by 'the restrictions of the enemy' – the Berlin and Milan decrees of Napoleon's Continental System – rather than 'the intercourse of neutrals with the Continent of Europe'.[45] Baring considered Stephen's pamphlet largely responsible for Britain's retaliatory Orders in Council, and deplored one commentator's disappointment that Britain had not taken the 'opportunity of going to war with America'.[46] All trade, Baring thought, should be encouraged: American neutral trade was 'politically inoffensive and commercially beneficial'. Britain's Orders in Council, he thought, should be repealed.[47]

But, until they were, American shippers were to find themselves in a dilemma. The Milan decree of 17 December 1807 had announced the French intention of detaining neutral vessels found trading with Britain. A series of

British Orders in Council had retaliated by requiring that neutral trade with French-occupied Europe should first pass through British ports, paying transit fees. As a result, Hickey argues, 'If American ships complied with the French decrees, they were subject to seizure by the British; and if they submitted to British decrees, they could be seized by the French.'[48] British concessions, such as reduced transit fees and the increased issue of licences to carry imports into Britain, did little to help, since the principle of Britain's perceived right to interfere with neutral American trade was not conceded.

Nevertheless, the level of American prosperity increased markedly until moderated by French decrees, British Orders in Council and Jefferson's anti-British embargo. It reflected the strength of American foreign trade, both rising exports and the level of imports, with important and lasting financial consequences for the government. Although the taxation of exports was prohibited by the Constitution, it proved possible to tax spending on imports.[49] As more American farmers, merchants and shippers became affluent spending increased on imported luxuries, including sugar, tea, coffee, wines and silks. Since the population of the United States grew between 1791 and 1801 by almost 35%, and its imports by over 280%, spending on imports could become the major source of government tax revenue by the imposition of customs duties on them. To these could be added, as a less important corollary, shipping registration and enrolment fees, and lighthouse dues.[50] Furthermore, although demand for such imports would rise as incomes increased, it would decline less than proportionally, if at all, when import duties raised the price. Internal excise duties, used by the opposing Federalists to pay for America's largely successful undeclared maritime war against France, had been unpopular, contributing to the Federalist's electoral defeat in 1800. Taxation of imports therefore seemed ideal in peacetime. While equitably targeting the rich it could be avoided by the poor and met the philosophical requirements of those who had read Adam Smith's topical 'Canons of Taxation', long available in America.[51] Being predictable, cheap and convenient to administer, as well as difficult to evade, import duties produced revenue so efficiently that Secretary of the Treasury Albert Gallatin argued that the Republicans' least unpopular import duties would allow progressive reduction of the United States National Debt, then considered an important objective. This proved so successful that, since 1805, as shown in Appendix B Table 4, the National Debt was still being reduced as late as 1813.[52]

But, however successful in peacetime, even allowing the avoidance of internal excise duties and 'direct' taxes on property, the United States government's almost sole reliance on import duties, providing more than 92.3% of its tax revenue in 1812, made it fiscally dependent on the continuation of normal trade relations with Britain, its major trading partner. However, both Jefferson and Madison after 1809 believed that Britain was vulnerable to the withdrawal of American trade and could be compelled to reduce the Royal Navy's interference with neutrals during its blockades of France and its reliance on impressment. Economic sanctions against Britain as an alternative to war, however, contradicted the taxation of imports for raising revenue and placed Gallatin in a difficult position. The political requirement to support the President's economic sanctions against Britain and the maintenance of sound government finances dependent on import duties would be extremely difficult to reconcile. Even the alternative of an American export embargo ran the risk of retaliation. Britain could find permanent sources of raw cotton in, for example, Brazil, Egypt or the East Indies, as an alternative to the southern United States.

After December 1807 Jefferson's export embargo and non-importation legislation, collectively known as the 'restrictive system', had damaged most sectors of the American economy. Officially recorded American total exports fell by almost 80%, from $108.3m in 1807 to $22.4m in 1808; they recovered by 1811, but to only $61.3m.[53] More importantly, however, and as shown in Appendix B Table 1, imports fell by almost 60%, from $144.7m in 1807 to $58.1m in 1808.[54] This effort to curtail British naval activity caused such serious damage to the American economy that even fellow Republican John Randolph compared it to an attempt 'to cure corns by cutting off the toes'.[55] Despite the unemployment, inflation and hardship caused by Jefferson's economic sanctions, which had brought no productive British diplomatic response, Madison persisted with Macon's No. 2 Bill and a Non-Importation Act which banned British imports from February 1811.[56] This did much to reduce Anglo-American trade. Furthermore, a severe shortage of specie in Britain made payment in cash for continuing American exports to Britain increasingly difficult.[57] Since, after the Non-Importation Act, Americans could not legally receive British manufactures in payment, credit built up in American accounts in London which holders became increasingly anxious to repatriate in some form. Some attitudes had also hardened. Some British opinion regarded American neutral trade as unprincipled profiteering on Britain's war against French tyranny, while some Americans resented British restrictions on maritime trade as an attempt at quasi-colonial subjection.

Madison was to compound the problem by the imposition of his own 90-day embargo on 4 April 1812, supplemented, before its end, by a declaration of war against Britain. This was to be without the prior introduction of a workable system of taxation of a wider cross section of the American population by either a 'direct' tax on property or the re-introduction of excise duties on internal production and trade or both. The pre-war American retention of revenue-raising methods so narrowly based on import duties and shipping fees demonstrates that few in Congress understood the vulnerability of the American economy or had forecast accurately the impact of either their own restrictive legislation or a British commercial blockade, much less the possibility of the two being in operation at the same time.

Gallatin had long intended that any war should be financed by government borrowing.[58] The prospect of borrowing being a sustainable success was rendered improbable by the Republican trade legislation. Such restrictions on American overseas trade, including the possibility of heavy financial penalties for noncompliance, would seriously damage the interests of precisely those people best placed to make long-term loans to the government. This would include farmers seeking to dispose of agricultural surpluses, merchants buying and reselling such goods, or the shippers arranging their transport. These men were often part of an articulate international network long practised in finding profitable alternative investments. The lost political support of those whose livelihoods were threatened was probably a foregone conclusion, but the forfeit of their loanable funds should also have been predictable.

Lending to the American government by buying its securities at par – at their face value – until then the usual practice, could well seem less attractive than investment in developing American industries such as textiles, largely freed of competition by British blockade, or in British government securities, readily available for cash, and at discount, in London or Canada. The potential lenders' cooperation was all the more unlikely in support of a war against the major maritime power best placed to impose a sea-based commercial blockade which would damage or destroy their livelihoods. Britain had demonstrated such competence in prolonged wars, inflicting real economic damage on France.[59] One, or even two, loan-calls might be made on affluent banks or wealthy and politically well-disposed individuals, but whether they could, or would, support an expensive war, as prolonged as Britain's against France, was of course untested and apparently un-investigated. Any expectation of financial aid from France, itself isolated from overseas trade by British maritime commercial blockade, was probably unrealistic. As Gallatin told the Senate in November 1811, 'In the present state of the world, foreign loans may be considered as nearly unattainable. In that respect, as in all others, the United States must solely rely on their own resources.'[60]

Anglo-American relations deteriorated quickly after February 1811. William Pinkney, the American Minister in London, returned to the United States, to be replaced only by a chargé d'affaires, Jonathan Russell, assisted by a consul.[61] The illegality of British imports, and potentially reduced government income from them, might reasonably have been expected to direct Congressional attention to fiscal alternatives. However, on 25 November 1811 Gallatin appeared cautiously optimistic. In his report on the 'State of the Finances' he informed the Senate that a forecast deficit of $1.2m for 1812 could be met from the surplus of $3.9m for the year ending 30 September 1811. He congratulated the administration on its use of import duties for reducing the national debt by $42m since 1805, despite the repeal of the duty on salt and 'the great diminution of commerce during the last four years'. This, he argued, 'considerably lessens the weight of the most formidable objection, to which that revenue, depending almost solely on commerce, appears to be liable.'[62]

He commented on the need for 'persevering application of the surplus which it affords in years of prosperity', and continued, 'if a similar application of such surplus be herewith strictly adhered to, forty millions of debt, contracted during five or six years of war, may always, without any extraordinary exertions, be reimbursed in ten years of peace'. 'But', he added, 'to be placed on a solid foundation, it requires the aid of revenue "sufficient at least to defray the ordinary expenses of Government, and to pay the interest of the public debt, including that on new loans which may be authorized"'. Disappointing proceeds from sales of public land could be rectified by 'an addition of fifty per cent to the present amount of duties'. 'This mode', he added, 'appears preferable for the present to any internal tax'. Another 50% on customs duties 'would', he said, 'with the aid of loans … be sufficient in time of war'. Together, this would later double the rate of import duties.

Having, so far loyally, followed the party line, Gallatin then allowed himself some moments of doubt.

> Whether it would be sufficient to produce the same amount of
> revenue as under existing circumstances cannot at present be
> determined. Should any deficiency arise it may be supplied without
> difficulty by a further increase of duties, by a restoration of that on
> salt, and a proper selection of moderate internal taxes.[63]

The fact that continued 'years of prosperity' could not be guaranteed impinged itself on Gallatin sooner than on most, apparently causing a perceptible reduction in confidence.

> The possibility of raising money by loans to the amount which may
> be wanted, remains to be examined: for, the fact that the United
> States may easily, in ten years of peace, extinguish a debt of forty-
> two millions of dollars, does not necessarily imply that they could
> borrow that sum during a period of war.'[64]

With war against Britain becoming ever more probable, Congress, its Committees and the Treasury Secretary belatedly gave thought to financing it. In a reply to the House Ways and Means Committee written on 10 January 1812 Gallatin proposed not only borrowing $10m, mostly for use in 1813, but also doubling the rate of import duties, already averaging 17%. His most controversial proposal, however, was his recommendation for raising $3m by a 'direct' tax on property, and another $2m by indirect taxes – specifically, internal excise duties.[65] He agreed to the Committee's earlier suggestion of issuing Treasury notes, to become in effect 'a part of the circulating medium', but warned that the amount should 'never exceed' that 'which may circulate without depreciation'.[66] Gallatin was immediately subjected to heavy, often libellous, criticism. Many, including Republicans, could not accept that – trade having been diminished by measures they had supported, together with currently rising interest rates – radical fiscal reform was required, even perhaps the re-introduction of internal excise duties, if the war that many of them had persistently advocated was to be paid for.

It was not as if Madison or Congress had lacked advice, based on varying degrees of expertise and political disinterest. On 17 February 1812, only four months before the American declaration of war, Ezekiel Bacon, Chairman of the

Ways and Means Committee, explicitly warned Congress. While almost wholly dependent for revenue on import and shipping duties, and especially when taking almost half its imports from Britain, 'which in a state of war must be entirely suspended', the United States, he said, could not afford to be subjected to British maritime commercial blockade. He advised Congress 'to estimate accurately ... not only [Britain's] military and naval strength, but what is of equal importance in modern warfare, her pecuniary and financial strength'.[67] 'We have been accustomed to consider the situation of British finances to be such that her Government must be on the very verge of bankruptcy.' By rejecting Gallatin's proposals to widen the American tax base, Bacon argued that 'we should advance much more rapidly in the road to national bankruptcy than Great Britain has ever done, with all her follies and all her prodigality'.[68] Major fiscal reform, including the raising of loans and the re-introduction of disused internal excise duties, was urgently required, if not already overdue. After much debate Congress agreed to borrow $11m, but would allow doubled import duties, 'direct' taxes and internal excise duties to be levied only after a declaration of war against Britain.[69]

Import duties would clearly prove crucial to any American war effort since net customs duties accrued during 1811, to be available as government income the following year, stood at $8,958,777 and comprised 91.41% of the American government's income for 1812 of $9,801,132.[70] Customs duties accrued in 1812 reflected that year's hurried importation into the United States of British goods into which American profits accumulated in Britain since the Non-Importation Act of 1811 had been invested. This raised net customs revenue to $13.2m, no less than 92.31% of the American government's income of $14.3m for 1813.[71] Without net customs revenue being supplemented by wider taxation and successful borrowing, war should surely be best avoided or, if already precipitately declared, quickly ended by armistice and negotiation, so minimising the damage. Although procrastination made a poor alternative to reform, Congress proved itself unwilling to demand financial sacrifices from voters until they became unavoidable.

THE BRITISH ECONOMY 1803–1815

Britain, meanwhile, had economic difficulties of its own. Harvests were poor in both 1809 and 1810, and average wheat prices rose by 18.6% between 1810 and 1811, reaching an unprecedented peak in 1812.[72] Despite the Non-Intercourse Act of 1809, which had replaced Jefferson's embargo and officially banned exports, 1.4m bushels of American grain and flour reached Britain that year, followed in 1810 by 786,889 bushels more.[73] Overall, bread prices in London rose by more than 15% between 1810 and 1812, despite a slight decrease in 1811.[74] Napoleon licenced the export of French and German wheat to Britain, perhaps seeking to worsen the developing currency shortage.[75]

Until 1810 British goods had been excluded from most European ports, excepting some in Portugal and on the Baltic coast, although in that year Russian ports were re-opened to Britain. The French invasion of Spain and then Portugal after 1808 weakened their control of their South American colonies, and British trade, particularly with Brazil, increased. British exports and re-exports to 'the foreign West Indies and South America' increased between 1807 and 1809 by more than 380% and imports by almost 280%. But, between 1810 and 1812, these exports fell by 31% and imports by 64.5%.[76] Additionally, the impact of the American Non-Importation Act of 1811 led to British exports to the United States falling from £10.9m in 1810 to £1.8m in 1811, a drop of 83.5%.[77] By 1812 over-production by British manufacturers misled by over-optimistic merchants had added to the cumulative effects of the American legislation, Napoleon's Continental System and the activities of French privateers in the Channel to suppress British business activity.

Despite numerous successful attacks on British merchantmen, including those by American privateers, the Royal Navy's protection of British trade, and therefore the country's economic and financial strength, was on the whole successful. Britain thus remained in a position to supply over £35m in subsidies to its European allies between 1810 and 1815 – £10m in 1814 alone.[78] Overall, between the periods 1804–6 and 1814–16, total British exports rose by 28.7% and imports by 29.2%.[79] Ultimately, Napoleon's Continental System had demonstrably failed. As shown in Appendix B Table 2, total British exports had fallen between 1810 and 1812, but, while American re-exports were to fall between 1812 and 1814, re-exports of British colonial produce had increased between 1804–6 and 1814–16 by 80.4%, contributing to a recovery of total British exports by 1814.[80]

However, the hardship caused among Britain's poor and unemployed was evidently real. By 1813, expenditure on poor relief in England and Wales exceeded £6.7m, 56% higher than in 1803, and fell by only 5.4% by 1814.[81] Complaints by some of the industrialists affected, and demonstrations by unemployed workers, provided valuable material for the government's Whig Opposition, notably for Parliamentary opponents of the Orders in Council, and particularly Henry Brougham.[82] Fear of popular unrest, and the assassination on 11 May 1812 of Prime Minister Spencer Perceval, long an advocate of the Orders, had probably contributed to their revocation, as far as the United States was concerned, on 23 June 1812 – ironically, five days after the American declaration of war on Britain.[83]

BRITISH TAX REVENUE AND BORROWING

But, although these economic problems were significant, neither the British government's tax income nor its borrowing position was ever seriously threatened. The government's gross tax income of £71m in 1812 was only 2.7% less than the £73m of 1811, the last year before war with the United States. The fall to £70.3m in 1813 was less than 1%, and by 1814 there was a rise, by 6.3%, to £74.7m. In sharp contrast to the United States, where net custom duties formed more than 92% of total government tax revenue in 1812, the British tax base was sufficiently wide for customs duties to form only 18.31% of the British government's total gross tax income in 1812; these rose comparatively little throughout the war and were still only 19% of total tax income in 1815, never having risen above 20%.[84] Revenue from British customs duties rose 7.7%, from £13m in 1812 to £14m in 1813, and almost another 3% to £14.4m in 1814. Customs and excise duties together formed 57.6% of total gross revenue in 1812. British 'property and income' taxes followed a similar pattern to the government's gross income, falling 2.2% from a pre-war yield of £13.5m in 1811 to £13.2m in 1812, and again by only 0.76% to £13.1m between 1812 and 1813. The yield of the British tax on land ownership was to rise by 7.8% between 1812 and 1814.[85]

The Royal Navy's protection of Britain's generally successful overseas trade position was therefore complemented by a comparatively widely based and crudely progressive system of taxation which, supplemented by the government's ability to borrow, was capable of supporting wars against both France and the United States. As shown in Appendix B Table 35, between 1812 and 1815 British customs duties yielded on average a gross £14.1m, 19.2% of total government income. During the same period gross excise duties yielded an average £27.7m, 37.7% of the total. Stamp duties produced £6.2m, 8.4% of total income. Land tax produced another £7.7m, a further 10.5% of the total. Property and income tax yielded £14m gross, 19.1%. Miscellaneous revenues gathered the remaining 5.1% of an average total government income of £73.5m.[86]

In contrast to the position in the United States after 1813, 'Nearly 60% of the extra funds raised by [the British] government to prosecute its wars between 1793–1815 ... came from taxes and not borrowing.'[87] The British tax strategy put most of the burden on domestic consumption, so that a wealthy minority's private investment, essential to maintained economic growth and to their taxable incomes, continued. Britain's interest rates remained relatively stable at 'just below 4% before the war to just over 5% during it.'[88] 'While the share of national income invested ... remained roughly constant ... consumption fell sharply, from over 83% of national expenditure in 1778–92 to around 72% in 1793–1812, and reached as low as 64% by 1813–15.'[89] While this may be borne out by United Kingdom sugar consumption per head, which may have fallen by 13.3% between 1813 and 1815, the basic cost of living for those in urban employment did not become excessive, as far as it can be measured by average London bread prices, which fell almost 33% from their 1812 peak by 1814.[90] The wages of agricultural workers, however, fell by 3 index points between 1812 and 1815.[91] Although unwelcome, privation in Britain was reportedly much less severe than in the United States, where prices rose by 45% between 1811 and 1814.[92]

In further sharp contrast to the United States, as will become evident in Chapter 7, British budget deficits were largely met by the successful sale of government securities worth over £440m between 1793 and 1815, covering between a quarter and a third of wartime government expenditure.[93] The British national debt rose from £299m in 1793 to £843m in 1815 'without', Kennedy concludes, 'any visible sign of the country going bankrupt or the lenders doubting the government's ability to repay in the future'.[94] Even a suspension of specie payments by the Bank of England in 1797 produced only short-term alarm, since the Bank

> had so secured itself in the public confidence that its now unbacked
> money was just as acceptable as when gold could be got for it at a
> fixed price ... The banking and mercantile community in London
> and the provinces, with virtual unanimity, pronounced its readiness
> to carry on business as normal with a paper currency.[95]

In contrast, Congress failed to renew the charter of the First United States Bank in March 1811, contributing to inflation by the resultant proliferation of state and private banks, many of which were later called 'unincorporated and irresponsible'.[96]

Especially since the renewal of war in 1803, some in Britain had advocated neutral trade with the West Indies, but encountered the view that such American trade in particular threatened the effectiveness of Britain's maritime commercial blockade of France. Furthermore, the Royal Navy's continued blockade of a militarily successful enemy remained vital to British trade, and was too costly and demanding to abandon before the war had been brought to a successful conclusion. Although not written until 1818, William James argued that Britain's Orders in Council were simply 'not permitting the subjects of the United States under the disguise of neutrals to be the carriers of France'. He continued that 'the ablest politicians in the republic were engaged to prepare a specious manifesto, representing the United States as the aggrieved, and Great Britain as the aggressive party'.[97]

For Americans, the British operation of the Orders in Council could prove costly, such as the loss to Brown & Ives, merchants and shippers of Providence, Rhode Island, when their ship *Arthur* and its cargo of cotton was captured by HM gun brig *Blazer* on 20 February 1810. On 25 February Captain Joshua Rathbun wrote to Brown & Ives from London about the trial before Sir William Scott that 'the disposition of the courts [of Admiralty] seem very unfavourable towards the Americans at this time, of the many which were sent in and tried, but few are Cleared'. The judge had condemned both ship and cargo.[98]

Nevertheless, one form of American maritime trade was so profitable that it continued up to and beyond the American declaration of war on Britain in June 1812. The poor harvests of 1809 and 1810 had been particularly inconvenient to the British government, since, with shortages of grain and flour at home, Britain was ill-placed to send supplies to its troops in Spain and Portugal after 1808. Despite the increasingly strained relationships over neutral trade, the American need to export its grain and flour surplus coincided with the British need to supply its Peninsula army. The 230,000 bushels of wheat sent directly under British licences from American ports to Spain and Portugal in 1810 increased to 835,000 bushels by 1811, an indirect contradiction of American attempts to apply economic pressure to Britain.[99] Britain's urgent need for specie, in sums of up to

£76,000 at a time, to pay for American grain, flour and biscuit cargoes caused recurrent crises for the Chancellor of the Exchequer, Nicholas Vansittart, and the Governor of the Bank of England, but each emergency was resolved in turn, after some anxiety. American attempts to capitalise on Britain's shortage of specie were forestalled by the timely arrivals of precious metals from the West Indies and the East India Company.[100] The strength of Britain's overseas trading position again provided the means for its financial survival.

Ex-President Jefferson's rationalisation of this situation may have influenced Madison's views on Britain's apparent inability to resist economic pressure and America's ability to finance dispute, or even war, with Britain. Jefferson had argued that

> If she [Britain] is to be fed at all events, why may we not have the benefit of it as well as others? Besides if we could, by starving the English armies oblige them to withdraw from the peninsula, it would be to send them here; and I think we had better feed them there for pay, than feed and fight them here for nothing. A truth too, not to be lost sight of is, that no country can pay war taxes if you suppress all their resources. To keep the war popular, we must keep open the markets. As long as good prices can be had, the people will support the war cheerfully.[101]

In time, however, the reverse of this view was to prove remarkably accurate, when British success in the Peninsula ended demand for American grain and flour, so reducing American earnings and taxable capacity.

While it lasted, the licenced export of American wheat, rye, flour, bread, crackers, rice and coffee to the Peninsula had certainly been profitable. On 1 September 1812 Brown & Ives' *Hector* sailed from Providence with a cargo of flour costing $13,000 which sold in Cadiz for $40,000, a net return of $27,000.[102] The possession of a British licence, however, did not necessarily protect against inconvenience. The firm's brig *Argus*, sailing for Cadiz on 10 September with flour and rice, was later stopped by the Royal Navy and taken into Gibraltar. Captain Noyce's production of a licence, apparently issued by Vice-Admiral Sawyer in Halifax, led the Vice-Admiralty court to restore both vessel and cargo. However, when the British need to issue licences for the export of American produce ended in 1813, a potential source of finance for the American war effort was also ended, without an apparent substitute.[103]

Despite the trade and personal links of the 'Atlantic economy', by 1812 some attitudes in both Britain and America had hardened further. The American Non-Importation Act appeared to be reducing British exports, however ingeniously it was said to be evaded there. British exports to the United States worth almost £11m at current prices in 1810 were reduced to £1.8m by 1811.[104] American agents in Britain, holding credit paid into their accounts for imports, were not buying British manufactures as they once did. In 1812, in London, John Croker, First Secretary of the Admiralty since 1809 and prolific writer, published a pamphlet called *A Key to the Orders in Council*, which reviewed the decrees and orders issued by France, Britain and the United States since 1807.[105] It also sought to explain and justify Britain's position and its treatment of neutral merchants and shippers, chiefly American.

Nevertheless, in Washington, two-thirds of Madison's address to Congress on 1 June complained of the effects of the Orders on the American economy. He argued that

> Under pretended blockades, without the presence of an adequate
> force and sometimes without the practicability of applying one, our
> commerce has been plundered in every sea; the great staples of our
> country have been cut off from their legitimate markets; and a
> destructive blow aimed at our agricultural and maritime interests.[106]

There were those present who understood the fiscal and financial consequences of this admission, but who evidently failed to explain themselves clearly enough to change the course of events. By 18 June both House and Senate had voted for war with Britain.[107] On 19 June a bill which would have raised revenue by allowing most British imports to be resumed was defeated by only five votes.[108]

For months after the American declaration of war it was hoped by some in Britain that revocation of the Orders in Council, as far as the Americans were concerned, would lead in time to a negotiated peace, allowing for unavoidable delays in communication. Conversely, on 2 August 1812, James Abernethy wrote to Lord Liverpool as 'one that entertains a different opinion', since the Americans sought 'rights which are infringements on our own maritime consequence'.[109] He was also 'sure that French influence and intrigues hath preponderated'. In order 'To conduct this war with as little expense' as possible, he enclosed a 'plan of a Naval War', which, had the same been adopted in what is called the 'American War' the issue to ourselves would have proved very different'. His scheme would 'effectually prevent the Enemy's Ships and Privateers from getting out of port, most certainly their re-entering with their prizes'. It would, he said, require two ships of the line, thirteen frigates and twenty-six sloops and brigs of war, forty-one vessels in all, to blockade the American coast, ranging from the 'Gulf of Florida and off New Orleans' to 'the Coast of New Hampshire, which offers partial security to our Newfoundland and Quebec Fleets'. The 'Line of Battle-Ships' would be particularly useful 'should there escape a Ship or two of that description from France, to guard against which, it might be advisable to have two Ships of the Line at Halifax'.[110]

As late as 3 October 1812 Lord Bathurst, Secretary of State for War and the Colonies and, until only weeks before, also President of the Board of Trade, was writing at length to the Prime Minister, Lord Liverpool.[111] Decisions were needed on the goods for so long imported from the United States, and on which Britain had come to depend. Lord Clancarty, he said, had also written to Liverpool on the subject some weeks before. Bathurst outlined again the arguments for and against importing under licence grain and flour, raw cotton, rice and tobacco in neutral, even American, ships. The only vessels to be disallowed with certainty would surely be French. The last three commodities were the products of 'the most Anti-Anglican' parts of the United States, the least deserving of benefit from continued trade.

Bathurst, who was clearly aware of the stocks already held in Britain, rehearsed all the arguments about alternative sources for each product, particularly cotton. Licence fees for importing cotton would be, in effect, a form of tax on textile manufacturers, and would 'at least limit their importation' of American cotton, one way of hurting its producers. Among the disadvantages of British blockade would be that American seamen would be diverted into manning privateers and the United States' men of war, well-constructed ships in a small but skilfully manned navy. Clearly, Bathurst wrote, these were all matters on which Liverpool must decide.

The decision was not much further delayed. On 13 October 1812 'HRH the Prince Regent in Council ordered that General Reprisals be granted against the ships, goods and citizens of the United States of America.'[112] According to the Edinburgh *Annual Register*, this Order in Council was in effect a delayed British declaration of war, made necessary both by unrecalled American letters of marque and the American decision not to ratify a suspension of hostilities agreed between Lieut General Sir George Prevost, Governor General of Canada, and the American Brigadier General Hull.[113] For American merchantmen and their crews, British General Reprisals, when eventually learned of in distant European ports, would mean internment and long detention. This included both Brown and Ive's *Asia*, stranded in Copenhagen, and the *General Hamilton* in St Petersburg: neither returned to Providence, Rhode Island, until 1815. For the Royal Navy in the waters of North America, it was to mean a renewal of arduous weeks of maritime blockade.[114]

Some British cotton spinners, dependent on imported raw cotton for their livelihood, had apparently long been opposed to Britain's efforts to regulate neutral American trade and, after the outbreak of war, the prospect of British commercial blockade completely preventing the importation of American cotton. In an open letter to Lord Castlereagh dated 2 March 1813 Charles Lyne reported that, having adapted their machines for its use, the spinners argued that superior 'bowed Georgia cotton wool' was essential, and unobtainable elsewhere.[115] They maintained that British blockade of American cotton supplies would be 'impolitic'. This view Lyne called 'very erroneous'. He calculated precisely that stocks held, even of Georgian raw cotton, would last 'from this time to 9 May 1814'. Additional imports from Brazil would postpone shortage until 27 November 1814. Imports from British colonies in the Caribbean and South America would maintain stocks until 3 March 1815, and Indian raw material, imported 'very cheaply' from Surat and Bengal, would allow production to continue until 17 July 1815. 'The additional quantity ... will probably be imported into Great Britain long before it is possible to consume what is now here.'

It was also the view of John Whitmore, 'Chairman of the Joint Committee of British Merchants Trading to and from the Brazils and Portugal', that these imports would be preferable as being 'from our own colonies and those of our allies, in our own ships, and payable in our own manufactured goods … thus proving to the enemy that we can do … without his assistance for the support of our manufactures'.[116] Whitmore had given evidence to the House of Commons that buying from sources prepared to take British cotton manufactures in payment would replace markets lost since the American Non-Importation Act. American manufacturers would admittedly benefit from a British blockade, but would be unable to export, and so confined to their own market, closed to Britain since before the war. The British cotton industry need not therefore oppose any proposed maritime commercial blockade of the Americans.

Lyne further reported that 'the Manufacturers, Exporters and Merchants of Glasgow' were in agreement. Even allowing American merchants to continue exporting in neutral vessels would 'lengthen this war to the detriment of our commerce, navigation, finances and national prosperity'.[117] They all recommended 'a strict blockade of the ports of the United States', which would be 'the most effectual means of distressing the enemy by excluding their produce from the markets of the world'.[118] Unknown to him, as Lyne wrote to the Prime Minister, Admiral Warren and Rear-Admiral Cockburn were about to begin the full-scale British blockade of the Chesapeake.

Unlike the United States, Britain had the means to protect its foreign trade, which in turn provided the wealth which could be efficiently taxed and borrowed to finance wars to successful conclusions, both in Europe and in North America.

CHAPTER 4

THE UNITED STATES BLOCKADED: ADMIRAL WARREN'S 'UNITED COMMAND', AUGUST 1812–APRIL 1814

Declaration of the Chesapeake and Delaware [to be] in a state of Blockade – This is to punish the Madisonians, by preventing their getting good prices for their produce – & to favour their opponents. (American consul Rueben Beasley to American charges d' affaires Jonathan Russell, London, 26 December 1812)[1]

HESITANT BEGINNINGS

The British application of naval and commercial blockades to the eastern seaboard of the United States suffered a series of setbacks at the outset, due in part to the pre-emptive action of Commodore John Rodgers of the United States Navy. Rodgers left New York harbour, unhindered by the Royal Navy, on 21 June 1812, three days after Madison's declaration of war on Britain. He sailed in USS *President*, a large American frigate, nominally of 44 guns, intending to cruise in squadron strength.[2] *President* was in company with the *United States*, also rated 44, the smaller frigate *Congress*, 36, the sloop *Hornet* and the brig *Argus*, altogether a powerful force. Rodgers was anxious to avoid the possibility of being blockaded in harbour by Royal Naval vessels off Sandy Hook, and hoped that

> should war be declared, & our vessels get to sea, in squadron, before the British are appraised of it ... we may be able to cripple and reduce their force in detail: to such an extent as to place our own upon a footing until their loss could be supplied by a reinforcement from England.[3]

He had also heard of a valuable British convoy homeward-bound from the West Indies, following the north-east trade winds before crossing on westerlies to the eastern Atlantic. There he hoped to intercept it.[4]

Rodgers left before receiving the orders of Secretary of the Navy Paul Hamilton, whose letter was delayed, possibly by his reputed inebriation by midday, his obsession with detail and the suddenly increased pressure of work and need for decisions.[5] Rodgers seems to have been remarkably well informed, having 'ascertained, & I think from a source that may be depended on, that the British naval force on this side of the Atlantic, consists of one sixty-four – seven frigates – seven sloops of war – seven Brigs, and two or three schooners'.[6] He also knew that the 'British frigate *Belvidera* & Sloop of War *Tartarus* were seen off Sandy Hook yesterday morning'.[7] Captain Richard Byron of HMS *Belvidera*, 36, was patrolling off Sandy Hook, although out of sight of land, in hope of intercepting the French privateer *Marengo*, expected shortly to leave the harbour of New London, almost due north of the eastern end of Long Island.[8]

However, at 6a.m. on 23 June, 'with Nantucket Shoal bearing NE, distant 35 leagues', *President* 'sighted a Large sail … soon discovered to be a Frigate'.[9] The frigate turned out to be the *Belvidera*, but, by 11.30p.m., after a day of unsuccessful attempts at disablement, miscalculations and accidents, including the bursting of a chase gun which killed three and wounded thirteen others, including Rodgers himself, the British frigate had escaped.[10]

The *Belvidera* reached Halifax on 27 June, having taken three small American prizes *en route*; the American squadron's having opened fire without any attempt at communication, killing two British seamen, had probably confirmed for Byron the outbreak of the long-expected war.[11] But in Halifax, Vice-Admiral Herbert Sawyer, commander-in-chief of the Royal Navy's North American station, remained characteristically cautious. On 9 May 1812 the Foreign Office had instructed the Admiralty to avoid precipitating war, and clear orders had been sent to Sawyer in Halifax that he was to await confirmation from Mr Augustus Foster, the British Minister Plenipotentiary at Washington, before sanctioning hostilities at sea.[12] Sawyer, therefore, released the *Belvidera*'s captures. This must have seemed an unexpected setback to Byron and his crew, both in terms of morale and eventual prize money. Sawyer also sent Captain Thompson in the sloop *Colibri*, 16, under flag of truce to New York, to obtain an American explanation and unambiguous information.

Rodgers had also noted in New York on 19 June that 'the schooner *Mackerel*, with Mr Ruff (the English messenger) sailed last evening for Hallifax', presumably without the news from Washington of Madison's declaration of war.[13] Despite this lack of confirmation, Sawyer now sent *Mackerel* under Captain Hargrave to England with his reports and dispatches.[14] According to the *Hampshire Telegraph* the *Mackerel* reached Portsmouth on 25 July, which caused the *Naval Chronicle* to publish a further cautious interpretation of *Belvidera*'s escape.

> Our Government has expressed an opinion that the attack made
> upon the *Belvidera* had neither resulted from any new orders of the
> American Government, nor was any proof that war had been
> decided on. The American frigates, it was thought, had acted in
> conformity to a previous order of the Government of the United
> States not to permit vessels of war belonging to foreign powers to
> cruise within their waters.[15]

Vice-Admiral Sawyer had also sent HM sloop *Rattler*, 18, to Bermuda, the *Hunter* to Newfoundland and other craft to the outlying cruising stations, with orders for all the vessels under his command to assemble at Halifax. This might enable them to intercept and defeat Rodgers' squadron. This concentration of the Royal Navy's strength at Halifax, including the elderly *Africa*, 64, had the effect of dismantling Sawyer's original intention, in the event of war, of blockading each major American port with one of his six larger serviceable ships. As one British officer was to complain, 'we have been so completely occupied looking for Commodore Rogers' [sic] squadron that we have taken very few prizes'.[16]

Whether deliberate or not, Rodgers' distraction of Sawyer's intended blockade allowed many returning American merchant vessels to reach their home ports safely and to replenish import stocks. The import duties on their cargoes added very significantly to customs revenues and, importantly, affected American government thinking. The New York legislature was told that 'Nearly as great a proportion of homeward bound merchantmen have escaped capture as has been customary during the last three or four years of peace'.[17] Rodgers, meanwhile, had abandoned his search for the returning West Indies convoy in the western approaches and had further failed to venture into the English Channel, Bristol Channel or Irish Sea, an omission since much criticised, particularly with regard to his failure to inflict on the Royal Navy the potential disruption of its blockades of France, while dealing with him.[18]

Although, as Mahan pointed out, the loss of one West Indies convoy would not greatly have affected the British economy, any merchant losses in British seas would be unwelcome, not least because of the possible adverse effects on the Stock Exchange, maritime insurance premiums, public morale and political stability.[19] The first round in Britain's maritime economic war with the United States was thus characterised by a succession of missed opportunities on both sides. Much more could have been achieved by a larger British blockading force, but, given the Royal Navy's current European commitments, this was impracticable.

DUAL OBJECTIVES: WAR AND DIPLOMACY

On 4 July Sawyer received confirmation from Foster in Washington that Congress had declared war on Britain. The following day he dispatched the packet *Julia*, which crossed the Atlantic with the news in a remarkable twenty-four days.[20] Therefore, it was not until 29 July that definite intelligence of the American declaration of war reached the British government. Even then, some in Britain hoped that once news reached Congress that Britain had revoked its Orders in Council on 23 June a diplomatic solution might still prove possible.[21] Revocation of the Orders, as far as they applied to American shipping, was worded so as to take effect from 1 August 1812. However, any reply from across the Atlantic could not be expected before the beginning of September at the earliest.

On the following day, 30 July, the British Government and Admiralty felt more free to act. Admiral Sir John Borlase Warren, a man with diplomatic experience as well as previous service in North American waters, was ordered by the First Lord of the Admiralty, Lord Melville, to 'come up to Town forthwith' to meet the Foreign Secretary, Lord Castlereagh.[22] The Foreign Secretary evidently read to Warren his 'Orders & Instructions', but left some possibilities unspecified. In a letter to Melville on 8 August Warren discussed the potential complications of the possible secession of the New England States from the Union, and how, in that event, the Royal Navy should conduct itself in relation, for example, to vessels from New England.[23] In a letter of 12 August Warren sought and received from Castlereagh clarification on the 'friendly disposition of parts of the United States' and the terms to be fixed for any cessation of hostilities for negotiation of a permanent peace.[24]

Warren was also to be entrusted with diplomatic responsibilities, since Foster, the British Minister, had left Washington, and had sailed from New York on 14 July in the sloop-of-war *Alecto*, not to reach Portsmouth until 19 August.[25] Warren was authorised to propose an armistice to the American Government to allow time for both parties to investigate the possibility of a peaceful resolution of Anglo-American differences following the revocation of the British Orders in Council, to take effect, as far as American vessels were concerned, on 1 August 1812.

EMBARGO AND CONVOY: OFFENSIVE AND DEFENSIVE ECONOMIC WARFARE

But, since diplomatic success could not be guaranteed, the legal framework for British commercial blockade was put in place nonetheless. On 31 July an Order in Council ordered that 'commanders of HM's ships of war and privateers do detain and bring into port all ships and vessels belonging to citizens of the United States'. A General Embargo was declared on American shipping and goods 'now within, or which shall hereinafter come into, any of the ports, harbours or roads within any part of His Majesty's dominions, together with all persons or effects on board'.[26]

The General Embargo contributed to an effective start to Britain's economic warfare against the United States. As Albion and Pope demonstrate, 46 of the 450 American ships libelled in the Vice-Admiralty Court in Halifax during the war were detained there before 17 September 1812, and included some of the largest American merchant vessels taken. They calculate that no less than 57% of the full-rigged ships and 26.5% of the brigs condemned in Halifax were taken in the first three months of the war.[27] While only just over 10% of the number taken, these vessels represent 'almost a quarter of the tonnage' taken during the entire war.[28] Most were probably seized in or near Halifax harbour, and were a serious loss even to often prosperous American owners whose incomes might otherwise have provided loans to the government.

British commercial sanctions against an American economy heavily dependent on trade with Britain began on 31 July with an order that 'no ships or vessels belonging to any of His Majesty's subjects be permitted to enter or clear out for any of the ports within the territories of the United States of America, until further order'.[29] The same issue of the *London Gazette* announced on 1 August 1812 that the Admiralty revoked 'all licences granted by us to any ship or vessel to sail without convoy to any port or place of North America, Newfoundland, the West Indies or the Gulph of Mexico'.[30]

The need for convoy often added considerably to delays and therefore costs, but unless given dispensation as particularly fast or well-armed, the penalties for masters of merchant vessels leaving without clearance as part of a convoy, or breaking away from the Royal Naval escort without permission, were severe. As well as invalidating the ship's insurance policy, punishment could include a prison sentence, such as that imposed on Mr Newlands, master of the *Coquette* of Glasgow. He sailed from St Thomas' Island in February 1813 under convoy of HMS *Kangeroo*, but 'ran away from the fleet' and received 'a month's imprisonment in the Marshalsea'.[31]

SIR JOHN BORLASE WARREN: ADMIRAL AND DIPLOMAT

The Admiralty now moved quickly and, on 3 August, Warren was appointed to take over the hitherto separate commands of Halifax Nova Scotia, Newfoundland, Jamaica and the Leeward Islands as a new 'United Command', an 'enlarged and important service', superseding their present commanders, Vice-Admiral Sawyer, Admiral Duckworth, Vice-Admiral Stirling and Rear-Admiral Laforey respectively.[32] On 6 August the Foreign Office issued to the Admiralty secret instructions similar to those given to Augustus Foster, the British Minister in Washington, on 8 July, but which had not reached him before he left on 14 July.[33] These instructions, and more dated 7 August, included a Foreign Office draft of the letter Warren was to send to James Monroe, Madison's Secretary of State, on arrival in America, and were received by Warren on 8 August, authorising him to 'suspend hostilities … in the event of the American Govt. revoking their letters of marque'.[34] He was to propose 'the immediate cessation of Hostilities between the Two Countries' provided that 'the Government of the United States of America shall, instantly, recall their Letters of Marque and Reprisal against British Ships, together with all Orders and Instructions for any Acts of Hostility whatever'.[35] On the same day Warren wrote a careful letter to Lord Melville, dated 8 August, in which he sought further clarification of his complex political and diplomatic instructions.[36] But even before leaving for Halifax Warren realised that, should diplomacy fail, the resources available in Nova Scotia were inadequate, and he wrote to the Admiralty that 'in the Event of its being necessary for the future prosecution of the War to harrass (sic) the Coast and destroy the Trade and Maritime Resources of America', he would need reinforcements including 'small vessels which may be navigated in Creeks and Shoal Waters'.[37]

On 12 August the Admiralty announced Warren's appointment as 'C in C of His Majesty's squadron on the Halifax and West India stations, and down the whole coast of America'.[38] After prolonged preparations, including the acquisition of a printing press for issuing future blockade proclamations, Warren left Portsmouth in his flagship *San Domingo*, 74, on 14 August 1812, accompanied by *Poictiers*, 74, *Sophie*, *Magnet* and the schooner *Mackerel*. The frigates *Tenedos* and *Niemen*, both 38s, were, according to the *Naval Chronicle* 'to follow as soon as possible'. Warren's diplomatic responsibilities were an open secret; the *Naval Chronicle* continued 'Sir John, we understand, is gone out with powers to negotiate [sic] as well as to act offensively with the ships under his orders; but proposals of conciliation are, in the first instance, to be made'.[39]

Ten days after Warren left Portsmouth, the Jamaica convoy arrived safely. According to the *Naval Chronicle*,

> Great expectations were formed in America of Commodore Rodgers falling in with the Jamaica fleet, and capturing the greater part of it. HMS *Thetis*, however, and the whole of the convoy from Jamaica, arrived in the Downs on 24th August. On the 6th, Commodore Rodgers's squadron hove in sight of the convoy, upon which the *Aeolus*, the *Shannon* and the *Belvidera* frigates, which were escorting it across the Atlantic, parted company, in chase of the enemy.[40]

However, whichever enemy the British frigates thought they were chasing, it cannot have been Rodger's squadron since, according to his own account, he had abandoned the chase on 13 July and turned south for the Azores.[41] Nonetheless, while employed in chasing Rodgers without success, the British frigates had been distracted from blockade duties which might have made a major contribution to a negotiated peace. Rodgers reached Boston on 31 August and explained, in a self-justificatory letter to Hamilton, that, with scurvy among his crews, he had captured only seven small prizes throughout his long voyage.[42]

Warren, meanwhile, was not to reach Halifax until 26 September after a 'boisterous passage' in which the accompanying sloop *Magnet*, Captain Maurice, was lost with all hands.[43] On arrival, Warren promptly set about both his naval and diplomatic responsibilities. On 30 September he wrote to the American Government proposing an armistice on the strength of Britain's revocation of its Orders in Council as they applied to American merchant ships, on condition that America withdrew its letters of marque, and began the long wait for a reply.[44] Warren had no unrealistic hopes of a diplomatic solution. On reaching Halifax he had quickly concluded that 'any alteration in the sentiment of the Eastern States respecting Great Britain, or a Separation from the General Union of the United States' had been 'too much relied upon: as the Whole Object between the Two Parties is only an Electioneering Struggle for Power'.[45]

WARREN'S UNITED COMMAND: PROBLEMS AND SOLUTIONS

Warren formally took over from Sawyer in Halifax on 27 September and found, perhaps not unexpectedly given Sawyer's reputation for inactivity, a number of immediate concerns, including the inadequate number and poor condition of the ships available. In Halifax, in addition to the 64-gunned *Africa*, launched as long ago as 1781, he found just five frigates, and in Newfoundland a 50-gun fourth rate and three frigates. Twenty-seven smaller vessels completed the North American part of his command. Altogether, his United Command consisted of eighty-three named 'Ships in Sea Pay' at Antigua on the Leeward Islands station and at Port Royal in Jamaica, as well as the thirty-seven in St John's, Newfoundland and Halifax. The list composed in August by Warren's meticulous Flag Secretary and prize agent George Hulbert had arrived at a total of seventy-nine ships for the United Command. Not all were seaworthy.[46] The disparity between these lists of vessels apparently available and the reality of those actually fit for service in American and West Indian waters was to remain a constant cause of concern for Warren.

On 5 October Warren wrote to John Wilson Croker, First Secretary of the Admiralty, reminding him that he had already lost nine vessels of his command to capture, loss or reallocation, and of 'the necessity of reinforcing the Squadron on this Coast and in the West Indies ... to meet the exertions of the Enemy, who seem to be determined to persevere in the annoyance and destruction of the Commerce of Great Britain and these Provinces'.[47] The list of losses included not only, on the afternoon of 19 August, the frigate *Guerriere* to the American *Constitution*, but also the frigate *Barbadoes*, which had struck a sandbar off Sable Island on 28 September, together with two convoyed merchantmen, resulting in the loss of £60,000 in specie intended as the payroll for Halifax Dockyard.[48]

Manpower shortage, of both seamen and dockyard workers, was another long-standing problem. On 5 October 1812 Warren issued a local proclamation, probably more in hope than realistic expectation, offering pardon to any Royal Naval deserters who returned.[49] Furthermore, on 7 October Warren wrote to Melville 'I am also sorry to say that Admiral Sawyer's Health will prevent him serving as Second with me at this Critical Moment and that the *Africa* is in so bad a State as to preclude me making use of her in the Line.' By 18 October he had informed Croker that Sawyer was too unwell to serve as his second-in-command, and sought his replacement.[50]

But, before leaving, Sawyer was to contribute to a problem which for Warren was to become serious: that of licences held by American and neutral trading vessels. Wellington's armies in Spain and Portugal had long relied on American flour, wheat, rye and dry goods shipped by American and neutral merchantmen. Now in wartime, these vessels had to be issued with British protections, licences to carry their cargoes through British blockades. Similarly, the British West Indian islands needed American grain, livestock and softwood, which had been traded in the past for sugar, tobacco, rum, hardwood and tropical fruit. Both American and Canadian merchants had long traded with the West Indies, and many felt that they faced financial hardship or worse if not supplied with such licences. On 5 August Sawyer had complied with the proposition of Andrew Allen, the British Consul in Boston, to 'give directions to the Commanders of

His Majesty's Squadron under my Command, not to molest American Vessels Unarmed and So Laden "bona fide" bound to Portuguese or Spanish Ports' or those of their colonies 'Whose Papers Shall be Accompanied with a Certified Copy of this letter Under Your Consular Seal'.[51]

But licences, genuine and suspect, together with the use of false neutral colours, had quickly proliferated.[52] As many as 500 licences had been issued by British naval, military and civilian officials in the first ten weeks of the war.[53] The unrestrained issue of British licences appears to have induced an air of complacency at least in some American merchants. On 11 September 1812 John Maybin of Philadelphia wrote to a business acquaintance in Providence, Rhode Island:

> I believe with some of our Merchants the Confidence they have that
> the British Cruisers will not Molest them going to Lisbon & Cadiz –
> others have a Pasport [sic] under the Authority from Admiral
> Sawyer and Mr Foster – for which I am told they pay one Dollar per
> Barrel.[54]

The availability of British licences created acute difficulties at sea, particularly for junior officers in command of British boarding parties, who were responsible for immediate decisions. Warren complained to Melville on 7 October 1812 that 'The applications for Licences are beyond all idea for Spain Gib'r & the West Indies from the Americans & I have not countersigned any', although adding pragmatically '... but for Importation into this Province', meaning Nova Scotia. Clearly irritated by the enemy's use of false neutral colours, he later added

> The Southern States, who are a composition of most Vile Materials:
> have sent to Sea Numbers of Ships under Spanish, Portuguese & of
> late obtained Swedish colours from St Bartholemews: the property
> is thus covered & leaves the field open to a war of privateers against
> the British Commerce.[55]

Meanwhile, senior serving Royal Naval officers seriously questioned Andrew Allen's widespread issue of British trading licences and his apparent personal gain, which, in turn, prompted immediate political enquiries.[56] Allen was also involved in the issue of licences to Americans trading with the West Indies in October 1812 as enquiries into his conduct began.[57]

A further problem, pre-dating Warren's arrival and hindering the prompt implementation of British blockades, was that of American privateers and merchant vessels with letters of marque. Before being relieved, Sawyer had informed Croker of his command's capture of nine American privateers, thereby 'protecting the Coast of this Province & the Trade'. Sawyer was 'much gratified that these Vessels were taken so soon after their Sailing, as they would doubtless have done much mischief'.[58] Similarly, Warren was anxious 'to clear that part of the Station of the Enemy's privateers, of which there are no less than Twenty that have much annoyed the Trade'.[59] Between 1 July and 25 August 1812 no fewer than twenty-four privateers, accounting for ninety-four guns and 963 men, had been captured, followed by two more by the end of the year.[60] On 7 October Warren had reported that 'privateers are innumerable there being not less than 10 off the Island of Cape Breton & having hitherto no frigates within my reach, I have been obliged to dispatch the *Africa* & *San Domingo* to clear that district of the Station'.[61]

These successes, in relation to the size of the problem, were small. The routes of British vessels travelling between Britain and the West Indies, or the ports of Lower Canada, all tended to converge off Halifax. Unless convoyed, these offered rich prizes to American privateers. Many vessels had hurriedly left American ports before 4 April 1812 in order to beat the start of Madison's 90-day embargo. On returning that summer, most of their seamen had escaped capture by the expected British wartime commercial blockade. Now, many of them took almost the only sea-going employment available, and joined crews of generously manned American privateers or sought to supplement their incomes in vessels on legitimate trading voyages with letters of marque. By American calculation, even 'before Warren's arrival' the number of British vessels captured by American privateers 'probably exceeded two hundred', three-quarters of them between the Bay of Fundy and Newfoundland.[62] Vociferous British traders in the West Indies and Canada were to complain about American privateers for the rest of the war, both to Warren and his successor and to the influential at home.[63] Warren was usually held responsible, by both Admiralty and merchants alike, for the escape of privateers to sea through a porous British naval blockade.

Warren's Order Book, for what he called his 'Halifax, Bermuda and West Indies Squadrons', reveals both the priorities he set for them and his initially limited resources. On 4 October 1812 Warren had ordered *Africa* and *San Domingo* 'diligently to cruise for the especial succour and protection of the Convoys', specifically those from Britain to Quebec and Nova Scotia and from the Gulf of St Lawrence 'as well as for the Trade in General and the Destruction & Annoyance of the Enemy'.[64] The order in which these tasks are set out is, at this stage of the war, very significant. Convoys were an important aspect of Warren's defensive economic warfare against the United States, although the escort by Royal Naval vessels of grouped British merchant ships, either outward or homeward bound, was, from the outset, difficult to coordinate with the implementation of blockades. With the Halifax squadron dispersed, Warren complained to Croker that 'until the several ships return, it will be impossible for me to send the Convoys directed by my Instructions'.[65]

Warren's second major order, dated 10 October, was for *Poictiers*, 74, and 'two frigates of Captain Epworth's Division', including *Nymphe*, 38; the sloop *Sylph*, 18, and the schooner *Herring*, 6. They were 'to Cruise off the Chesapeake & Cape of Delaware, taking care to Station some vessels off Cape Hatteras', some 150 miles south of the Chesapeake 'to intercept any Ships from the East Indies, or Ships of War from France as well as for the protection of the Trade from the West Indies stretching occasionally towards the Delaware ... and Sandy Hook but not further to the Northward'.[66] As if this were not enough, they were also to inform Warren 'from time to time of any movements of the Enemy or any intelligence of importance', sending information to Halifax until 15 November and thereafter to Bermuda. They were to 'continue upon this service for the space of Eight Weeks … or until you are joined by a Flag Officer, and detaching one Ship as occasion may permit, to refit & complete Stores and Provisions and Water'.[67] This was indeed a tall order for only five vessels, especially at this stage of the war, when the intervention of the French was not thought an impossibility. By March 1813 Warren was to estimate that double that number of vessels would be needed for efficient blockade of Chesapeake Bay and the Delaware River alone. By then he would consider three 74s, three large frigates and at least four smaller vessels the essential minimum. Moreover, additional vessels would be needed to form a relieving squadron to fill gaps made by exhaustion and storm damage.[68]

GENERAL REPRISAL: THE WIDENING OF ECONOMIC WARFARE

In London on 13 October 1812 an Order in Council provided the legal basis for a wider and more offensive commercial blockade at sea, not only by Royal Naval vessels but also by holders of Letters of Marque and Reprisal. It sanctioned their 'apprehending, seizing and taking of the ships, vessels and goods belonging to the Government of the United States of America or the citizens thereof' or 'others inhabiting the territories'. British captors should 'bring the same to judgement in any of the Courts of Admiralty within His Majesty's domains'. Importantly, however, 'nothing in this Order contained shall be understood to recall or affect' Warren's authorisation to 'sign a Convention recalling and annulling, from a day to be named, all hostile Orders issued by the respective Governments'.[69] Furthermore, not wishing to miss any opportunity for taxation, the British Government had printed in the *London Gazette* for 31 October its 'regulations for the distribution of Prizes' which could be 'sold and disposed of' by the takers 'for their own use and benefit after final adjudication' but 'subject to payment of customs duties as if imported'.[70]

As a further indication of the complexity of the situation in which Warren and his squadrons found themselves, on the same day a further Order in Council was made 'permitting trade between Bermuda and the United States in neutral vessels' in essential commodities.[71] Although necessary for normal life on the island which would serve as Warren's winter base, this trade would inevitably help the American economy, a perverse contradiction to economic warfare. The Royal Navy was further instructed 'not to molest American vessels that have taken Grain &c to Lisbon on their return to the United States provided they have Licence from His Majesty or Mr Forster [sic]', the British envoy to Washington.[72] Until 13 October, such American vessels were supposed to return from Spain or Portugal in ballast, but could now carry return cargoes of 'lawful merchandise' as well as specie taken in payment, making the detection of false licences still more important, but no easier.

In his orders to Broke's squadron on 14 October Warren, significantly, gave priority to their using their 'utmost exertions for the protection and support of the Trade and Commerce of His Majesty's Subjects', and only then 'for the destruction and annoyance of the Enemy'. Warren also confirmed an established tactical principle, warning Broke to 'be careful not to weaken the strength of your Ships by sending into Port any vessels of small Value'. Sending away experienced junior officers and seamen as prize crews would leave British vessels shorthanded in the event of more important action, although burning or sinking insignificant prizes once stripped of anything useful was not popular with either officers or men deprived of even long-postponed prize money.[73]

As Warren waited for the American government's reply to his armistice proposal of 30 September the *London Gazette* noted that Congress had refused to ratify the ceasefire arranged on land between Sir George Prevost, the British Governor-General of Canada, and General Dearborn of the American Northern Provinces Army, and had directed that 'hostilities should be recommenced'.[74] Personally, Warren might have felt that General Reprisals could not be implemented until he received the American answer; certainly, the Bermuda 'Copy of Records in Vice-Admiralty Court' kept by George Hulbert, Warren's meticulous flag secretary and prize agent, does not begin until 25 November 1812.[75] Some prize taking by both sides, however, seems to have continued uninterrupted.

Economic sanctions at sea would not necessarily have been incompatible with Warren's suggested armistice and potential diplomatic solution, however, in that sanctions could be withdrawn and reversed in the event of peace. Following a negotiated settlement, captured vessels and cargoes could be restored, prisoners released and even compensation paid. A generous British policy after a display of force might have proved persuasive in the long term.

The American reply arrived at Halifax in the *Junon* on 16 November 1812. Not unexpectedly, Monroe's answer, dated 27 October, referred back to the issue of impressment, suggesting that it should be suspended pending Congressional legislation to prohibit the employment of deserting British seamen on American merchant or 'public' naval vessels. That same day Warren found unacceptable 'the surrender, even for a short period of one of the most antient (sic) and essential of the Maritime Rights of the British Empire'. 'The Presidents [sic] Speech Containing a refusal of the propositions, render any further observation unnecessary'.[76]

Now that *Junon* had returned with Monroe's inadmissible counter-proposals General Reprisals could be put into effect legitimately, although hostilities had never been completely suspended; American prizes had continued to arrive at Royal Naval bases. In anticipation of commercial blockade begun in earnest, Warren sought to rectify the shortage of both adequate resources and clear instructions from London. From Bermuda, on 7 November, Warren had written to Melville that

several points of this Command require a much more numerous Force
than I have under my orders & I trust you will, as soon as convenient
with your other Engagements think of our situation, as well as some
Decisive Orders respecting the number of American ships that have
been brought into this port as well as in the West Indies.[77]

The want of decisive orders, and of adequate means of implementing them, were
to remain among Warren's major problems.

VICE-ADMIRALTY COURTS AND PRIZE MONEY

Despite Albion and Pope's apparent assumption that 'the best prize money for the
Royal Navy was won in the first three months' of the war, the early embargo
captures did not mean promptly paid prize money for British crews.[78] The
protracted process of condemnation of prizes by the various Vice-Admiralty
Courts of Warren's United Command, especially when conducted as punctiliously
as at Halifax, meant that payment of prize money was long delayed. Warren was
concerned that this lowered the seamen's morale[79] and, certainly, delay in the
payment of prize money can have done little in reducing the rate of desertion.

On the Jamaica station the hazards of navigation produced another setback
for Warren, and the inadequate resources with which he sought to implement
the multi-faceted policy of commercial and naval blockade, as well as the
protection of British business property in the Caribbean, were further reduced.
On 22 November 1812, Captain James Yeo in the British 32-gun frigate
Southampton captured without difficulty the American 14-gun brig *Vixen*, but
in returning to Port Royal, just after midnight on 27 November, both vessels
struck a reef and sank. Both crews landed on Conception Island and later reached
Jamaica, but the need for a Court Martial was inevitably added to Warren's
responsibilities for operational planning.[80]

Towards the end of November Warren complied with the Admiralty's order
to establish his winter headquarters in Bermuda, at least until March, when the
weather generally moderated. Although 600 miles due east of Cape Hatteras,
North Carolina, and 700 miles from New York, it was 'admirably calculated …
for an advanced post or a port of equipment in time of war, to guard our West
India trade from the enterprises of the enemy's cruisers, and in particular, those
of America.'[81]

Despite an immediately apparent lack of resources relative to the task in hand
anywhere in his United Command, it was clear from the outset that Warren knew
what he was about. As early as 18 November 1812 Warren requested from Melville

Ships of the Line to Blockade the Chesapeake and to move to any
part attacked in the West Indies or this Province [Nova Scotia] &
likewise by stationing Divisions of Frigates & Sloops off the Ports of
Charlestown New York & Block Island in order to cut off the
Enemy's Commerce & Resources. This mode of action in the
Prosecution of the War which is unavoidable with the American

> Govt: has allways (sic) appeared to me as the most likely to prove
> beneficial to the Interests of the United Kingdom.[82]

Nine days earlier he had spelled out the expected consequences:

> I therefore should hope that a few Months will produce a great
> change in the people of the Country & the Numbers of their Ships.[83]

DIPLOMACY SUSPENDED: BLOCKADE IN EARNEST

Although as yet unaware that Warren had received Monroe's unhelpful reply, the British government seems to have been prepared for an American rejection of Warren's diplomatic approach. His commercial and naval blockades of the United States could now proceed less constrained by diplomatic considerations.

Even by early November, apparently unconstrained by Warren's diplomatic effort, a British commercial blockade of the southern coast of the United States was underway over 500 miles west of Bermuda. Extending from Charleston, South Carolina, southward to St Mary's, Georgia, then the southernmost Atlantic seaboard state, this blockade sought to disrupt all southern trade, particularly Georgia's timber trade which supplied America's shipbuilding and repair yards, such as Portsmouth, New Hampshire, and New York; this gave the blockade a strategic importance which would grow as it continued. As early as 7 November 1812 the uncertainty of Savannah timber supplies made one American buyer with responsibility for naval ship repairs insist that 'the Government also bear the risque of capture.'[84]

Then, on 21 November 1812, Lord Bathurst, British Secretary of State for War and the Colonies and, until September, also President of the Board of Trade, wrote to the Lords Commissioners of the Admiralty. He formally instructed them on this first occasion to order Warren that 'in the Event of the American Government having refused to conclude a cessation of Hostilities by Sea and Land', he should 'forthwith institute a strict and rigorous Blockade of the Ports and Harbors of the Bay of the Chesapeake and of the River Delaware', and 'maintain and enforce the same according to the Usages of War in similar Cases'. Mindful of the 'Law of Nations', Bathurst then added 'in the Event of the Blockade … being *de facto* instituted, that he do lose no time in reporting the same, that the usual Notification be made to Neutral Powers.'[85]

As evident from Map 2, such a blockade would hinder American use of the major ports of Baltimore and Alexandria, as well as the harbour at Norfolk, Virginia, and disrupt internal trade and communication between the smaller towns and settlements on each river. Blockade of the Chesapeake alone would hinder commercial traffic on the James, York, Rappahannock, Potomac and Patuxent Rivers. Bathurst's proviso 'in the event' of American refusal of peace feelers implies that British commercial blockade of the Chesapeake and Delaware had not so far been rigorously applied while any hope of a diplomatic solution remained, even if it had been further south.

The Admiralty issued these initial orders to Warren on 27 November, and then, perhaps reflecting the uncertainties of trans-Atlantic communications, re-iterated them on 26 December, this time sending Warren a copy of Bathurst's letter of 25 December, which repeated his instructions. Warren was again ordered to conduct 'the most complete and rigorous Blockade, of the Ports and Harbours of the Bay of the Chesapeake and of the River Delaware', to 'establish' the blockade 'and to maintain and enforce the same according to the usages of War under the Regulations pointed out in his Lordships said Letter'.[86]

However, any such blockade would be rendered largely ineffectual if the United State's overseas trade could simply be conducted for the duration of the war by neutral shippers. Although such a situation would be less than ideal for the Americans since tonnage duties on American vessels would be lost, import duties would still be payable and the American Treasury partly replenished. Therefore, Bathurst's instructions to the Admiralty would have to address the question of how neutral vessels making for, or leaving, blockaded American ports were to be dealt with by the Royal Navy. Accordingly, Bathurst's letter of 25 December importantly instructed the Admiralty that 'all Measures Authorized by the Law of Nations and the respective Treaties' between Britain and 'the said Neutral Powers will be adopted and executed with respect to Vessels attempting to violate the Blockade after such notice'. The Admiralty was to 'give Instructions to the Commanders of His Majesty's Squadrons and Ships of War', including 'Cruizers', and 'particularly to the Senior Officer employed … to stop all Neutral Vessels destined' to the blockaded ports. If they appeared ignorant of the blockade, and had 'no Enemy's Property on Board', British blockading vessels were only to 'turn them away apprising them' of the situation, and 'writing a Notice to that Effect upon one or more of the Principal Ships Papers'. 'But if any Neutral Vessel which shall appear to have been warned, or otherwise informed of the existence of the Blockade, or to have sailed from her last clearing Port after it may reasonably be supposed that the Notification before mentioned may have been made public there, yet shall be found attempting or intending to enter' any blockaded port 'such Vessels shall be seized & sent to the nearest Port for legal adjudication'.[87] Similarly, any neutral ship leaving a blockaded American port with a cargo 'appearing to have been laden after knowledge of the Blockade' would also be seized and sent in. Any in ballast, or loaded before notification, unless previously warned, would be 'suffered to pass, unless there be other just Grounds of detention'. Even then, such vessels would have 'notice and warning' written on their papers, prohibiting further attempts, and 'stating the reason for thus permitting them to pass'.[88] Such a comprehensive grip on enemy and neutral vessels and command of American waters would, if practicable, be likely to make an impact on the United States overseas trade and tax revenues.

Therefore, on 26 December, as part of the British government's effort to keep neutrals informed, the *London Gazette* announced that Viscount Castlereagh

> signified … to the Ministers of Friendly and Neutral Powers … that
> the necessary measures have been taken … for the blockade of the

ports and harbours of the Bay of the Chesapeake and of the River
Delaware in the United States of America, and that from this time
all the measures authorised by the Law of Nations will be adopted &
executed with respect to all vessels which may attempt to violate the
said blockade.[89]

After a period of four or five weeks to allow for the slowness of communication,
neutral European merchant shipping could not claim to be unaware of this
development and could, if it chose, avoid confrontation with the blockading
vessels of the Royal Navy.

There was certainly no shortage of American merchant vessels to intercept.
Despite American non-importation and 'enemy trade' legislation designed to
prevent such trade, some American-owned merchandise continued to cross the
Atlantic throughout the summer and autumn of 1812.[90] Especially after the
revocation on 23 June of Britain's Orders in Council concerning American
shipping, many American merchants in Britain, including Jonathan Russell, the
United States chargé d'affaires in London, apparently expected a negotiated
settlement and the resumption of Anglo-American trade.

Their financial assets frozen in cash form by the British shortage of specie,
American merchants were obliged to convert their capital into British
manufactured export goods or processed re-exports, which were strongly
demanded in America.[91] Russell advised them to dispatch their goods to America
and ostensibly 'thought it his duty to countenance the idea that shipments made
after the revocation of the orders would be admitted into the United States'.[92]

Even when British newspapers published the American declaration of war
on 30 July, Russell's advice to American merchants in Britain and British
colonies was to ship their goods to America. Similarly, Anthony Baker, the
British chargé d'affaires in Washington, expressed hopes to Castlereagh that
revocation of the Orders in Council meant that such American shipments would
be allowed under special British licences.[93] In November 1812 the American
Secretary of the Treasury Albert Gallatin believed that 'On the 30th of July, the
account of the declaration of war having reached England, a temporary embargo
was laid on American vessels; but on the following day, they were by order of
Council [sic] permitted to take cargoes of British merchandise and to proceed
to the United States, being for that purpose provided with licenses protecting
them' at least until 15 September.[94] But all were mistaken. Such shipments
remained illegal, contravening both American non-importation and enemy
trading laws until Madison made a specific proclamation suspending the acts,
which he chose not to do.[95]

By December 1812 American customs officials had impounded illegal
imports with a 'prime' – that is, cost-price – value of 'about £4m sterling', then
officially worth almost $18m, and accepted bonds on them for that amount. The
goods had an American market value nearer $30m.[96] After suggestions that the
merchants should pay $9m, only half the value of the bonds, even this was waived

by Congress. Later, Gallatin's plans to modify the Non-Importation and Enemy Trade laws to allow the collection of revenue on hitherto illegal imports, failed to gain Congressional approval.[97] These procedural obstructions would later prove very costly.

SHORTAGES AND INTERNAL DISSENTION

Even before the Admiralty's orders of 27 November for the commercial blockade of the Chesapeake and Delaware can have reached him Warren wrote to Croker complaining of the paucity of his resources relative to the demands on them. On 29 December he wrote from Bermuda, observing bluntly that

> the Force under my Orders is extremely small, the extent of Coast very considerable, and with many Convoys to furnish, it is impracticable to cut off the Enemy's resources, or to repress the disorder and pillage which actually exists in a very alarming degree and will continue, both on the Coast of British North America, and in the West Indies, as will be seen by the Copies of the Letters enclosed from Sir George Beckwith and Governor Elliot upon that subject.[98]

The demands of Beckwith, Governor of Barbados, and Elliot of the Leeward Islands, represent the relentless pressures indirectly exerted by the wealthy and often influential British owners in the islands, to which Warren was to be subjected during the twenty months of his 'United Command'.

It soon became evident that Warren's United Command was not to be entirely based on friendly cooperation. Sawyer's eventual departure from Halifax had overlapped with difficulties with the West Indies. In February 1813 Warren had confided to Melville that the West Indies had already cost him 'more trouble & pain than it is easy to Describe', especially 'Jamaica: where I am sorry to say that Admiral Stirling is acting in a very unhandsome way'. Stirling had been dispatching ships and allocating men without consulting Warren, aiding 'political intrigue or outcry ... against the Administration' and laying 'all the odium of every protest ... upon my shoulders'.[99] Warren hoped that, 'after receiving their Lordships Orders', Stirling would cooperate, and that 'the Board will perceive the necessity of making that Officer answerable for the employment of the Ships left under his Immediate Direction', especially since 'a few privateers is the only warfare waged in that Quarter: & which with 13 or 14 sail of Pendants I should think he might prevent; if he employed the Ships upon the Public Service instead of Convoying Money'. Stirling had been benefiting personally by illicitly charging for convoy protection as well as for bullion shipment, and was eventually court-martialled and replaced, but Warren's perceived mismanagement of the West Indies Station was to prove a recurrent problem for all involved. Warren hoped in vain that Melville would 'arrange this Disagreeable business & relieve me from such Insidious combinations that would require every Moment of my Time to revisit'.[100]

Earlier, however, Warren had made some well-informed and partly practicable suggestions:

that the Squadron would be much benefited by Six or Seven good
Sailing, old Ships of the Line, such as the Canada, Captain, Bellona,
Monarch, cut down and reduced as Razies, to Carry their Lower
Deck Guns and heavy carronade on their Quarter Deck, Gangways
and Forecastle, manned with three hundred Seamen and Sixty
[Marines].

In view of the size of the crews of the large American frigates, Warren went on,
'likewise ... twenty five or thirty Marines and some Seamen should be added to
the complements of the Frigates on this station'.[101] Given the demands on the
Royal Navy of the ongoing war in Europe, these manning suggestions were, for
the time being at least, unrealistic.

BLOCKADE IN PLACE: CHESAPEAKE BAY AND THE DELAWARE RIVER

On 6 February 1813 Warren supplemented the London proclamation of the
Chesapeake and Delaware blockades with a local declaration to neutrals.[102]
Meanwhile, he learned in a letter from Melville dated 3 December 1812 that Rear-
Admiral Sir George Cockburn had been appointed as Warren's second-in-
command in place of Sawyer, and that he was 'understood to be a very intelligent
and enterprising Officer'.[103] In the same letter Melville had confided:

> You will receive an Order for instituting a rigorous blockade of the
> Chesapeake and Delaware, & I must confess that I have been
> surprised that some measure of that description had not been
> already resorted to in regard to the Enemy's Ships although of
> course it required an Order from hence to extend it to Neutrals. I
> presume their can be no difficulty in anchoring at all times of the
> year within the Chesapeake & that the Delaware may also be
> rendered very unsafe for the Enemy's cruisers to enter.[104]

Cockburn was ordered to leave Cadiz on 18 November and join Warren in
Bermuda. Sailing on 23 November, he arrived there on 17 January 1813, to learn
that he was to be responsible to Warren for the Chesapeake blockade. After
urgent repairs to *Marlborough*, he left for the Bay on 18 February, although he
did not arrive until 3 March.[105] Warren's assurance to Melville on 19 February
that Cockburn 'immediately went into the Chesapeake and placed that Bay and
the Delaware in a State of Strict and Rigourous Blockade' was, therefore,
somewhat premature. He was also compelled to refer to a problem perhaps all
too easily overlooked in the comfort of an Admiralty office in London: 'The Port
of Boston and Rhode Island cannot be blockaded; without much loss of men &
risk of Ships, from the Month's of Nov[ember] untill March;(sic) owing to the
Snow Storms & severity of the Climate.'[106] Nonetheless, by 21 February Warren
felt able to inform the Admiralty that the blockade was in place, although so far
comprised of only four vessels.[107] But, by then, the American Secretary of the

Navy had already complained that 'The enemy having penetrated the Bay …
with their tenders and Boats, … are now greatly annoying the trade.'[108]

When the frigate *Narcissus*, 32, arrived in company with the *Dragon*, 74, and
the 44-gun frigate *Acasta* in Lynnhaven Bay, at the entrance to Chesapeake Bay,
on 4 March 1813, Captain Lumley found that *Marlborough*, *Poictiers* and
Victorious, all 74s, had arrived the day before. He also found that the 36-gun
frigates *Maidstone* and *Belvidera*, and *Junon*, 38, together with the smaller
Laurestinus, had been in Chesapeake Bay since 4 February and had already
'Formed the Blockade previous to our arrival with Rear-Admiral Cockburn', to
whom the *Maidstone*'s Captain Burdett now relinquished command.[109] Burdett's
force, augmented by *Statira*, had already captured the American armed schooner
Lottery en route from Baltimore to Bordeaux with a valuable cargo of coffee,
sugar and logwood.[110]

By now, despite Warren's estimate of ten vessels being necessary for
Chesapeake Bay and the Delaware together, the blockading force in the
Chesapeake alone now consisted of more than ten vessels; four 74s, six frigates
of between 44 and 32 guns and several smaller vessels. This situation may have
been temporary, however, as Captain Lumley's list, adopted by Hulbert, shows a
rotation of vessels, some arriving and others leaving within days for
replenishment or deployment elsewhere.[111]

Cockburn's arrival in force coincided with an attempt by Captain Charles
Stewart in the American heavy frigate *Constellation* to reach the open sea beyond
Hampton Roads. Stewart retreated, initially to Norfolk, and then further up the
tidal river, beyond the reach of potential cutting out expeditions, but was
nevertheless unable to escape. To commercial blockade had been added naval
blockade. *Constellation* was to remain incarcerated for the remainder of the war
and was therefore unable to attack vessels of the British blockading squadrons
or, by doing so, mitigate the economic effects of British commercial blockade.

Warren himself arrived in Chesapeake Bay in *San Domingo* on 22 March, his
initial stay lasting until 5 May. On 23 March Rear Admiral Cockburn made an
evaluation of British progress to date in blockading the Chesapeake. He reported
to Warren that even with the collaboration of a captured American pilot, all
efforts to reach the blockaded *Constellation*, now in the shallow Elizabeth River,
were seen as impracticable. Boats from his squadron did, however, capture some
American merchant vessels, and 'it appears the Capture of these Ships so high
up one of their Rivers' and 'the probability of their other Rivers being subject to
similar visitations' contributed to 'the state of alarm in which our arrival has put
the whole country'.[112] The residents' 'ineffectual application to Government for
means of defence' added to 'the rigorous blockade of the bay and the Delaware,
and the check lately given to the Licence trade … have caused the continuation
of Hostilities with us to be now as unpopular in this as it has been in other parts
of the United States'. 'The Virginians', he added, 'who a few Months back so loudly
called for war, are beginning to be as clamorous and a[n]xious for Peace'.[113]

An 'intelligent Merchant of Richmond' had, Cockburn reported, 'never seen since his entering into Business such Commercial activity in America, offering such Prospects of general Profit to all concerned' as in the first four or five months of war. The needs of the British army in Spain, and of the British Caribbean colonies, had increased demand for grain and flour, while 'the Superabundance of British Licences ... at a reasonable Rate' had meant that 'the Shipowners were able <u>without risk</u> to get Freight the moment their ships were ready to receive it'. Meanwhile, 'Merchants had more orders for Shipments to Europe &c than they could well execute and Farmers ... consequently got higher prices for the produce of their Labor than had been known for many years.'[114] Cockburn's informant maintained that the British blockade of the Chesapeake had 'not only put a Stop to these advantageous prospects but having also thrown back into the Country an immense quantity of last year's produce and caused an entire and complete stagnation of all Commerce and profit'. This, the merchant said, had 'a proportionate effect on the minds of the People, and there was now only to be heard from one end of the Country to the other Lamentations of Individuals who were now beginning to suffer from the effects of the war'. The American 'added with much apparent pleasure that Mr Maddison had lost all the latter measures he had proposed to Congress ... for prosecuting the War with rancour, and he assured me from the present state of the Country the President would neither be enabled nor permitted to continue it'.[115]

As a matter of course, Warren would have expected a situation report immediately upon his arrival at the scene of operations. However, in the absence of independent confirmation, Cockburn's report of the naval, economic and political consequences of the blockade of the Chesapeake, so soon after its beginning, might seem premature, exaggerated or even sycophantic – designed to tell Warren what Cockburn thought he wanted to hear. It might merely reflect Warren and Cockburn's conversations in Bermuda between Cockburn's arrival in mid-January and his departure in mid-February, in *Marlborough*, for Chesapeake Bay. No American merchant, keen for largely commercial reasons to see the end of Anglo-American conflict, can be seen as an entirely disinterested commentator.

Further, the apparent results so quickly observed by the Richmond merchant so clearly match the ideal outcome of British strategy as to invite some scepticism. While the cancelled plans of American farmers to grow for the international market and the fears of shippers who cancelled attempts to reach the open sea are no doubt significant, they are difficult to measure. Similarly, and most importantly, both the merchant's impressions and Cockburn's report are wholly subjective, where an objective analysis of commercial captures and their fiscal, financial and – therefore – political consequences would have been much more valuable.

However, a letter written by a committee of Baltimore insurance underwriters to Secretary of the Navy Jones in February 1813, pre-dating Cockburn's somewhat effusive report to Warren, to an extent vindicates the impression given by Cockburn's informant and reflects the concern felt by some other American businessmen. Having begun their letter 'Under the Circumstances of the present

Blockade of the Chesapeake, and the extraordinary Hazards to which our Commerce is exposed', the underwriters proposed a measure of self-help by providing up to four 'fast sailing and well equipped and well armed Schooners' to oppose the British blockading squadron's tenders and launches allegedly being used to 'decoy and intercept' American merchantmen, causing their insurers financial loss. Apparently anticipating rejection, the underwriters disingenuously added that they were 'aware that the protection of Commerce is the proper provence [sic] of the General Government, with which they do not desire to interfere' in suggesting their 'auxiliary measure'.[116]

Jones replied promptly on 16 February 1813 that he would put the suggestion to Madison, unknowingly naming the now blockaded 'Frigate *Constellation*' and '17 Gun boats and a Cutter now at Norfolk' as the existing American naval defences of the Chesapeake 'now directly menaced with an attack'.[117] He also made a realistic assessment of the American capacity to defend their overseas and coastal trade against British blockade, writing:

> It is true that the Government of the United States is Constitutionally charged with the protection of Commerce, but its means are limited and inadequate to protect at all points our extensive Coast and coasters against a powerful Naval foe whose Superiority enables [them] to attack a vulnerable point with a celerity and force that cannot be repelled but by the Cooperation of the voluntary local force, whose interests & feelings are directly assailed.[118]

Less realistically, Jones also hoped that 'if it were practicable to get below their tenders and launches in the night so as to intercept them and chastise their temerity, it would probably confine them to their ships in future'.[119] In the event, even a combination of federal government and local forces were unable to offer sufficient resistance to British blockades of increasing scope and power.

Throughout the early spring and summer of 1813 the thirty vessels named in Captain Lumley's list of the 'Blockading Squadron in the Chesapeake' arrived to maintain the naval and commercial blockades of the Chesapeake or left for resupply, refit and repair.[120] An early indication that the Admiralty's orders were being carried out was a report in Baltimore's Niles' *Weekly Register* that the American ship *Emily*, carrying flour from Baltimore to Lisbon apparently with a valid British licence, had been stopped in Chesapeake Bay and its papers 'indorsed' with a statement that the bay had been placed under rigorous blockade.[121]

In the months that followed *Narcissus* initially captured vessels in ballast, which were usually sunk or burned, but later took four ships carrying flour. The *Rolla*, from Norfolk, Virginia, bound for Lisbon, was followed by the *Finland* and two others unnamed in Hulbert's list of captures up to 12 June 1813. The schooner *Flight*, returning from Bordeaux to its home-port of Baltimore with a cargo of silks, brandy and wine, was a richer prize; while the schooner *Vista*, also *en route* from Bordeaux to Baltimore 'with Oil, Brandy and Wine', was 'Drove on shore, the Cargo sav'd by *Victorious* and *Spartan*'. Two Baltimore schooners,

Racer and *Lynx*, each laden with coffee, sugar and flour for Bordeaux, were captured, as were two schooners and a sloop, each carrying maize, described as 'Indian corn'.[122]

The *Narcissus* was obliged to share many prizes with other vessels present at the time of capture, but the ship *Beauty of Baltimore*, laden with 'Whiskie and Iron', and the sloop *Butler* of New Bedford, carrying corn, were unshared. While the majority were commercial vessels, some were out of the ordinary. The schooner *Dolphin*, listed as 'on a Cruise', was apparently a privateer, for which 'head money' was later paid on each prisoner taken. *Narcissus*' list of prizes ends on 12 June 1813 with the capture of the American Revenue cutter *Surveyor*, of ninety-six tons, with twenty-six men and six guns.[123] For the American administration, as well as for merchants and owners, the accumulation of such losses was becoming financially more significant, as well as a source of inconvenience and irritation.

These blockades, of the southern coast and of the Chesapeake and Delaware rivers, were accelerating a process of erosion of many American livelihoods and living standards. The Royal Navy's method is exemplified by Warren's order to Broke's squadron, composed of *Shannon*, *Nymphe*, *Tenedos* and *Curlew*, dated 27 November 1812. Broke was 'occasionally to Cruise with the whole or part of your Squadron, for any period not exceeding five or Six weeks, upon St Georges Bank, and as far as Block Island and Montauq (sic) Point, so as to intersect the passage to Long Island Sound, Rhode Island and the Ports near Boston'. This work was not without its navigational hazards. He was to remember that 'when employed Cruising upon that station or upon St Georges Bank and off Nantucket Shoals, great attention is to be paid to Sound every two hours'. Broke's squadron, later joined by *Valiant* and *La Hogue*, was to be deployed 'so that a Division may always occupy the Quarter Specified for Cruising and cutting off the Enemies Supplies'.[124]

Among the consequences of this rigorous commercial blockade was the isolation of Nantucket Island, thirty-five miles off the Massachusetts coast, eventually reducing the population to extreme poverty, a consequence later to have significant political results. By depriving many Americans of their capital and markets the blockades eroded their means of generating incomes and their ability and preparedness to continue to finance a war by an increasing number and level of taxes, and the government's repeated calls for loans, well beyond the end of 1814. While they were of necessity a protracted process, and not obviously successful at the outset, these commercial blockades, supplemented by naval blockade, were nevertheless the beginning of the end for any realistic hope of achieving American war aims.

Nonetheless, the defensive aspect of economic war with the United States could not be overlooked, including the protection of Britain's important trade in North American timber. As a result, on 2 December 1812 Warren had issued orders for a squadron to 'take the Merchant Vessels Laden with timber for the Several Ports of the United Kingdom under your protection and afford them Convoy 150 Leagues to the Northward and Eastward of the Grand Banks of

Newfoundland and having done so you are to cruise in search of the Enemy's Ships reported to be at Sea'.[125] Reconciliation of the defensive and aggressive priorities in these instructions necessarily heightened the need for quick decisions by watch keepers over whether to remain with the convoy or investigate potential enemies, with potentially grave consequences for mistakes. Trade protection by convoy escort was, however, to remain a vital part of Britain's economic war with the United States, although one never easy to coordinate with blockades.

In addition to the operational decisions for the blockades of the Chesapeake and Delaware, Warren was occupied in corresponding with London, both privately with Melville and more officially with Croker. However, in a letter to Croker marked 'private' for official reasons, dated 25 January 1813, Warren alluded to the important intelligence-gathering function of the Royal Navy's blockade of the United States. Warren's squadrons occasionally collected both informative American newspapers and onshore agent's reports, usually brought out by boats prepared to trade with British vessels, not only in fish, fruit and vegetables, but also in intelligence, often remarkably well-informed, accurate and up to date.

The role also included monitoring and, where possible, intercepting American communications with potential European allies, as well as the interrogation of captured crews. On 25 January Warren informed Croker that he had 'sent for their Lordship's Information Two Dispatches in Cypher from the French Consul in Carolina to the Minister for Foreign Affairs at Paris. The Cypher may be Discovered at the Office in Downing Street by my old friend Broughton, or some of the Gentlemen in that Department'.[126]

While writing from his flagship 'off New York', Warren had clearly decided, in advance of any formal orders to do so, to add that port to those to be blockaded. Earlier in January 1813 he had ordered Byron in *Belvidera*, with *Spartan* and *Tartarus*,

> forthwith to proceed off Montaug Point, long Island (sic) & Cruise
> for the Destruction of the Enemys Commerce & Ships and
> protection of the Trade of His Maj. Subjects between the East Side
> of Long Island & Block Island, & from thence 20 Leagues to the
> Eastward for the Space of Nine Weeks ...[127]

By February, Baltimore's *Weekly Register* reported that 'They are blockading the Chesapeake and the Delaware, and are occasionally off New York.'[128]

Warren's letter to Croker of 25 January 1813 gives an insight into local tactical dispositions, and into their underlying strategic purpose:

> You are aware that the *Dragon* 74 *Statira* 38 and *Colibri* Brig are
> with me: we have Taken and burnt since our being out 16 sail of
> Ships and Vessels. – I may probably produce some Deficit ere long
> in the Revenue of the United States: If all my other Divisions are
> equally active and successful:[129]

The same letter also revealed an anxiety:

> I am anxious to Take or Destroy some of the Enemys Frigates as
> they are called but in reality they are small Two Decked Ships: I
> trust their Lordships will not be displeased with my having enclosed
> a Newspaper containing an Official Report of the Committee upon
> their Naval Affairs; and particularly the size Descripsion and Force
> of the American frigates.

Returning to the themes of earlier letters, Warren also added:

> I wish you would send me some Razees of the Descripsion I have
> stated: and the *Indefatigable* as well as 8 Gun Brigs for New
> Brunswick the Gulph of St Lawrence; and another Ship or Two of
> the Line would render our Force here more useful and
> respectable.[130]

At this stage, the Royal Navy's commercial blockade of the United States was still beset with complications. The treatment of apparently neutral shipping remained a problem, as some American vessels had reregistered in neutral countries, and neutral vessels, unless clearly carrying contraband, were still, thus far, allowed access to such New England ports as Boston. The proportion of apparently foreign ships entering American harbours was rising steadily. Such vessels imported, for example, iron and glass from Swedish ports and sugar, molasses and rum from the Swedish West Indies, returning with American flour, tobacco and timber.[131] Both these export markets, and the materials bought, with the tonnage and import duties payable on them, were useful to the enemy, and so long as neutral vessels were allowed the use of American ports Britain's commercial blockade would remain only a partial success. Even as late as February 1813 Warren sought Admiralty clarification as 'it was impossible to Institute a Blockade of the Enemies Ports in the Face of Neutral Licences and Protections without Number'.[132]

From the assumption of his united command Warren had been subjected to the lobbying of the entrepreneurs of both Halifax and the West Indies. Few approaches, however, can have been as naively self-interested as that of the merchants of St John, New Brunswick, who demanded that the gypsum trade they conducted with American vessels should be allowed to continue, yet somehow 'consistently with effectual Prosecution of the War against an enemy whose proceedings are by none held in greater Abhorence than these Memorialists'.[133] However, since long-term British interests, as in the Peninsula, were occasionally served by connivance with some short-term American benefit through continued trade, more was required of Warren than merely mechanistic application of his instructions. Therefore, when even some American merchants made similar requests, Warren needed a strategic understanding wider than that of merely immediate tactical concerns. He received one such approach from a group of Boston merchants as early as December 1812, requesting that they should be allowed to use a licence purportedly acquired from the British Home Secretary Lord Sidmouth to carry grain from Alexandria and Norfolk to Britain's army in Spain. On the back of the letter Warren pencilled and initialled 'No vessel, either with or without Licenses can go out of a Port under Blockade, the orders upon this subject are Strict and Decisive.'[134] The letter then appears to have been filed unanswered. By the time Warren drew the attention of the Admiralty to this matter, exactly a year later, Wellington's progress in Spain had made such licences unnecessary, and Warren's approach to American grain exports could be really unambiguous. Until then, implementation of blockade on the North American station was seldom uncomplicated.

KICKS AND HA'PENCE: CRITICISMS AND REINFORCEMENTS

Warren's persistent requests for reinforcements, as in early November and late December 1812, met with varied responses. In mid-November Croker insisted that 'their Lordships have already placed under your orders … 3 sail of the line exclusive of the *Africa*', as well as twenty-one large and small frigates, twenty-nine sloops and fifteen smaller vessels, with even more promised.[135] In a private letter of 3 December 1812 Melville informed Warren that he would then have 'in the number of pendants under your orders … about one seventh of all the Sea-going Vessels in the British Navy', with the apparent implication that the Admiralty was expecting better results.[136]

Official correspondence from London also brought implied criticism and news of an appointment likely to lighten Warren's administrative burden. On 9 January 1813 Croker first re-iterated Admiralty dissatisfaction:

> My Lords Commissioners of the Admiralty had hoped that the
> great force placed at your disposal, as stated in my letter of 18th
> November, would have enabled you to obtain the most decided
> advantages over the Enemy, and to blockade their Ships of War in
> their Ports, or to intercept them at Sea if they should escape the
> vigilance of your blockading Squadrons.[137]

Even the promise of help was not without, at least, irritation. Now that reinforcements, once arrived, would give Warren a force including 'ten sail of the Line, my Lords have thought fit to appoint a Captain of the Fleet to serve with your Flag'. Customarily, Warren could expect to be consulted on such an appointment, but, Croker continued, 'as they were not aware of any individual among the senior Captains of the Navy to whom the appointment must be limitted, who would be more acceptable to you, they have appointed Captain Henry Hotham to that Situation'.[138]

A possible indication that Warren might have preferred an alternative, having met and disliked Hotham, is perhaps evident in a letter Melville had written to Hotham earlier. 'There can be no question that whatever may be the habits of private intercourse on which you may have hitherto been with him, he will be glad to avail himself of your professional assistance.' Hotham had previously received commendations from very senior officers, and was highly regarded.[139] In the months that followed, Hotham would send regular instalments of a Journal to the Admiralty via Second Secretary John Barrow, always openly acknowledged in a letter from him to Hotham in Bermuda, noting that it would be 'laid before their Lordships'.[140] Warren's staff, including his Secretary George Hulbert, would surely see these acknowledgements, weakening the suggestion that Hotham had been 'carefully chosen' to report secretly on Warren's performance.[141]

Originally intended to leave on 5 January 1813 with *La Hogue* and *Valiant*, Hotham left on 8 January to take up his appointment in March, raising a broad pendant. Another of Croker's letters followed, also dated 9 January 1813. It noted that the Admiralty 'understood that several Captains and Commodores, officers of His Majesty's Ships ... have been in the habit of taking their Wives and other Females to Sea, and disapproving as they most strongly do of this irregularity', called upon Hotham to 'prevent in every instance the recurrence of a practice which must be extremely injurious to His Majesty's Service'.[142] A professional approach to maritime blockade and economic warfare was required.

The reinforcements reaching Warren early in 1813 were, however, a disappointment. '[T]he wretched State of the Ships that joined me singly rendered it impossible to make use of them without Refitment.'[143] Moreover, the fulfilment of Croker's promise on behalf of the Board that 'Such an addition will also be made to your force in frigates and Sloops as will place 30 of the former and 50 of the latter at your disposal', was clearly improbable given Britain's continuing war with France and the Royal Navy's current world-wide commitments.[144]

Warren had certainly inferred Admiralty criticism even if none was intended. He replied to Melville: 'I have felt much hurt that the Board Should Suppose that any Exertions on my part should be wanting; were the means in my power of Distressing the Enemy.'[145] Perhaps as partial proof of his exertions, he enclosed in a letter to Croker at the Admiralty dated 28 March 1813 a table entitled 'Coast of America – Proposed Division of Ships & their Stations'.[146] Although, as he wrote, Warren knew that most of these 'proposals' had already been carried into effect, they serve to show exactly how Warren saw the Royal Navy's role at this stage of Britain's economic and naval war with the United States.

WARREN'S DISPOSITIONS: 'COAST OF AMERICA – SHIPS AND THEIR STATIONS'

Warren's proposals reveal a pattern of at least one 74 and up to five other vessels on each of the three major stations. Of Warren's dispositions, the first station was for the blockade of the Chesapeake, performed by *Marlborough* and *Victorious*, both 74s, the frigates *Maidstone* and *Junon* and the sixth rate *Laurestinus*, 26, *Fantome*, 18, and an 8-gunned tender. Their purpose was 'To intercept the Enemies' Trade and Cruizers from Washington & Baltimore & to prevent the produce of Virginia from going to market'. The squadron was not only 'To destroy their Revenue' but also their 'Resources, there being the greatest No. of

Privateers from those Ports upon the whole Coast of America'. The second station was for the blockade of the Delaware, where *Poictiers*, 74 *Narcissus*, 32, and *Paz*, 10, were to perform an identical function. The third station, kept by *Dragon*, 74, and one other unnamed vessel, was 'Off New York', to perform the same roles as the first two squadrons. Warren further speculated that

> This Port may be Blockaded by taking possession of Sandy Hook
> with Troops & anchoring some Ships within it, & by another
> Squadron off Mont[a]uk Point to anchor, Water and Refit in
> Gardiner's Bay E. end of Long Island where 18 Sail of the Line
> under Adml. Abuthnot in the old American War used to lay.

The other, fourth, squadron Warren referred to 'Off Nantucket Shoal, Block Island' and 'Montuk Point' was composed of *Belvidera*, 36, and *Acasta*, here described as having 40 guns. Five smaller vessels, the largest with only eighteen guns, were all that was available for the Bay of Fundy and 'To protect the Coast of New Brunswick from Invasion'. Nova Scotia was better provided for. Three 38-gun frigates, *Shannon*, *Tenedos* and *Nymphe*, were 'To cruise upon St George's Bank, off the Gulf of St Lawrence & on the Banks of Newfoundland'. A seventh squadron was allocated to the southern coastline. *Aeolus*, 32 and *Sophie*, 18, were posted 'Off Charleston, Beaufort, Ocracoke and Roanoke' in order 'To intercept Trade, Privateers & to destroy the Revenue'. Warren added that he was aware that 'several additional Vessels must be added to distress this part of the Enemy's Coast'. Only the 14-gun *Viper* was allocated to watch Savannah and St Augustine, despite their having 'The most implacable & virulent people in the whole Union'.[147] It was through this area, however, that clandestine cargoes of American raw cotton began their voyages to Britain, having been transferred in exchange for British manufactures to the neutral Spanish Amelia Island through a commercial blockade at this point deliberately left porous.[148]

Meanwhile, Warren's flagship, the *San Domingo*, in company with *Ramillies*, also a 74, *Statira*, 38, and *Orpheus*, 32, together with *Colibri*, 18, and a tender, were held in reserve 'To unite to meet an Enemy, or to Cruize occasionally whenever an additional No. of Frigates or Sloops arrive so as to afford relief upon the several Stations'. He hoped for an additional 'two Frigates & two Sloops of War' to allocate to 'any given point wanting Force or in search of any of the Enemy's Ships'.

Despite its already being the end of March before the schedule was dispatched to London, Warren went on 'In the month of March it will be necessary to add a new Squadron to attend to Boston & Rhode Isld., as the weather will then be sufficiently mild to admit of Ships keeping that Station'. He also wrote of then being able to add to the responsibilities of the three frigates currently off Newfoundland.[149] Warren's proposed dispositions emphasise just how thinly spread his resources had to be to meet the Cabinet's intentions and the Admiralty's instructions, over enormous distances and facing navigational hazards and frequently foul weather.

To add to Warren's discomfort, Croker had relayed in a letter dated 10 February 1813 that the Admiralty found his reports on the number of active American privateers 'in a great degree exaggerated'. Further, that,

> they cannot suppose that you have left the principal Ports of the American Coast so unguarded as to permit such multitudes of Privateers to escape in and out unmolested; and their Lordships are quite sure that by preventing our Merchant Ships from running [away from convoy protection] and by carefully blockading the Principal Ports the trade of privateering will be made so hazardous and expensive that its objects will be in most instances frustrated.[150]

But it was not just a question of America's 'principal ports'. On an indented coastline of prodigious length, the number of small inlets and harbours able and willing to support privateers was one of many factors inadequately allowed for in the Admiralty's assessment of Warren's performance to date. Whatever the Royal Navy's other commitments, a shortage of suitable resources would always be a limiting factor in conducting efficient blockades and dealing with privateers. For both tasks, sufficient substantial vessels, capable of penetrating estuaries and inlets, would be essential.

On 3 March 1813 Warren made an attempt to nullify the efforts not only of several American public warships but also of the privateers based around Boston, as well as those Bostonians engaged in overseas trade. He ordered Broke to 'use every exertion in your power to intercept the Enemys Frigates coming out or going into the Port of Boston as well as the Privateers Prizes & Trade returning to the Northern Ports'.[151] Boston at this time, however, was still open to neutral merchant vessels. Warren's initiative seems likely to have coincided with a discussion of the need for it in London.

In a very long letter dated 20 March Warren was to receive further Admiralty evaluation of his progress as expressed by Croker, who initially conceded that 'With regard to the watching Boston ... my Lords are aware that this Port cannot be effectually blockaded from November to March', but nonetheless recorded Admiralty disappointment that Rodger's squadron had escaped in October, as if the weather conditions permitting it complied to a precise timetable. The Admiralty also deplored the escape of Bainbridge in December and

> Tho it was not possible perhaps to have maintained a permanent watch on that Port yet having ... precise information that Commodore Bainbridge was to sail at a given time, My Lords regret that it was not deemed practicable to proceed off that Port (at a reasonable distance from the land) and to have taken the chance at least of intercepting the Enemy if the weather should not have permitted you to blockade him.[152]

Croker continued, 'With regard to your future operations and the disposal you propose to make of your force, I have to express to you their Lordships approbation of the general arrangement', although Warren was reminded that four more ships of the line had been allocated to him, two of which should apparently have reached him by 20 March.[153] 'My Lords are glad', Croker went on, 'to think you will consider the amount of force now under your orders as most ample – It exceeds very much what a mere comparison with the means of your Enemy would appear to make necessary'. This comment, however, takes into account only the naval blockade Warren was expected to conduct, and the relatively few American 'public' warships he faced; but not the numerous American privateers nor the American and neutral merchant vessels which Warren's forces were expected to intercept and detain as part of the Royal Navy's commercial blockade.

Warren's references to the French in demanding reinforcements were deemed 'by no means just' since, so far in this war, no French fleets had been deployed in Caribbean or American waters. Should the French Navy escape its Royal Naval blockade, Croker asserted, Warren would be proportionately reinforced. Finally, Croker added, 'My Lords … recommend to you the most active and vigorous prosecution of the War during the Season when the whole of the American Coast is accessible by your Squadron, and which will admit of your placing all the Enemy's Ports in a state of close and permanent Blockade.'[154] This, however, implied simultaneous commercial and naval blockade, for which Warren's resources remained inadequate.

Some news from London was more encouraging. In the letter of 10 February, Croker referred to Warren's proposal of razees, adding that 'their Lordships have already turned their attention to this point; and had ordered four 74 Gun ships to be cut down and fitted in the manner you recommend, with a view to their being employed on the American Station in lieu of Line of Battle Ships'.[155] By 23 March 1813 Melville could be more specific, assuring Warren in a private letter that 'when *Majestic* and *Goliath* are completed as razees we propose sending them to you'.[156] Melville continued, 'We wish also to give you not less than 30 Frigates for the whole of your command, besides a due proportion of smaller vessels amounting altogether perhaps, with the Line of Battle Ships and Frigates to 120 pendants, and we calculate that this will allow for your various blockading convoy and cruising services, and also a full third in port refitting and repairing.'[157] Whether this part of Melville's promise could be fully kept seems doubtful, although the cause of this apparent largesse was about to become clear.

As he outlined his current dispositions for the Admiralty in March 1813 Warren was unaware that, in London, both the Admiralty in formal orders and Melville in a private letter were framing instructions for the blockade of the United States to be extended. In his letter of 26 March 1813 Melville informed Warren that he should expect an Admiralty order 'for blockading all the principal Ports in the United States to the southward of Rhode Island & including the Mississippi', and added, 'we calculate that your force is amply sufficient to enable you to execute this service effectually'. Intending that Warren should comply as far as possible with the British perception of the 'Law of Nations', Melville went on, 'We do not intend this as a mere <u>paper</u> blockade, but as a complete stop to all trade and intercourse by Sea with those Ports, as far as the wind & weather, and the continual presence of a sufficient armed Force will permit and ensure.' More practically, Melville added, 'If you find that this cannot be done without abandoning for a time the interruption which you appear to be giving to the internal navigation of the Chesapeake, the latter object must be given up, & you must be content with blockading its entrance & sending in occasionally your cruisers for the purpose of harrassing & annoyance.'[158]

Warren's Admiralty orders, bearing the same date, required him to 'institute a strict and rigorous Blockade of the Ports and Harbours of New York, Charleston, Port Royal, Savannah and of the River Mississippi'.[159] He had already been blockading the northern approaches to New York; these orders sanctioned his blockading the more difficult southerly approach and legitimised what he had been doing in the north. This extension of the blockades passed into British law with an Order in Council dated 30 March 1813, and the *London Gazette* duly published its usual warning to neutral shipping.[160] To an extent, Warren's Admiralty orders followed events, sanctioning what was in fact already happening. A letter from the port authorities in Charleston to American Secretary of the Navy Jones dated 1 March 1813, pre-dating Warren's new orders, reported that 'The Frigate *Eolus* [*Aeolus*] and Brig *Sophie* with the two Small Privateers are still off our bar', although 'by information received from the Fishing Smacks, they have made no Captures of Consequence, five schooners and Several Ships Sailed on Saturday for france, unobserved by the blockading Squadron'. Nevertheless, the writer found it necessary to add that

> it appears that Lord Townsend [*Aeolus'* commander], is perfectly acquainted, with the State of this harbor, and also the destination of every vessel in it, with the politics of their owners &c ... I regret that I am not authorized to prevent the fishing smacks from going out while the Enemy remains off the bar; no doubt but that all the information goes out through that channel, altho rigidly searched at the Guard vessel.[161]

Nonetheless, the British blockade of Charleston was, at this stage, clearly under-strength and Warren's repeated calls for reinforcements were understandable. Warren's appreciation of his crucial need for all the means the Admiralty could spare to implement effective commercial blockade is expressed in his letter to Melville on 29 March 1813. If American overseas trade, especially imports, could be sufficiently reduced,

> It is possible that the everlasting Demand for Cash & Consequently Taxes may occasion Convulsion & Disorder among the Several States, which may urge the President to more explicit & acceptable Terms, of which, should such an event arise, your Lordship will receive the Earliest information.[162]

The British, however, were not alone in experiencing shortages. American resistance to British blockade seems to have been hampered in places by a shortage of suitable manpower, as at Norfolk, Virginia. By April 1813 Secretary of the Navy Jones had to admit that '... our efforts to recruit for the Gun Boats have failed at Baltimore, and progress very slowly at Philadelphia, even for the small force ordered for the defence of the Delaware, now as effectually blockaded and annoyed as the Chesapeak'. The range as well as the psychological impact of the British blockades is revealed by Jones' further comment that 'The presence of a powerful hostile squadron is naturally calculated to excite alarm; thus we have urgent calls from Maine to Georgia, each conceiving itself the particular object of attack.'[163] In April 1813, while 'off Annapolis in the Chesapeake', Warren remained 'persuaded that the Blockade of the Enemies ports here & the Chain of Ships established along their Whole Coast, has already, & will produce more beneficial Effects to our Arms than any other Measure Whatever'.[164]

Warren's earlier service in North America between 1777 and 1778 contributed to his sound grasp of the economic and political geography of his United Command. An American strategy, early suggested from alternatives by Commodore Rodgers, consisted of attacking British vessels in squadron strength. This led Warren to 'endeavour to send something off the Stream of the St Lawrence towards Newfoundland', since Rodger's 'Objects will be the Taking of any of our Convoys with Reinforcements & Supplies to Quebec or the Destruction of the Fishery ... & afterwards, the West India Convoys'.[165] This dictated an initial concentration on the American eastern seaboard. Later, the extension of the blockades in March 1813 would cause Melville to add his 'trust' that Warren would 'be able effectively to put a stop to all trade in the Mississippi'. As importantly, Melville had also insisted that, despite Warren's initial enthusiasm, New Orleans was 'beyond our reach in point of force, both for its capture and still more for its retention', a point of view which Melville might have been very wise to retain.[166]

The Chesapeake certainly was being 'blockaded and annoyed'. During April and May 1813 Warren exploited his almost complete command of Chesapeake Bay, with Cockburn leading an expedition into the Bay and landing without, at this stage, much effective opposition. An interim convoy of forty prizes was dispatched to Bermuda on 17 May – a useful measure of success to date. In June, however, an amphibious assault on Craney Island, at the western entrance to the Elizabeth River and vital to an attack on Norfolk, was repulsed.[167] Amphibious forces later briefly occupied Hampton near Newport News, where French auxiliaries fighting for the British behaved with barbarity, contributing to Cockburn's not wholly deserved reputation for brutality. Many soundings were taken and much useful intelligence was gathered, to be used with great effect the following year.[168]

The impact of the British commercial blockade was also being increased by a change in the type of vessel detained. It appears that from April 1813 the Royal Navy sought to intercept not only the ocean-going ships and large schooners of often-wealthy owners but also smaller coastal vessels, often the only physical capital of modest entrepreneurs who were sometimes undertaking the journey themselves. When maintained from one year to the next, this policy would disrupt the coastal trade on which many local economies relied, eventually with serious consequences for the American government. By May 1813 a Captain Dent complained from Charleston that 'our port continues Blockaded by a sloop of war and two brigs' in company with a privateer, making 'a number of captures, principally coasters'.[169] By the end of April 1813 no less a commander than Captain Sir Thomas Hardy in *Ramillies* led a squadron off Block Island, north-east of Long Island Sound, attacking the coastal trade seeking to approach New York. His squadron also sought to deny access to privateers and those with letters of marque, and used boats such as those of the frigate *Orpheus* for pursuit into inlets and estuaries.[170]

On 26 May 1813 Warren issued from Bermuda a local proclamation of the commercial blockade of New York, so that vessels attempting to leave the port could not claim ignorance. Additionally, on 2 July 1813, Thomas Barclay, the former British consul, still in residence as agent for British prisoners of war, wrote a letter to the Russian vice-consul in New York specifying the blockade's significance to neutrals.[171] This letter was published there on 6 July. So far, the commercial activities of the ports and harbours on Long Island itself were excluded.

Although on 28 March 1813 Warren had proposed stationing *Aeolus* and *Sophie* off Charleston, North Carolina, to blockade Beaufort, Ocracoke and Roanoke, south-west of Cape Hatteras, it was not until September that he named such places in a proclamation. Since in the meantime American vessels used the innumerable local inlets, Warren authorised an attack on Ocracoke, made by Cockburn with marines and other troops on 12 July. British boats captured the privateering brig *Anaconda* and the schooner *Atlas*, with letters of marque. Those landing 'purchased Cattle &c' from cooperative local inhabitants.[172]

The following week Cockburn explained at length how the 'Blockade of the Chesapeake is very materially, if not entirely frustrated by the Port of Beaufort and the Ocracoke Inlet not having been hitherto declared to be also in a state of Blockade', linked as they were by 'an easy inland navigation from Norfolk and Elizabeth Town'. 'Flour and other Produce of the neighbourhood of the Chesapeake, which can no longer be sent by the Capes of Virginia is now sent in numerous small Craft to the Neutrals & other large vessels safely laying at Ocracoke and Beaufort.' They should be blockaded 'as well as the Chesapeake of which in fact they now form a part owing to their immediate water Communication with it'. They were 'a Depot likewise for whatever is to be important to it'. Estimating the cargo of the *Atlas* alone to be worth '600,000 Dollars', such vessels were, Cockburn wrote, 'kept in constant activity from the immense Quantity of Goods ... sent from and received at the various Towns situated on the Shores of the Chesapeake'.[173]

Perhaps partly as a result, when, on 1 September, Warren sent a copy of his current proclamation to the Crown Commissioner's agent, dated 26 May 1813, publishing the blockade of New York, Charleston, Port Royal, Savannah and the River Mississippi, he took the opportunity to announce an extension and to explain the reason for it:

> From the first of September 1813, all outlets from the Albermarle & Pamlico Sounds, connected by inland navigation with the port of Norfolk, the ports of Beaufort and Ocracocke (sic) North Carolina, Cape Fear river & Georgetown, South Carolina, and Sunbury and Darien in Georgia, [were] in a state of strict and rigorous blockade.[174]

Although barely begun by 1812, the network of canals so far completed potentially gave better access to blockaded ports from further along the coast than was immediately obvious. The Dismal Swamp Canal, opened in April 1812, offered escape from Norfolk in Chesapeake Bay south into Albermarle Sound and out into the Atlantic.[175] Although often so narrow as to accommodate only twenty- or even ten-ton vessels, these canal entrances could, if unwatched, significantly reduce the efficiency of a coastal blockade. Waterways provided New York with 'ample channels of communication with the interior by water', making it a 'centre of domestic distribution … the whole range of coast from the Connecticut to the Shrewsbury River, and remotely inland – can be reached in perfect safety from this city in a sloop of 20 tons'.[176] An efficiently applied close blockade of the coast would drive internal traffic onto such inland waterways, with their connections to the sea. In the absence of cost-effective road transport, canals would do much to gather exports and maintain local distributive trade and communication; therefore, as far as possible, access to them would have to be closed.

Furthermore, by naming specific ports and the vessels allocated to blockade them in a proclamation, Warren complied with what was then generally understood to be legally necessary for a maritime blockade. Aware that the named squadron had to be an apparently adequate force for the blockade to be complete and uninterrupted, Warren had carefully added to his proposal in March that 'several additional Vessels must be added'. Extension of the blockade to hinder the American's use of inland waterways was therefore not only expedient but also legally respectable.[177]

By September 1813 a more objective appraisal of British progress with the blockade of the United States than Cockburn's attempt in March was possible. Throughout the spring and summer of 1813 the Royal Navy's commercial blockade had gathered pace; between 30 March and 22 July 1813 Warren's squadrons made 138 captures, all but two of which were merchant vessels. The exceptions were the American heavy frigate *Chesapeake*, taken by the *Shannon* on 1 June 1813, and the US revenue schooner *Surveyor*, taken by *Narcissus'* boats on 12 June. After a succession of keenly felt defeats, these captures were seen in Britain as vital progress in the war with the United States, although in the long run they were less important than the impact made on the American economy by the cumulative effect of the seizure of American merchant vessels. Continued commercial blockade was made practicable by the Royal Navy's successful blockade, capture or destruction, by the beginning of December 1813, of the fifteen named American warships shown in Appendix A as Table 2.[178]

Of the 136 trading vessels taken during those sixteen weeks, 110 were American, of varying sizes and with a range of cargoes. Of the twenty-six non-American vessels, most were Spanish, Portuguese or Swedish, although four were 'English' recaptures, with other British vessels detained for 'illicit trading'.[179] Of these prizes twenty-four were sent under prize crews into Halifax, twenty-two to Bermuda, eight into Nassau on New Providence Island and seven to Jamaica for adjudication by their respective Vice-Admiralty Courts, and one into Porta Corbello. Twenty-six were burnt or destroyed and two simply 'set adrift', while eight of the faster prizes were pressed into service as tenders for larger British ships and one, captured by Warren's *San Domingo*, was 'fitted as a watering vessel'.[180] Despite its being illegal, one American ship, the *Montesquieu*, 'laden with tea, nankeen, silk, copper and cassia, from Canton, bound for Philadelphia, captured by the *Paz* March 27 1813', was 'ransomed for 180,000 dollars'.[181]

Whereas, earlier in the year, the voyage of the 409-ton American ship *Star*, carrying grain from Alexandria to Lisbon, would have been licensed and condoned, Wellington's recent progress in the Peninsula now rendered such shipments less necessary. *Marlborough*'s capture of the *Star* on 14 June 1813 showed that the British could now strike at American grain exports without hindering efforts against Napoleon's armies in Spain. Only four days later *Marlborough* took the 292-ton ship *Protectress*, also laden with American flour; together these were a significant success for Cockburn's 'Chesapeake Squadron' and a powerful disincentive to American farmers, processors and shippers.[182]

While the schooner *Ploughboy*, sent by *Ramillies* into Halifax on 16 April 1813, carried 288 bales of cotton, other cargoes were more varied. The 150-ton American brig *Valador*, flying Portuguese colours when captured by *Statira*, *Spartan* and *Martin* on 1 June, carried silk, ribbon, window glass and some specie.[183] The 35-ton American sloop *Butler*, taken by *Narcissus*' boats on 9 June 1813, had carried merely 'corn meal and fish', but was nevertheless sent into Bermuda for adjudication. Other mundane cargoes included groundnuts, potash, potatoes, barrel staves, roof shingles and sundries, while more exotic ones included valuable mahogany, indigo, tea, sugar, wine and skins.[184]

Often vessel and cargo together must have represented a considerable investment. The 457-ton ship *Volante*, laden with 'Brandy, Wine, Silks, Dry Goods, Iron &c', was captured *en route* from Bayonne to Boston by *La Hogue*, *Valiant* and *Curlew* on 26 March 1813 and listed as 'condemned'. So was the 293-ton brig *Diomede*, captured on 10 May by *La Hogue* and *Nymphe* exporting 'Redwood, Indigo, Sugar, Tea, Oil & Ships Blocks' from Salem to Manilla.[185] Later, on 3 September 1813, the 750-ton ship *Jerusalem*, importing '2,000 boxes of Sugar, Coffee, Copper, and Hides', from 'Havannah to Boston' was captured by *Majestic* and 'taken into Halifax'.[186] These three losses alone must have had an adverse effect on the preparedness of all those involved to continue with American international trade. Both exports and imports were also disrupted in the timber trade. On 14 March 1813 the 120-ton American brig *Commerce*, 'with lumber from Rhode Island bound for Havannah', was captured by *Colibri* and burned, while on 31 March the American ship *Franklin* 'of 171 tons and ten men', importing timber from Cayenne to New York, was captured and sent by *Ramillies* into Halifax.[187]

Internal American trade in a range of commodities, including cotton, was also being disrupted by captures such as that of the American schooner *Rising Sun* of '100 tons and 8 men laden with cotton from Charleston to New York', captured by *Atalante* on 31 March 1813 and sent into Halifax. Similarly, the American brig *Cornelia*, laden with cotton from Savannah, bound for Boston's growing textile industry, was taken by *Ramillies* on 26 April 1813 and sent to Bermuda.[188] Conversely, the recapture by HMS *Opossum*, on 2 February 1813, of the 250-ton British brig *Bowes*, laden with a cargo of cotton being imported from Pernambuco in Brazil to Liverpool, must have brought relief to owners and insurers alike, if not its prize crew.[189]

Taken together, these lists suggest that by September 1813 most sections of the American economy were being affected, rather than, as earlier, the profits of just a minority of shipowners and wealthy merchants. Although neutrals were not unaffected, of a list of seventy-seven of Warren's captures taken up to 19 July 1813, all but fifteen were American. Eight were 'English' recaptures. Forty-four were definitely 'condemned' and thirteen more looked likely to be. Only ten were 'restored', of which seven had produced licences, one was 'part condemned' and another one 'cleared'.[190]

Warren's pencilled note, added to the list of captures and detentions ending on 26 September 1813, testifies to the slowness of the Vice-Admiralty Court's adjudication system by recording that '121 sail at Halifax, 113 at Bermuda, 68 at Leeward Islands, 70 at Jamaica' were still 'unaccounted for, total 372'.[191] Warren reported to Croker, as tardily as 11 November 1813, that between 20 April and 20 September that year his squadrons had sent a total of 115 vessels into Halifax alone for adjudication in its Vice-Admiralty Court. At the time Warren wrote, the outcome of just sixty-eight of these cases was fully recorded. Twenty-nine vessels, almost 43% of the cases decided, were 'condemned', together with the cargoes of two more. Fifteen vessels, 22% of those decided on, were found to be recaptured British vessels, and twenty-two vessels, almost 32%, were 'restored' by the laboriously thorough court proceedings. The ultimate fate of the remaining forty-seven vessels was unrecorded. This list of vessels sent into Halifax does not refer to those sunk, burned or unofficially ransomed at sea.[192] By December 1813 Warren's squadrons had sent no fewer than 231 prizes into Bermuda alone, 54 up to the end of 1812 and a further 177 during 1813, of which only five appear to have been restored, and one recapture, which was placed 'under Admiralty Orders'.[193]

To complement these successes in the Royal Navy's commercial blockade, some progress was made with a British naval blockade. On 1 June 1813 initial American plans for Decatur to attack the British squadron blockading Charleston – later amended to molesting British trade in the West Indies – were frustrated at the outset. His heavy frigate *United States*, together with the now American *Macedonian* and the sloop *Hornet*, were intercepted by the *Valiant*, 74, and *Acasta*, 44, although Decatur later reported that as many as seven British vessels had blockaded the eastern exit of Long Island Sound.[194] The American vessels took refuge in the port of New London, north of Long Island, outside which a reinforced British blockading squadron became permanent. Only the *Hornet* was to escape, in November 1814, to take any further part in the war. Captain Oliver of the *Valiant* reported to Warren that he took 'great consolation in having prevented their getting to sea from both ends of Long Island [Sound] and from knowing that they are now in a situation where perhaps they can be more easily watched than in most others'.[195]

But, despite this clear progress, and having kept a 74 and three frigates outside Boston, Warren had to admit in a letter to Melville dated 1 June 1813 that 'in a fog which is prevalent at this Season ... Commodore Rogers with the *President* and the *Congress* had got out'.[196] Warren's letter, in fact, crossed on its journey to London with a letter to him from Melville and the Admiralty, dated 4 June 1813, which seems somewhat critical in its tone.

> We hope soon to have further accounts from you & to learn that your most important object, the blockading [of] the Enemy's Ships of War in their Ports has been attained, as also the other objects of putting a total stop to their trade and the annoyance of the Coastline.[197]

This order of priority obviously reflects the possibility that major American warships, if unblockaded, could attack and disrupt, if not potentially remove, the British squadrons conducting the commercial blockades making a progressively less ignorable impact on American trade and Customs revenues.

Melville was also 'very solicitous that the Ports of New York and Boston should be watched by a force fully equal to encounter the Enemy in the event of their putting to Sea', and that any escaping should be pursued. Further, that Warren's 'Squadrons off New York and Boston will be on their guard against being caught between two fires by the junction of the Enemy from those Ports'. Melville then combined good news with bad. 'Some of our Fir Frigates have been launched; and others are coming forward. The whole will probably be completed in the course of this year, but we have great Difficulty in procuring men for them.' He continued, 'We are building these Ships of the same size and force as the large American's & shall probably build a third'.[198]

By June 1813 Warren felt the need to postpone his return to Halifax until the autumn 'if the Service will admit for a few weeks for the benefit of my health and Refitment of the Ships'. On 22 July he said he would return to Halifax in September, but meanwhile intended 'to attend a little to my health, which has suffered by so long a period at Sea'.[199] By September, however, serious sickness among British crews in Halifax was 'prevailing', although temporary.[200] Further, in September and into October, the Caribbean and more southerly American states could expect hurricanes.

Occasionally, provisions for the British blockading squadrons came from captured cargoes, but others were supplied by Americans at a profit. This 'palpable and criminal intercourse' became sufficiently widespread for American Secretary of the Navy Jones to 'call for the vigilant interposition of all the Naval Officers of the United States'. In an order dated 29 July 1813, Jones complained that

> This intercourse is not only carried on by foreigners, under the
> specious gard (sic) of friendly flags, who convey provisions water
> and succours of all kinds (ostensibly destined for friendly ports, in
> the face too of a declared and rigourous blockade,) direct to the
> fleets and stations of the enemy with great subtlety and treachery by
> profligate citizens who under cover of night or other circumstances
> favouring their turpitude find means to convey succours or
> intelligence to the enemy.[201]

Provisions were indeed supplemented by 'constant intelligence of our naval and military force and preparation'.[202] From later accounts, American attempts to restrict, much less eradicate, these transactions were largely ineffective. Meanwhile, the clandestine showing of 'blue lights' at night continued to alert British blockading vessels outside New London to American intentions to leave harbour and to infuriate pro-government sections of the American press.[203]

Warren was still so short of reinforcements that the relief of vessels on blockade duty was often delayed, with a corresponding reduction in efficiency. On 22 July, Warren wrote to Melville from the 'River Potomac 40 miles below Washington' that he was

> pleased that some Razees are likely at last to come here: & when
> these additions arrive I shall place a strong Division as has already
> been the case off Boston & New London, this place & the Delaware
> – but it requires many ships to afford a relief to the several
> Divisions: added to which our supply of provisions at Bermuda has
> failed us much & must be remedied.[204]

These complaints contrast strangely with the Admiralty's version of the vessels at Warren's disposal. In comparison with the eighty-three vessels on the North America and West Indies stations in July 1812, only seventy-nine of which are recorded by Warren's flag secretary by 7 August of that year, by 1 July 1813 the Admiralty listed no fewer than 129 vessels allocated to Warren's United Command.[205] The North America station at Halifax was listed as having sixty vessels of various sizes, including a prison ship, while the Leeward Islands station had thirty-nine. The Jamaica station had seventeen and Newfoundland thirteen, including its prison ship, but excluding numerous troopships. The North

America station was listed as having ten 74s and one razee described as having 58 guns, two large frigates – *Acasta*, with 44 guns, and the *Loire*, with 40 – and seven 38-gun frigates. Seven further frigates carried between 36 and 32 guns, while two sixth rates carried either 24 or 20 guns. Twenty-eight vessels with fewer than 20 guns were listed, together with three unarmed vessels. The Leeward Islands station was given as having two 74s and a 50-gun fourth rate, three 38-gun frigates and four smaller ones, and three sixth rates with 20 guns. A further twenty-six smaller vessels with fewer than 20 guns were also listed. Similarly, Jamaica was given as having two 74s and a 44-gun fifth rate; all the rest, excluding the unarmed receiving ship, were described as sixth rates with fewer than 22 guns. The list gave Newfoundland one 74, one fifth rate with 40 guns, one with 38 and two with 36. Seven sixth rates with 20 or fewer guns and an unarmed prison ship completed the United Command's allocation, approximately one-fifth of the 624 vessels given by the General Abstract as the Royal Navy's strength on 1 July 1813.[206]

By July 1813, Rear Admiral Griffith had been appointed as Flag Officer to lighten the administrative load at Halifax. He was, Warren said, 'already known to me', and 'will be of infinite Service; as I can then Depend upon the Ships being sent out to their several stations after re-equiptment; (sic) and also the unreasonable Demands & Alarm of the Merchants answered and attended to in Time'.[207]

Despite all of Warren's often-valid complaints, the British naval blockade was achieving a measure of success. By July 1813 the Royal Navy had blockaded or captured eight named American warships and destroyed or captured numerous smaller 'public' vessels.[208] The best of the smaller craft left afloat were often used as tenders by the British blockading squadrons. Warren was later to inform Croker of his purchase of nine such vessels, two brigs and seven schooners, all captured with American letters of marque and 'particularly fine Vessels of their Class and extremely fast Sailers'.[209]

Warren's private letter to Melville on 6 September 1813 revealed his misgivings at apparent machinations in London. He wrote:

> I am sorry to Observe in the Orders received from the Board; that Directions have been given to Rear Admiral Griffith to Direct the Blockading Squadrons without their going through me as the Senior and Commanding Officer; which is not a pleasant circumstance.[210]

Clearly deciding just to get on with the job, however, Warren continued, as if reminding London of his function: 'I shall however endeavour to arrange the System of Blockading Boston and the Eastern ports with Rr Admiral Griffith as well as selecting a certain number of Ships for that Service & Directing the Rear Admiral to See them relieved by fresh Ships occasionally throughout the Winter.'[211] With hindsight, perhaps, Warren should have complained more loudly.

By 27 September 1813 Warren wrote from Halifax of his intention to 'proceed to Bermuda' and direct Cockburn to 'Employ the Flying Corps in Harrassing the

Southern Coast of America and attacking such places as may be most Vulnerable and Destroying the Enemies Ships & Commerce', while leaving in Halifax 'a strong Division of Ships with Rear Admiral Griffith for the Services of the Blockade of this Quarter of my United Station – so as to ensure their being regularly relieved'. Then, despite his usual plea that 'some fresh ships may soon arrive upon this Station', he wished that 'Orders were given to include the Port of New Haven & perhaps also New London ... within the Blockade of New York, or it will be impossible to prevent the Trade and Vessels entering the latter port by passage of the Sound'.[212] If granted, this second wish would significantly increase the demands on his resources.

Indeed, the cumulative wear on such British ships as *Nymphe*, *Orpheus* and *Statira*, long employed on both naval and commercial blockades, was to contribute to another embarrassing failure of the British blockades. While *Nymphe* was in Halifax, withdrawn from her station for a routine refit, *Orpheus* sprang her mainmast and was obliged to join her there. *Statira*, meanwhile, was 'so very bad in her topsides, knees &c', that Warren proposed sending her temporarily to join the New London blockade, then to the West Indies, to return to Britain with a convoy. On 16 October Warren had to admit in a letter to Croker that Rodger's *President* had again evaded the British blockading squadrons, and had re-entered Newport harbour from a five-month North Atlantic cruise.[213]

Despite this obvious reversal, by October 1813, after the tentative start complicated by belated diplomatic overtures, shortage of resources and undeniable shortcomings, the beginnings of naval success must have seemed within reach. Warren's disposition of available ships and personnel seem to reflect much of what the British Government had in mind at the outset. On 26 October Warren informed Melville that he had 'directed Rear Admiral Griffith to superintend and direct the Blockade of Boston and the Bay of Fundy & the Convoys from thence in addition to the Port Duty'. He also proposed 'having Rear Admiral Cockburn with the Ships off New York & moving myself occasionally towards Chesapeake & along the line of Coast'. He could not, however, avoid adding that he

> should hope that all the Razees may be sent direct to me and an additional number of the new large frigates as I have not by 30th last so many as proposed in your Lordships former letter, and with the numerous blockades all of which require a relief of ships to preserve them.[214]

Although Oliver's reports to Warren and the American warships trapped in New London harbour both show that the British naval blockade of New York was in place by the summer of 1813, neutral merchant ships continued to enter and leave New York harbour as well as Boston. While the decision still stood to allow Boston to continue its trade with neutrals, in the hope of widening to the point of secession the political gap between the Republican administration and the increasingly prosperous, and largely Federalist, New England, any such hopes concerning New York were unrealistic. An opportunity for inflicting further economic damage on the United States clearly existed, as the continued arrival and departure of neutral merchant vessels in New York still allowed its dealers their stock in trade and resulted in continued Customs contributions to the American Treasury. By November 1813 the Royal Navy's slowly increasing resources on the American north-eastern seaboard probably meant that this trade could be curtailed.

Warren's proclamation on 16 November 1813 legally extended the commercial blockade everywhere south of Narragansett Bay, importantly noting that 'the Ministers of Neutral Powers' had 'been duly notified', and 'that all the Measures authorized by the Law of Nations would be adopted and exercised with Respect to all Vessels which may attempt to violate the said Blockade'. Equally essential legally was his declaration that he had 'stationed on the Sea Coasts, Bays, Rivers and Harbours of the said several States, a Naval Force adequate and sufficient to enforce and maintain the Blockade thereof, in the most strict and vigorous Manner'.[215] Warren's letter to Croker of 20 November enclosed a copy of the proclamation detailing the additional blockade, which included Long Island Sound and 'the line of Coast from the entrance by the Sound into New York to the Southern Ports & River Mississippi', and which would seek to end neutral trade with New York.[216]

Ostensibly, the extension was due to the Americans 'establishing at the Port of New-London a Naval Station to cover the Trade to and from the Port of New York' and having 'through the Medium of Inland Carriage established a Commercial Intercourse between the said Blockaded Ports', weakening 'to a certain degree' the existing blockade.[217] Warren's proclamation, however, sought to legitimise what he had already been doing, both in Long Island Sound and between Charleston and St Mary's, Georgia, and off the Mississippi estuaries, since 1 September. By December, Americans in Baltimore and beyond could read an announcement of Warren's extended blockade in Niles' *Weekly Register*, and would soon be able to measure its adverse economic effects.[218]

When extended on 16 November 1813 the commercial blockade of New York was to include all the 'ports and places' on Long Island itself, especially on its northern and eastern coasts. An American writer later conceded, however, that 'the inhabitants were not molested in peaceful pursuits'.[219] On 2 December 1813 Captain Oliver of the *Valiant*, the Senior Officer in Long Island Sound, wrote to the Spanish consul in New York that 'after 6 December, no vessel whatever will be permitted to sail from any port in Long Island Sound', and asked him to 'communicate this intelligence to the neutral consuls in your district'.[220]

Towards the end of 1813, perhaps not surprisingly after 15 months' effort sometimes under difficult conditions, Warren's health and temper began to fail. His letter of 26 October had been written with 'the assistance of his confidential friend owing to a cold in my eyes', and had contained the sort of pessimistic 'reflections' later to be expressed more strongly. In early November 1813 Warren's letter to Melville again referred to the 'gale of wind & fog which so frequently occurs on this coast'. He went on to 'Earnestly request that some Reinforcement of Ships be sent to preserve the Blockades', adding with a touch of asperity 'as well as to keep the Gentlemen of Jamaica in good humour'.[221] On 30 November he complained in another letter to Melville that he found it increasingly difficult to maintain and relieve blockades, guard the West Indies and meet the constant demand for convoy escorts. Apparently anxious to continue the commercial blockade, he concluded that 'I shall if possible be in Bermuda in about three weeks & send Rear Admiral Wimburne to attend to the Duty off New York & the Albermarle.'[222]

By 30 December 1813 Warren had reached a low point. He was obliged to write to Croker that 'Several large Clipper Schooners of from two to three hundred Tons, strongly manned and armed have run thro' the Blockade in the Chesapeak, in spite of every endeavour and the most vigilant attention of our Ships to prevent their getting out, nor can anything stop these Vessels escaping to Sea in dark Nights & Strong Winds.' He also referred to Capt. Barrie's enclosed report which described 'an instance of Several of these Schooners passing out in a Squadron, & outsailing every Ship in Chace'.[223]

In a less guarded letter to Melville he wrote, 'I am sorry to say … that the American Small Vessels, notwithstanding the Vigilance of the Blockading Squadron; from the severity of the weather and in the Dark Snowy nights Do get out, & it is almost impossible to prevent it'. Furthermore, 'The Assembly at Jamaica are caballing & demonstrating about Ships; I have sent all in my power.'[224] The incessant lobbying of the influential West Indies merchants had again touched a nerve. He added, 'I really am left so base to keep in check the Enemies Cruisers & new Ships which must be soon expected out, and that I am in no serviceable State but trust you will soon reinforce this Squadron with some of the new large Frigates: the *Endymion* is an Excellent ship & also the *Goliath* & *Majestic*.' Warren then wrote resignedly that earlier reinforcements had never been enough.[225] In fact, in December 1813, Warren appears to have had thirty-eight warships in Jamaica and the Leeward Islands, and in Halifax, Newfoundland and Bermuda combined 'a dozen ships of the line & 56 cruisers', apparently a total of 106 ships, although not including all the smaller vessels in his United Command.[226]

With this force, by the beginning of December 1813, the Royal Navy had blockaded, captured or caused to be destroyed a total of fifteen named American naval vessels, ten of which were major ships of more than 20 guns.[227] Warren's health had, however, suffered in ways unlikely to improve either his temper or his optimism. His letter to Melville of 30 December complained that 'Cruising on the Edge of Nantucket Shoal & off Rhode Island: the cold has occasioned a Rheumatic Illness from which I am but just recovering.'[228]

As long before as 26 February 1813, as Mahan notes, Warren had himself suggested to the Admiralty that his United Command should be redivided, and that the Jamaica and Leeward Island stations should be given local autonomy, keeping his right to direct all North American and Caribbean stations only as exceptional circumstances demanded. However, on 30 March 1813 the Admiralty had disagreed; the war required his unified command to remain unaltered.[229] Now, however, the West Indies station was to feature once more in correspondence with London, in a reversal of the Admiralty Board's decision.

Warren had almost certainly not yet received, while writing to Melville on 30 December, either an Admiralty letter of 4 November or one from Melville dated 24 November, notifying him of an essentially unjust Admiralty decision. The injustice lies not so much in the decision to reseparate the unified commands, but in the reasons given for it. Melville wrote 'You will receive by the present opportunity, the Official intimation of the measure we have been compelled to adopt of again placing the Leeward Island and Jamaica stations on their former footing of <u>chief</u> commands, the former under Rear Admiral Durham who succeeds Sir F[rancis] Laforey & the latter under Rear Admiral Brown.'[230] However, Melville's letter continues 'This arrangement became unavoidable (though much against my inclination) by the repeated and well founded complaints from Jamaica of the almost total want of protection on that station.'[231]

Only on 30 December had Warren once more attempted to draw the Admiralty's attention to this precise problem. He had again asked for a force more appropriate to the length of the American eastern seaboard, and for the three roles his force was expected to perform on it, as well as the British American coasts and the Caribbean. He had specifically requested Croker

> to acquaint my Lord Commissioners of the Admiralty that having
> sent the *Barrossa* to Jamaica to carry home specie, and every other
> Ship that could be spared without raising the Blockaded ports of
> America, I lament to find that both the Leeward Islands and
> Jamaica are very deficient of a Force adequate to their protection, or
> to perform the various extensive Convoy Service required to be
> done in those places.[232]

Warren was as aware as any naval officer of the Royal Navy's limited means in relation to its world-wide commitments; therefore, his being held responsible for these particular consequences of the shortage, and the Admiralty's apparent failure to comprehend his requirements in dismissing his closely reasoned and often repeated requests for reinforcements, seems harsh.

Melville, moreover, continued:

> This evil was also liable to be increased by the order which Admiral
> Brown had received from you to send away to join your flag any
> Vessel whose commanders might happen to die, in order that the
> vacancy might be filled up after such situation instead of an acting
> Captain being put in immediately. Under all those circumstances it
> became necessary to attach a certain number of Ships to each
> Admiral [and] to make him responsible for their being properly
> disposed of, according to the Wants of his station.[233]

Warren had presumably made these promotions from Bermuda in order to retain control, without preferment being decided by admirals subject to local lobbying. The 'wants' of the West Indies stations appear to have been given preference, without proper recognition of all of Warren's other responsibilities, which the Admiralty, if not the local administration and sugar plantation owners, should have been in a position to appreciate. However, although now less critically short of specie, the British government was still anxious to safeguard shipments of money from the Caribbean, and it was, therefore, expedient to attend to the views of its providers. Melville was careful to continue,

> As the sole reason for the appointment of an Officer senior to Vice
> Admirals Stirling & Sawyer was the Union of the three commands, I
> do not think it fair either to you or to the latter officers to expect or
> direct that with your work in the Service you could continue merely
> as the successor of Admiral Sawyer on the Halifax Station. No
> person has yet been selected for that command, which if the latter
> had remained there would actually have reverted to him: but it will
> probably be either Sir Alexr. Cochrane or Sir Richard Keats.[234]

Being too senior to command any one part of a redivided command, Warren would have to be recalled, probably to be replaced by the newly promoted Vice-Admiral Sir Alexander Cochrane, with whom he had had his differences some years before. In his reply, dated 3 February 1814, Warren professed himself 'extremely surprised in being recalled at this moment' having 'zealously and faithfully served my Sovereign and Country, under so many Disadvantages'.[235] He was also surprised at the decision 'having undertaken the Command in the Situation in which I was placed at the Time', an apparent reference to his additional diplomatic responsibilities at the outset. Disappointingly, however, Warren resolves to 'forbear saying any further upon the Subject untill my arrival in Great Britain'.[236]

Warren had also received on 28 January Croker's letter of 4 November 1813, officially notifying him of his replacement on the reseparation of the North American and West Indies stations, and the necessary reallocation of vessels. Warren should 'return in *San Domingo* or other convenient vessel needing urgent return, leaving at Halifax 10 line of Battle Ships or razees, 20 frigates, 25 twenty-gun ships or Sloops, and all smaller vessels on station'.[237]

Moreover, while the Admiralty's letter to Warren was being delivered, his naval critics currently in Britain were quick to capitalise. Captain David Milne of HMS *Bulwark*, then in Portsmouth, gossiped on 2 January 1814 that 'Sir John Warren is coming home. I believe he has not at all given satisfaction; but the Prince is his friend'.[238] Warren had, however, done little to help his current reputation. During Cockburn's attack on Havre de Grace, Maryland, in early May 1813, John Rodgers' home there had been partly burned in his absence, and valuable possessions looted. Part of a British effort to bring the war home to the Americans, not themselves blameless in Canada, it nevertheless gave detractors like Milne the opportunity to add 'Commodore Rodgers' house has been plundered; his pianoforte is in Sir John's house at Bermuda, and he was riding in his, the Commodore's, carriage in Halifax. What do you think of a British Admiral and Commander in Chief? This is not the way to conquer America.' In addition to the old accusations of indecisiveness, Warren had renewed his reputation for acquisitiveness, perhaps even adding one for impropriety.[239]

Vice-Admiral Cochrane's orders to succeed Warren were dated 25 January 1814, and he arrived at Bermuda in HMS *Tonnant* on 6 March. Warren delayed the actual handover of command until 1 April, and finally sailed for England on 8 April, never afterwards to hold an active naval command, or to receive much public recognition.

By November 1813 the whole American coast except New England had been, as far as his resources permitted, under both commercial and naval blockade. The British government had not apparently ordered Warren to abandon the exemption of largely Federalist New England in the hope of separating it from the more strongly Republican remainder of the United States. Until Warren's recall, the ports of New England had continued to supply British needs in Canada and the West Indies as the government had intended.

In the twenty months since Warren's appointment, up to 1 April, both American international and internal trade had been significantly reduced. According to Warren's own pencilled calculations, his squadrons had accounted for 971 prizes, 300 of which had been 'burnt or sunk'. He records 210 'prizes sent into Halifax', 263 into Bermuda, 138 to the Leeward Islands and 60 to Jamaica, and to them added 'Burnt or Sunk in the Chesapeake, Long Island Sound, Delaware, Boston Bay – Large Vessels & Small Craft – 300 Sail', making his total of 971.[240]

He seems, however, to have gained little contemporary credit, either for his diplomatic efforts with the Americans on the British government's behalf or for his naval and commercial blockades. Warren's obituary in the *Annual Register* for 1822 makes no reference to his services between 1812 and 1814.[241] The entry for Cochrane in a series of naval biographies, published almost immediately after Warren's death, gives Cochrane sole credit for having 'not only put a stop to the trade of that country but kept the whole line of sea coast in a continual state of alarm', with no mention of Warren's initial contribution to either.[242] A more objective evaluation of Warren's efforts is probably best attempted after a review of Cochrane's time in command.

CHAPTER 5

BLOCKADES AND BLUNDERS: VICE-ADMIRAL COCHRANE'S COMMAND, APRIL 1814– FEBRUARY 1815

Admiral Warren also told Levitt Harris ... that he was sorry to say
that the instructions given to his successor on the American station
were very different from those under which he had acted and that
he apprehended that a very serious injury would be afflicted on
America (Gallatin to Monroe, 13 June 1814)[1]

VICE-ADMIRAL SIR ALEXANDER COCHRANE wrote a formal acceptance
of command from the *Asia* at Bermuda on 1 April 1814.[2] Much was expected of
Warren's successor, although some of his earlier senior officers had found him
difficult. Ten years earlier Lord Keith had called him 'a crackheaded, unsafe man
... one with others who endeavoured to stir up dissensions in the fleet'.[3]
Conversely, Robert Dundas, Lord Melville, First Lord of the Admiralty, was a
fellow Scot, and since their two families had been friends for generations
Cochrane was not without 'interest'.[4]

His record was nevertheless impressive. He had commanded successfully the
now reseparated Leeward Island station in 1805, and had fought well under
Duckworth at the Battle of San Domingo in February 1806. He had led the capture
of the French island of Martinique in 1809, and of Guadaloupe in 1810, of which
he had since been Governor.[5] His promotion to Vice-Admiral of the Red had
come on 4 November 1813, the very day on which Croker had written to Warren
to notify him of his recall. Not yet 56 years old, Cochrane was expected to remain
energetic. He was also reputed to feel a more than professional antagonism
towards Americans. His elder brother had been killed by the rebellious Colonists
more than thirty years before, and this probably coloured his views.[6]

As his newly printed letter-heads showed, his responsibilities covered a vast
geographical area. He commanded 'Ships and Vessels employed & to be
employed in the River St Lawrence, and along the Coast of Nova Scotia, the
Islands of Anticosti, Madelaine, St John & Cape Breton, the Bay of Fundy', and
the entire North American eastern seaboard, as far as 'at and about Bermuda or

Somer's Island, the Bahama Islands, & the Gulph of Mexico to the Tropic of Cancer &c, &c'.[7] Containing an energetic enemy over such a wide variety of theatres, with limited resources, was part of a great range of responsibilities.

Throughout April Cochrane was much concerned with victualling since 'the Crews of His Majesty's Ships in this Port have not had a Day's fresh Provisions since my arrival here'.[8] Beyond this implied criticism of his predecessor's arrangements, however, Cochrane was turning his mind to more important matters. As yet unknown to him, Napoleon's abdication on 11 April 1814 had reduced the need for a British blockade of France. This, however, was not to mean an immediate increase in either ships or manpower at his disposal. Although the *Tonnant*, intended as Cochrane's flagship, was delayed, the *Superb*, *Bulwark* and *Saturn* had left Portsmouth for Bermuda with a small convoy in January 1814. The *Saturn* was 'a cut-down 74, of course a match for any American frigate'.[9]

Morale on the North America station seems to have been varied. Captain Milne of *Bulwark* was depressed by reports of the imminent launch of heavily armed American warships, including a 74, and felt it 'a disgrace to the British nation to have such ships as we have. There is none of our new two-decked ships that can carry her lower deck guns out if there is the least wind, and hardly one of them that does not need a thorough repair in less than two years after she is launched.' American ships, he felt, were better built than either British or French, and would 'give both nations a lesson'.[10] Milne also saw manning as a problem: 'we are not near as we ought to be either in number or quality of the men; and as for the marines they hardly deserve the name of men'. With other priorities met, those marines allocated to ships were 'bad enough ... this ship is really not manned as she ought to be; yet there are few in the service better'. Such pessimism was either not universal, or remained unexpressed. Milne was 'ordered to sail in a few days to cruize in Boston Bay'.[11]

Rear-Admiral Cockburn had been retained as second-in-command on the North America station and the Admiralty left him conducting operations in Chesapeake Bay, where the blockades had continued uninterrupted even throughout the winter months. Captain Robert Barrie's letters home from the *Dragon* in Chesapeake Bay testify to the Royal Navy's endurance in adverse weather, its unrelenting persistence with the blockades and the professional aggression of its onshore raids. Barrie had written in February 1814 that, despite being 'so severely cold', his crews had 'destroyed and taken upwards of eighty-nine of the Enemies Vessels, besides frequently annoying them on shore'.[12] In March he wrote 'we have a squadron of Frigates & there is another squadron cruising within the Capes so that the Chesapeak is completely blockaded ... we have turned back at least fifty vessels so the trade within the Chessapeak is done up while we remain here'.[13] The British naval blockade of the Chesapeake was so remorseless during March that its efficiency had been admitted by the American Commodore Barry to Secretary of the Navy Jones. '[A]ny attempt' by the American ship sloop *Erie* trapped at Annopolis 'to get out would be imprudent, the season is past and the enemy concentrated near the entrance of the Bay in such a manner as to defeat all prospects of escaping'.[14]

Routine for the blockading squadrons continued. Returns began to be made at Bermuda of blockading progress made under Cochrane's command. One return detailed twenty-five vessels totalling no less than 1,778 tons 'captured, recaptured, detained or destroyed' in a nine-week period between 1 April and 22 May 1814.[15] Less routine for a force of 136 seamen and marines from the squadron blockading New London was a raid up the Connecticut River on Pautopang Point on the night of 7/8 April. They 'destroyed all the vessels afloat or on the stocks', including three large privateers and twenty-four other vessels totalling over 5,000 tons and worth $140,000.[16] That clandestine American support for the blockading squadrons continued, despite this sort of exercise of British sea power, is shown by Cochrane's reports to Croker of his having authorised British vessels to obtain cattle and vegetables for cash more successfully than as originally suggested, by offering Americans British bills.[17]

Warren had earlier decided to facilitate British blockading and raiding operations in Chesapeake Bay by the occupation of Tangier Island. As shown on Map 2, it was almost centrally placed, and was only intermittently inhabited. Warren had been recalled before putting the plan into practice, but in early April 1814 it was implemented by Cockburn. The island would serve as a collecting point for British prizes and captured goods and, although relatively infertile, 'Excellent water' was 'to be obtained in any quantity'. Moreover, boats could 'Land with perfect facility at all Times and in all Weather', while Tangier Bay offered a convenient and safe anchorage for larger ships. A redoubt and guard-houses were built with timber and roof shingles from a captured American schooner.[18] On 2 April 1814 Cochrane had issued a proclamation encouraging those wishing to 'withdraw from the United States', specifically runaway slaves, to become 'Free Settlers in British Colonies', or to join the British forces. Many joined the black Colonial Marines, later to use Tangier Island as their training base.[19]

It was from Tangier Bay that Cockburn assured Cochrane that he would 'carry on the requisite offensive attacks at different and distant places across the Bay, by which in spite of every Effort of the Enemy, who cannot possibly guard every point, we manage at times to surprize his Vessels where he deems them to be most secure'. He strove to 'Keep him continually on the Fret, much harass his Militia and Oblige them to always under Alarms' and aimed to be 'a most serious Inconvenience and Annoyance to the Country in general'. He also informed Cochrane of intelligence that 'the *United States*, *Macedonian* and *Hornet* are secured as high as possible above New London and <u>dismantled</u>', with their crews redistributed. He would convoy recent prizes to Bermuda, while continuing to 'Service the Chesapeake Blockade' with 'Two Frigates – a Line of Battle ship &c', all to be used 'stretching across in a Line' in Lynnhaven Bay, although he could 'offer full and useful service to twice the number'.[20]

Meanwhile, in Washington on 30 March the United States government had abandoned its final attempt to coerce Britain by the use of economic sanctions as

Madison recognised the failure of the widely evaded American export embargo. Lacking the Senate's support for the idea, Madison had imposed his embargo by executive decree on 29 July 1813.[21] Reluctantly ratified by Congress only on 17 December 1813, it was suspended on 31 March and finally repealed on 14 April 1814.[22] In recommending this course of action President Madison had called on the House Foreign Relations Committee to forecast such a repeal's financial consequences, and a copy of their report, dated 4 April 1814, was soon in Cochrane's hands. Cochrane claimed to be 'in possession of <u>private</u> information' of the embargo's repeal, and 'from the same Channel received a Copy of the report of the Secret Committee'.[23] The most far-reaching decisions implementing the British commercial blockade of the United States continued to be intelligence-led.

Cochrane was concerned by the report's predictions of increased neutral imports into the ports of New England, with the resultant augmented customs revenue financing new American warship building, and was disturbed at 'obtaining a knowledge of the Enemy having received his Supplies for the equipment of his Navy ... by Neutral Trade carried on with the Northern States'.[24] He was similarly concerned that 'the executive Government having in great measure failed in obtaining supplies for carrying on the War' was now 'principally depending on Revenues collected on Cargoes of Neutrals trading with the Eastern Ports'.[25] Cochrane therefore informed Croker that he 'judged it of national importance to extend the Blockade to all the other Ports to the Eastward of Long Island not hitherto under blockade, which I shall take care to enforce de facto by placing a sufficient number of Ships before these Ports'.[26] In anticipation of Cochrane's arrival, Warren had prepared in March a 'Schedule of Orders in Council, Circular Orders, Letters etc' to inform him of the complex situation existing as command was transferred on 1 April.[27] Among these documents, Cochrane had almost undoubtedly seen Croker's 'Secret' letter to Warren of 28 April 1813, giving him Admiralty authority for 'de facto' blockades, those not specifically announced in the London Gazette or by local British proclamations, and was presumably confident of Admiralty approval for blockade without the legal niceties.[28]

Nevertheless, despite the Admiralty's willingness to condone undeclared blockades, as soon as 25 April 1814 Cochrane issued a local proclamation which further extended the British naval and commercial blockades to the whole American coast 'from Black Point', eight miles west of New London, 'to the Northern and Eastern boundaries of the United States' with British New Brunswick.[29] The British blockades now included neutral trade into New England.

Also, on this occasion, Earl Bathurst's notification to the 'ministers of friendly powers' of the proclamation of 25 April by 'the commander in chief of His Majesty's naval forces off the coasts of the United States of North America' appeared in the London Gazette of Tuesday 31 May. It followed the usual formula of 'declaring all the ports, harbours, bays, creeks, rivers, inlets, outlets, islands, and sea-coasts of the said United States ... to be in a state of strict and rigorous blockade'. European neutrals should be aware that 'All the measures authorised by the Law of Nations will be adopted and executed with respect to all vessels attempting to violate the said blockade.'[30] This time it was more likely to be true since, as the *Naval Chronicle* noted, 'A late *Gazette* contained an Order in Council releasing from the restrictions of blockade, all such ports and places in France as now are, or may be, placed in the military occupation or under the protection of His Majesty.'[31]

In Europe, Paris had fallen to the Allies on 30 March and Napoleon's war had also, for the time being, come to an end with his first abdication on 11 April. With this welcome interruption to war in Europe Britain could divert ships and men to the American war. On 30 April the Admiralty recorded its intention of withdrawing ships from Europe, although the 'unjust and unprovoked aggression of the American Government' did not 'permit them to reduce the Fleet at once to a Peace establishment'. For the Board, the vital question remained the 'Maintenance of Maritime Rights'.[32] For Madison, any remaining hope of French diplomatic or financial help was now gone.

Publicity for the extended blockade was also widespread in Britain, and the *Naval Chronicle*'s reprinting of the Foreign Office's announcement, under 'State Papers', included the confident assertion that 'All the measures authorised by the Law of Nations will be adopted & executed.'[33] To comply with what the British government maintained were the requirements of international law, the force deployed for such a blockade was carefully described as 'adequate'.[34] While seeking to end American trade with neutrals, as well as both their coastal and ocean-going trade, this force should also prevent American warships from getting to sea or making any attempt to lift the commercial blockade.

'ALL AMERICA BLOCKADED': LT. NAPIER IN HMS *NYMPHE*, 22 MAY 1814[35]

The British government's notification of the extension to neutrals completed the British naval and commercial blockades of the entire Atlantic coast of the United States, from Maine's border with the British province of New Brunswick to Georgia's frontier with Spain's East Florida at the St Mary's River, and to West Florida and the Mississippi estuaries. This now included Newport, Boston 'and the Eastern Ports', and so finally interdicted all American seaborne trade, including that with neutrals. New England had prospered from neutral trade during its exemption from British commercial blockade, but no longer. This would at last effect American economic isolation, with profound fiscal, financial and political consequences. For the American war effort, this was the beginning of the end.

Cochrane promptly ensured that the extended blockade was to be strictly enforced. On 26 May he gave an unambiguous answer to a query from Cockburn: 'With respect to the Ship *Emilie* – as the whole of the Ports of the United States are now declared in a state of blockade you will be pleased to withdraw the permission you have given for her proceeding from Newport with a Cargo: she can only be allowed to sail in Ballast.'[36]

The number and the quality of vessels eventually available to perform the naval and commercial blockades of the North American eastern seaboard and the Gulf of Mexico are revealed in a table enclosed in the same letter to Cockburn. Two 'Line of Battle Ships', *Bulwark* and *Ramillies*, with four frigates, eleven sloops and a schooner, were to blockade out of Halifax, to include Boston Bay. Two frigates patrolled Nantucket Shoals from the south-east. Two 74s were stationed off New London and Rhode Island, together with one frigate and two sloops. Two frigates, the *Nieman* and *Narcissus*, were responsible for the Delaware. The Chesapeake, under Cockburn, was allocated two 74s, two frigates, a sloop and a schooner. The razee *Majestic* and three sloops patrolled between Cape Hatteras and St Mary's River, while just one frigate, two sloops and two schooners covered the Gulf of Mexico to the Tropic of Cancer. Altogether, the list includes six Line of Battle Ships, two razees, thirteen frigates, nineteen sloops, four schooners and a gun-brig. Forty-five vessels were named, far fewer than the number of familiar names appearing on blockade service would seem to suggest; this was clearly explained by the postscript: 'The same force or as near as possible will be kept on those Stations altho' the Ships will be occasionally changed', by both wear and tear and convoy duty.[37]

On 31 May the Board of Admiralty drew conclusions on the feasibility of maintaining a year-round blockade of the whole American eastern seaboard. It had consulted Warren, just returned to Britain, Rear Admiral Sir John Beresford and Captain Philip Broke 'late of the *Shannon*'. They advised that it was not possible to maintain 'a strict blockade north of Cape Cod'; while, for eight months of the year, blockade was 'possible to the extent as to render all vessels attempting to sail out as in extreme risk of capture', during the winter months only between a third and a half of such ships would be taken.[38] On 5 July Cochrane ordered Captain William Percy of the *Hermes* to take command of the small British squadron in the Gulf of Mexico and maintain a blockade of the Mississippi estuaries; therefore, for the whole American coast, from Maine to Louisiana, a long summer and autumn of both commercial and naval blockade was considered practicable by those who had first-hand experience.[39]

Cochrane's proclamation meant that the New England coast, so far almost untouched, began to experience both blockade and raids. By July, Niles' *Weekly Register* reported that now 'The eastern coast of the United States is much vexed by the enemy' who 'seem determined to enter the little outports and villages, and burn everything that floats'.[40]

Madison's last embargo had included a ban on American coastal traffic, and its eventual repeal on 14 April might have led to a revival of such trade by small vessels but for the almost relentless application of the British commercial blockade after 25 April, except where conducted to mutual advantage. Some trade continued between Americans seeking outlets for food and information and British offshore squadrons and British forces in Canada, but generally, at sea, the strangulation of the American economy and tax base continued. Usually untroubled by the prospect of American naval intervention, the British blockading squadrons took what appeared to be available. For the Americans, escape from harbour and evasion of British blockade was proving easier in smaller vessels. As the larger ships and brigs became scarcer, the faster and handier schooners and sloops began to replace them as prizes.[41]

Such smaller prizes feature in the journal of Lieutenant Henry Napier, who arrived in the frigate *Nymphe*, in company with the *Ramillies*, off Boston Bay on 6 May 1814, for three months of blockade duty. Their blockade was to be hampered even in May by 'heavy rain and fogs, thunder and lightning', in July by a dangerous three-day gale, and in August by the start of the hurricane season.[42] This blockade was usually conducted with propriety, sometimes even generosity, although occasionally with impropriety and harshness. On 25 May *Nymphe* captured 'four sloops and a schooner' but 'took cargoes out and restored the vessels'.[43] While loss of the cargoes, often by now uneconomic to insure, would have damaged incomes and the local, and cumulatively national, economies, restoration of the vessels might have retained some goodwill among Americans.

This might have been seen as necessary since *Nymphe* intended to 'oblige the Yankees to supply us with stock and vegetables at the market price. This is very reasonable; we leave all fishermen unmolested.'[44] Although this last assertion proved unfounded, *Nymphe* was brought 'green peas and fruit, with stock of all kinds, books and newspapers wet from the press, by our friends here'.[45] Despite helping to prevent the scurvy suffered by both British and American seamen, this trade prompted Napier to make accusations of American 'venality'.[46]

On 5 June *Nymphe* was 'laying in wait for coasters' off Halibut Point in Ipswich Bay, and 'took an empty sloop of 100 tons', which was released, and the schooner *Maria*, laden with potatoes, later 'distributed between the two ship's companies'. More importantly, they took the American schooner *Welcome Return*, 'a good prize worth $4,000', prosaically 'loaded with notions' – vegetables.[47] High values of this sort led to the unofficial transactions practised by both sides which discredited the operation of maritime commercial blockade. Captured merchant vessels were occasionally ransomed to evade the often-lengthy process of condemning prizes, and the legal fees involved. Following cash payments to captors, journeys were resumed, cargoes delivered, and the vessels themselves remained available for continued use. The real possibility of merchants and shippers having to add ransom payments to the costs of a voyage might discourage some American maritime trade, usefully reducing tax revenues and shipper's preparedness to lend to the government and thus increasing British pressure on the American economy, but the ransoming of prizes was illegal, the practice having become sufficiently widespread for both British and American governments to forbid it. Nonetheless, between May and July 1814 Lieutenant Napier recorded the ransoming of at least ten American vessels, presumably unreported.[48] His conscience was occasionally troubled. *Nymphe's* taking $200 from a Cape Cod fisherman demonstrably unable to afford it prompted Napier to write 'This is an ungenerous war against the poor, & unworthy of Englishmen. I am ashamed of Captain Epworth's conduct.'[49]

Nevertheless, on 6 June, the *Maria*, now apparently *Nymphe's* tender, and the ships' boats took two sloops laden with timber, which, 'having supplied the ships', were burned. They also 'set fire to a schooner of 100 tons with wood, sails anchors &c'. The next day they 'burned two fine sloops with wood', to which a now unrepentant Napier added 'much better to have ransomed them'. On 9 June a 'flag of truce came out' to negotiate for the *Welcome Return*, later ransomed for $3,500, a sum shared with *Junon*.[50]

The alternative threat of destruction was very real. On 11 June Napier wrote 'the boats returned after having been amazingly successful in capturing and destroying about 800 tons of shipping ... Destroyed all the vessels in Scituate Harbour but one'.[51] Men as well as vessels were ransomed by the blockading squadrons. That same day, the *Nymphe* ran 'the *Concord* loaded with iron, on shore and detained the skipper as a hostage for the ransom of $1000'.[52] The virtual British exclusion of neutral shipping from the harbours of New England continued. On 12 June Napier recorded that *Nymphe* 'Weighed and chased a Swede, whom we warned off the coast'.[53]

By late July 1814, as shown in Appendix A Table 4, Cochrane had a total of eighty vessels on his North American Station, comprised of nine 74s, four razees and twenty-four frigates of either 40, 38 or 36 guns. Particularly useful for reaching into estuaries and harbours were thirty-seven smaller craft including two fast schooners, three bomb-vessels and a rocket vessel. While four 74s, three 38-gun frigates and seven smaller vessels remained 'with the flag', two 74s, two frigates and five smaller craft were allocated to Chesapeake Bay. Rear-Admiral Griffith's northern division of *Bulwark* and *Spencer*, both 74s, two razees, five frigates and sixteen vessels of fewer than 20 guns blockaded the area from Halifax to Nantucket. Meanwhile, the *Superb*, 74, a 50-gun razee, six frigates and four smaller vessels closed the sealanes between Nantucket and the Delaware.[54]

The British offshore patrols imposing the naval and commercial blockades had long isolated islands such as Nantucket, thirty-five miles from the Massachusetts mainland. Nantucket was particularly unfortunate since it was passed by both Griffith and Captain Sir Edward Troubridge, specifically ordered to patrol south of the island.[55] Few American vessels around Nantucket escaped the Royal Navy's attentions. Its deep-sea whaling fleet, consisting of forty-six vessels in 1812, had been halved by 1814. Those inhabitants not engaged in distant whaling had long been dependent on local offshore fishing and imported food and fuel from the mainland. Despite having survived one wartime winter, by 21 July 1814 the largely Republican citizens were ready to approach Cochrane.[56]

On 28 July 1814 Cochrane wrote to Commodore Henry Hotham: 'I send you herewith Copies of Petitions received by Capt Barrie of His Majesty's Ship the *Dragon* from Selectmen of the Island Nantucket representing the Inhabitants of that Island to be in a state of Starvation.'[57] Cochrane sought to drive a hard bargain, writing:

> The request they make to be permitted to carry on their Fishery
> cannot be complied with, but if they actually are in the distressed

114

state they represent, permission may be granted them to import from the Continent supplies of Food provided they will declare themselves Neutral and deliver up all such Artillery, Guns & Ammunition as may be on the Island and submit to His Majesty's Ships getting from them whatever refreshments the Islands will afford ... Cause inquiry to be made into the truth of the enclosed statements and act as you deem circumstances to require.[58]

An enclosed petition described Nantucket as 'in a distress[ed] situation for Provisions and Fuel', asking that the 'sloop Earl Jacob Barney' be allowed 'to pass ... to bring Corn and Bread stuff for the relief of this Island ... as there is from six to seven thousand Inhabitants which have got the most of their subsistence out of the Seas, by the Whale fisherys (sic) which', they argued 'precludes us from any concerns of War'.[59] On the islanders' agreement both to stop paying Federal taxes and to water passing British warships Cochrane would agree to their resumption of fishing and trading for food and fuel with the mainland.[60] Accordingly, on 28 August, Hotham, off Gardener's Island in *Superb*, had ordered that an unarmed Nantucket sloop be allowed to cross Buzzard's Bay, between the Massachusetts mainland and the island, with fuel and without interference.[61] The *Surprise* was to allow Nantucket vessels to pass for as long as no evidence was found of any tax being paid; if it was, permission was to be revoked.[62] Nantucket vessels, trapped by the British blockade of coastal traffic, were to be allowed as neutrals to regain their homeport. Cochrane also undertook to facilitate the release of Nantucket's prisoners of war, but this arrangement was to be overtaken by eventual peace.[63] Nantucket was not alone in its predicament; other American communities, such as that on Block Island, agreed to supply British blockading vessels in return for exemption from raids or naval bombardment.

Cochrane's application of British commercial blockade seems, as Warren's had been, more than a merely mechanistic execution of a precisely pre-defined duty, but the thoughtful implementation of an essential part of a thoroughly understood strategy of economic warfare. Therefore, when Sir John Sherbroke, Governor of Nova Scotia, passed on to Cochrane the requests of the Halifax merchants to be allowed to conduct a licensed trade with blockaded American ports, he denied them. Cochrane's reply to Sherbroke emphasised that the American government had not long repealed its latest embargo on 'trade with the enemy' precisely because of its increasing difficulties with tax revenues and loans, and that any trade with American ports would help the American administration rather than the long-term interests of the Halifax merchants.[64]

Throughout the remainder of 1814 the British exerted further pressure on the American economy and administration in a way more likely to produce political stability and long-term wealth for Nova Scotian merchants than rejected requests for licences to trade with American ports. This began with the British government's order to Sherbroke in June 1814 to occupy the eastern parts of the American border province of Maine, which stood between Nova Scotia and Lower Canada and seemed a potential threat to both. Sherbroke was to occupy 'that part of the District of Maine which at present intercepts the communication between Halifax and Quebec'.[65] On 11 July Rear-Admiral Griffith's command of the northern American coastline, including Penobscot Bay, made possible the occupation of Eastport on Moose Island and, by 2 September, the seizure of the port of Castine. On 3 September an almost unopposed British advance up the Penobscot River resulted in the Americans burning their 26-gun corvette *Adams*, blockaded at Hampden, and the capture or destruction of American merchant-ships at Bangor. The later occupation, until the war's end, of the coastal town of Machias, almost ninety miles north-west of Castine, strengthened the Royal Navy's control of the Bay of Fundy between Nova Scotia and Maine. By 27 September Griffith was able to report to the Admiralty that all of Maine between Passamaquoddy Bay and the Penobscot River was under British control.[66] It was to remain so for the rest of the war.

Castine was well placed to trade with both the British provinces of New Brunswick and Nova Scotia. This offered those of the population who accepted occupation a chance to prosper when Griffiths, and Sir George Prevost, Governor-General of British North America and Governor of Lower Canada, jointly issued a proclamation giving local inhabitants the option of pledging allegiance to the British Crown or leaving the area.[67] Those taking the oath gained protection and the right to trade with neighbouring British provinces. British manufactured goods and re-exports were imported into Castine and then smuggled into the United States through, among other places, Hampden. The lost tax revenue from unpaid customs duties contributed to a major problem for the American administration, which both ambiguous legislation and half-hearted enforcement failed to alleviate significantly.[68] Many in Castine therefore embraced a situation, which, in any case, the United States administration lacked the funds, or sufficient unblockaded warships, to alter.

Similarly, Cockburn's increasingly complete command of the Chesapeake was allowing him to make often ineffectually opposed attacks on military and economic targets in the Bay. Cochrane told Bathurst on 14 July that he had 'sent about Nine Hundred Marines to the Chesapeake to act under Admiral Cockburn – who has been Annoying the Americans a good deal of late – with this force making partial Attacks and Shifting from place to place I trust to be Able to find the enemy full employment for all his troops in Virginia, Maryland and Pensylvania – without detaching to the Canada Frontier'.[69]

Three days later, in a letter to Melville, Cochrane had gone into detail. He pointed out that 'Philadelphia can be Approached within fifteen miles by a Ship of 64 Guns – to attack it part of the Army may be Landed at N[ew]castle upon the Delaware – Six miles from which thier (sic) Principal <u>Powder</u> and <u>Corn</u> <u>Mills</u> are situated … those of course will be destroyd.'[70] Beyond the immediate tactical advantage of limiting the number of American troops sent north, the repair or replacement of mills, foundries, factories, stores and warehouses destroyed by Cockburn's landing parties would be a further drain on the American administration's increasingly strained financial arrangements.

Like Cochrane, Cockburn seems to have sought tacit agreements with local inhabitants that, if not attacked, his forces on land would respect their lives and private property, and that goods supplied to them would be paid for in specie 'at the time, to the uttermost farthing', in preference to paper assets difficult for Americans to dispose of without their neighbour's opprobrium or heavy discounts.[71] Despite some serious lapses, often duly punished, this policy was followed such that the Captain of the Fleet responsible for provisioning established a table of prices to be paid to American civilians 'with a view to prevent imposition'.[72]

Cochrane's letter to Bathurst of 14 July revealed more of his views on Americans, and future British conduct of the war. 'I have it much at heart to give them a complete drubbing before Peace is made – when I trust their Northern limits will be circumscribed and the Command of the Mississippi wrested from them'.[73] His thoughts were to turn again later to New Orleans and the Mississippi, but, for the present, taking Washington seemed attractive. 'If Troops Arrive soon and the point of Attack is directed towards Baltimore I have every prospect of Success and Washington Will be equally Accessible. They may be either destroyed or laid under Contribution, as the Occasion may require … '.[74]

Three days later Cochrane reminded Melville that all 'the principal Towns in America' were 'Situated upon navigable Rivers – but none of Them Accessible to a direct attack from Shipping only, although open to a combined one with a land Force'.[75] The successful delivery of sufficient British troops to either Baltimore or the American capital clearly required Royal Naval command of Chesapeake Bay and its rivers, including the Patuxent River on its eastern side, to avoid any interference with British troop carriers in confined waters, but by July 1814 at least eighteen named warships of the United States Navy (listed in Appendix A, Table 2) had been either blockaded, taken or destroyed, and were in no position to intervene.[76] Secretary of the Navy Jones' report to Madison on American naval forces in the Chesapeake in June 1814 had listed two gunboats, thirteen barges, a 5-gun cutter, a schooner and a pilot boat, clearly a limited but potential threat. This situation was to change.[77]

THE BRITISH IN WASHINGTON

The extent of British command in North American waters paid remarkable dividends in August 1814. The containment or elimination of American fighting vessels in Chesapeake Bay, especially after the self-destruction at Pig Point of Commodore Barney's flotilla of a large sloop and gunboats, gave British land forces unhindered access to the Patuxent River, as shown on Map 2.[78] After a short running battle at Bladensburg, this allowed a successful British attack on Washington on 24 and 25 August. During a deliberately brief military occupation, until 26 August, much of Washington was burnt, the proximity of British forces leading the Americans to burn Washington Navy Yard with its valuable timber stores and ropewalks.[79] American losses also included two almost completed warships, the heavy frigate *Columbia* and the sloop *Argus*.[80] In Madison's absence the British Army briefly occupied and burned the White

House and other large government buildings, causing the 13th Congress to meet in Washington's Post and Patent Office, the only adequate venue remaining. Important financial results followed; the British action caused a major run on Washington, Baltimore and Philadelphia banks, where many deposits were withdrawn, mostly as specie. Especially following the earlier export of $3.8m of specie to Canada, largely used to buy British Government securities, this contributed to the American administration's critical shortage of coin, soon to have far-reaching fiscal, financial and political consequences.[81]

The degree of British control in Chesapeake Bay also gave access to the Potomac River, allowing the port of Alexandria to be attacked on 28 August and occupied until 2 September. Twenty-one American merchant-ships with cargoes of tobacco, sugar and wine were either captured or destroyed, as were weapons and 'public stores'. The British force made an opposed but successful withdrawal down the Potomac River.[82]

THE BRITISH 'ESSAY ON BALTIMORE'[83]

After success at Washington and Alexandria the next logical step was the proposed British attack on Baltimore, the largest port at the head of Chesapeake Bay, which Cochrane believed was 'the richest in the Country'.[84] Before the British commercial blockade of the Chesapeake, Baltimore's exports of grain and flour and its imported luxuries had made a significant contribution to American overseas and internal trade. These were now heavily curtailed, but the port remained populous, important and accessible. Furthermore, despite the British naval blockade, it still remained a base for persistent American privateers. There had been anti-Federalist riots when news of Madison's declaration of war first reached Baltimore, and even after damage to livelihoods by blockades its largely Republican population remained fiercely anti-British. '[T]his Town' Cochrane was convinced 'ought to be laid in Ashes'.[85]

However, precautions against a British attack had begun early in 1813, when Samuel Smith, a Senator and militia major-general, had begun earthworks and the recruitment of volunteers. Around 4,500 British troops landing under Major-General Ross on 12 September were heavily outnumbered by regular American troops and militia, and Ross was killed by an American sniper during a pyrrhic British victory at North Point. The absence of close naval support contributed to a decision to abandon further frontal attack on 13 September. Cochrane's failure to capture Fort McHenry overnight on 13–14 September, and a barrier of scuttled American ships, meant that even the lightest British warships could not reach Baltimore harbour to fire on the American lines. Since Cochrane also failed to silence the American guns on Lazaretto Point, and an attempt to attack Baltimore with 1,500 men in barges from the Patapsco River was defeated by fire from the shore, the whole raid was abandoned.

While off Baltimore, Cochrane had written to Cockburn ashore: 'It is impossible for the Ships to render you any assistance – the Town is so far retired within the Forts. It is for Colonel Brook to consider under such circumstances whether he has Force sufficient to defeat so large a number as it [is] said the Enemy has collected.'[86] As a result, Brook called a Council of War which concluded that 'from the situation I was placd in they advised I should Retire'.[87] Extraordinarily, in view of his earlier enthusiasm for an attack on Baltimore, on 17 September Cochrane wrote to Croker that high tides produced in Chesapeake Bay by a concurrence of a new moon with the equinox had made leaving the Bay 'unsafe', and had led him to decide on a mere 'demonstration upon' Baltimore. Cochrane then asserted that since 'the primary object' – the relief of pressure on the British Army in Canada – had 'been already fully accomplished … it was mutually agreed we Should withdraw'.[88]

The same day, in a private letter to Melville, Cochrane wrote,

> Your Lordship will see by my Public letter that we have made an
> Essay on Baltimore, an attempt Contrary to my Opinion, but
> extremely urged by the General, to which I reluctantly consented,
> but to preserve Unanimity between the two services; I have not
> stated my Objections to the measure in My letter to the Admiralty –
> I now exceedingly regret My deviation from my Original plan.[89]

As late as 3 September Cochrane had expressed a preference for leaving Chesapeake Bay and sailing northward to refresh troops and ships at Rhode Island, and had told Melville that 'About the close of October we will move to the Southward', and 'if the reinforcements arrive I propose an attack upon Baltimore'.[90]

Although New York had always conducted more trade, in failing to occupy or destroy Baltimore, Cochrane had missed a significant opportunity in economic warfare. Tight commercial and naval blockades, preventing movement in or out of Baltimore without British agreement, would have been effective without giving the Americans the propaganda value of a repulsed attack. However, War Office instructions clearly gave Cochrane the right to select objectives, and his name remains associated with failure at Baltimore.[91] By October, news of British failure at Baltimore had reached both the British negotiators and the American Peace Commissioners at Ghent. Even then, there was still time to give further thought to the British decision to attack New Orleans.

Long before the British attack on Baltimore Cochrane had written in June to Croker that 3,000 regular troops, the Creek Indians and the local French and Spanish populations 'would drive the Americans entirely out of Louisiana and the Floridas'.[92] In July he wrote to Bathurst that 'Two Thousand Men would give to Gt.Britain the Command of That Country and New Orleans'.[93] In early September Cochrane still felt able to write 'hitherto what I promised has been effected & if Peace makers will only stay their procedings until Jonathan is brought to the feet of Gt. Britain, future Wars will be prevented'. To that end, and to avenge what Prevost had reported as American barbarities in Canada, Cochrane suggested that 'As the Season advances I propose going to the Carolinas Georgia &ca. and ending at N Orleans which I have not a doubt of being able to Subdue & thereby hold the Key of the Mississippi.'[94]

On 17 September 1814, the same day that he had written to Croker about the abortive attack on Baltimore, Cochrane received a secret letter from Melville, dated 29 July, sanctioning an attack on New Orleans.[95] Despite the enthusiasm with which Cochrane had written of such an attack on 3 September his letter to Melville was still at sea, and would be for at least another two weeks; however, his earlier letters recommending an attack on New Orleans seem to have agreed with current thinking in London. Melville's letter giving permission to attack New Orleans therefore long pre-dated London's receipt of news of the defeat at Baltimore, but could still have been reconsidered when it arrived. The net cost of defeat at Baltimore could have been reduced by taking from it useful lessons in evaluating Cochrane's long-held aspirations for an attack on New Orleans.

Cochrane immediately left the Chesapeake for Halifax on 17 September.[96] Cockburn also left on 26 September to refit in Bermuda, leaving Rear-Admiral Malcolm in the Chesapeake until relieved by Barrie, currently refitting in Halifax, so that the blockades and attacks on the shore should continue uninterrupted.[97] On 1 October Cochrane ordered Cockburn to attack Cumberland Island off southern Georgia, partly to disguise his own preparations for the attack on New Orleans.[98]

THE BRITISH COMMERCIAL BLOCKADE CONTINUED

Captain Barrie in the *Dragon* returned to the Chesapeake late in September, and by November could write 'There is no trade going on in the Chesapeak', with only 'meagre pickings' coming from ashore.[99] Nevertheless, in December 1814 Cockburn ordered Captain John Clavell in the frigate *Orlando* 'to use every Effort and Exertion to maintain in the most strict and rigid manner possible the Blockade of the Chesapeake'. He was also 'to interrupt and prevent ... the Communications by Water which the Enemy by small Vessels occasionally endeavors to renew and keep up between different Towns and Places in the Upper Parts of the said Bay'.[100]

Meanwhile, Rear-Admiral Hotham's blockading squadron off the River Delaware had reported to him that between 6 August and 9 October 1814 a total of eighty-three vessels had been 'captured, burnt, and destroyed' in only two months.[101] Significantly, all were American. Such a list the year before would have included neutral vessels, which had evidently been deterred by the Royal Navy's commercial blockade from attempting further use of American ports. Of these, only two, less than 2.5% of the total, were described as 'ships', both captured by the British frigate *Narcissus*. The remaining eighty-one were smaller, either sloops, schooners or brigs, while five were listed as 'schooner boats'. Despite the list's unambiguous title, five of the vessels appear to have been taken more than once by the blockading squadron, including the sloop *Sally*, apparently captured twice by the British gun-brig *Nimrod* early in the period covered, and, later, for a third time by the British frigate *Pomone*. Similarly, the American sloop *Two Friends*, taken by the *Pomone* twice towards the end of the list, is apparently the same vessel. This strongly suggests, as in Lieutenant Napier's earlier experience aboard *Nymphe*, that, despite being illegal, some prizes were being ransomed and released, to be taken again.

While the rig of prizes had generally changed, to the faster sloops and schooners rather than the American ships taken so frequently the year before, Hotham's nine blockading vessels included such powerful warships as the *Superb*, 74, the razee *Saturn*, 55, the new fir-built fourth rate *Forth*, 50, and four frigates, including *Niemen* and *Loire*, 40, and two brig-sloops.[102] One of the smallest, the 18-gunned brig-sloop *Nimrod*, accounted for no fewer than thirty-eight of the eighty-three prizes named, more than 45%, while the other brig-sloop, *Dispatch*, took only one. The *Pomone* took nineteen, the *Loire* and *Niemen* seven each, the *Forth* six and *Narcissus* and *Saturn* two each. Even the heavier *Superb* is credited with one prize. The *Niemen's* capture of the American schooner privateer *Daedalus* on 18 September, and the capture by the boats of *Narcissus* and *Dispatch* of the American revenue schooner *Eagle*, are listed separately.[103]

The Royal Navy's domination of the American coastline was everywhere becoming total, and the economic effects of the commercial blockade a stranglehold from which neither American population nor administration could realistically expect to escape. In the six months between 12 May and 14 November 1814 109 vessels 'captured, detained or destroyed' were recorded at Bermuda alone. Among these was one ship of 400 tons, but eighty-three others, more than 76%, were either schooners or sloops.[104] The size of enemy vessels available as prizes was definitely decreasing. New vessels built to replace those lost to the Royal Navy's commercial blockade show an evident demand for smaller, handier and perhaps faster vessels. In 1813, 371 American vessels of all types had been built, totalling 32,583 gross tons, an average of 87.4 gross tons. By 1814 490 vessels totalling 29,751 gross tons were built across the country, an average of only 60.7 gross tons. Carrying capacity was apparently being sacrificed in an attempt to escape the British commercial blockade.[105]

THE BRITISH ATTACK ON NEW ORLEANS

By November 1814, although with fewer troops than he had expected in July, Cochrane had planned an attack on New Orleans, 100 miles up the Mississippi estuary, and, with a population of 25,000, the largest city west of the Appalachians. Successful occupation of New Orleans by a British force of 6,000 men would deny Louisiana access to the sea and make a useful bargaining point in peace negotiations. Cochrane's preliminary occupation of Pensacola, a Spanish harbour on the Gulf coast potentially useful in attacking New Orleans, was initially successful, but the American General Andrew Jackson re-occupied it with overwhelming numbers on 7 November, despite risk of an American war with Spain.[106]

Cochrane's gathering of troops and ships in Negril Bay, Jamaica, implied for the Americans an attack either on Mobile or New Orleans, especially since any more northerly British objective than Cumberland Island, off the coast of Georgia, was unlikely in winter.[107] On 17 September, however, a British force including the sloops *Hermes* and *Carron* had attacked Fort Bowyer, commanding Mobile Bay, but the *Hermes* had run aground in range of American guns and had been burned by her crew to prevent her capture.[108] The British force had withdrawn, focusing attention on New Orleans. The British forces left Jamaica on 26 November, not reaching Ship Island, still 70 miles from New Orleans, until 8 December.[109] American preparations had begun slowly until energetically directed by Andrew Jackson, who had arrived in New Orleans on 2 December.

Having dealt successfully on 14 December with a potentially dangerous flotilla of American gunboats, ideally suited to the relatively sheltered waters of Lake Borgne, Cochrane faced a shortage of suitable landing boats, despite having written to Melville as early as 17 July that 'Mobile and New Orleans are equally [accessible] but the necessary Craft are wanting', his having 'only Three Flat Bottomed boats in the Country'.[110] Eventually the British troops were ferried ashore in less suitable boats. The British army commander Major-General Sir Edward Pakenham, who had not arrived until 25 December, was killed on 8 January 1815 as the Americans defended prepared positions, which Jackson successfully resisted British attempts to outflank.[111] The *Carolina*, 14, an American naval vessel firing from the river, was belatedly destroyed on 27 December, but quickly replaced by the *Louisiana*, which was better positioned to avoid British gunfire.[112]

By 18 January it was obvious that further costly frontal attacks were unlikely to succeed, and British forces withdrew, capturing Fort Bowyer off Mobile in their retreat, a new attack on Mobile being forestalled only by news of peace. An Anglo-American Peace treaty had been signed at Ghent on 24 December, although it was not yet ratified by Congress or President. News of Cochrane's second failure in attacking an American land target might have encouraged either Congress or President to withhold their ratification, but for the United States' by now untenable fiscal and financial position, which had been increasingly obvious since August 1814 and was well understood by the American Peace Commissioners. One of them, Albert Gallatin, had himself – until his effective resignation in March 1813 – been Secretary of the United States Treasury, and was well aware of its predicament.[113]

With a letter of recall dated 30 December 1814, Cochrane sailed for the Chesapeake on 15 February 1815.[114] Perhaps partly out of loyalty, on 14 March Warren's former secretary and still prize agent, George Hulbert, commented on the debacle at New Orleans to James Fraser, his 'substitute' at Halifax. 'It has made a sad finish of the war', he wrote 'but it has shown the World who [were] dissatisfied with the small achievements of the former C in C how much less his successor has achieved with the most powerful means'.[115]

Meanwhile, the Admiralty had ordered that British operations should not stop until definite news of American ratification had been received. Therefore, the Royal Navy's naval and commercial blockades of the United States continued until the Ghent Treaty was passed unanimously by the Senate, signed by President Madison on 16 February 1815, and exchanged with Anthony Baker, the British envoy, the following day.[116] Together, the blockades had brought about decisive commercial, fiscal and financial consequences, with conclusive political results.

FIGURE 1.
James Madison (1751–1836), the Republican Party's fourth President of the
United States in 1809, remaining in office until 1817.

FIGURE 2.
Admiral Sir John Borlase Warren RN (1753–1822), Commander in Chief of the United Command of the North America and West Indies stations between August 1812 and April 1814.

FIGURE 3.
Rear-Admiral George Cockburn RN (1772–1853), Warren's second-in-
command after November 1812. His blockade of the Chesapeake from
February 1813, facilitated the British burning of Washington in August 1814,
seen in the background. Cockburn was knighted in January 1815.

FIGURE 4.
Vice-Admiral Sir Alexander Cochrane RN (1758–1832), Warren's successor as
Commander in Chief of the reseparated North America station from April
1814 until the peace.

FIGURE 5.
Albert Gallatin (1761–1849), Swiss-born Secretary of the Treasury since 1801 and retained by Madison until March 1813. Gallatin effectively resigned to become an American Peace Commissioner in Europe until the signing of the Treaty of Ghent.

FIGURE 6.
James Monroe (1758–1831), American Secretary of State from 1811 to 1817,
and Secretary of War, 1814–1815.

FIGURE 7.
Robert Banks Jenkinson, 2nd Lord Liverpool (1770–1828), Tory and British
Prime Minister, 1812–27.

FIGURE 8.
James Madison after leaving office.

CHAPTER 6

TRADE AND WAR: THE EFFECTS OF WARREN'S BLOCKADES

For war is quite changed from what it was in the time of our forefathers; when … the matter was decided by courage; but now the whole art of war is in a manner reduced to money.[1]

BOTH AT THE TIME AND SINCE, events seem to have conspired to disguise the impact of the British commercial and naval blockades of the United States, implemented after its declaration of war on Britain in June 1812. Yet, in thirty-two months of war, a British naval blockade was to contain most of the American navy such that it was unable to prevent a British maritime commercial blockade. This, in turn, bankrupted a United States government heavily dependent on customs revenue and credit, and led to the abandonment of its original war aims in peace negotiations.

When news of Madison's declaration of war was finally confirmed in London on 30 July 1812 the British Cabinet's priority was to use the occasion of Warren's arrival in North America to find a diplomatic solution to this additional problem while still at war with France. It was posed by an American refusal to accept the restraints on neutral trade made necessary by Britain's need to blockade France, which some Americans had seen as a trading opportunity. The Royal Navy's efforts to recover apparently British seamen from neutral vessels had exacerbated the problem. Should Warren's diplomatic efforts fail, naval and commercial blockades of the United States would be added to the world-wide commitments of a hugely expensive and already overstretched Royal Navy, now in the ninth year of its renewed war with Napoleon.

The lack of conclusive naval action against American naval vessels and privateers during the unavoidably long wait for replies to Warren's diplomatic overtures can readily be represented as a lack of British incisiveness.[2] One suggested 're-assessment' of the effectiveness of British blockades argues that Warren had missed the opportunity to 'cripple' the American merchant marine, and by December 1812 had established only a 'tentative military blockade – little

131

more than a patrol – of New York and Boston'. In fact, Warren did not receive Monroe's rejection, dated 27 October, of Britain's armistice proposal, until 16 November 1812. Largely confining the United States Navy to port and 'crippling' the 1m ton United States merchant marine had to await the rebuff of Britain's attempts to reach a diplomatic solution, and might be expected to take more than a few weeks.

This alleged lack of application is said to be most evident in the British implementation of economic warfare against the United States. On 23 June Britain had revoked its Orders in Council interdicting neutral trade with France as far as American vessels were concerned, and still waited for a reaction to what might be seen as a conciliatory gesture.[3] Although by 16 November 1812 Warren had received Monroe's rejection of British armistice proposals, it had not reached London. There, Warren's wait for an American reply was misrepresented as prevarication, perhaps most importantly by George Canning, Castlereagh's opponent in the House of Commons. 'The arm which should have launched the thunderbolt was occupied in guiding the pen.'[4] In a long speech Canning argued that

> the best way to carry on any war is the way that will lead soonest to
> peace; it is by vigour, not by forbearance and hesitation; it is by
> exertions calculated to make an enemy feel a dread of our power.[5]
> … It never entered into my mind that we should send a fleet to take
> rest and shelter in our own ports in North America, and that we
> should attack the American ports with a flag of truce.[6]

Delay, he concluded, had handicapped American opponents of the war, and reduced the proponents' 'notion of the mischiefs which we could inflict upon the coasts and navy of the United States. How they must now laugh at their own apprehensions.'[7]

Nevertheless, investigation of the possibilities of a diplomatic settlement was considered worthwhile on economic as well as humanitarian grounds. Continued trade was thought preferable to expensive warfare. Moreover, aggressive action during negotiations might be counter-productive, and expected to harden American resolve, while money spent fighting a war which the British government avowedly sought to avoid, could be seen by its taxpayers and domestic political opponents as money wasted, as well as apparent evidence of hypocrisy. Nonetheless, the delay in Warren's implementation of British naval and commercial blockades, damaged his reputation both then and since.

The range of Warren's diplomatic and naval responsibilities, including convoy protection and the safeguarding of influential West Indian interests with relatively limited resources, meant that progress in any one direction was to be constrained. Warren's scope for initiative was further limited by his knowledge that failure in any one objective could seriously damage both Britain's prospects of eventual success and his own professional reputation. Among the policies so handicapped was British maritime commercial blockade. In June 1812 potential

British blockading forces outside several major American ports were diverted by Sawyer's unsuccessful search for Commodore Rodger's American forces, which the British government had feared would attack valuable British convoys. By early November 1812 the number of American merchantmen reaching their homeports safely approached peacetime levels.[8]

Lord Bathurst, Secretary of State for War, had also been, until September 1812, President of the Board of Trade. His letter to the Prime Minister, Lord Liverpool, therefore clearly shows that the British Government was well aware of American vulnerability to war on its economy. At the same time, letters to Liverpool from British cotton manufacturers assuring him of their ability to survive American non-export legislation meant that it could feel free to act on its perception, while the Royal Navy provided it with the means to do so. Attack on the American's trade, tax base and financial position, and thereby the American government's credit, would ultimately erode American ability and political preparedness to continue the war they had themselves declared.[9]

On 31 July 1812 the Privy Council issued a General Embargo on American merchant shipping found anywhere in the British Empire. This was to prove immediately effective, and demonstrates the potential economic consequences of British commercial blockade. The forty-six American vessels quickly seized by the Royal Navy and brought into Halifax, Nova Scotia, before 17 September 1812 represented more than half of the full-rigged ships, and more than a quarter of the brigs detained and brought there, during the entire war.[10] Even the temporary loss of such valuable vessels and cargoes, often made permanent in due course by the Halifax Vice-Admiralty Court, sobered the most prosperous American owners, shippers and merchants, as well as their insurers and bankers. This served to reinforce their already considerable opposition to the war they had so long predicted and tried to prevent,[11] a warning to the Republican administration which brought little constructive response.

Even before the British General Embargo was implemented in earnest, Thomas Ives, a rich and influential American merchant, complained in November 1812 that 'the course that our public affairs have taken seems to paralize all business & if the War with England is to be continued, this part of the Country must suffer great inconvenience'.[12] By mid-January 1813, as the number of American vessels taken into Halifax as prizes by the Royal Navy grew to 125, the psychological and financial impact of the British strategy increased.[13] Ives now felt that 'the value in this Country of most foreign merchandize must in a great measure depend upon the continuance of the War in which we are foolishly engaged'. Funds had become difficult to 'remit – the risk of Specie by water being too great'.[14] The pressure of British commercial blockade was clearly felt even in Rhode Island, the smallest of the New England states, so far deliberately excluded from the imminent British commercial blockade of the Delaware and Chesapeake in the hope of separating them from the Union.

As shown earlier, the level of American imports, on which government revenue so heavily depended, was extremely vulnerable to trade restrictions, whether self- or enemy-imposed. The speed and direction of changes in import levels, as well as the duties on them, reflect the significance of these restraints of trade, whether American embargo, British commercial blockade, or occasionally both acting together. The American reliance on trade with Britain and fiscal dependence on customs revenues made import levels of crucial importance to the attainment of Madison's ambitions while at war with a former major trading partner. Although American consumers had long been prepared to pay duties to obtain imports, and so add to American Treasury funds, they were to be prevented from doing so, such that the American government was forced to borrow in an increasingly disrupted economy and to attempt belated fiscal reform, only ever partially successful.

It is difficult to determine to what extent the marked reduction in the level of American imports for much of the war was caused by the British commercial blockade, facilitated by the Royal Navy's restraint of an American navy potentially capable of lifting it, or by the American legislative restrictive system, occasionally concurrent with the blockade, but widely evaded. However, it can shown that, unsupplemented by American embargoes for the last ten months of the war, the British commercial blockade and its consequences contributed hugely to the American government's insolvency and, by making the original American war aims clearly unattainable, hastened a negotiated peace. Falling import levels and therefore customs revenue forced upon Madison fiscal, financial, economic and political realities which induced him to end the war from a weakened position. In making significant reductions in American imports, successful British commercial blockade would cause the American government, at the very least, temporary financial embarrassment and, at worst, a need for peace at almost any price.

The availability of reliable American import statistics between 1800 and 1820 is, therefore, crucial in measuring the effectiveness and relative importance of American embargoes and the Royal Navy's commercial blockade of the United States. However, as shown in the notes to Appendix B Table 1, total import figures were not recorded in the United States before 1821, incomplete figures being supplemented by later estimates.[15] The United States import figures for 1800–1815, compiled and adjusted by North in 1960 and given in Appendix B Table 1, show the size, pace and direction of the changes, revealing the impact of successive American legislative trade restrictions and the British maritime commercial blockade. From a record figure of $144,740,342 in 1807, American imports fell by almost 60% to $58,101,023 in 1808, measuring the effect of Jefferson's Non-Importation Act of 1806, implemented on 14 December 1807, which banned most British imports.[16] This was followed by the Embargo Act of 22 December 1807, prohibiting exports and American ships, from leaving port; together these theoretically curtailed almost all American overseas trade.[17] Both measures were widely evaded. Because of this evasion, and despite the embargo's reportedly serious economic effects, the initial decrease in imports was followed by a recovery to $61,029,726 in 1809, and to $89,366,069 by 1810, an increase of 53.8% on the figure for 1808. The extent of evasion resulted in the Congressional

Act for Better Enforcement of the Embargo of 9 January 1809, and its replacement on 1 March that year by the Non-Intercourse Act, allowing repeal of the original embargo a fortnight later. Macon's No. 2 Bill of 1 May 1810 re-opened trade with Britain and France, but would then withhold it from whichever European belligerent failed to remove its restrictions on neutral American trade. In August 1810 Champagny, Duc de Cadore, Napoleon's Minister of Foreign Affairs, implied that France intended to end its depredations on American shipping, provided that the United States resisted British trade restrictions.[18] Either from credulity or for convenience Madison accepted this apparent change of policy at face value. Accordingly, from 2 February 1811, the Non-Importation Act was applied solely to Britain. American imports of $57,887,952 in 1811, only about a third less than 1810's, suggest that evasion of the restrictive system remained widespread.[19] It was against this background that Madison and much of Congress saw increased imports and customs revenue in 1812 as vindicating their hopes of financing war with Britain without the need for fundamental tax reform, leading to fiscal difficulties, financial failure and eventual bankruptcy.

Customs duties were usually recorded with other duties reflecting the level of imports, such as tonnage and lighthouse dues, but nothing illustrates with greater clarity the impact of even the threat of British maritime commercial blockade on American government income than the raw data of the United States net customs revenue. This was gross customs duties, less the expenses of collection and 'drawbacks' – the rebate of duty on some re-exports – as shown in Appendix B, Table 3.[20]

Therefore, an increase in American imports, and consequently of the United States net customs duty revenue, would seem to imply that Britain's first attempt at economic warfare in this war had proved an abject failure. Seybert's figures for Net Customs Revenue were actually over 20% higher in 1812 than in 1811.[21] Indeed, the perceived threat of British commercial blockade had apparently proved counter-productive. However, increased imports were not to last beyond the scramble to bring back to America those imports often already paid for by exports to Britain before the war. In 1812, anticipation of a British commercial blockade had produced consequences which seem to have lulled American fiscal decision makers into a false sense of security. American fear of economic isolation – the psychological impact of British commercial blockade – had the initial effect of increasing American government revenue from import duties, appearing to justify the position of those in Congress who had argued that no fundamental changes in American revenue collection were necessary, certainly, not in their view, before war had been declared.

The potential effectiveness of Britain's limited blockade policy of the first six months of the war had been disguised by a backlog of $18m worth of British manufactures which their American owners sought to dispatch to the United States. The American declaration of war had found some of the goods already loaded onto American vessels in British ports; other American merchants sought exemption from restrictive legislation to fetch their property from Canada or the West Indies.[22] The importers had been anxious to avoid the anticipated tightening of the British commercial blockade once war began in earnest. They had been convinced by the advice of Jonathan Russell, the American chargé d'affaires in London, that, after 1 August, the recent revocation of the British Orders in Council affecting American vessels would allow them to return fully laden from Britain to the United States. They also knew that Madison's first 90-day embargo on American foreign trade had ended on 3 July. Given Gallatin's prediction in November 1811 of a $2m budget deficit for an 1812 at peace, both President and Treasury were understandably keen to collect the normal import duties, despite the merchants' and shippers' view that leniency was appropriate in these unusual circumstances.[23] By November 1812 Madison noted that 'a considerable number' of previously stranded vessels had arrived in the United States. Despite Madison's announcement that the matter would be resolved by Congress, the owners, he said, had been 'under the erroneous impression that the Non-Importation Act would immediately cease to operate', and resisted compromise.[24]

On 4 November 1812 Madison felt able to tell Congress, somewhat disingenuously, that 'The duties on the late unexpected importation of British manufactures will render the revenue of the ensuing year more productive than could have been anticipated.' While conceding that America was 'not without its difficulties', Madison added that 'the view here presented of our pecuniary resources' was an 'animating consideration'.[25] This situation was not to last; Madison was living in a fiscal fool's paradise. Within days letters were to be written to the American Secretary of the Navy complaining of a British blockade of southern American ports, while, in London, letters left Downing Street formalising British blockades of Chesapeake Bay and the Delaware.[26]

The threat of British commercial blockade, even when barely started, and certainly before being fully implemented, had a measurable effect on the level of American imports, then a sensitive barometer of the United States' fiscal and financial climate. As shown in Appendix B Table 1, the prospect of British commercial blockade had the effect of raising total American imports from 1811's $57.9m to 1812's $78.8m, an increase of more than 36%. Madison's use of the then-current uncorrected estimated figures probably led him to suggest a bigger increase to Congress, one of over 43%.[27] This appears to have induced Congressional, even Presidential, complacency. Madison was apparently encouraged by these figures to believe that increased rates of customs revenue, supported by loans, could produce sufficient funds to support the war, and would continue to do so long enough for the British to concede what Madison now asserted to be America's major grievance, Britain's alleged right to stop and search neutral vessels at sea, followed as necessary by the impressment of apparently renegade British seamen. Those Americans whose incomes had up to this time been maintained, or even increased, by this temporary artificial boost to the United States imports may have contributed to the first partially successful loan of $11m to the American government authorised on 14 March 1812. Later calls for loans were to be less successful, once British maritime blockades became tighter and wider.[28]

Nor can Madison have been unaware that the deceptively encouraging total customs revenue, accrued in 1812 and available for government expenditure during 1813, was in part due to American customs revenue figures having been inflated since 1 July 1812 by the Congressional decision to double all rates of import duty once war had been declared.[29] This had allowed Congress to postpone the necessity of re-introducing internal excise duties and what they called 'direct' taxes. Allowance for the increased rate of customs duties for the second half of 1812 reduces the net customs duties accrued for that year by 25%, from $13,331,467 to an adjusted $9,998,600.[30] Even so, this adjusted figure for 1812 shows an increase in the real level of accrued net customs duty at original rates of approximately 21.6%. This reflected the increased level of imports from $57.9m in 1811 to $78.8m in 1812, and served to hide the fiscal impact of Madison's 90-day embargo and the limited British commercial blockade to date. It may even have diverted some attention from the number of commercial sea voyages cancelled under such American legislative restrictions as the Non-Importation Act, as well as the threat of wider and stricter British commercial sanctions. In analysis of later years, it will be possible to allow for the increased rates of import duties during 1813–14, to permit more accurate use of net customs revenue as a partial measure of the effectiveness of British commercial blockade, using as data the decreasing accrued totals for each of the war years.[31]

The customs revenue figure for 1812 enabled Madison to dismiss temporarily the criticism levelled at the consequences of his 90-day embargo on foreign trade, which had operated from 4 April to 3 July 1812. This banned first imports and then American exports to Britain, but was in operation for only two weeks of the war.[32] However, although Madison's export embargo ended on 3 July, imports remained prohibited by the Non-Importation Act of 1811, an earlier part of his 'restrictive system' designed to gain concessions on British Orders in Council and impressments by withholding trade. Many Congressmen, notably John Calhoun, thought that the 1811 act should be modified or suspended to allow duties on imports from Britain to add to government revenue; leaving it in force, Calhoun thought, would 'debilitate the springs of war'.[33] Others, including the House of Representatives Speaker, Henry Clay, successfully argued that restrictions on Anglo-American trade would be as effective as war in obtaining concessions, and bills to allow the resumption of British imports were narrowly defeated.[34] Thereby, the United States continued to place itself at a fiscal and financial disadvantage.

The restrictive system, including Madison's short-lived second embargo of 1813, further complicates the use of American net customs revenue as a measure of the effectiveness of the Royal Navy's wartime commercial blockade up to April 1814. However, the intermittent nature and relative brevity of the embargoes and the widespread evasion and uneven enforcement of the Non-Importation Act all limit the validity of the criticism, reducing the usefulness of American restrictive legislation as an alternative explanation to British commercial blockade for a debilitating decline in net customs revenue. Later, when neither of Madison's embargoes nor any legislative restrictions were in force, the reduction in American overseas trade may be safely attributed to the British commercial blockade alone. It was by then largely protected from American naval interference by the British naval blockade which progressively contained American warships as the war continued.[35]

Memories of the severe unemployment and other adverse economic effects of Jefferson's earlier embargo increased the determination with which Madison's first embargo was evaded. Merchants' efforts to 'palsy the arm of government' were duly reported by contemporary American commentators. Niles' *Weekly Register* for 12 April 1812 asserted that in a frantic five days before the embargo came into force goods worth $15m, including 200,000 barrels of flour, left American ports in defiance of the export ban.[36]

Despite such resistance and evasion, the effects of Madison's 90-day embargo, operating alone, would have been the temporary reduction of both American overseas trade and tax revenues. Many inward and outward sea voyages were reportedly embargoed, with American vessels left idle, but the value of American foreign trade lost is difficult to quantify beyond its apparent effects on employment and prices. The embargo's ending on 3 July, the Congressional doubling of import tax rates after 1 July and the American merchants' attempts to retrieve their stranded goods each increased 1812's imports and customs duties revenue – effectively offsetting much of the embargo's impact. As a result, according to Madison's account to Congress, the total net customs revenue accrued in 1812 had been inflated to $13,331,467 by the 'unexpected' increase in the arrival of imports, apparently serving to disguise from him, as well as from later observers, the effectiveness of the threat implied by early British efforts to impose a commercial blockade on the United States. Madison, however, made no apparent attempt to adjust the annual net customs revenue to under $10m to allow for the doubled rate of duties in July. Had he chosen to emphasise the impact of doubled customs duty rates since 1 July, and the temporary nature of the fiscal windfall from the merchants' scramble to repatriate their profits as imports, Congress might have been less compliant, and a more urgent attempt at major tax reform might have been made before the limited success of government borrowing became all too apparent.

Since even the adjusted net customs revenue figure for 1812 exceeded that of 1811, its value as a measure of the effectiveness of the British maritime commercial blockade at the beginning of the war is limited, except perhaps as a starting point. Until Madison's second brief embargo and the Non-Importation Act were repealed in April 1814, the responsibility for any economic changes in America have to be shared between a range of factors, including both British maritime commercial blockade and self-imposed American handicaps. However, despite these complications, adjusted net customs revenue can for later years, when the relatively brief and intermittent embargoes and the equally evaded Non-Importation Act were repealed, be used as a measure of the effectiveness of the Royal Navy's commercial blockade of the United States.

By December 1812, after six months of war with Britain, the American budget deficit was more than predicted. Seybert gives net customs revenue of $8,223,715, collected in 1811 and forming the bulk of the United States government receipts for 1812.[37] Dewey raises that to $8,900,000 when including other import-related taxes such as Registered and Enrolled tonnage duties, lighthouse dues and revenue from passports, and, by adding miscellaneous income of $800,000, reaches a total available for 1812 of $9,700,000.[38] However, total expenditure for 1812 appears to have been $20,280,000, creating a shortfall of $10,580,000, summarised in Appendix B as Table 5.[39] Authority to raise a loan of $11m at 6%, gained on 14 March 1812, was clearly necessary, but was not unopposed in Congress.

Critics doubted whether loanable funds existed for so large a demand without the imposition of internal excise revenues to create confidence that interest would be paid and the principal eventually redeemed. However, after a slow start, the call produced $6,118,900 at par in only two days; then, however, the supply of funds faltered such that by 24 June 1812 only $6,500,000 had been collected.[40] The prices of existing government stock fell by between 2 and 3% while the 1812 loan was available, and Gallatin suggested renegotiating its terms; he should perhaps have made the introduction of new taxes to meet interest payments the price of his remaining in office. While the banks were willing to lend the government another $2,150,000 in short-term loans, only $8,180,000 of the $11m sought for this first war loan was ever eventually raised, resolving conclusively the subsequent protracted discussion of its relative success.[41]

From the outset, therefore, even before the end of 1812, the unpopularity of the war, the restrictive legislation and the so far limited British commercial blockade had evidently damaged the preparedness of some wealthy American citizens, particularly prosperous New England merchants and bankers, to lend to a government they had outspokenly criticised as having already damaged their interests by embargo, restrictive legislation and the prospect of wartime commercial blockade.

Therefore, on 30 June 1812 the American government had resorted for the first time to an issue of $5m worth of Treasury notes in denominations of $100 or more. These were short-term loan certificates bearing 5.4% annual interest, redeemable by the Treasury a year after each issue. To create wide acceptability and to stimulate their circulation they could, despite not being intended as legal tender, be used to pay duties and taxes or buy public lands. They enabled the government to receive money in anticipation of future tax revenues and long-term loans. Gallatin and others had insisted that, not backed by precious metal, their success depended on internal excise duties to meet the interest, and on issues being limited to avoid the notes being discounted during transactions and to retain public confidence in government credit.[42] In ignoring this advice the American government was to embark on an ultimately disastrous monetary policy.

The American government relied less for its revenue on the taxation of exports, so much so that tax initially paid by importers on goods they intended to re-export could be reclaimed by them as 'drawback'. These tax rebates, on such products as coffee, cocoa, sugar and pepper, fell from $2,227,245 in 1811 to $1,542,623 in 1812, reflecting a 30% decrease in the re-export of products subject to rebate.[43] Most other goods intended for re-export paid *ad valorem* tax on importation according to their value; such goods were valued at $8,815,291 in 1811 but only $3,591,755 in 1812.[44] Even by the end of 1812, therefore, the fall in the level of American exports was significant. As is apparent from Appendix B Table 15, American total exports fell from $61.3m in 1811 to $38.5m in 1812, a fall of more than 37%.[45] Notwithstanding Madison's 90-day embargo on American overseas trade, in force between 4 April and 3 July 1812, this decline remains remarkable, since American and neutral ships with British licences continued to carry grain and flour from such American ports as Baltimore and Alexandria to British and allied armies in the Peninsula. Furthermore, in December 1812 the ports of New England were to remain exempt from British commercial blockade for almost another sixteen months. Exports of grain and flour from each reduced the fall in American exports.

The decline in the level of American re-exports was even more marked. From over $16m in 1811, they fell to $8.5m in 1812, a fall of almost 47%, although how much of this decline is due to Madison's three-month embargo and how much to the Royal Navy's embryonic commercial blockade remains problematic.[46] Traditionally an important component of the United States' total exports, re-exports still comprised 26% of American exports in 1811, but only 22% in 1812, beginning a catastrophic decline until after 1815.[47] In later years, greatly reduced re-export figures during wartime periods without American legislative trade restrictions measure the effectiveness of the British commercial blockade. These falls in American exports and re-exports would reduce the incomes of growers, merchants and shippers, consequently their spending, and eventually the employment of others. This would reduce the general ability to pay taxes and the preparedness of many to lend to the government held responsible for the decline in American overseas trade.

However, as late as October 1812 the level of wages and employment in the maritime sector of the American economy seemed buoyant. While attempting to refit and man his command, the American frigate *Constitution*, Isaac Hull complained on 29 October 1812 that competition for seamen and dockside workers from the American merchant service, and those fitting out privateers, had raised wages and created maintenance and manning difficulties for him and the United States Navy.[48]

But fiscal, financial and economic conditions for the American administration were about to worsen. Anticipating that Warren's diplomatic efforts would fail, the British Privy Council had, on 13 October 1812, issued General Reprisals against American ships, vessels and property wherever found, a *de facto* declaration of war. On 16 November Warren had received the expected rejection of his armistice proposals, together with unacceptable American counter-proposals.[49] On 21 November Earl Bathurst, British Secretary of State for War, ordered the blockade of Chesapeake Bay and the Delaware river, and on 25 November the Admiralty relayed this order to Warren.[50] By 26 December the *London Gazette* made the customary formal notification of the blockade to neutrals.[51] On 6 February 1813 Warren made a local declaration that Chesapeake Bay and the Delaware were under blockade[52] and, on 19 February, he assured the First Lord of the Admiralty that the blockade was in place.[53] He also announced that American vessels apparently with British licences would no longer be allowed to enter or leave the Chesapeake. His earlier demands for reinforcements, and clarification from London of the issues raised by the proliferation of British licences to trade, had been partly resolved.

Since its arrival there in 1808, the British Army in the Iberian peninsula had depended on American grain and flour, accounting for over 60% of American grain exports in 1811, including those to Britain.[54] However, on 3 February 1813 the British Foreign Secretary informed Anthony Baker that American grain and flour would no longer be needed by the Army in the Peninsula.[55] By May Wellington had authorised the purchase of grain from Egypt and Brazil, despite which American deliveries to the Peninsula continued throughout the remainder of 1813 until largely replaced by restored supplies from the Baltic.[56] The American vessels engaged, officially intended to return in ballast, in fact returned to the United States with British specie and such valuable cargoes as salt, activities incompatible with any form of economic warfare. Madison, too, had long regarded such trade as inconsistent with the American restrictive system, and in May 1813 had finally succeeded in persuading Congress to ban the American use of British licences.

Significantly, from the summer of 1813 the possession by American merchantmen of an apparently British licence to trade would become a progressively less effective protection against detention by a British blockading squadron and the possible confiscation by a Vice-Admiralty Court of both cargo and vessel. The over-supply of grain and flour formerly exported from Baltimore appears to have depressed its price there by two dollars a barrel, a quantifiable link between export prices, American legislation and British commercial blockade, to become increasingly important as the blockade was extended.[57]

The first British blockade, planned for Chesapeake Bay and the Delaware, had been supplemented in early November 1812 by a squadron stationed off Savannah, intended to intercept American shipments of timber and raw cotton. Increasingly important strategically, the interruption of southern timber supplies to the north caused American anxiety over repairs and maintenance of both the United States Navy and the merchant fleet.[58] More importantly, by beginning to restrict American foreign trade Warren could hope that, by January 1813, he 'may probably produce some Deficit ere long in the Revenue of the United States: If all my other Divisions are equally active and successful'.[59]

Warren had in fact extended the commercial blockade in anticipation of written Admiralty orders.[60] By February 1813 Niles' *Weekly Register* reported from Baltimore that British vessels were 'blockading the Chesapeake and the Delaware and are occasionally off New York'.[61] On 26 March the commercial blockade of New York was officially sanctioned in both personal correspondence and official orders. Privately, Warren was told to expect 'an order for blockading all the principal Ports in the United States to the southward of Rhode Island & including the Mississippi' to put a 'complete stop to all trade & intercourse by Sea'.[62] Officially, the Admiralty ordered him to 'institute a strict and rigorous Blockade of the Ports and Harbours of New York, Charleston, Port Royal, Savannah, and of the River Mississippi'.[63] Quoting the Order in Council of 30 March 1813, the *London Gazette* gave the usual notification to neutrals, and, on 26 May, Warren issued from Bermuda a copy of his orders as a local proclamation.[64]

Throughout the spring, summer and autumn of 1813 a series of local proclamations spelled out precisely which coasts, ports and estuaries were blockaded by Warren's squadrons, while Niles catalogued American complaints.[65] Improving weather conditions in the spring allowed British blockading squadrons closer inshore. As early as April 1813, agents' reports suggested that the commercial blockades were proving effective in curtailing American coastal trade and communication. One letter intercepted by inshore blockade in April revealed the American writer to be thinking that 'all Water communication with you had ceased, order from head Quarters having been issued to stop all Bay Craft &c for fear they should fall in the hands of the Enemy ... The War as you say now assumes a serious aspect'.[66]

By 5 April 1813 Thomas Ives, a prominent Rhode Island shipper and businessman, well aware of the commercial significance of developments at sea, complained that

> British Cruisers are actually in the Sound and have taken one of the
> New York Packets, Capt. Walden, also a number of Coasting and
> other Vessels ... as the communication by water with New York is of
> great importance to the trade carried on by New England with the
> Middle States, Govt. ought immediately to send a force sufficient
> into the Sound to give it ample protection – part of our naval force
> could not otherwise be so well employed'.[67]

This demanding attitude, in view of New England's relative prosperity and frequently outspoken opposition to the war, and a general failure there to contribute proportionately to the Government's call for loans, was precisely the sort of view which drew hostility towards New England, both during and especially after the war, when the records of its contributions became better known.

By 15 June Ives was being forced to admit that 'the British force off N[ew] London is vigilant & employs a number of small vessels in all directions so that we consider the coasting trade between this [i.e. Providence R.I.] & New York thro' the Sound at an end for the present'. His Boston agent replied the same afternoon that the price of 'soft flour' was even 'advancing in consequence' of 'the probable rigorous blockade of the Sound'.[68] The American coasting trade was economically important in gathering exports and distributing imports, and the interruption of both was evidently reflected in producers', shippers' and merchants' incomes, and in consumer prices.

Warren gained invaluable secret intelligence, presumably gathered at considerable personal risk, from agents ashore. In April, a British agent reported that

> Rigidly cutting off all trade between towns in the bays, particularly
> Baltimore, disrupts the neighbourhood very much. Wood and
> several other articles from the Eastern coast are now very scarce,
> and commanding exceeding high prices. This plan ... if persevered
> in, would injure them more than in any other way; great complaints
> are already made of the War.[69]

Another, apparently American 'Federalist', agent significantly noted in April that 'A very high traffic was carried on between Baltimore and Philadelphia by water before the Squadron [arrived], but ... this trade is now stopped ... as it cannot be carried by land'.[70] Nevertheless, efforts were made to replace blockaded coastal traffic with land transport. One commentator, writing in 1819, noted that 'Before the war, there were but two wagons that plied between Boston and the town of Providence, and soon after its commencement, the number increased to two hundred.'[71]

The extent to which American coastal trade could be replaced by land transport was by all accounts very limited, however. The quantity of goods that could be carried by either wagon trains or packhorses was restricted, and the rates expensive. Canals were often unavailable as an alternative and, where present, were often short, shallow and discontinuous; in any case, transhipment added greatly to costs. After the war Seybert attributed the dislocation to the British coastal blockade, adding that

> The inhabitants ... in the immediate vicinity were not alone
> affected by the enemy; his operations extended their influence to
> our great towns and cities on the Atlantic coast. Domestic
> intercourse and internal commerce were interrupted, whilst that
> with foreign nations was in some instances entirely suspended,
> everything had to be conveyed by land carriage; our
> communication with the ocean was cut off.[72]

'Our roads', he wrote earlier, 'became almost impassable in consequence of the heavy loads'.[73] Since 'a wagon trade between points as widely separated as Savannah and Boston' would take 115 days in peacetime, only serious inflation in the price of American-produced cotton goods would make such land transport of raw cotton from the Southern states to New England remotely feasible in wartime.[74] Generally 'turnpikes were unable to offer cheap transport for long distances. To haul a ton from Philadelphia to Pittsburgh ... cost $125. To move a bushel of salt 300 miles by any road cost $2.50 ... to transport goods, wares or merchandise cost $10 per ton per hundred miles.[75] Hauling a ton from Philadelphia to Pittsburgh had cost $90 in peacetime, and now cost almost 40% more, making the land haulage of even moderately heavy goods, such as grain and flour, uneconomic over more than 150 miles.[76] In April 1813 the same 'Federalist' agent reported to Warren the impact of British blockade and substituted land carriage on American prices. 'Wood is 10 and 12 Dollars per load at Baltimore – Indian Corn cannot be got, with grain for Horses, Fish is very dear, and every other Eatable is high except flour which is 6 and a half and 7 Dollars per Barrel.'[77] Seybert later saw the impact of British commercial blockade as being 'not only deprived of revenue': 'The expenses of the government, as well as of individuals, were very much augmented for every species of transportation.'[78]

From 1 September American access to inland waterways in Virginia, North Carolina, South Carolina and Georgia was to be curtailed.[79] By 16 November 1813 Warren's proclamation extending the blockade to Long Island Sound and southward of Narragansett Bay down to the border with Florida interdicted neutral trade with New York,[80] while by 2 December 1813 a local proclamation by the squadron blockading New London announced the closure of the northern approaches to New York.[81] Only the neutral trade of the ports of New England remained excluded, as Britain sought to widen their political differences with the rest of the Union.

By April 1813 the economic effectiveness of the British commercial blockade was being recognised by those directly affected. Vincent Nolte, a New Orleans cotton merchant, complained to Alexander Baring, a London merchant banker, that interrupted trade with the Atlantic states was causing 'very heavy sacrifices on our part and bears so hard on all classes of citizens'. Only two foreign vessels had arrived at New Orleans in the past nine months. He suggested that Baring should charter neutral Swedish vessels in England and send them to him in ballast, to export raw cotton to the Peninsula or Gothenburg before returning to Britain under licence.[82]

Similarly, in May 1813 an unnamed Baltimore merchant wrote to a Nova Scotian newspaper that 'Our situation is more distressing than pride or obstinacy will permit most to allow.' The condition of Baltimore was 'exactly that of a besieged city'. 'All business' was 'at a stand', with 'nothing talked of but the enemy and the war. What an enormous tax upon us is the war! The price of every thing almost doubled, and our supplies by water totally cut off!' Unemployment in Baltimore was evidently becoming serious. 'If no change takes place in a few months the middling classes of society must leave the place, and go where they can get employ and support their families.'[83] Holding, and being prepared to express, such opinions, once prosperous merchants would be unlikely to pay tax increases willingly or to lend to the administration responsible for the war. For the American government, this created increasingly serious difficulties in meeting wartime expenditure.

In addition to their damage to trade and shipping and the fiscal consequences, Warren's blockades of the Chesapeake and Delaware provided access for British amphibious forces raiding strategic targets in Virginia, Maryland and Delaware. On 3 May 1813, for example, Cockburn reached Havre de Grace, at the head of Chesapeake Bay. There he 'gained Intelligence' of the Cecil cannon foundry at Principio, three miles further north, and 'one of the most valuable Works of the Kind in America'. He caused 'its destruction, and that of the Guns and other Material we found there' with 'several Buildings & much complicated heavy Machinery'. As Cockburn reported to Warren, his 'small Division' had 'been on Shore in the Centre of the Enemy's Country and on his high Road between Baltimore and Philadelphia'. Other boats had penetrated the Susquehanna river, 'destroying five Vessels in it and a large Store of Flour'. With only one officer wounded, they had destroyed fifty-one guns and '130 Stand of Small Arms'.[84]

Actions of this sort created financial as much as practical problems for the Americans. The import-substitution made possible by the capacity of more than 200 powder mills of firms such as the Dupont Company of Delaware had long since solved the gunpowder shortages of the Revolutionary War.[85] The United States was virtually self-sufficient in powder and no longer so dependent on imported weapons, but commercial organisations still needed paying, while British attacks on trade and tax revenue had eroded both the administration's ready cash and credit. In the long term, therefore, it was not the damage to strategic targets that proved most effective, but the damage to the American economy and government creditworthiness that most reduced the administration's preparedness to continue the war. However, the raids do appear to have forewarned the Americans of the probability of a British attempt to capture Baltimore, and gave those like Senator Samuel Smith time to prepare its effective defence.[86]

Any successful British commercial blockade of the United States would have to include New York, a port of enormous commercial and therefore fiscal importance. On average between 1803 and 1812, its registered tonnage employed in foreign trade was 122,603 and the net revenue derived from customs $3,687,075.[87] With a population in 1808 of 83,530, it was the most populous as well as the most productive of customs revenue, its population having grown almost 40% since 1801 and more than three and a half times since 1786.[88] As well as being 'the centre of local distribution' it was also 'the leading place in the foreign trade of North America'. As a result, John Lambert, an Englishman travelling in America before the war, could write that 'the moneys collected in New York for the national treasury, on the imports and tonnage have for several years amounted to one fourth of the public revenue'.[89]

On 5 May 1813 the Philadelphian merchant John Maybin wrote that 'the Report of the Day is that New York is Blockaded – Should that be the case, the Middle States will then be completely Shut in'. By 13 May his correspondent feared that 'our coasting trade is nearly destroyed & it is found extremely difficult to supply the Town & Country with Corn, which has become very scarce as well as dear'.[90] In June, he found 'the passage thro' the sound is at present completely shut up – by the British force stationed off New London watching commodore Decaturs Squadron'.[91] As soon as 21 June Maybin wrote 'I fear the blockade of the Sound Will Prove an Injury to the Eastern States as they will Not be Able to get a Supply of Bread Stuffs – this wicked and unnecessary War is Ruining our Country – and it do not appear that Congress is doing anything to put a stop to it.' By 14 September 'The British have moved their Squadrons in the Sound down towards New York so that it is impossible for Coasters to pass.' Four days later Maybin assessed the consequences 'It is a lamentable thing that this Country is deprived of its regular Traid (sic) and Imports in General have got so high' [i.e. in price]', '– which operates both ways against the Citizens.'[92]

Consequently, while in December 1812 New York's registered merchant tonnage was 162,885 by 31 December 1813 it had fallen to 146,512.[93] By 27 September 1813 'the number of ships and brigs laid up and dismantled in New York City was 122', together with eighteen sloops and schooners. In the same month, the privateer *Governor Tompkins* was sold at auction in New York for $14,000; her cost the year before had been $20,000.[94]

In the House, in June 1813, Jonathan Fisk of New York had declined to argue that his electorate was 'more exposed and less efficiently defended' than elsewhere. 'It would be sufficient', he said, 'to state that three fourths of our seacoast had been declared in a state of blockade; that our waters were infested, and coast lined with the armed boats and barges of the enemy, which were engaged in marauding and destroying the property of our citizens, with an impunity that was deeply to be regretted'. He asked whether gunboats or 'any means could be devised to defend our coast from a warfare so distressing and vexatious'.[95]

By the end of 1813 the interruption of American imports, caused at this stage by both British commercial blockade and American legislative restrictions, was having a measurable effect on customs duties payable in New York. In 1810 New York State had contributed $4,419,060 to net customs revenue, almost 35% of the national total. Raised in 1812 by New York's share of the 'unexpected' British imports to $2,885,102, net customs revenue had fallen in 1813 to $1,368,618, a decrease of almost 53%.[96] When allowance is made for Congress having doubled the rates of customs duties from 1 July 1812 the real decrease in net customs revenue collected in New York State between 1812 and 1813 is over 68%.[97]

Shortages of previously imported commodities contributed to quantifiable inflation. An all-commodity index of New York wholesale prices, standing at 127 in June 1812, when America declared war, rose to 160 by June 1813, by which time Warren's initial blockade of New York was officially sanctioned. By December 1813, with all approaches to New York strictly blockaded, it rose to 189.[98] How far the lives of ordinary people were adversely affected is measured by changes in the basic commodity index of New York's wholesale prices between the declaration of war and December 1813. This index for June 1812 was 128;

by June 1813 it was 163 and, by December 1813, 198.[99] Although far worse was to come, the end of 1813 saw the beginning of a marked decline in New York's standard of living, its shipping and tonnage duties, its overseas trade and customs revenue – even the city's population.[100]

New York was not alone. Throughout the summer of 1813 operation of the British commercial blockade of the Chesapeake had proved effective. By September its commander, Captain Robert Barrie, wrote that 'as Nathan has not had <u>any</u> trade whatever during the summer', he wondered whether the Americans would 'venture to run any of their French traders during the winter', and hoped that they 'will dash a little now the bad weather is coming on'.[101] Perhaps more trustworthy than Barrie's enthusiasm is the more quantitative list showing that in less than three months, between 6 September and 25 December 1813 alone, his squadron went on to capture or destroy seventy-two American merchant vessels, and, in addition to those 'libelled' in Halifax, over the twenty-week period from 6 September 1813 to 12 January 1814 eighty-one vessels totalling more than 4,000 tons were registered in Bermuda as 'captured burnt or destroyed' in Chesapeake Bay.[102]

With the British commercial blockade of the Delaware River and Bay also strictly enforced, the state of Pennsylvania, including Philadelphia, was similarly affected. Even by the end of April 1813 the unemployment of seamen along the Delaware was being attributed to the British blockading squadron and 'the depredations committed by these Vessels'. Despite this, however, 'the people who from the interruption of the Navigation are at present without employment' remained disinclined 'to enter on board the Gun Boats' which might have provided some defence.[103]

Occasionally, the psychological effect of British maritime blockade becomes evident. The usually pragmatic Maybin wrote from Philadelphia on 5 May:

> Messers Myers wrote to me from Norfolk that the Squadrons are
> close in with their Capes & make many Captures, I hope you are
> safe – should the Fleet visit Newport which is very much Exposed –
> in case the War is continued any length of time, I fear the British
> will act with more vigour along the coast the next Summer than
> they did the last.[104]

Even rumours of British commercial blockade were thought likely to have an impact on prices. On 16 June 1813 Ives described price changes 'probably owing to the *expectation* of an immediate rigorous Blockade & the Stoppage in a great measure of the Coasting trade'.[105]

By late July 1813 Maybin records just how severe the impact of the British blockade was becoming. '[A]t present', he wrote, 'prices are merely Nominal as No Sales are making – Coffee Sugar and Pepper are articles also Expected to advance in prices as they are getting Scarce in our Markets. Indeed goods Generally are getting Scarce and if we do Not get an additional Supply soon, prices will be very high for Articles of Necessity.'[106] An index of Philadelphia wholesale import prices standing at 155 in 1812 reached 185 by 1813.[107] Although American agricultural wages had risen in 1813, rising prices and maritime unemployment would mean that demand for many goods, including imports, would fall.[108] As a result, having contributed $2,439,018 to net customs revenue in 1810, and $2,090,298 in 1812, Philadelphia produced only $311,030 in 1813.[109] This represents a decrease in Philadelphia's contribution to net customs revenue between 1812 and 1813 of 85.1%. When allowance is made for the doubling of the rate of customs duties on 1 July 1812, the real decrease over the same period is a remarkable 90.1%.

Similarly, Maryland, which had collected $1,780,365 net customs revenue in 1812, paid in only $182,006 in 1813, an unadjusted decrease in its contribution to net customs revenue of 89.8% and an adjusted decrease of no less than 93.2%.[110] With British commercial and naval blockades in place, even with the non-importation act as widely evaded as ever, according to Adams 'after the summer [of 1813], the total net revenue collected in every port of the United States outside New England did not exceed $150,000 a month', producing only $1,800,000 a year.[111] This did not bode well for meeting the almost inevitably high wartime expenditure of the following year.

The current fiscal situation was becoming critical. Given the disparity between United States revenue in 1813 – essentially the net customs revenue of $13.2m accrued in 1812 – and the current level of expenditure in 1813 of $31.6m, as measured by Dewey, and shown in Appendix B as Table 5, virtual dependence on net customs revenue alone was clearly no longer adequate.[112] Especially following the shortfall of $10.6m in 1812, a deficit of no less than $17.3m in 1813 began to look serious.

By the end of 1812 the prospect of borrowing all of the $11m loan at par began to look poor. Until now this had been the usual American practice for such government loans as that authorised in the spring, but the outlook for the coming year was worsening.[113] The immediate shortfall had been met on 30 June 1812 with a $5m Treasury note issue and a $5m windfall tax yield from the 'unexpected' British imports, but, despite Gallatin's views, Congress had later cancelled the merchants' tax debt, costing the Treasury $9m in revenue.[114]

By mid-1813 all this had contributed to the first serious American financial setback of the war. Faced by Madison with the irreconcilable tasks of financing the war by taxing shipping and imports, while at the same time expected to support the administration's increasingly draconian enforcement of the government's trade restrictions, Gallatin's continued success at the Treasury looked improbable. Gallatin had long held that any war with Britain could be financed by borrowing, but only with continued foreign trade and the resultant prosperity of farmers, bankers, merchants and shippers, all traditional lenders to the government. He agreed that proposed 'direct' taxes, internal duties, additional tonnage duties and 'the diminution of drawbacks' could all be avoided, but only 'in the event of the suspension of Non-Importation'.[115] In this he was again frustrated by Congress, although unemployment and hardship were reportedly increasing under the Republicans' legislative trade restrictions, and increasingly by British blockade. Already, preparedness to lend to the government was demonstrably less than required.

In January Gallatin's revised estimate of outgoings for 1813 had been $36m, while expected income was only $17m: a shortfall of $19m.[116] On 8 February 1813 Congress authorised the call for a second, larger, wartime loan, this time for $16m, initially at 7% interest. To complete this loan it was necessary from the outset for the American government to accept bids below par, despite which not all American banks considered themselves to be in a position to help. After Congressional failure to renew the charter of the First United States Bank in February 1811 state and local banks had proliferated, but their capital was often in credit rather than assets, making them wary of long-term commitments. The American government had missed the chance of creating a major lender, and of launching a paper currency, thereby making itself dependent on private and state banks in which politicians often had a personal interest. On 5 March 1813 Gallatin had to inform Madison that 'We have hardly money enough to last to the end of the month.'[117]

Furthermore, the worsening shortage of British manufactures on the American market, caused by American restrictive legislation and British commercial blockade, was sheltering previously uncompetitive American manufacturing businesses from British competition. The prospect of abnormal profits attracted as financial capital those funds which might otherwise have been lent to the government.

On 25 February 1813 another $5m in Treasury notes was issued, paying little regard to Gallatin's advice for strict regulation of their number. Congress still made no provision for internal duties or 'direct' taxation to provide funds for the interest payments, and still refused to repeal the Non-Importation Act.[118] The loan subscription books were opened to the public on 18 March, with less than $4m subscribed.[119] The government's financial difficulties could not be kept confidential. The perceptive Providence merchant Thomas Ives had deduced by 19 March that 'The Loan Subscription must have fallen very short of the Sum proposed, & if money is found difficult to raise, it may tend to bring our Rulers to thinking seriously of their Ruinous War.'[120] The loan was filled only in April, after the books had been officially closed, when three foreign-born financiers were approached who between them produced almost two-thirds of the $16m needed. Even this was at a 12% discount, producing only $88 in specie and Treasury notes for every $100 in bonds. This stratagem was probably unrepeatable, having caused at least one lender financial embarrassment.[121]

Gallatin's frustration with continued Congressional obstruction, especially in the Senate, and disputes with John Armstrong, the Secretary of War, would end for the time being with the adjournment of the 12th Congress on 3 March 1813. But the arrival in Washington of the Russian government's offer of mediation on 8 March had presented Gallatin with an alternative to accepting personal responsibility for increasingly likely American fiscal and financial collapse and its resultant military and political defeat. On 11 March 1813 Madison had accepted the Russian offer, and Gallatin had at once offered himself as one of the team of American Peace Commissioners to be needed in Europe, which would necessitate his leaving both Treasury and Cabinet, although, perhaps, not immediately.[122]

Extraordinarily, Madison agreed, persuading Gallatin to remain at least nominally at the Treasury while someone was sought to deal with the Department's daily affairs, an arrangement never likely to succeed. Nevertheless, on 9 May 1813, before Congress reconvened, Gallatin left the Delaware for Europe.[123] Madison had lost his most experienced and financially best-qualified advisor. A special session of the 13th Congress began on 24 May 1813. On 3 June Madison still insisted that the Treasury office was not vacant, but on 7 June he declared William Jones, already Secretary of the Navy, as also Acting Secretary of the Treasury.[124]

Gallatin's wish to avoid supervising financial failure cost Madison much standing in Congress. Even after Gallatin had reached St Petersburg on 21 July 1813 Congress still refused to endorse his appointment as Peace Commissioner. Although his ability was widely recognised, he had long been resented as foreign-born. Some Senators thought he would be better kept at the Treasury; for others, the opportunity to defy and embarrass Madison proved irresistible. Gallatin was eventually 'appointed in recess of the Senate' on 29 March 1814.[125] He may not have been, as Adams later asserted 'the most fully and perfectly equipped statesman', but in losing such an experienced Cabinet colleague this early in the war, Madison lost his best hope of financing it to a successful conclusion.[126]

The $16m loan of 8 February had been filled, but at the cost of the breach of a number of important principles. The first had been Gallatin's own: that any war could be funded by borrowing only so long as neither domestic embargo nor British maritime commercial blockade interrupted American overseas trade, which could be relied on to provide the necessary funds and cooperative attitude. Madison's initial 90-day embargo had ended on 3 July 1812, but continued neutral and collaborative trade with the British were leading him towards suggesting another.[127] Having seen previous embargoes erode government revenue, Gallatin would not welcome another. Gallatin had also called in past favours to affluent friends, who had made very large personal contributions at some risk.[128] Almost certainly, this could not be repeated.

Formerly, American stock had been issued at par; bids for this loan had been accepted at a discount from the outset. Conventionally, bids were made before subscription lists closed; now, apparently, they could be re-opened. The Treasury was becoming reliant on the routine issue of Treasury notes to supplement loans, without repeal of the Non-Importation Act or the introduction of new taxes to guarantee that funds would be available to meet interest payments.[129] The Treasury notes of 1812 had been of $100 denomination, deliberately too large for general circulation. Those of 25 February 1813 were for $20, more likely to be commercially discounted for cash-in-hand, eroding their status, value and future usefulness. Meanwhile, the government itself would have to accept them at face value in loans and taxes. Once relinquished, all these principles were unlikely to be successfully re-established. By preventing net customs revenue from meeting wartime expenditure the British commercial blockade had forced the American government to borrow on increasingly vulnerable terms and, once established, the blockade was unlikely to be relaxed.

Meanwhile, British naval squadrons had continued their intelligence-gathering role. As early as March 1813 Warren's apparently well-informed contacts ashore clearly led him to believe that the Royal Navy's commercial blockade was proving effective. Prizes listed as carrying American grain and flour show that unlicensed exports of such commodities were becoming more difficult. On 9 March 1813 Warren wrote to Melville that he was 'happy to observe that the blockade established has already produced great Effect as the Farmers and others are under great apprehension of their produce not being sold: & the Distress it must occasion in the Eastern States'.[130] The reduction of imports by the British commercial blockade was also contributing to increasingly evident fiscal and political problems for the American administration. Even while at sea, Warren was able to write to Melville on 29 March that 'Madison is alarmed from not obtaining Cash … & the apprehension of the Discussion which must ensue in the Congress from the Necessity of Imposing Taxes to Pay the Interest of the Debt already created by the War'.[131]

Among other reports Warren forwarded to London on 5 June was an agent's 'letter out of Boston', dated 24 February 1813. It asserted that

> the American Government will be compelled by internal causes to
> Request peace before the ensuing Winter. The unpopularity of the
> War is Rapidly extending … and distress increases among the
> general classes of Society. [I]n the Eastern Country … a state of
> want little short of famine has forced the people to enlistment

obliging the government to increase expenditure it was already struggling to finance. Perceptively, the writer continued:

> The actual funds of the Government have been suddenly dissipated,
> and debts accumulated beyond the power of liquidity, of any yet
> arranged plan of finance, and public credit has received a mortal
> blow. From despair at receiving money (aggravated by the
> important events in the North of Europe) dismay has spread among
> the members of the administration in Washington.[132]

He forecast that 'propositions' would soon be made 'for discontinuing the War'. Less than three weeks before the date of the letter Congress had sought the $16m loan. The day after it was apparently written, the relative lack of response had prompted the second $5m issue of Treasury notes.

Madison had indeed called Congress to a special session on 24 May 1813, again recommending the internal excise duties and 'direct' taxes which his party had repealed on gaining office, in order to meet its mounting budget deficit.[133] The letter even forecast that 'the machine of Government must soon Stop', with the resignation of the 'Supreme Executive' and the 'Secretaries of State for War and the Treasury etc ... without waiting for the appointment of successors'. Madison was still in office, but, on 9 May, Gallatin had in effect done precisely as the letter had predicted. All Britain had to do, the writer suggested, was maintain its 'vigourous plan of hostility'.[134]

Throughout 1813 the level of American imports had continued to fall. According to North's corrected figures, shown as Appendix B Table 1, total imports had fallen by almost 72%, from $78,788,540 in 1812 to only $22,177,812 by 31 December 1813.[135] This had a predictable effect on net customs revenue. Even without taking into account the doubling of customs duty rates in July 1812, by 31 December 1813 the unadjusted totals of net customs revenue, intended to provide the bulk of tax revenue for 1814, had been almost halved, having fallen by more than 48%.[136] When adjusted for the changed rates of duty, net customs revenue for 1813 had fallen by no less than 65%.[137] Recognition of the sharp decrease in the major source of tax revenue in wartime was to lead during the summer of 1813 to urgent Congressional debate on alternative ways of raising revenue.[138]

The size of discount evidently needed to fill the $16m loan apparently concerned even those Congressmen reluctant to offend their constituents by supporting legislation for higher taxes formerly used by Federalists. In July 1813 Congress belatedly ended its almost sole dependence for revenue on customs duties by passing laws for a duty on imported salt, stamp duty on bank notes and bills of exchange, and internal excise duties on stills, sugar refining, carriages and auctions, and for gathering $3m in 'direct' taxes on the ownership of land and slaves. Including an additional duty on foreign tonnage, these were intended to produce net revenue of $5.6m.[139] Congress still contrived to drag its feet, however; these laws would not come into effect until 1 January 1814.[140]

By the summer of 1813 the impact of the British commercial blockade was discussed in Congress in terms which reflected the warnings given by, for example, Ezekiel Bacon before the United States declared war. On 21 July 1813 the Senate heard a letter from the still 'Acting Secretary of the Treasury' William Jones, which revealed that an 'additional sum of about $2m' would be needed before the end of the year to avoid 'delay and embarrassment'. This was in addition to $5.5m needed for the first quarter of 1814. Significantly, Jones estimated that 'custom-house duties' payable during the first three months of 1814 would provide only $1.5m. Another $250,000 might come from the sale of public lands and the new 'internal duties' due in operation on 1 January 1814. An additional $250,000 from the Treasury balance should make up the $2m.[141]

This, however, left a shortfall of $5.5m in meeting the $7.5m total expenditure until the end of March 1814, including $6m for the War and Navy departments, $400,000 for miscellaneous and diplomatic expenses and $1.1m 'for public debt', exclusive of the Treasury notes falling due in the new year. Senators heard that, without a further loan, in addition to that of $16m agreed on 8 February 1813, 'there would be, at that time, in circulation the sum of seven millions of dollars' in Treasury notes 'a sum greater, considering the limited state of our commerce, … than might perhaps be maintained in circulation without some difficulty or depreciation'. Jones sought Congressional authority for a further loan, this time for $7.5m, allowing the issue of another two million dollars' worth of Treasury notes to be postponed until after those issued in 1812 had been redeemed.[142]

This loan was sanctioned on 2 August, on condition that the stock was not sold at less than 88, a 12% discount.[143] It was completed at a lower discount of 11.5%, perhaps reflecting hopes of peace after the Russian offer of mediation. But, during 1813, the American government had sought to borrow a total of $28.5m in support of the war, and after this occasion no further attempt to borrow would be more than partially successful. Even the success of this loan would later be questioned.[144] Furthermore, the administration's overuse of Treasury notes, and a developing shortage of specie to redeem them or pay their interest, contributed to their becoming an unpopular liability.

During October 1813 Warren seems to have feared that the effectiveness of the British commercial blockade had been undermined by the American government's ability to borrow the $7.5m sought on 2 August, albeit at a discount. Warren appears to have been convinced that the British banker Alexander Baring, who had acted since before the war for both American merchants and the American government in London and Europe, had contributed towards the $7.5m government loan. On 26 October he wrote to Melville, evidently angered that 'British money' had been lent towards 'the vindictive war carried on against us'.[145]

Not having received an answer on this specific point from Melville, on 16 November 1813 Warren wrote a private letter, in his own hand, to Prime Minister Lord Liverpool:

> I wrote to your Lordship some time ago from the Chesapeake and stated my opinion respecting the Embarrassment of the American Government from the pressure of the War: I am however sorry that the great Source of their Difficulties have been removed, in obtaining an additional Loan of seven Millions of Dollars, through the aid of Messers Parish of Philadelphia, & the Mr Baring who was settled belonging to that House in America; consequently British Money is now used in the vindictive War carried on against us: and from his supply it is supposed the Government party may be enabled to continue their operations: without levying Taxes for another Year.[146]

Although partly perhaps because of his American marriage and business connections, Baring was later prepared to lend the American government small sums of money to avoid immediate embarrassments, nothing suggests his ever having lent enough to make any real difference to the outcome of the war. Baring was not unpatriotic by contemporary standards, much less traitorous. He was forthright in his condemnation of American opposition to British impressment.

Writing from London on 22 July 1813, as the American Peace Commissioner's bankers, to Gallatin in St Petersburg, Baring insisted that,

> highly as I value a state of peace and harmony with America, I am so sensible of the danger to our naval power from anything like an unrestricted admission of your principles, that I should consider an American as an inevitable concomitant of a French war, and to provide for it accordingly. It is useless to discuss the abstract question of right when it becomes one of necessity, and with us I sincerely believe it to be so.[147]

He even went so far as to continue

> If therefore, the disposition of your government be to adhere pertinaciously to the determination to give us no better security than the Act of Congress lately passed, I should certainly think your coming here or negotiating anywhere, useless for any good purpose.[148]

These opinions leave little room for doubt on Baring's support for Britain's position. Even if Baring had lent a significant sum to the American government at this stage, for which no evidence seems to exist, it would certainly not have allowed Madison's administration to meet an annual expenditure of $31.6m in 1813 without further taxation. As shown in Appendix B Table 5, the customs revenue of $13.2m for 1813 was added to by only $1.1m of miscellaneous receipts, making total receipts of $14.3m. This left a deficit of $17.3m. Even completely filled, the $7.5 loan would still have left $9.8m unfound. If all of the proceeds from the 25 February 1813 issue of $5m of Treasury notes had remained unspent, this would still have left an annual deficit of $4.8m. In this sense, even in 1813, the American administration was already bankrupt.

Warren concluded his intemperate letter to the Prime Minister with the incautious hope that 'the success of the Allied arms in Europe' might make possible 'some decisive strokes against the Enemy either upon the Lakes … or by a vigorous attack to the Southward in taking Possession of New Orleans.'[149] A private letter from a naval officer, written over Melville's head to the Prime Minister, is unlikely to have improved Warren's standing at the Admiralty, despite his earlier achievements and the clear effectiveness of his current commercial blockade.

Certainly, throughout 1813 the level of American exports had continued to decrease. According to Seybert total exports had fallen from $38.5m in 1812 to $27.9m in 1813, a further fall of almost 28%.[150] North's corrected statistics produce almost identical results.[151] The continuation into 1813 of licensed sales of American grain and flour, largely to the Peninsula, had so far slowed the rate of decline in domestic exports.[152] No such British needs protected the American re-export markets. The trans-oceanic import to America of exotic products such as cocoa and pepper was vulnerable to British commercial blockade, as was their re-export to Europe in American and neutral vessels. Traditionally, the British had an interest in the development of their own colonial re-export markets, increasingly threatened before 1812 by Americans.[153] Consequently, the fall in the American re-export trade was much more pronounced, from nearly $8.5m in 1812 to almost $2.9m in 1813, a decrease of 66.5%.[154] Although not as important to government revenue as falling imports, these figures meant unemployment at a time of rising prices, and falling incomes for merchants and shippers, good customers of the banks, potentially the administration's most reliable lenders.

Madison was apparently concerned not so much by the level of American exports as by their destinations. Foodstuffs especially were being sold to the vessels of the British blockading squadrons offshore and exported by American producers to British land forces in Canada and to the West Indies. Despite American use of British licences having become illegal in May 1813, grain and flour was still being shipped from the United States to Spain in useful quantities until October. Furthermore, the ports of New England were still, so far, open to neutrals.[155] The British maritime commercial blockade was clearly being selectively applied.

After failing to obtain a Congressional ban on this 'insidious discrimination' Madison made an Executive Order on 29 July 1813 making such trade illegal, to be implemented by the Secretary of the Navy and the War Department.[156] Illicit trade nevertheless continued in both American exports and British imports, as well as in supplies and intelligence between the American shore and British blockading vessels.[157] Madison's final embargo, including its ban on coastal trade and the ransoming of ships and cargoes, was eventually ratified by Congress on 17 December 1813.[158] However, its enforcement by the limited means at the Americans' disposal, especially around New Orleans, Savannah and Charleston, was later described by Mahan as 'manifestly impossible'.[159] Smuggling methods included the ransoming of vessels and cargoes, mock 'captures' by privateers and unofficial clear passages given in exchange for services rendered, but, most significantly, such smuggling, however achieved, added nothing to American government revenue.[160]

New York was not unique in experiencing price instability by 1813. By August 1813 something was having an effect on the prices producers received and consumers paid throughout the United States. How far these changes were caused by the American's own restrictive system, or by British maritime commercial blockade, or by both in unquantifiable proportions, is of fundamental importance. Attribution remains as difficult now as it seemed then. Writing in the mid 1890s, and citing Niles' *Weekly Register*, Henry Adams appears to have had no reservations in asserting that 'the pressure of the blockades was immediately felt'.[161]

The pressure included increasingly serious congestion of American ports by unused shipping. In early September 1813 Boston was reported to be holding ninety-one redundant square-rigged ships, usually employed in international trade, contributing to a total of 245 unemployed vessels, importantly excluding coasters.[162] By 25 September the *Columbian Centinel* reported that the interruption of coastal traffic was widening the economic impact of British blockade and American legislation. '[T]he long stagnation of foreign and embarrassment of domestic trade, have extended the sad effects from the seaboard through the interior, where the scarcity of money is severely felt. There is not enough to pay the taxes.'[163] By December 1813 200 square-rigged vessels reportedly lay idle in Boston harbour.[164] Efforts were made to supplement reduced coastal traffic with overland transport. A Senate Committee discussed a Chesapeake and Delaware Canal, to cost $850,000, but postponed any decision until the next session of Congress.[165]

The difficulties agrarian producers experienced in reaching markets by overseas shipping, traditional coasting, inland waterways and overland transport were evidently beginning to produce local gluts and distant shortages, and the dislocation of international and local trade inevitably made an impact on prices. Niles recorded for August 1813 that superfine flour sold in the port of Baltimore for $6.00 a barrel. Nearer its source, in Richmond, Virginia, it cost only $4.50, while in Boston the same quantity cost $11.87.[166] Similarly, upland cotton sold at Charleston, South Carolina, for 9 cents per lb, and in Boston for 20 cents a pound. In both Charleston and Savannah, Georgia, rice sold at $3.00 a hundredweight, but cost $12 in Philadelphia. A hundredweight of sugar fetching $9 in New Orleans cost $18.75 in Boston, between $21 and $22 in New York and Philadelphia and $26.50 in Baltimore. Adams concludes that 'Already the American staples were unsalable at the place of their production. No rate of profit could cause cotton, rice or wheat to be brought by sea from Charleston or Norfolk to Boston.'[167] Land transport was prohibitively expensive over long distances, and inland waterways were narrow, discontinuous and difficult to approach; finding their entrances often needed detailed local knowledge.[168]

Adams notes that 'soon speculation began', arguing that price inflation for imported commodities was due principally to scarcity created by British commercial blockade.[169] Certainly, by December 1813 price inflation in such commodities had become marked. A pound of coffee, which had sold for 21 cents in August 1813, cost 38 cents by the end of the year, an increase of almost 81% in five months.[170] The price of tea also rose by between 76 and 135%, having risen from $1.70 a pound in August to between 'three and four dollars in December', by which time sugar had almost doubled in price.[171] However, what proportion of these changes was attributable to British commercial blockade alone remains problematic.

Contemporaries had similar difficulties in attributing changes to either British blockade or American trade restrictions. On 21 December 1813 John Sheldon wrote a report to Congressman William Lowndes to 'assist in forming an opinion on the number of American seamen thrown out of employ by the war ... or the embargo'.[172] Without referring to their reduced wages or ability to pay, Sheldon reported that four-fifths of merchant seamen were unemployed by the end of 1813. This produced a sharp decline in revenue from a seaman's hospital tax, levied on wages decreased by competition for work, and increasing reluctance to pay such contributions among those still so far employed. The employers' use of casual labour at lower wage rates reduced the seamen's concern for their own future welfare, that of others, and hospital incomes.

The repeal of Madison's last embargo within four months of Congressional approval, together with repeal of the Non-Importation Act, would resolve the problem of whether British maritime blockades or the American restrictive system had been more responsible for American economic difficulties. After these repeals, American economic problems may be attributed more safely to British maritime blockades, which no longer at times coincided with American restrictive legislation. Madison became prepared to consider these repeals largely as a result of important news from Europe, which served to sharpen perceptions of reality among those Americans hitherto reluctant to face unwelcome truths.

On 30 December 1813 the British schooner *Bramble* arrived at Annapolis with a letter from British Foreign Secretary Castlereagh to Secretary of State Monroe, offering the American administration direct peace negotiations at Gothenburg in Sweden, in preference to Russian mediation. Constant awareness of British blockades, damaging both United States overseas trade and government revenue, as well as virtually preventing American naval intervention, may well have made immediate acceptance of the offer seem attractive, especially when considered with discouraging news of recent American progress in the land war. Disconcertingly outspoken criticisms of the war continued, especially from New England. First reports came from New London, Connecticut, of 'blue lights' being shown at night, apparently by traitors, to warn the British blockading squadrons of vessels attempting to break the blockade of the Thames. These alone might have induced in Madison's Cabinet an increased sense of realism.[173]

The *Bramble*, however, had also brought British newspapers. These included official reports of a comprehensive French defeat by Austrian, Prussian, Russian and Saxon Allies at Leipzig between 16 and 19 October 1813, which frustrated Napoleon's campaign in Germany. Just as British maritime blockade had hindered the American government's communication with potential European allies, this 'Battle of the Nations' ended any hope of financial, diplomatic or military help from France. Furthermore, it also meant that European markets were once again open to British exporters, making the French decrees which had formed the Continental System wholly ineffective. With British manufacturers and processors also importing their raw materials from alternative sources – such as raw cotton supplies from Brazil, adding to what could be smuggled from the southern United States – any further hope of the economic isolation of Britain was clearly unrealistic. As well as stopping Napoleon, the battle of Leipzig appears to have brought Madison to the conclusion that the last parts of the American restrictive system might as well be repealed.

ECONOMIC WARFARE IN THE PACIFIC

During 1813, in addition to Warren's commercial blockade of the American Atlantic coast, the Royal Navy's economic warfare against the Americans had also been extended into the Pacific. By the end of November the British government, the Admiralty and a London-financed fur-trading company had achieved their joint ambition to seize American assets in a contested area of Oregon, on the Pacific north-west coast of North America. The decision to attempt this had been taken as long before as the previous March. The British North West Company had successfully convinced the government that the seizure of an American fur-trading settlement on the Columbia river would serve national as well as their commercial interests. As a result the company storeship *Isaac Todd*, with partner Donald McTavish, had left Portsmouth on 25 March 1813, escorted by the frigate *Phoebe*, 36, commanded by Captain James Hillyar. His sealed orders were to proceed to the settlement known as Fort Astoria and 'totally annihilate any settlement which the Americans may have formed either on the Columbia River or on the neighbouring Coasts'.[174]

The trading post was named after John Jacob Astor, the same foreign-born entrepreneur who had earlier been sponsored by Secretary of the Treasury Gallatin, and who had, in return, raised over $2m of the $16m lent to the American government in April 1813. Astor had suspected British intentions, and had in June written two warnings to Secretary of the Navy Jones, but, despite having given financial help to the government, had been told that naval resources needed on the Lakes could not now be spared to help him.[175] This may very well have affected his preparedness to contribute further financial help to Madison's administration when, later, the need was even more urgent.

Reinforced with two 18-gunned sloops at Rio de Janeiro by Rear Admiral Manly Dixon in July, Hillyar rounded Cape Horn with his squadron, but lost touch with the *Isaac Todd en route*. Near the equator in October, however, Hillyar sent the sloop *Racoon*, under Commander William Black, onto the Columbia river alone, while diverting himself southward into the Pacific to search for the American heavy frigate *Essex*, known to be preying on the British whaling fleet there.[176] However, before HMS *Racoon* reached Fort Astoria, McTavish had arrived with a party of seventy-one trappers, and by 12 November had persuaded the local Americans to transfer the fort to North West Company ownership.[177]

On his arrival on 30 November Commander Black had only to formalise the arrangement, claiming sovereignty and renaming the settlement Fort George. By mid-December 1813 Black could inform Croker in London that the Americans were 'quite broke up' and left with 'no settlement whatever on this River or Coast'. While provisions lasted he would endeavour to destroy enemy vessels said to be 'on Coast and about Islands' in weather which had 'set in very bad'.[178] As on the other side of the Continent, the Royal Navy's world-wide reach had contributed to the erosion of the American financial capacity to sustain the war it had declared on the predominant naval power. When compared to the cumulative damage to the American economy and its taxable capacity, the loss of an enterprise on the Pacific seaboard is less important, except perhaps in its impact on morale in Madison's administration.

Other aspects of the ongoing economic warfare were also discouraging for the Republican administration. Throughout 1813 the ports of New England, primarily Boston, had remained open to neutral shipping, largely Swedish, Spanish and Portuguese, which Britain had allowed to continue in the hope of widening New England's differences with the rest of the Union. Nonetheless, New England's merchants, shippers and shipyards had suffered a marked decline in trade. Some referred openly to 'Mr Madison's War', and had long called the inverted tar barrels on the mastheads of disused vessels, intended to inhibit rotting, 'Madison's nightcaps'.[179] Some trade in grain and flour to Canada continued, but, by 1813, the re-export of West Indian products from New England in American vessels had fallen by 94.9% since 1811, to only just over 300,000 tons.[180]

By 15 December 1813 Boston harbour held ninety-one ships, two barks, 109 brigs and forty-three schooners, totalling 245 vessels excluding coasters, an accumulation Mahan attributes to the 'lack of employment'.[181] Similarly, Niles' *Weekly Register* recorded that, from 1 December to 24 December 1813, forty-four vessels were cleared from Boston for abroad, only five of which were American.[182] Evidently, by the end of 1813, even where neutral vessels were still so far allowed, and the cargoes imported in them paid some customs duties, the United States was not paying for its war by taxing foreign trade.

By orders dated 25 January 1814 Warren was to be replaced by Vice-Admiral Sir Alexander Cochrane, although his command was not to include responsibility for the reseparated West Indian stations. Cochrane was quick to express concern that the volume of apparently neutral trade through New England ports such as Boston could increase to such an extent that duties paid on imports arriving there might make a significant contribution to American fighting funds.[183] Cochrane officially assumed command on 1 April 1814, and promptly took steps to address the problem. The foundations for effective British naval and commercial blockades had been laid under Warren's direction, despite his multi-faceted responsibilities and numerous constraints. How effectively his successor might build on these foundations remained to be seen.

One measure of the effectiveness of the British blockades under Warren might be the amount of prize money made during his United Command. His estimated earnings of almost £100,000, including flag-money shared with junior flag-officers, were exceeded by very few commanders in other contemporary theatres.[184] Warren's earnings apparently became one of his major concerns, and so accurately reflected the intensity of the British commercial blockade. His reputation for avarice again surfaced in the correspondence of his prize agent and flag secretary George Hulbert, who wrote in November 1813 to his brother that Warren was 'growing so miserably stingy & parsimonious, that nothing occupies his thoughts but remittances, and it is an increasingly worrying conversation ten times a day'. This may have been something of an exaggeration, since Hulbert continued that 'but for getting rid of the Flag occasionally, and the prizes having been tumbling in pretty thick, I should desire to quit the concern'. This seems improbable, as Hulbert too was to make a fortune of perhaps £40,000 while in Warren's employment.[185]

Another measurement of its effectiveness might be the impact of the British commercial blockade on the political thinking of some Americans. As early as June 1813 a Philadelphia merchant confided his opinion of 'the great folks at the Capitol' to a friend, impugning even their motives.

> [W]as their intrigue for the advantage of their Country – they
> would not be Sencureable [sic: Censurable] but Everything that
> they do appears to Sink the nation further into distruction [sic]. I
> Expect the administration will be obliged to Treat for peace after
> the Nation is involved in a debt that the present generation will Not
> get clear of Should the Union remain.186

Neither the near truth of this prediction nor the effectiveness of Warren's blockades were yet as evident as they were to become.

Consequently, contemporary maritime historians were later unjust to Warren. Among them, William James, for all his meticulous recording of the numbers of guns, crews and tonnages of British and American antagonists, seems in his summary of Warren's command in North America to have missed the point of his successful application of economic warfare. In 1826 a second edition of James' *Naval History of Great Britain* was to maintain that 'After 15 or 16 precious months had been wasted in the experiment, the British government discovered that admiral sir John Warren was too old and infirm to carry on the war, as it ought to have been carried on, against the Americans'.[187] James failed to appreciate that, in laying the foundations of maritime blockade despite serious obstructions, Warren had begun the effective denial of American war aims.

CHAPTER 7

CAPITAL AND CREDIT: THE IMPACT OF THE FINAL PHASE

> I will yet hope we may have no more war. If we do, alas … we are not
> making ready as we ought to do. Congress trifle away the most
> precious of their days. (Mrs Madison to Mrs Gallatin, 7 January 1814)[1]

ON 1 JANUARY 1814 THE NEW TAXES authorised by Congress the previous
August came into effect. These internal excise duties, on the distillation and sale
of spirits, sugar refining, auctions, carriages, bank notes and 'negotiable paper',
were accompanied by 'direct' taxes on land, property and slaves. Customs duties
alone were failing to meet wartime expenditure and, with public borrowing
becoming increasingly difficult, taxation of a wider range of spending had
become unavoidable. But these distasteful revivals of earlier Federalist taxes
would, as before, have to be paid by the affluent, be predictably unpopular and,
if possible, be evaded. Worse, they were together estimated to yield no more net
revenue than $5.6m, not enough when set against the government's increasingly
urgent need.[2] Funds for the first three months of 1814 had been sought as an
additional loan of $7.5m, agreed in Congress the previous summer: a fiscal and
financial consequence of the United States declining overseas trade.[3]

By February 1814 Federalist Joseph Pearson of North Carolina told the House
that 'the expenditures of the Government, from January 1812, to January 1815,
will have exceeded ninety millions of dollars, exclusive of many millions of
outstanding claims'.[4] They had, in fact, exceeded $96.5m by December 1814.[5]
Pearson's estimate that 'the public debt will, at the close of the present year, exceed
one hundred and five millions of dollars' was particularly apposite in view of
Gallatin's reduction of the national debt to $48m in 1812 and $45.2m in 1813.[6]
Representative Pearson worried that 'the proportion which my constituents will
have to pay … unless you restore peace and commerce' would be 'more than they
are able to pay'.[7]

Pearson was in no doubt as to the cause of these reverses and the administration's
financial difficulties.

> Blocked up as we are by the enemy's squadron on our coast; corked
> up by our still more unmerciful Embargo and Non-Importation
> laws, calculated as it were, to fill up any little chasm of ills which the
> enemy alone could not inflict; the entire coasting trade destroyed,
> and even the pittance of intercourse from one port to another in the
> same State prohibited; the planters of the Southern and Middle
> States finding no markets for their products are driven to the
> alternative of wagoning [sic] it hundreds of miles ... or permitting it
> to rot on their hands.[8]

Given the country's reduced overseas and internal trade, he doubted whether sufficient credit could be found, or relied on in future, to support the Government's wartime financial demands. The administration's position would be 'bottomed on credit alone and therefore may fail'. 'If we had,' he said, 'a flourishing commerce between the States ... especially between the moneyed men and the moneyed institutions in all the States ... credit might be relied upon to almost any imaginable extent'. Since, however, the British commercial blockade's restriction of coastal traffic was hindering inter-state trade, 'the balance of trade, if trade it may be called ... being so entirely against the Southern and Middle States, the whole of our specie is travelling to the North and East'.[9]

It was precisely this difference between the interests of the different States which Warren's commercial blockade had sought to exacerbate by excluding New England from its restrictions. This division was now reflected in the varying prosperity of the different parts of the Union, even in the way in which the bank notes of one area were unacceptable in another, and in how specie was being concentrated in New England, so long opposed to the war.[10] Pearson put his finger on the vulnerable inter-relationship between the banks and the Government:

> Suppose some of the principal banks were to contract for the
> greater part of the proposed loan, and issue their own paper on the
> credit of the stock to be created; these bills not finding general
> circulation, or a shock given to the institutions, either by accident or
> mismanagement, what would be the situation of the Government?
> Their finances would be deranged, their credit impaired – enriched
> with debt, but their coffers empty.[11]

The Madison administration was to find obtaining credit increasingly problematic.

Until February 1814 William Jones, Secretary of the Treasury, was also Secretary of the Navy, probably an impossible combination of responsibilities for any man. He was by then anxious to leave the Treasury. His replacement was to be Senator George Campbell of Tennessee, who did not inspire confidence since he 'wanted promptness of action & more knowledge of finance'.[12] Madison had indeed offered the job to abler men, who had declined it. Before leaving office Jones presented his budget for 1814. He estimated government revenue for the year at $16m and outgoings as $45.4m, leaving a shortfall of $29.4m to be raised by loans and Treasury notes.

The growing lack of confidence in government creditworthiness meant that general interest rates were rising, so that, as foreign trade and therefore government revenue fell, money was being borrowed to pay interest on existing loans. As a result, Jones had also to recommend further new taxes.[13] This situation was described by Federalist Alexander Hanson as 'deceptive and disingenuous ... a most desperate system of fiscal gambling'.[14] Before the war, Gallatin had insisted that a war could be paid for by borrowing loanable funds created over time by profitable foreign trade, which would provide enough customs revenue to cover interest and finance the government's ordinary expenditure.

Nevertheless, on 24 March 1814 Congress authorised another loan of $25m and a further issue of $10m of Treasury notes. The Chairman of the House Foreign Relations Committee, John Calhoun, argued that 'The sum proposed' was 'indispensably necessary to meet the expenses of the ensuing year'. Even now some denied the need for further credit. Such opponents, Calhoun insisted, appeared 'bold in facing bankruptcy'.[15] Without these steps, the pro-government *National Intelligencer* predicted 'the bankruptcy of the Treasury; confusion and anarchy at home; and ... an ignominious submission to whatever terms the arrogance of the enemy might dictate'.[16] This was, however, to be remarkably similar to what was going to happen within a year, when the loan failed.

Meanwhile, the American strategy of maritime economic war on Britain remained theoretically unchanged into 1814. On 5 January Secretary of the Navy Jones had written to the commander of the *Constellation*, blockaded in Norfolk, Virginia, repeating his view that 'The Commerce of the enemy is the most vulnerable interest we can assail, and your main efforts should be directed to its destruction.' Optimistically, he had continued 'The ports of Georgia and North Carolina are the safest and easiest of access, for your prizes', before adding more realistically 'but the chances of recapture are so great, that no attempt should be made to send in a distant prize'.[17] Jones had earlier ordered that since 'the chances of safe arrival of the Prize are so few', both vessel and cargo should be destroyed.[18] The *Constellation*, moreover, was to remain blockaded for the remainder of the war, its crew progressively transferred to the Great Lakes.[19]

BRITISH NAVAL BLOCKADE

British counter measures to attacks on its merchant vessels had included both convoy and the naval blockade of American warships. As shown in Appendix A Table 2, by the end of 1813 the Royal Navy had blockaded in American ports, harbours, rivers and estuaries at least nine United States naval vessels, with more to be blockaded, captured or destroyed in 1814, four in Washington alone. Even according to a contemporary American account, British naval blockade had proved so effective that, of 1,613 British ships taken or destroyed by the Americans, throughout the war and across the world, only 172 had fallen victim to United States 'public vessels'.[20]

The British naval blockade, however, had not been an unqualified success. Poor winter visibility offshore contributed to occasional American blockade breaking. USS *President* had escaped from Providence, Rhode Island, on 4 December 1813, and the *Constitution* from Boston on 1 January 1814.[21] Every escape potentially threatened British shipping, but on this occasion the frigates appear to have taken only four prizes between them, owing partly to the rigorously enforced British convoy system. Eventually, each proved able to evade British patrols to regain an American harbour.[22] Admiralty instructions not to tackle the large American frigates single-handed had meant that HMS *Loire*, of 38 guns, had allowed the *Constitution* to return to Marblehead unmolested. The American brigs *Rattlesnake* and *Enterprise* also escaped into the Caribbean from Portsmouth, New Hampshire, in early January 1814, but of their eleven interceptions before their return in March only two were British: one a merchantman and the other a privateer.[23]

An important aspect of the success of the British maritime blockades of the United States, both naval and commercial, remained the number of British and neutral merchant vessels recaptured by the Royal Navy while sailing under prize crews to American ports. As shown in Appendix A Table 1, of the 121 prizes taken into Halifax, Nova Scotia, by the Royal Navy during the remaining twenty-eight weeks of 1812 after the American declaration of war, thirty-four had been recaptures – a substantial recovery rate of 28.1%. In 1813 the Royal Navy took 209 prizes into Halifax; excluding those of British and Canadian privateers, forty-two had been recaptures: a lower recovery rate of 20.1%. During 1814 of 135 Royal Naval prizes sent into Halifax thirty-six were to be recaptured British or neutral merchantmen, a rate of 26.7%. During the war and its aftermath, until May 1815, Halifax Vice-Admiralty court was to receive 473 of the Royal Navy's prizes. Of these, 116 were recaptures, an overall recovery rate of 24.5%. Other Vice-Admiralty courts operated in Antigua, Bermuda, New Providence in the Bahamas and Port Royal in Jamaica. If, overall, as Lloyd's of London reported to the House of Commons in December 1814, as many as 373 British vessels out of 1,175 captured by the Americans had indeed been recovered, a rate of 31.7%, then the Royal Navy prevented almost a third of American prizes reaching a port in the United States.[24] In preventing this proportion of United States captures reaching American ports the Royal Navy significantly offset the impact of the American strategy against British maritime commerce.

Measurement of the effects of British commercial blockade necessarily involves allowing for the comparative impact of the at-times-contemporaneous American restrictive legislation, especially Madison's second embargo, theoretically in operation until mid-April 1814. By the end of July 1813, concerned by exports of American grain and flour to the British army in the Peninsula and in Canada, food and timber to the West Indies and provisions supplied to British blockading squadrons offshore, Madison had convinced himself of the need for another embargo. Congress having refused to ratify his suggestion, Madison had imposed it by Executive Order through the Secretary of the Navy on 29 July 1813.[25] As shown in Appendix B Table 6, when first applied, and thought likely to be rigorously enforced, Madison's final embargo appears at first to have raised New England commodity prices considerably, notably sugar prices. In August 1813, within days of the imposition of Madison's second embargo, sugar prices in Boston had risen to 31 cents per lb, although by the new year they had fallen again by almost 42% when the embargo proved largely ineffective.[26]

Congress had been extremely slow to endorse Madison's demand for another embargo, but had finally agreed on 17 December 1813.[27] By then, however, much of its initial impact seems to have been lost. On 23 December 1813, still unaware that the rumoured Congressional approval had been given, a Boston business agent, Charles Greene, wrote 'We have no embargo yet, but we are in no hurry to receive it.'[28] With the embargo apparently not as strictly applied as had been feared, by late January 1814 sugar prices had reverted to an average of 18 cents per lb.[29] As evident from Appendix B Tables 7–12, average Boston prices of other commodities, including molasses, coffee and tea of various sorts, followed a remarkably similar pattern. News of the embargo thus had an effect on New England commodity prices which was marked but short-lived.[30]

Moreover, since the *Bramble*'s arrival on 30 December 1813 with news of Napoleon's comprehensive defeat at Leipzig implying more normal trade in Europe, any hope of an American embargo on trade hurting Britain more than the United States was seen by many to be unrealistic. In time, Madison himself reversed his opinion on his second embargo's likely effectiveness and, although no longer as directly concerned, the recently replaced Secretary of the Treasury, William Jones, also recommended lifting the embargo in order to gain revenue from trade, which in any case could not be stopped.[31] On 30 March 1814 Madison again addressed Congress on the embargo, but this time recommending its repeal, together with that of the Non-Importation Act. Operation of the embargo was immediately suspended and, despite outspoken opposition, the Act was repealed on 14 April 1814.[32] Madison's final embargo had lasted only eight months after his Executive Order, with less than four months between Congressional ratification and its suspension and eventual repeal.

The repeal of the embargo and Non-Importation Act creates an opportunity for comparison of apparent consequences, and the relative importance of American restrictive legislation and British commercial blockade as causes of the United States fiscal, financial and economic difficulties. The New England prices of a range of commodities can be systematically observed over the successive time periods covering the operation and repeal of Madison's final embargo, during the interval when neither American embargo nor British commercial blockade was in operation, and also during that period after 25 April 1814 when British commercial blockade was widened to include New England.

WIDER BRITISH BLOCKADE AND NEW ENGLAND PRICES

Commodity prices included in the correspondence of Brown & Ives, a long-established firm of import/export merchants of Providence, Rhode Island, in

New England, provide just such an opportunity for analysis of this kind. This prosperous and influential business, usually represented during these periods by partner Thomas Poynton Ives, had agents in Boston, New England's major port, Philadelphia and New York, and, despite the war, maintained contacts with both Washington and London.[33]

Prices in Boston, as reported to Providence, were sensitive both to events in Europe and to American political developments. On 25 April 1814 Thomas Ives wrote to Brown & Ives' commission agent in Boston about a cargo of sugar, newly shipped from New Bedford, Connecticut, to Boston. 'This article', he wrote, 'as well as several others has fallen very considerably [in price] since the Presidents (sic) recommendation to repeal the non-importation & Embargo Laws.'[34]

From averaging $22.19 a hundredweight on 19 March 1814, with the embargo still legally, if not very effectively, in operation, the price of sugar fell to an average of $15.32 on 16 April, by which time news of Madison's suspension, although not Congress's repeal, would have reached Boston – unwelcomed by those used to speculating on the short-lived panic caused by the 'restrictive system'.[35] News of the repeal of Madison's last embargo caused a fall of almost 32% in the price of sugar in New England since 19 March.[36] By 26 April the price of sugar in Boston had rallied slightly to $15.50, or $16.00 for those needing credit. Then, during three successive sales up to the 16 May, the average price of sugar in Boston settled at around that price, as shown in Appendix B Table 6.[37]

Boston prices were also responsive to British blockading activity. Charles Greene, Brown & Ives' Boston agent, wrote to them on 15 March 1814 that 'The recent captures by the British in the W[est] Indies have occasioned considerable demand for goods coming from there', and consequently higher prices for them.'[38] On 1 April 1814 Vice-Admiral Cochrane had succeeded Warren as commander of the British North America Station and had acted quickly on concerns that increased neutral trade with New England might contribute sufficient customs revenue to the American government to enable it to fund new naval building and finance further fighting.[39] On 25 April 1814 he had, therefore, issued a proclamation from his Bermuda headquarters instituting a British commercial blockade of the entire coast of America, including for the first time the ports of New England. The impact of this decision is reflected in Boston commodity prices.

Eight days later, on 4 May, Brown & Ives sent their Boston agent important instructions. Partner Thomas Ives wrote to Charles Greene:

> We are just informed of an arrival this morning at Boston from
> Bermuda bringing information of a Blockade of the whole Coast –
> this unexpected intelligence must have the effect to enhance the
> value of all foreign productions & you will doubtless avail yourself
> of it to dispose of our sugars for a good price.[40]

Only the day before – the last before Boston's dealers took the extended British blockade into account – Greene had informed Brown & Ives that the auction price of sugar in Boston had been $15.75 per short hundredweight. By 27 October 1814 the last date available from this correspondence before the end of the war, the price for the same amount of sugar had risen to $22.50, an increase of over 45%.[41] As shown by Appendix B Tables 7–12, average Boston prices of other commodities, including coffee, molasses and various teas, followed a strikingly similar pattern over the same periods, showing that the maritime British commercial blockade of New England made a greater proportional impact on Boston commodity prices than the former American 'restrictive system'.

The British commercial blockade became a major consideration for bidders and sellers at Boston commodity auctions. The day after the news reached them of its extension to New England, the price of 'Havannah' brown sugar fetched $16.00 cash, and $16.25 for those needing credit, beginning its climb to $23.00 by the end of September 1814, another increase of almost 43%. Greene noted the increased prices of sugar on 5 May and added that 'it is thought that they will improve still more in consequence of the news of the blockade'.[42]

The price of sugar in New England had fallen sharply with the repeal of Madison's final embargo, measuring the extent by which it had been inflated by the shortage it had caused. After a period of stability, when neither embargo nor blockade were in force, the British blockade was applied to New England. The price of sugar then rose by a considerably larger percentage margin, indicating the greater relative impact of the British commercial blockade. Comparison of New England sugar prices between the relevant time periods appears to provide empirical evidence of the relative importance of the United States restrictive legislation and British commercial blockade in imposing economic difficulties on the American economy. These difficulties, including inflation and unemployment, in turn produced fiscal and financial problems for the American government, determining its ability and preparedness to continue the war and influencing the terms on which it was ended.

After initial enthusiasm, both embargo and Non-Importation Act had been demonstrably ineffective for much of that time. In Eastport, Maine, for example, army officers expected to repress it had shown a 'blind indifference and an almost total disregard ... to the prosecution of an illicit trade'.[43] Conversely, the British maritime commercial blockade was to continue with reinforced squadrons, uninterrupted except by foul weather, for almost another ten months, from 25 April 1814 until peace on 17 February 1815. Measurement of its impact during this time is uncomplicated by American restrictive legislation other than a residual ban on importing British-owned goods, holding a British licence or trading directly with the enemy. The last restriction was certainly ignored, as when HMS *Nymphe*, off Boston, was supplied in June and July 1814 with stock, fruit, vegetables, books, newspapers and information from American boats.[44]

The entrepreneurial flair for which New England was famous meant that the implications of the extended British blockade were quickly investigated and put to the test. Business intelligence in New England was both quickly gathered and acted upon. By 24 May 1814 Thomas Ives knew of a letter from 'Captain Milner of the British ship *Bulwark* dated 4th inst. To the Spanish Consul at Newport

Communicating Ad Cochrane's proclamation [which] States that "no vessels will be suffered to depart with Cargoes" – it seems to imply that those in ballast will not be molested'.[45] His commercial agent in Boston quickly discovered that a Russian ship already in America when the blockade was extended, the *Nicholas Paulowitch*, could be insured there for $8,000. For a 5% premium of $400 the vessel would be covered to sail in ballast from Newport, Rhode Island, to the Spanish-held Amelia Island off the Florida border '& during the time she will be taking in a cargo' of raw cotton 'possibly for Gothenburg'.[46] The cover specifically excluded 'British capture from Newport to Amelia Island', and the whole contract pre-supposed that the Russian ship was not one of the three neutrals already 'ordered back to Rhode Island' for attempting to contravene the new British blockade. The plan came to nothing – the *Nicholas Paulowitch* was detained by the Royal Navy and sent back to Newport, presumably for trying to export a cargo to the Spanish on Amelia Island.[47] By 31 May the official *London Gazette* had informed neutral European governments that the whole American coast was under 'strict and vigorous blockade'.[48] It was also public news in American cities.[49] On 9 July 1814, in Baltimore, Niles' *Weekly Register* reported that 'The eastern coast of the United States is much vexed by the enemy'.[50] Consequently, when in July Greene attempted to insure the Russian ship for another attempt, he had to report to Brown & Ives that 'the underwriters decline altogether the risk of British capture'.[51]

The extended British blockade now clearly affected the volume of American trade, even when conducted in neutral vessels trading in and out of New England. Between 4 May 1814 and the peace, fourteen vessels attempting to reach Boston and other New England harbours from foreign ports were detained by the Royal Navy's blockading squadrons and sent into Halifax Vice-Admiralty Court for adjudication. Over the same period, privateers sent in two more. Between 4 May 1814 and the end of the war, the Royal Navy took and sent into Halifax alone a total of 130 prizes, both neutral and American. Both the *Boston Gazette* and the *Columbian Centinel* reported that, by the end of the war, foreign trade shipping movements from New England's major port had fallen to zero.[52]

Nor was the British commercial blockade extended to New England at the cost of relaxing it elsewhere; it remained rigorous and effective on other parts of the American coast. Pressure was maintained, for example, on New York by blockading the passage between the Connecticut coast and Long Island. When relieved from his station off New London on 30 May Captain Milne of HMS *Bulwark* wrote that 'The blockade has annoyed them very much, for they thought they would be allowed just to trade as usual on their taking off the embargo, and they were very much disappointed when I would not even allow them to trade along shore'.[53]

The crucial New England price changes during 1814 are reflected in Warren and Pearson's yearly and monthly indexes of 116 American wholesale commodity prices for 1814, shown as Appendix B Table 13, which provide evidence of the same pattern of price movements for the United States as a whole.[54] The monthly figures show that, having been constant at 182 for both March and April 1814, the index falls to 179 for May and June, reflecting the reduced opportunities for exploiting shortages formerly offered by the now repealed restrictive legislation. The index shows a continued fall for the summer months of 1814, from 178 in July to 177 for both August and September, partly as American entrepreneurs evaluated the possibilities of evading the widened British commercial blockade imposed on 25 April. This decrease is unlikely to be merely seasonal, as the index for these months in other years often rises. The index may also show a time-lag in the movement of wholesale prices in response to the extended blockade as rumours of peace persisted and as long as speculator's current stocks lasted. The deterioration in the condition of some stocks might make selling them increasingly necessary, thereby stabilising prices.

By October 1814, however, by which time neutral trade with America had been curtailed, even with New England, the wholesale price index rose sharply by six points to 183, the largest change in the index since the nine-point rise, apparently caused by Jefferson's embargo, between February and March 1809. The index rose further to 187 in November 1814, and again to 193 in December, making an increase since September of sixteen points. Without the interfering effect of restrictive legislation, the impact of the British commercial blockade of the United States, now including New England, is measured by the index of these American wholesale commodity prices rising by a remarkable ten points between October and December 1814, as shown in Appendix B Table and Graph 13.

Indeed, the only comparable changes in the index are the sharp declines, totalling seventeen points, between January and March 1815, when ratification of peace brought the British blockade to an end. It falls from 185 in February 1815 to 176 in March, a startlingly clear measure of the effectiveness of British maritime commercial blockade, and falls another twelve points between March and May 1815 as trans-Atlantic trade resumes. The decline is seen to continue until the end of 1816, when the resumption of American foreign trade appeared to be lasting, and the peace not merely an armistice The effectiveness of Britain's commercial blockade can probably be most clearly measured when the application of the strategy is ended. The same pattern is evident in a weighted annual index of all United States wholesale commodity prices 1800–1820, shown in Appendix B as Table and Graph 14.

Even while increasingly short of funds, the American government had apparently decided against redoubling of the rate of import duties on 1 January 1814, as Niles had pessimistically predicted in December 1813.[55] This decision was justified by the precipitate fall in American imports, shown in Appendix B Table 1, which had already fallen almost 72% between 1812 and 1813.[56] They were to fall almost another 42% between 1813 and 1814.[57] American imports between 1812 and 1814 had therefore fallen almost 84%.[58] For just over the last eight months of 1814 this fall had been due solely to the British commercial maritime blockade.

Decreased imports had produced a marked decline in net customs revenue receipts. As shown in Appendix B Table 3, net customs revenue for 1813 had shown a real decrease of over 65% with allowance made for the doubling of the rates of import duties on 1 July 1812.[59] By the end of December 1814 net customs revenue had fallen another $2.2m to an unadjusted $4,694,318, a further fall of almost a third, the imports of both years being taxed at the higher rates.[60] With adjustment made for those periods subject to the doubled tax rate, during the years from January 1812 to the end of December 1814 net customs receipts had fallen by no less than 76.5%.[61] The absence of adjustment for the American doubling of import duty rates in July 1812 has in the past partially obscured the impact of the British commercial blockade of the United States.[62]

Comparatively, Jefferson's embargo, in force between 22 December 1807 and 15 March 1809, had reduced government income, almost entirely composed of net customs revenue, from $17.1m in 1808 to $7.8m in 1809, a fall of almost 55%, eroding Gallatin's accumulated surplus of $17m.[63] Any decrease in revenue of over 50% was serious, but is supplanted by one of over 76% which necessitated government borrowing under difficult circumstances. Adjustment for change in the rate of duty therefore allows a comparative assessment of the fiscal impact of Jefferson's embargo with that of the British maritime commercial blockade between 1812 and 1815. For less than a third of the war, British commercial blockade was accompanied by American restrictive legislation which was clearly intermittent, unevenly applied, poorly enforced and widely evaded.[64] The major cause of the loss of more than three-quarters of American net customs revenue between 1812 and 1814 may therefore be attributed proportionately to British commercial blockade.

BRITISH COMMERCIAL BLOCKADE AND AMERICAN TRADE: EXPORTS

Exports were not taxed, but the unemployment, inflation and disruption resulting from the loss of overseas markets further damaged the American economy and government creditworthiness.[65] As shown in Appendix B Table 15, American total exports had fallen from $27.9m in 1813 to only $6.9m in 1814, a decrease of more than 75%.[66] During Seybert's accounting period from 1 October 1813 to 30 September 1814 fear of loss had deterred many American exporters from shipping goods and produce worth more than three-quarters of the value of the previous year's exports; others made the attempt. Seybert records the value of cargoes reported as having left American ports, not the value of exports successfully reaching foreign harbours. Between 1 October 1814 and peace on 17 February 1815, the Royal Navy detained and sent into Halifax ten vessels ranging from 250 to 17 tons which had left American ports with cargoes for foreign destinations in breach of the British commercial blockade.[67]

The loss of American exports during the six months from the embargo's suspension on 30 March to 30 September 1814 was due wholly to the British commercial blockade. But while American exports condemned by British Vice-Admiralty Courts during the last three months of 1814, and until 17 February 1815, will have reduced exports during the accounting year from 1 October 1814 to 30 September 1815, the figure is probably impossible to separate from the great increase in American exports after peace was ratified.[68]

Even in the early stages of the war the prosperity of American foreign trade had been heavily dependent on the export of wheat, oats, maize, rice, barley and rye, together with flour, bread and biscuits. Five hundred licences had been issued to American shippers to allow supplies to continue to the British Army in the Peninsula.[69] Lisbon prices, 'frequently double' those elsewhere, had 'spurred the American farmer and merchant to greater and still greater effort'.[70] However, after May 1813 the Peninsular Army no longer relied on American grain and flour. Supplies of American flour to Spain and Portugal peaked during 1813 such that saturation point was reached and prices fell.[71] The issue of new British licences was suspended. Usually valid for three or six months, genuine licences became scarce and forgeries more obvious, and during 1814 this once lucrative trade collapsed. If Congressman Timothy Pitkin's high estimate for 1813 is accepted, sales of American flour to the Peninsula between 1813 and 1814 fell by more than 99%. With Madison's embargo suspended after March 1814, the British commercial blockade ensured that this trade was not replaced by sales elsewhere.[72] By the end of 1814 overall American wheat and flour exports had fallen since 1813 by more than 85%, maize and meal exports by more than 90%.[73] Comparatively, even Jefferson's 1808 embargo had been less severe: although it reduced such exports by 81% they had largely recovered in 1809.[74]

AMERICAN RE-EXPORTS

Most American imports intended for re-export were entitled to a rebate of the import duty paid on entry, known as 'drawback', less a small administration charge. Other re-exports, such as foreign wines, teas, coffee and spices, were not, so their import for sale abroad added to government revenue, as did the tonnage, lighthouse and harbour dues paid by all exporters. However, as evident from Appendix B Table 15, by 30 September 1814 American re-exports had fallen precipitously from $2.8m in 1813 to only $145,000, a decrease of almost 95%.[75] Between 1811 and 1814 American re-exports of sugar fell by more than 99%, cocoa by 98.8% and coffee by almost 98%. Pepper re-exports of 3m lbs in 1811 fell to nil in 1814.[76] The contribution of re-exports to American revenue, while never large, fell from $123,418 for the year ending 30 September 1813 to $7,932 by the same date in 1814, a fall of almost 94%.[77]

BRITISH COMMERCIAL BLOCKADE AND AMERICAN TRADE: ECONOMIC EFFECTS

For comparison, Jefferson's 1808 embargo had caused a fall of over 68% in the overall foreign trade of the United States (imports and total exports combined), shown in Appendix B Table 16.[78] This, however, had been followed by a 40% recovery in 1809.[79] Combination of import and export figures reveals an *average* value of overall American trade in 1810–11 approaching $138m, as the effect of Jefferson's embargo receded.[80] By 1812 it had fallen to $117m, by 1813 to $50m and by 1814 to less than $20m. American restrictive legislation and British commercial blockade, at times contemporaneous, were making a marked impact.

The decrease in overall American foreign trade during 1812 had not been as great as pessimists had feared, with the effect of Madison's first embargo offset by determined attempts to beat it, the prolonged dispute over its terms and delayed British commercial blockade. Total American foreign trade decreased from $119.2m in 1811, to $117.3m in 1812, a fall of only 1.6%. The fall in total American foreign trade between 1812 and 1813 was caused by the continued effect of Non-Importation legislation and escalating British blockade, and exceeded 57%.[81] It was followed not by recovery but by a further fall of over 60%.[82] Most significantly, between 1812 and the end of 1814, United States total foreign trade fell by more than 83%, reduced after April 1814 by British commercial blockade extended to the whole American coast, unaccompanied by the effects of domestic legislation.[83]

BRITISH COMMERCIAL BLOCKADE AND THE AMERICAN MERCANTILE MARINE

Jefferson's year-long embargo is held by Gardiner to have caused the unemployment of 55,000 seamen and 100,000 ancillary workers.[84] The cumulative effects of two successive years of reduced American foreign trade are likely to have been greater. Incomes lost in maritime unemployment and depression would have reduced total spending and other employment, and the ability to pay tax or lend to the government.

In 1811 the British merchant marine was comprised of over 20,000 vessels and, with a combined tonnage of almost 2.25m, was the world's largest.[85] However, in the course of Britain's war against Napoleon, the blockade of French merchant shipping by the Royal Navy had allowed neutral shipping, especially American, to expand rapidly. Gallatin estimated that between 1803 and 1807 the American merchant fleet had grown by 70,000 tons a year and had become the largest neutral fleet.[86] By 1807 over a million tons of American merchant shipping carried the United States' foreign trade, almost 93% of all vessels doing so, including foreign 'bottoms'.[87] As is clear from Appendix B Table 17, Jefferson's embargo of 1808 reversed the trend. Nevertheless, in 1811, 948,247 tons of American shipping had carried the United States' foreign trade, still almost exclusively in its own ships. Madison's 90-day embargo and British blockade together were to reduce this by almost 30% to 667,999 tons by the end of 1812.[88]

By the end of 1813 British blockade of Chesapeake Bay, the Delaware River and some American southern ports had produced a further 65% decrease in the tonnage of American shipping carrying United States foreign trade.[89] These blockades had been supplemented to some extent after August by Madison's Executive Orders banning exports and coastal traffic, although widespread corruption and collaboration had done little to reduce their evasion.[90] By mid-April 1814 these restrictions were lifted. Thereafter, decreased United States foreign trade was due solely to British blockade, now extended to the whole

American coast. The tonnage of American vessels engaged in United States foreign trade between 1813 and 1814 fell by almost 75% to only 59,626 tons.[91] This shows the final strangulation of the American foreign carrying trade exclusively by British blockade for the eight and a half months from mid-April to the end of December 1814.

Before the war, larger ocean-going vessels had conventionally been 'Registered' for each separate voyage, a fee going to the Treasury. Coastal vessels could be 'Enrolled' – licenced for a fixed annual payment for an unspecified number of voyages.[92] A fee was also paid for fishing vessels when in use, although the extent of smuggling, informing and collaborative victualling of British blockading squadrons meant that these were not used exclusively for fishing. Whether or not fees were actually paid for registration, enrolment or fishing depended on the current level of American legislative restriction, the prospects of profitable trade in competition with the still-expanding British merchant fleet, and the likelihood of British capture. Although American embargoes were in force for less than one-third of the war's duration, the Non-Importation Act had forbidden American imports until mid-April 1814. Its repeal, however, had almost coincided with an increase in the range and severity of British blockade. The sense in an American ship-owner paying to take part in either overseas or coastal trade therefore remained limited.

As is shown in Appendix B Table 18, of almost 675,000 tons of American shipping potentially available for foreign trade in 1813, only 37% was thought worth registering for specific voyages.[93] As Mahan argues, of these 'many doubtless sailed under British license'.[94] By the end of 1814, when British commercial blockade alone constrained American trans-oceanic trade, the proportion of suitable shipping with registration duties paid had fallen to 8.7%.[95]

The annual enrolment fee, paid irrespective of the number of voyages made, left operators free to exploit opportunities to leave port as they arose, and enrolments rose by almost 40% between 1812 and 1813.[96] Despite this, the proportion of enrolled vessels for which duty was paid also fell, from almost 54% in 1813 to 41% in 1814.[97] As British maritime blockade tightened even the proportion of fishing vessels actually paying duty fell between 1813 and 1814 by 11.2%. Between 1813 and 1814 total new building also fell by 8.7%, from 32,583 to 29,751 gross tons, reflecting a lack of demand for shipping space. This rate was probably too low to offset the rapid depreciation of the under-used United States merchant fleet, but fails to justify Mahan's assertion that American shipbuilding had 'practically ceased'.[98]

The widening British maritime commercial blockade severely affected the American whaling 'fisheries' in 1814. The total tonnage of American deep-sea whaling vessels had fallen from 2,942 in 1813 to only 562 in 1814, a decrease of over 80%. Settlements largely dependent on whaling, such as New Bedford, Connecticut, began a long-term diversification into textiles. The number of vessels whaling from Nantucket had halved since the war began, adding to the island's isolation and hardship and to its need for a negotiated neutrality.[99]

BRITISH COMMERCIAL BLOCKADE AND THE SIZE OF PRIZES

Further evidence of the ever-tightening British commercial blockade by 1814 can be found in the smaller average size of the ship-rigged vessels and brigs brought into Halifax as prizes as the war progressed. Risk limitation also explains the *rising* average size of the faster schooners and sloops detained by the Royal Navy and brought into Halifax until May 1815.[100] The average size of ship-rigged vessel detained by the Royal Navy and brought into Halifax in 1812 had been 317.2 tons. By 1813 this average had fallen to 309.7 tons, and to only 263.1 tons by 1814. No ship-rigged prizes were recorded as having been brought into Halifax between then and May 1815. The average size of brig sent into Halifax as a prize in 1812 had been 191.4 tons, falling to an average 176.0 tons in 1813 and to 166.4 tons in 1814. The four brigs detained in Halifax early in 1815 averaged only 165.3 tons. The average size of all American vessels newly built as replacements was also decreasing.

Conversely, the average size of schooners and sloops seems to have risen, as these were faster and more frequently used in attempts to evade American customs officers (while restrictive legislation still applied), as well as British blockading squadrons. The average size of schooner sent into Halifax in 1812 had been 71.3 tons. By 1813 this average had risen to 93.4 tons and, by 1814, to 135.7 tons. The size of the three schooners sent into Halifax in early 1815 averaged as much as 144.0 tons. The average size of sloop detained also rose as the British blockade tightened. Averaging only 55.5 tons in 1812, sloops detained in Halifax averaged 69.3 tons by 1813 and 73.6 tons by 1814, although carrying relatively little to earn revenue when compared with the ships and brigs they displaced. The average size of American schooners and sloops newly built as replacements, was also increasing.

The unrelenting British blockade and the occasionally contemporaneous American restrictive legislation until mid-April 1814 appear to have induced an unwillingness to risk the capture of larger and more valuable vessels and cargoes, not to mention their crews. Prohibitively expensive insurance premiums would have added to this reluctance, especially when payment by insurance companies might fail to meet litigation costs. Financial capital would tend to become scarce and expensive as the risks of using larger vessels became more evident and alternative investments progressively more attractive, among them cotton processing and textile manufacture, ironically protected by the blockade's exclusion of normally cheap British cloth.[101] For those remaining in shipping, smaller cargoes in faster vessels, preferably on inshore journeys, would become a more acceptable risk than a trans-oceanic voyage risking confiscation of a larger vessel and its costlier cargo.

The average tonnage of prizes at different times seems at first to indicate that the British commercial blockade was at its most successful during Warren's United North America and West Indies command in 1813, not in 1814 when, after 1 April, Cochrane assumed command of the reseparated North America station. Considering the Halifax Vice-Admiralty Court alone throughout, in 1812 a total of 121 captures amounted to 17,702 tons with an average of 186.34 tons. In 1813 a total of 209 vessels reached 26,795 tons, albeit producing a lower average size of 161.42 tons as smaller schooners and sloops began to be used in preference to larger ships and brigs. In 1814 135 vessels were sent into Halifax, together making a total of 15,212 tons, with an average of a still-lower 139.56 tons. Although the Treaty of Ghent received American ratification in mid-February 1815 prizes continued to arrive in Halifax until May 1815: eight, totalling 1,093 tons, produced a higher average of 156.14 tons, perhaps indicating shippers' attempts to 'jump the gun' with larger vessels before ratification. However, after 1 April 1814, when Cochrane took over, a higher proportion of vessels detained may have been sent to other ports, many in the now reseparated West Indies stations, in preference to Halifax, since Vice-Admiralty Courts also operated in Bermuda, the Bahamas, Jamaica and Antigua.[102]

BRITISH COMMERCIAL BLOCKADE AND THE AMERICAN FISCAL PROBLEM

Throughout the war the British commercial blockade remained selective. In Britain, the Opposition referred throughout to industrial unemployment caused partly by overproduction in anticipation of new South American markets. This was, however, eased to some extent by continuing American demand for British manufactured goods met by imports through British occupied Castine and Spain's Amelia Island. The British commercial blockade had never sought to prevent American trade entirely, nor had British policy-makers ever intended that it should. It was clearly in British interests that American flour, livestock and timber continued to reach the British West Indies and the army in Canada, and it was similarly important that supplies reached the blockading squadrons at sea and the Lancashire cotton mills. Nevertheless, the British commercial blockade had been sufficiently effective to ensure that, as import duty revenues failed, the American government turned for war finances to the 'direct' taxes and internal excise duties they had once opposed in principle, and to progressively less productive borrowing. By 1814 the fiscal effects of reduced trade, worsened by persistent and self-interested Congressional procrastination, had accumulated. As shown in Appendix B Table 19, a shortfall in American total revenue in relation to total expenditure had become evident well before the end of 1812.[103]

The 'direct' taxes on property, in effect from 1 January 1814, were initially fairly successful in their first year, producing $2.2m of the $3m due, almost 74% of their expected yield. In 1815, however, they actually collected less money when their expected yield was doubled to $6m. Internal excise duties were less successful in 1814, collecting only $1.9m of the $3.3m expected, less than 59%. Internal duties were also inefficient. Writing in 1818, John Bristed recorded the cost of their collection, calculated to be as high as 8.5% of their actual receipts in 1814 and still 5.9% even in 1815, most of which was in peacetime.[104] While the war lasted, even taxes once used by the government's Federalist opponents would do little to rectify a growing shortage of revenue.

As Ezekiel Bacon, among others, had warned Congress before the war began, as British commercial blockade continued and war costs mounted, customs revenue increasingly failed to meet expenditure. As is evident from Appendix B Tables 19–21, total tax revenue in 1812 had been less than 44% of total government expenditure, in 1813 under 42% and, by 1814, only just over 28%.[105] Even including miscellaneous receipts, total government income excluding borrowing formed less than half of government expenditure in 1812, and less than a third by 1814. Customs revenue of only $7.3m in 1815, just $1.3m more than for the last whole year of war, suggests that the British commercial blockade remained effective up to, and perhaps someway beyond, the Treaty of Ghent's ratification, and that the Connecticut Federalist Timothy Pitkin's figures, purporting to measure the post-war recovery of American foreign trade, are a serious over-estimate.[106]

BRITISH BLOCKADE: SPECIE, CAPITAL AND CREDIT

Between 1812 and 1814 the United States had an adverse Balance of Trade: the total of goods imported had exceeded that of goods exported by over $40m.[107] This relative lack of American exports meant that goods imported – either brought legitimately into the United States in neutral vessels or smuggled – usually had to be paid for with money in the form of precious metal. Since only New England's ports were open to neutral shipping before April 1814, internal American trade in imported goods brought much of the specie formerly held in the middle and southern states into the New England states. By June 1814 Massachusetts banks had accumulated $7,326,000 as specie holdings, compared with $1,709,000 in the same month in 1811.[108] According to Niles, in 1810 Massachusetts bank deposits had totalled $2,671,619, of which 58% was specie; by 1814 deposits had grown to $8,875,589, of which 72% was precious metal.[109] In March 1814, shortly before Cochrane's extension of British commercial blockade to New England, Charles Greene, Brown & Ives' agent in Boston, could report to them that

> Money has been very abundant here, but I observe that some of our own capitalists who have had 30 to 70,000 dollars in the bank have disposed of their Surplus funds.[110]

The risks imposed by the British commercial blockade, although at that date still excluding New England, ensured that many such funds were to be diverted away from traditional shipping into, for example, textile production.[111]

This accumulation of money by the merchants and bankers of New England sometimes led to the unrealistic expectation of their lending much of it to the American government. Greene had continued 'I believe some have bo't [bought] govt paper, altho' many think it will experience a very great Depression.'[112] Elsewhere, this reluctance caused caustic comment and peremptory demands.

Greene further reported that 'The New York banks have agents here to raise money, and it is asserted that the Manhattan bank has requested from the Boston bank a loan of 300,000 dollars!!'[113]

Moreover, specie flowed out of New England not only in payment for imports but also in the search for a safe return in securities other than the American government's bonds, despite its increasing need for funds. Nevertheless, in April 1814 both houses of Congress had rejected a bill to forbid the export of specie on the grounds that it was probably impossible to prevent. Federalist Elisha Potter had argued in the House that 'you might as rationally [seek to] prevent the ebb and flow of the tide'.[114] This goes far to explain Greene's revelation that in Boston

> Gold grows scarce. Several persons have been engaged in carrying it to Canada for the purchase of [British] Govt bills; 60,000 dolls in gold were carried in the last weeks for one merchant. These trips consume from 8 to 12 days and leave a net profit of from 4 & 5 per Cent.[115]

Probably impossible to keep confidential, such profit-maximising activities were seen elsewhere in the United States as unpatriotic, even traitorous, especially since the American government was becoming increasingly short of funds. In the House as early as February 1814 Republican John Jackson of Virginia had described money lenders withholding funds as unpatriotic, and his fellow representative Felix Grundy had repeated an earlier description of those who, by such measures as exporting specie, 'combine together for the purpose of preventing loans being filled' as 'guilty of treason from a moral point of view'. Grundy invoked the Federalist's Sedition Act of 1798, passed during America's Quasi War with France, which had made it illegal to 'combine or conspire together, with intent to oppose any measure … of the Government of the United States'.[116] The export of specie nevertheless continued; on 3 August Greene again noted that 'very large quantities of Specie have been sent to England and its possessions'.[117] Throughout 1814 about $3.8m in specie left the United States for Canada to buy British government bonds and commercial bills of exchange.[118] Those who seek to deny the existence of such an outflow of specie from the United States by 1814 are clearly mistaken.

THE BRITISH IN WASHINGTON: MANIFESTATION, CAUSE AND EFFECT

By 26 August 1814 British command of the American eastern seaboard, and the ability to mount complex and logistically demanding amphibious operations without effective opposition, had borne fruit in the form of the successful capture and brief occupation of Washington. The financial and political effects of its seizure were to be far-reaching. The loss of the almost complete heavy frigate *Columbia* and sloop *Argus*, and the burning of Washington Navy Yard with its timber-yards and ropewalks, were relatively unimportant. The yard's $417,745 net repair costs were comparatively trivial. And more significant in the long run than the destruction of the unfinished Capitol building, Treasury and War Office, and the burning of the President's House, was the reaction of American banks.[119] Unsurprisingly, an immediate run on Washington banks denuded them of most of their specie. On 31 August banks in Baltimore and Philadelphia announced that they too had suspended specie payments, as did banks in the southern and middle states, to protect their already depleted reserves. Significantly, the presidents of six Philadelphia banks began their 'public proclamation' of their suspension of specie payments with:

> From the moment when the rigorous blockade of the ports of the United States prevented the exportation of our produce, foreign supplies could be paid for in specie only, and as the importations … into the eastern states had been very large, occasioned a continual drain on the banks. This drain has been much increased by a trade in British government bills of exchange which has been extensively carried on, and has caused very great sums to be exported from the U. States.[120]

In their estimation, British commercial blockade had been a direct and immediate cause of their need to suspend specie payment.

On 1 September New York banks declared their suspension permanent. Then came news that, between 29 August and 2 September, the port of Alexandria had accepted terms offered by another British amphibious force, by which twenty-one American ships, stores and merchandise were surrendered.[121] On 6 September the shockwave reached Boston where, Greene wrote, 'All classes of people have been drawing specie out of the banks today'. By 12 September 'The panic' there was 'almost universal'.[122] When Congress reconvened on 19 September the government had to admit that specie suspensions by those banks 'most important in the money operations of the Treasury, has produced, and will continue to cause difficulties and embarrassments in those operations'.[123]

The British action also had adverse commercial effects. 'The Suspension of Specie payments by the Banks in Phila. and New York', complained Ives in October, 'causes great difficulty and renders it almost impossible to draw funds from New York … little or nothing is doing in business and our goods remain as yet on hand'.[124] He received scant sympathy from Philadelphia, where suspension was 'considered a prudential matter, and unless your Eastern banks adopt the same plan, they will be drained of their Specie should the war continue much longer'.[125] To remain solvent, even New England banks with large specie reserves, and regulated by State laws, were ultimately obliged to suspend cash payments.

Suspensions of specie payments also created immediate problems for a government needing to buy unprecedented quantities of manufactured goods, primary products and services. The wartime proliferation of banks had complicated all transactions, since banknotes were not always acceptable at face value. Compared with 1811, when eighty-nine banks had a combined capital of $52m, by 1815 208 banks had a combined capital of $82m. Over the same period note circulation increased by more than 100%, from $22m to $45m, while specie holdings increased by only 67%.[126] While this increase in money supply alone would not make inflation inevitable, it made those supplying goods and services to the government wary of accepting banknotes which eventually might prove worthless.

An under-appreciated link clearly exists between British naval blockade, which prevented the intervention of American naval forces in British amphibious operations, and the serious financial consequences of the British incursions. The over-issue of banknotes had already been causing their depreciation, but British landings, largely protected by the Royal Navy's containment of American warships, and the subsequent occupation of Washington, had made American monetary problems considerably worse. As a result, paper currency now circulated 'at a discount of 7% in New York and Charleston, of 15% in Philadelphia, of 20 and 25% in Baltimore and Washington, with every other possible variation in other places and States'. Congress heard that banknotes had been 'placed on a new and uncertain footing', affecting 'the pecuniary operations of the citizens in general'.[127] In Boston, instead of cash, the government offered holders of maturing bonds either discounted Treasury notes, inconvertible Massachusetts State banknotes or the undemanded new government bonds.[128] The discount rate on Treasury notes, a useful barometer of public confidence in the government's financial credibility and the plausibility of current peace rumours reportedly varied between 15 and 25%.[129]

BRITISH BLOCKADE AND THE COLLAPSE OF AMERICAN PUBLIC FINANCE

The American government's accounts for 1813, published in 1814, showed, encouragingly, that the $16m loan Congress had authorised on 8 February 1813 had been raised, even slightly exceeded.[130] No less than $534,200 had been raised with 6% Stock bought at par by early subscribers, also given thirteen-year annuities with 1.5% interest to compensate for the better deal given to latecomers, who got a 12% discount, receiving $100 in stock for every $88. This had raised another $15,468,800. Altogether, Stock for a nominal $18,112,377 had been issued to raise $16,003,000.[131]

Since this last success, however, the lack of overseas and domestic trade had further reduced loanable funds and the government's credit. Of the $7.5m loan sought on 2 August 1813 only $3,907,335 had been raised in 1813, leaving $3,592,665 still to be found. This would involve selling each $100 worth of Stock for $88.25.[132] By this time, however, the Treasury's need for funds was such that Congress sanctioned a $10m issue of Treasury notes and, on 24 March 1814, authorised an attempt to raise an unprecedented $25m in three instalments.

Even before the new loan stock went on sale the public attitude to the loan was unpromising. One Philadelphia merchant wrote 'as yet the Govt meet with little Success in this City in obtaining Money ... at this date I have No Idea that it will fill'. More specifically, he added that neither 'Banks nor Insurance offices

… intend to take any … Mr Girard do not intend to Loan them any and I believe Mr Parish has as much as he can well get along with.'[133] The reply confirmed his news that a prominent shipping business had stopped payment 'in consequence of New York failures', and predicted that 'establishments of considerable consequence will follow'. He added that 'the Govt … has obtained only a very limited sum in New Eng'd'.[134]

When, after 2 May, the Treasury offered the first $10m of securities, subscriptions were initially received for $9.8m. However, $5m of this was offered by the New York banker Jacob Barker, whose ability to find the money had been doubted at the outset. Jones wrote to Madison describing Barker as a 'speculative individual' and his offer as the 'bold effort of a gambler'.[135] Barker eventually paid $3.5m into the Treasury, but defaulted on the remaining $1.5m. As predicted, others had defaulted on another $400,000, and, of the $10m hoped for, the government received only $7.9m, even when offering a 12% discount.[136] Early buyers, finding latecomers getting a better price, insisted on additional stock as compensation, making it in their interests to depress the price further by pessimism and delayed payment, then buying more at better retrospective terms. William Jones, the previous Treasury Secretary, was right when he told Madison on 6 May 'that the stream is nearly dry unless new sources can be opened'.[137]

Barker himself correctly identified the cause of his, and the American government's, borrowing difficulties when on 17 May he wrote to John Armstrong, the Secretary of War, that

> The success of the allies, and the general blockade, operate very
> much against the loan; so difficult is it to raise money that Mr
> Parish told me it was impossible to raise a single $100,000 in
> Philadelphia on a deposit of United States Stock.[138]

By 25 May Madison was sufficiently anxious to write to Campbell, Jones' replacement at the Treasury, urging him to find such new sources of finance 'with less scruple as to the terms'.[139]

Nonetheless, on 22 August 1814, the government offered another $6m in bonds, but even at a 20% discount subscribers offered only $3.5m, of which the government only ever received $2.5m 'in money'.[140] Again, subscribers defaulted on $410,000. When state banknotes worth only 65% in specie were accepted for some stock, early subscribers demanded supplementary stock to make up the difference.[141] The government returned to the original subscribers at 12%, and improved their terms, but for bonds worth $4m received only $2.5m in cash.[142] The high point was reached in late July 1814, when, of the $25m sought, $10.4m in cash had been received. The 4 March issue of $10m of Treasury notes only ever brought in $7.2m. Of the final $9m instalment authorised, nothing was ever raised.[143] It now remained only for the government itself to default.

FINANCIAL EMBARRASSMENT AND POLITICAL IMPLICATIONS

Before this point was reached the fiscal and financial predicament of Madison's administration had become evident even to well-informed outsiders. Rear-Admiral Cockburn, in Chesapeake Bay, knew in May, by 'Intelligence from the Shore', that 'the Money voted by Congress ... cannot be obtained'. '[I]t is therefore doubtful whether the [American] Government will be able to Act up to its Intentions with Respect to Canada.'[144] The French Minister at Washington, Louis Serurier, thought that 'The Cabinet is frightened, it tries however to keep a good face externally, but the fact is that it has the consciousness of its own weakness, and the full strength of the enemy.'[145]

As this level of financial embarrassment becoming increasingly evident, Madison put 'Motion 2' before his Cabinet meeting on 23 June 1814. It dealt with the matter which Madison and Monroe had made the crucial point of Anglo-American dispute in October 1812. It asked 'Shall a treaty of peace silent on the object of impressment be authorised?' When asked for their opinion the following day, all voted 'no' except William Jones, until so recently Secretary of the Treasury, and John Armstrong, Secretary of War, 'who were aye'.[146] These were precisely the two who knew just how weak the United States had become, both financially and therefore militarily. On 27 June, exactly the day on which the French Minister wrote of their 'fright', Madison again consulted his Cabinet. According to Madison, 'in consequence' of Bayard and Gallatin's letters, and 'other accounts from Europe as to the ascendancy & views of Great Britain & the disposition of the great Continental powers, the preceding question No 2' was again put to the Cabinet.[147] This time it was unanimously 'agreed to by Monroe, Campbell, Armstrong and Jones, Rush being absent'.[148] Secretary of State Monroe was instructed to inform the American Peace Commissioners that an American insistence on a British end to impressments, as a prerequisite of peace, had been abandoned.[149] Nor would government revenues meet the cost of an American occupation of Canada. British commercial blockade without American prior fiscal reform, and now no longer accompanied by any American legislative trade restrictions, had eviscerated American war aims.

The British had earlier rejected offers of Russian mediation in its war with the United States, and had insisted on direct negotiations, originally intended to take place at Gothenburg in neutral Sweden. The effectiveness of the British blockade of the United States eastern seaboard was such that the American government felt it necessary to apply to Rear-Admiral Cockburn for a safe-passage across the Atlantic for its Peace Commissioners and their staff. Cockburn wrote to Cochrane on 9 May 1814, hoping that he would 'approve of my having granted the Passports to Gothenburg requested by the American government'. He confessed to having 'not the most distant Idea' of how many more such requests were likely, but thought that 'negotiations may offer plausible excuse for it'.[150]

When Madison's hopes for a 'well-digested system of internal revenue' and of 'improving terms on which loans may be obtained' had both been disappointed, he looked speculatively towards Europe.[151] On 25 May 1814, exactly a year after last addressing Congress on the 'State of the Finances', Madison wrote to Secretary of the Treasury Campbell that,

> as money is cheaper in Europe than here, especially while disaffection withholds the greater part of the capital for Market, it is obviously desirable that we should avail ourselves of the foreign market, now become the [more] practicable in consequence of the repeal of the Non-Importation law.[152]

Apparently oblivious to the British effort and expenditure in securing it, Madison saw the newly restored 'Independence of Holland' as an opportunity. Dutch bankers had largely financed the Louisiana Purchase in 1803 and, now that Napoleon had abdicated, would perhaps refinance the United States war against Britain. He would seek advice, and gain Congressional approval.

Accordingly, on 1 August 1814, Campbell wrote to the bankers Wilhelm and Jan Willink of Amsterdam, asking for their help in negotiating a European loan. Copies were sent to Gallatin and John Quincy Adams in Ghent, and William Crawford, the 'Minister at Paris', authorising them to act. Campbell's letter to Willink & Co did not specify the amount sought, but the Treasury agreed to send United States 6% stock worth $6m to Crawford in Paris, already made out in the name of the Dutch bankers. The whereabouts and value of this stock was later to prove problematic.[153]

On 1 September the British government received confirmation of the failure of the American's latest loan attempt, and of Barker's bankruptcy, from a Dr Bollman, a Hanoverian resident in America for nineteen years, who had acquired Federalist sympathies before his appearance in London. He also told the British Treasury that each of the proliferating American banks had

> found it necessary to collect as much Specie as possible; that this rendered it quite impossible for the American Government to supply itself with the Specie wch its wants required; that for a considerable time back Specie was becoming very scarce in America owing to many Causes, among others to its being smuggled into Canada.[154]

He further warned against Britain seeking to impose harsh peace terms and 'humbling the United States', since this would unite and stiffen American resistance. He argued that British moderation would gain Federalist approval and noted that, after the war, it would be in Britain's interests 'that other nations should be rich customers instead of poor ones'.[155]

By 19 September 1814 Madison found it necessary to summon Congress to another special session, now obliged to meet at the Post and Patent Office, the only undamaged public building available in Washington. He hoped to 'replenish an exhausted Treasury and restore public credit'.[156] During the following weeks 'direct' tax for 1815 was to be doubled to $6m and the internal excise duty on carriages raised. The duty on distillers was to be continued and the duties on alcohol retail licences and auction sales were to be increased.[157] However, as Bristed explains, taxes accrued in one year were very often not paid until the next. This late in the financial year, these new taxes were clearly not going to produce the amounts hoped for in time.

For domestic party-political reasons Madison found it necessary to tell Congress on 20 September 1814 that citizens were 'everywhere paying their taxes, direct and indirect, with the greatest promptness and alacrity'.[158] The assertion was unsupportable. As shown in Appendix B Tables 19–21, while in 1814 'direct' tax gathered almost 74% of its expected yield, indirect excise duties realised less than 59%. By 1814 total tax revenue was less than 30% of Dewey's outgoings for nine months. Even total receipts, excluding loan contributions, raised less than one-third of that expenditure. When writing to Alexander Dallas, about to become Campbell's successor as Secretary of the Treasury, Jones' summary of this dire state of the national finances was again accurate. On 15 September he wrote 'Something must be done, and done speedily or we shall have an opportunity of trying the experiment of maintaining an army and navy and carrying on a vigorous war without money.'[159]

By 23 September 1814 this financial crisis was evident from Campbell's report to Congress. It revealed that $20m had been paid out by the Treasury between January and July 1814, with another $27m payable between that July and January 1815.[160] While Treasury income for the nine months ending 30 June 1814 had been $32m, expenditure already exceeded £34m.[161] On 1 July the Treasury held $4,722,639 and expected revenue of $4,840,000 during the remainder of the year, which, together with $4,320,000 from the loans already contracted, made a total of $13,882,639, about half of the $23,327,586 needed.[162] At best, Campbell estimated a shortfall of $11,660,000 for the remainder of 1814.[163] He even doubted the possibility of borrowing more, admitting in his report that 'The experience of the present year furnishes ground to doubt whether this be practicable.'[164] This reflects the effectiveness of British commercial blockade in reducing both the ability and preparedness of Americans to lend the government more in order to continue the war. Campbell's dismissal of customs revenue, which in 1812 had been the mainstay of government income, measures the success to date of the British commercial blockade. He admitted to Congress that 'While the whole navy of the enemy is disposable for the interruption of our trade, this source of revenue cannot be very productive.'[165] This is precisely what the British had intended at the outset.

For the Americans, a European loan would partly resolve such problems, at least temporarily. After some delay, on 3 October 1814 Gallatin wrote at some length directly to the Willinks, seeking 'a sum not exceeding six millions of dollars or part there of' and, trusting that they would keep the matter 'perfectly confidential', enquiring about the American government's current financial standing in Europe.[166] On 6 October, however, Crawford wrote to Gallatin from Paris stating baldly that he had 'made sufficient enquiry to ascertain that no loan can be obtained in France, upon terms which can be accepted'. He was also 'apprehensive that the same difficulty will be found to exist in Holland. The Capture of Washington will no doubt [have] increased the obstacles which previously existed.' Crawford also reported a remark made by 'the Prince Benevent', better known as Talleyrand, 'to a person on holding a large amount of the funded debt of the US, that he would not give one sou for the whole of it'.[167] This was, from him, unlikely to be an unconsidered outburst. The wily Talleyrand, a political chameleon who had held office in both Revolutionary and Napoleonic governments, had survived Napoleon's initial downfall to become Minister of Foreign Affairs to the newly restored Louis XVIII, and was anxious to gain influence with the British representatives among the occupying Allied Powers in Paris.

As soon as 11 October 1814 Gallatin received an answer from Amsterdam. The Willinks had consulted another important Dutch banking house, Nicholas and Jacob van Staphorst, and both firms felt that they

> must candidly confess that the late untoward circumstances & the
> fear of what may further happen has operated forcibly on the minds
> of our monied people so much so that we consider it not advisable
> to come forward at this juncture with any proposal of Loans,
> because it would never do to offer terms of too favourable a nature
> or such as would not be deemed decent.[168]

The Dutch bankers added that 'The abatement of Spirits is such that Louisiana Stock whose interest is payable here was in the beginning of the Year at par and is now as low as 76 to 78%.' The latest 6% American stock now sold at 72%.[169]

As well as appearing to be a poor loan prospect, the United States was becoming diplomatically isolated. Britain had gained the agreement of the other Allies against France not to intervene in its war with the United States. This precluded their financial intervention, even assuming that they were in a position to do so. Russia, Prussia and Denmark were all seriously in debt to Britain themselves, and Russia had made no repayments, of either principal or interest, since 1812. Moreover, since Gallatin's original approach, Britain had signed a peace treaty with Holland on 13 August 1814, linked with a British loan to the Dutch government at a preferential 2.5% interest rate. This may well have affected Dutch willingness to lend any money to the United States while it was at war with Britain.

By 25 October Crawford in Paris became anxious that the implications of American failure to borrow European money were worse than he had realised. In a partially coded letter to Gallatin in Ghent he wrote 'From the answers to your inquiries the inference is almost necessary that the US have not in the hands of their bankers funds sufficient to discharge the interest of the publick payable in Europe on the first of Jan'y next', meaning the interest payment due on the United States Louisiana debt. It would be 'too late to make remit[t]ances for the purpose after they are advertised of the failure of our efforts. In this event the credit of the US will become worse instead of better.' Despite being 'fearful that no effort that can be made will be attended with success', he insisted that 'the sum necessary to make the payment of the interest due ... ought to be raised upon any terms which can be arranged'.[170]

On 26 October Gallatin and Adams wrote jointly to Campbell from Ghent telling him formally that 'Although the prospects of success may improve after the 1st of January, we think that it would be unsafe for Government to place any reliance on that resource' – that is, borrowing in Europe.[171] That same day, Gallatin wrote Campbell a more forthright letter in his own hand. 'I think that you should not place the least reliance on obtaining a loan in Europe.' 'Breaches of faith' having 'taken place everywhere', real interest rates had 'risen from less than 4 to more than 7%'. 'Nor is our past fidelity', he added, 'considered as a sufficient pledge of our ability hereafter' of 'fulfilling our engagements'. 'On the contrary, I apprehend that owing to' the war '& to our distance which increases the fears of the result, we cannot at this time borrow on as good terms as European powers'. Moreover, Britain had exerted diplomatic pressure on Holland to enact laws 'forbidding foreign loans', forming, he thought, 'another formidable obstacle'. Britain had contrived to preclude the possibility of itself financing continued American war efforts since, even if such laws were repealed, there was, ironically 'no prospect of borrowing elsewhere than in England'. Gallatin had 'thought it right to prevent any unfounded hopes being entertained by our Government'.[172] On the same day Gallatin also wrote to Secretary of State Monroe, simply stating that 'No loan can be obtained in Europe, and our financial resources will be deficient.'[173]

Meanwhile, in Washington, after submitting his 'Financial Statement' to the Senate on 26 September, Campbell had resigned as Secretary of the Treasury, later admitting to Madison that he had been 'humbled' by the task.[174] He was replaced by the able, respected, but not popular Alexander Dallas, whose appointment was not confirmed until 6 October. By 17 October Dallas had estimated a shortfall in revenue for the remainder of 1814 of $13.8m, and argued for further loans and Treasury note issues. The smaller Treasury notes, in denominations down to $3, would, he said, have to be non-interest-bearing, since interest payments would require further cash.[175] Apart from the convenience of using them as an unofficial currency, as a substitute for increasingly scarce specie, it is difficult to imagine what motive the public might have for accepting notes of such small value.

The $8m of Treasury notes already issued circulated only at an increasing discount, representing a potential loss for holders. On 19 October they were discounted at between 10 and 11%, and a further issue in Boston on 27 October led Greene to comment that 'Treasury notes are selling here today ... but I think they will fall'. By the 29 October he noted them 'selling from 15 to 20 per Cent disco'nt, at the latter rate the Sailors have been selling the paper paid for their wages'.[176] Dallas was aware of how unpopular Treasury notes had become, and rejected a suggestion that they become an official medium of exchange. They were, he said, 'an expensive and precarious substitute' vulnerable 'to every breath of popular prejudice or alarm', although still acceptable in payment of taxes or as subscriptions to government loans.[177] Discount rates continued to rise when, without further options, the government issued another $3m of Treasury notes on 15 November. Although theoretically giving the administration more time to collect revenue, so being able to redeem them later, in practice Treasury notes would now seem acceptable only to those with limited options, such as those owed money by the government.

AMERICAN FINANCIAL FAILURE

By this time, however, the government had reached the point of actual bankruptcy, more technically 'insolvency', but in either case an inability to access either saved or borrowed liquid assets when required. It was not a matter of the United States' long-term potential, which remained under-developed and enormous, but of its present ability to pay those with an immediate and unassailable right to be paid.[178] For most contemporary Americans, this meant payment in specie, a universally acceptable currency, not discounted State or private bank notes, or more Treasury notes. The first formal notification of the government's inability to meet even interest payments on the National Debt was sent by Dallas to the Boston Commissioner of Loans on 9 November 1814 and later published by the normally pro-government Niles' *Weekly Register*.[179]

By 27 November even Dallas appeared dejected, and wrote that his 'means consisted first of a fragment of an authority to borrow money, when nobody was disposed to lend, and to issue Treasury notes, which none but necessitous creditors or contractors in distress ... seemed willing to accept'.[180] On 29 November failure abroad was narrowly avoided when $132,000, due in Holland as interest on the Louisiana loan stock, was paid to the Willinks by the British banker Alexander Baring, although, according to Gallatin, other Dutch bankers were still owed money for diplomatic expenses.[181]

By 2 December Dallas had admitted that $200,000 in dividends in America were unpaid.[182] On 16 and 31 December 'two temporary loan repayments of $250,000 each, which became payable to the State Bank in Boston were not paid, it having been impracticable in consequence of the general suspension of payment in specie' precipitated by the British occupation of Washington. Dallas told Congress on 6 February 1815 that 'they remain unpaid'.[183] 'From the same causes', he said, Treasury notes also due for redemption and worth $2,799,200 went unpaid, like the loans still unpaid in February 1815, since 'The Treasury was unable to make any other provision than that of Treasury notes'.[184] The worsening shortage of specie made the redemption and interest of Treasury notes an increasingly serious problem (Appendix B Table 34).

Unsurprisingly, respect for Treasury notes, unacceptable to several Boston banks a year before, continued to fall. By 14 December they passed at a 25% discount, and, according to Greene, 'the expectation of a new emission renders their further depreciation very probable. You had better avoid having anything to do with them, for I tell you <u>in confidence</u> there is very little probability of the govt being able to redeem them.' In Boston alone a total of $1.7m was payable in interest and dividends on the 'funded debt' at the beginning of January 1815. Greene informed Ives that 'A loan to the Govt will prob'y be made for the express purpose of paying the Int. & div'd, but not for the payment of the Treas'y notes.' Nor were Treasury notes any longer universally acceptable, even to a loan-hungry government prepared to accept a 20% discount. 'The Loan office told me today that the T'sy notes payable on 1st Oct last ... were receivable for stock of the 6 million at 80 per Cent, but no others.'[185] On 29 December he wrote that 'The Interest' on government loan stock 'will be paid on the Next monday in Treas y notes for am'ts [amounts] over $100, & no provision is made for those under.'[186]

On 14 December 1814 Wilhelm Willink and Nicholas van Staphorst had informed the American envoys in Ghent that 'we may have a chance' to find purchasers for 'more or less' all of the $3m stock in a way which would 'avoid the difficulties' of 'a general or usual' loan. The terms, however, would be punitive. The 6% stock would be discounted at 75, a 25% discount, for a maximum of ten years, at 8% annual interest. At the outset, the bankers would get a commission of 1% of the $3m and their expenses, and, on completion, another 0.5% of the principal. Throughout, they would also get 1% of the annual interest 'to be remitted in Amsterdam in Dutch hard money before falling due'. The stock was to be bought, and the interest paid, at a fixed exchange rate. The putative purchasers were unnamed, but their opportunity for abnormal profit was to be overtaken by the peace negotiations in Ghent, by then making progress.[187]

Relatively recent suggestions that the United States did not go abroad for finance during its war with Britain include the assertion that 'The government did not borrow internationally during the War of 1812.'[188] It had certainly not been for want of trying. Initial American intentions are confirmed in the Peace Commissioner's first letter to Dallas, referring to their 'instructions from the Treasury having been given with a view to the continuance of the War'. But, with Dutch financial help available only illegally, and on such disadvantageous terms, the Commissioners concluded that 'we will not now act on the subject without hearing from you'.[189] Meanwhile, the British banker Alexander Baring's timely financial help, given perhaps in part because of his American marriage and business ties, had almost certainly been on too small a scale to affect the war's outcome.

BRITISH TRADE IN THE DISTRICT OF MAINE

The effectiveness of the British naval blockade had contributed to such a degree of control of the American eastern seaboard as to allow the practically unchallenged occupation of the ports of the District of Maine.[190] Eastport fell on 18 July and Castine surrendered on 3 September. The British also passed virtually unopposed up the Penobscot River, taking '120 vessels of all descriptions'. At Hampden the Americans burned the *Adams*, a 24-gunned sloop of war, and at Bangor twelve vessels were captured and other property destroyed. In addition to the immediate tactical gains, this amphibious operation brought the British the benefits of newly unhindered overland communication between Halifax and Quebec and commercial use of the Penobscot River and eastern Maine's ports, all useful for bringing British manufactured goods into the United States.

After 21 September the local population had been encouraged by Sir John Sherbroke, Governor of Nova Scotia, and Rear-Admiral Edward Griffith to swear an oath to keep the peace or leave the area. Those swearing allegiance to the Crown gained a certificate of protection, British commercial rights and a Coasting Licence.[191] It was soon reported 'that trade in Castine is very brisk; that there is a great and constant influx and efflux of traders to such an extent that the town is overflowing'. A vessel was 'warped backwards and forwards laden on the British side and unladen on the American'. As a result, Niles reported that

> Specie is travelling rapidly from Boston &c to Castine, and the want of it is about to be as severely felt by the late purse-proud people of that quarter as anywhere else. If the enemy is not driven from that post, between smuggling and dealing he will soon drain the whole eastern country that has nothing else but *cash* to give in exchange for his goods.[192]

Although the British occupation continued until the end of the war, official figures show total British exports to the United States in 1814 as only £8,000; neither the British nor the American government was able to quantify the amount of smuggling.[193] American efforts to control illicit imports cost both money and lives, although their attempts showed the level of government concern.[194] Illegal imports paid no customs duties; nor were questionable incomes going to be lent to the government for fear of the questions raised.

In May 1814 Rear-Admiral Cockburn had felt secure in Tangier Bay in the Chesapeake, and thought that the American 'Government not being able to obtain Money to go on with is not likely to improve their Means of Resistance'.[195] In July he conceded that the American defence of some 'exposed' towns such as Norfolk had been organised, but 'In the Mean time the total Stop to the Trade & other resources, renders it extremely difficult for them to pay the War Taxes.' He presumably meant internal excise duties and 'direct' taxes, but in any case thought them 'inadequate' to prosecute the war 'with Vigor'. He concluded that 'the Treasury is at this Moment without sufficient Funds to pay the various Demands on it, in short it is quite impossible for any Country to be in a More unfit State for War than it now is'.[196] The defeat of the British attack on Baltimore in mid-September was to prove such a view to be complacent.

However, by October shortage of government funds was presenting practical difficulties. When Congress refused compensation to the unpaid men of Barney's Chesapeake gunboat flotillas for clothing lost in action, but nonetheless ordered them to recover merchants' property from Baltimore harbour, their commanding officer offered his resignation.[197] Secretary of the Navy Jones instructed one Navy agent that debts should be paid only in Treasury notes 'or in money 60 or 90 days after purchase'.[198] But the naval contractors A. & N. Brown, employing 'one thousand Carpenters' building warships on Lake Ontario, protested that 'it will ruin us if money is not Sent from the Navy Department that will pass in this State'. '[O]ne hundred thousand Dollars was Due on 22nd December 1814, and the Like Sum on the first of febuary 1815 … if we are to be paid in money Seven Per Cent under par we never will be able to fulfil our contract'.[199] The American government's poor payment record can have done little to motivate its contractors, thereby limiting American naval superiority on the Lakes.

In Maryland, a bill of exchange for the Mint's purchase of copper for striking cents was 'protested and returned unpaid'.[200] The Mint's last supplies of copper were exhausted in 1814, and no cents were struck in 1815.[201] The repercussions of British commercial blockade were reaching even the everyday transactions of ordinary people.

'NEW ENGLAND SEDITION': THE HARTFORD CONVENTION

By the summer of 1814, particularly in New England, increasingly serious hardship was being attributed to the cumulative effects of 'the predatory system of the English on the Coast', now no longer accompanied by any component of American restrictive legislation.[202] Although Massachusetts alone still owned more than a third of American merchant tonnage, New England's share of the United States reduced exports had been more than halved.[203] Such trade had been transferred to the Southern and Middle states, where it was easier to evade customs and blockade. By October a Federalist told the Massachusetts Legislature that

> We are in a deplorable situation, our commerce dead; our revenue gone; our ships rotting at the wharves … Our Treasury drained – we are bankrupts.[204]

As difficulties accumulated expressions of discontent, not always from New England, appear to have become more extreme. On 12 October John Maybin wrote from Philadelphia to Rhode Island: 'I look for something decisive from your Quarter to oblige our worthless President to resign – untill that is done, I fear the Br. government will not make peace with us.' He added as a postscript that the previous day's elections had produced 'a 1,200 Federal majority in the City', overturning the 500-vote 'Democratic majority' of the previous year.[205] Some in New England had begun to discuss more radical political change. Madison's second embargo and, later, the depression caused by the wider British commercial blockade had revived talk of a New England Convention for the first time since of the summer of 1812. The federal government's right to deploy local militia was still hotly debated, but the desire expressed by some New Englanders for constitutional reform and peace came partly from anxiety over an increased risk of British invasion. Thomas Ives, in Providence, Rhode Island, feared 'that attempts will be made to burn the Shipping in our port', and wrote that 'it has been decided to fortify a point of land about three miles below the Town, &

application is already made to the Pres. for Guns & Ammunition. We are about thirty miles from the Sea, & until latterly have considered ourselves safe from the British.'[206] The defeat of France led Maybin to think that 'The wicked and unjust war which our Mad Rulers thought proper to declare, is only just commencing on the part of Gt Britain.' In September he was 'fearful for the safety of the goods' in his care; 'at Washington Private property was not Molested but at Alexandria' British 'conduct was very Extraordinary'. By October he thought that Ives had 'good reason to fear that the British will take up their Winter quarters at Newport'.[207]

Some Federalist newspapers aired extreme views. The Salem *Gazette* called for the sequestration of federal taxes, a separate peace with Britain and a 'convention of neighbouring states in an alliance of amity and commerce'.[208] On 19 October 1814 the Massachusetts Legislature chose delegates for a Convention at Hartford, Connecticut, to meet on 15 December. The other New England states were invited to send representatives to discuss their 'affinity of interests'.[209] At least one Boston newspaper openly advocated secession, describing the appointment of, first, Connecticut's and then Rhode Island's Hartford delegates as the 'raising of the Second' and 'Third Pillars ... of a new Federal Edifice'.[210]

But, while Massachusetts would send twelve delegates, Connecticut seven, and Rhode Island four, Vermont declined to send any delegates, only an unofficial observer. New Hampshire also wavered, sending only two unofficial observers. Nonetheless, Republican Charles Ingersoll reported to Congress that the Convention intended 'to proceed deliberately to the disintegration of New England from the Union'.[211] Its meeting in secret was seen by some as confirmation of a treasonable intention to secede, although known extremists had been deliberately excluded from both its morning and evening sessions.

In the event, the seven moderate resolutions for amending the federal constitution adopted at Hartford and taken to Washington were overtaken by the end of the war, but not before the Convention had had its effect on Madison personally. He had been described as early as October as 'miserably shattered and woe-begone. In short, he looked heartbroken. His mind is full of New England sedition.'[212] In fact, the disaffection had been more severe and widespread than Madison may have known. Perhaps, like Gallatin, fearing a British attack on Boston, Governor Caleb Strong of Massachusetts had sent an agent to Sir John Sherbrook in Halifax to discuss a separate peace, a move again overtaken by progress at Ghent. Earlier, Ohio and even Virginia had threatened sequestration of customs duties gathered there, during their financial disputes with the federal government.[213] Some Federalists remained unrepentant. '[T]he report of the convention at Hartford you must have seen', Ives wrote to Maybin on 20 January 1815, '& we think you must be much pleased with the course taken by that body of enlightened Statesmen ... as being prudent and correct'.[214] Economic difficulties and social distress caused by the skilful and persistent application of British commercial blockade had evidently contributed to political as well as fiscal and financial effects, all making American success less likely.

Not until 14 October 1814 had the House of Representatives received documentary evidence of the Cabinet's decision of 27 June to abandon American insistence on a British ending of impressment as a prerequisite of any peace treaty.[215] Madison had first referred to the American plenipotentiaries' new instructions on 10 October, and then only in a message to Congress, by which time an inkling of their contents may have leaked. Federalist Thomas Oakley of New York speculated that 'the Administration ... must have been prepared to abandon some of the grounds on which it [the war] had been declared.'[216]

Since hearing of Britain's suspension of its Orders in Council in 1812, Madison had made impressment the war's major issue. It had been the central point of Monroe's answer to Warren on 27 October 1812 rejecting Britain's offer of an armistice. Monroe's letter of 25 June 1814, two days before the crucial Cabinet meeting, told the American Peace Commissioners that 'on the subject of impressment, on which it is presumed your negotiations will essentially turn', they might 'concur in an article stipulating that the subject of impressment, together with that of commerce between the two countries, be referred to a separate negotiation.'[217] A postscript which the Commissioners received on 2 August insisted that 'all American citizens who have been impressed into the British service shall be forthwith discharged.'[218]

Long after Britain had rejected the Russian offer of mediation Gallatin and Bayard had eventually left St Petersburg, ostensibly on their way home, but, having reached Amsterdam, obtained agreement to their passing through London. There, they remarked on the hostility of British public opinion, which ascribed the American declaration of war 'solely to a premeditated concert with Bonaparte at a time when we thought him triumphant and their cause desperate.'[219] This contributed to an apparent British intention to drive a hard bargain in any peace negotiations. The British right of impressment was to remain a priority. On 22 April 1814 Gallatin had written from London to fellow Commissioner Henry Clay, noting that British success in Europe now left the Americans 'ill prepared' to continue the war alone 'in a proper manner', giving 'room to apprehend that a continuance of the war might prove fatal to the United States.'[220]

In June Madison had received, via William Jones, Reuben Beasley's account from London dated 18 May 1814 that, in any peace negotiations, Britain expected the United States to renounce its traditional Newfoundland fishing rights and any American trade with the West Indies and beyond the Cape of Good Hope, and to cede Louisiana to Spain.[221] These views, taken into Madison's meetings with his Cabinet on 23 and 24 June, together with continued difficulties with loans, seem likely to have promoted pessimism.

Then, on 26 June 1814, Madison saw Gallatin and Bayard's dispatch from London to Monroe dated 6 May. In addition to Beasley's fears, it said that the British sought to curtail America's northern boundary and exclude all American shipping from the Great Lakes. Furthermore, Madison now discovered that Britain had extracted promises from its European allies not to become involved in its war with the United States. With the defeat of France, the issue of impressment amounted 'to little more than questions of abstract rights', best left out of a negotiated settlement.[222] The dispatch also sought Monroe's leave to transfer negotiations from Gothenburg to the newly liberated Ghent. Significantly, Britain's senior negotiator there would be Lord James Gambier, a retired Admiral rather than career diplomat or politician. Another was to be Dr William Adams, an expert on maritime law.[223] In Washington, Monroe asked the French Minister to delay the return of the dispatch vessel *Olivier* to France for a second time, in view of the need for a further letter to the American Peace Commissioners.[224]

Madison took the Peace Commissioner's views and the diplomatic news, together with the knowledge of his administration's dire financial straights, to a further Cabinet meeting the next day, 27 June. During it, he set aside earlier hopes of dealing separately with Britain's major requirement and, instead, sought and gained the Cabinet's agreement to the abandonment of any reference to impressment in the peace treaty, should it prove necessary. The letter Monroe was instructed to write on 27 June 1814 had informed the Commissioners, in a different tone, that

> On mature consideration it has been decided that, under all the
> circumstances above alluded to, incident to the prosecution of the
> war, you may omit any stipulation on the subject of impressment if
> found indispensably necessary to terminate it. You will of course
> not concur to this expedient until all your efforts to adjust the
> controversy in a more satisfactory manner have failed.[225]

Any remaining doubt Madison might have had on his decision, and the Cabinet's advice, would have been reduced by a letter from Gallatin to Monroe written from London on 13 June 1814. Gallatin had thought 'it probable that Washington or New York are the places the capture of which would most gratify the enemy'. This letter had arrived in late August, after the British capture of Washington had in fact occurred. Gallatin had also added

> I have the most prefect conviction that, under the existing
> unpropitious circumstances of the world, America cannot by a
> continuance of the war compel Great Britain to yield any of the
> maritime points in dispute, & particularly to agree to any
> satisfactory arrangements on the subject of impressment; & that the
> most favourable terms of peace that can be expected are the *status
> quo ante bellum*.[226]

With its contents unknown outside the Cabinet, even to Congress, Monroe's letter of 27 June had reached the Commisioners in Ghent on 10 August. By October Oakley was insisting in Congress that 'The government's conduct could not be properly estimated until the instructions to our Commissioners are laid before the House.' It would then 'appear how far they had thought it important to maintain the grounds on which they had deemed it expedient to commence a war; the conclusion of which was not now within their control, and [which] appeared to be removed to a hopeless distance'.[227]

Just how distant the original American war aims now were was shown by the government's fiscal and financial predicament. Total expenditure for 1814 had been estimated at $47.3m, later amended to $57.7m, while actual receipts for the year, including borrowing, were only just over $40m – despite which, on 3 December, Congress had rejected a proposed income tax as 'inexpedient'.[228] The decision of Congress on 23 December to increase internal excise duties by 50% would do little to help.[229] On 26 December Congress authorised the issue of another $10.5m in Treasury notes, despite the $1.9m already owed on those which, having 'fallen due, remain unpaid'.[230] By the end of the year an attempt to raise a loan of $3m, authorised by Congress on 15 November, had clearly failed. Three New York banks offered to take $600,000 in bonds for cash, but paid in depreciated notes worth only $390,000 in specie.[231]

A second United States national bank, another potential solution to the government's crucial shortage of cash or credit, was, however, foundering for lack of public support. Ives wrote from Providence that '[W]e very much doubt whether the new Bank – should it go into operation will gain any confidence – mixed up as it must be, with depreciated public Debt'.[232] With a capital of $50m, subscribed as specie and government 6% stock, it could lend to the government $30m at 6%.[233] By January 1815, however, United States 6% stock was reportedly quoted at a 40% discount, and although post-war publications, shown as Appendix B Table 22, recorded the discount as having been 24%, such wartime accounts as those in Niles' *Weekly Register* would have damaged the government's financial standing.[234]

Congress, as so often before, procrastinated and, Ives suggested, 'does not appear to know what to do – the Bank bill, we see is bandied between the two Houses & will be lost most probably'. In any case, he thought 'it will not answer' as a means of providing 'a general currency while the War lasts – all the advantage to the Govt would be to absorb part of the National Debt thereby making room for the circulation of a new emission – this relief they would find only temporary and a most miserable expedient as a financial Scheme'.[235] News of peace arrived before even an emasculated Bank bill could both pass Congress and avoid the President's veto. Congress had repeated the self-interested inertia which had resulted in its failure to renew the charter of the First United States Bank, even when already contemplating a declaration of war on Britain.

On 17 January, with news of peace still almost a month away, Dallas estimated 1815's income as $15.1m, to meet expenditure of more than $56m. This included $15.5m interest on debts of $40.9m to be incurred as new loans and Treasury notes.[236] Interest payments greater than income would be a nadir in American public finance which 'filled them [the Republicans] with dismay'. When John Eppes read Dallas' report to the House, one hearer said 'All his former communications were but emollients and palliations, compared with this final disclosure of the bankruptcy of the nation'.[237] To raise the $40m needed for 1815

Dallas sought to borrow $25m and issue $15m worth of Treasury notes, aims which Congress dismissed as unrealistic given the recent failure to borrow less than an eighth of this amount. Congress authorised instead $25m Treasury notes, only $8.3m of which were ever issued.[238] News of the Treaty of Ghent and the completion of its ratification by the Senate on 16 February came before the American need to borrow as much as $40m while still under British commercial blockade was put to the test.

During December and into January 1815 Cochrane had implemented his long-held intention to attack New Orleans, and had been bloodily repulsed by American defenders given time to prepare and led by the determined General Andrew Jackson. Even the decision to appoint Jackson to organise the defence of New Orleans was to reflect the financial standing of an administration deprived of sufficient overseas trade and revenue. Jackson had been told, probably unconstitutionally, that he could draw on Monroe's personal funds to finance the transfer of troops to New Orleans.[239] Nevertheless, a British frontal attack on 8 January was heavily defeated, and by 18 January it became clear that British forces should be withdrawn. Their capture of Fort Bowyer in the course of their retreat, in apparent preparation for a second attack on Mobile, was rendered unnecessary by news of a peace treaty having been signed on 24 December.

A land attack on New Orleans had, in any case, been unnecessary. Resources spent instead on the stringent enforcement of the British maritime commercial blockade of New Orleans would have denied Louisiana much of its access to the sea, exerted further pressure on the American economy and further restricted their political options, without Cochrane's involvement in a second unsuccessful British assault on a land target. This should have become apparent, especially after news of the successful American defence of Baltimore had reached Ghent in October 1814 and so changed the outlook of all involved in negotiating a settlement.

It was agreed at Ghent that enemy vessels captured on the American coast would still be 'good prize' for only twelve days after the treaty's ratification, although for thirty days on the Atlantic and for longer 'on distant seas'. The Admiralty therefore recalled Cochrane by a letter dated 30 December 1814, anticipating that, by the time it was delivered, Britain's commercial blockade would be successfully completed, largely on lines established by Warren.[240] Cochrane's decision to close Boston to neutral as well as to American shipping was to remain his most significant contribution.

Although unmeasured at the time, evidence is available of real and contemporary damage to the American economy due less to an intermittent American restrictive system than to the British commercial blockade. In addition to the wholesale commodity price rises in New England and across the United States, discussed earlier, other economic indicators show adverse trends which would have made an impact on the everyday lives of the majority of the American population. The impact of the war in general, and the British commercial blockade in particular, on the consumer prices paid by ordinary people can be seen in a composite consumer price index. That constructed by McCusker, shown as Appendix B Table 23, peaks in 1814, rising thirty-two points between 1812 and 1813 during Warren's blockades, and a further nineteen points between 1813 and 1814, before falling twenty-six points by 1815, during three-quarters of which period the blockade was not in force.[241] These levels of American consumer prices, as measured by the same index, were not to be reached again until 1919–20.

According to Rockoff, 'prices rose 45% between 1811 and 1814'. As shown as Appendix B Table 24, his index of American wholesale prices, based on those of 1811, peaks in 1814 and falls by ten index points in 1815, despite both the amount outstanding in Treasury notes and the value of commercial banknotes issued continuing to rise.[242] This suggests that, by late 1814, Britain's commercial blockade had been, by constricting imports, and largely preventing the exports which might have paid for them, more responsible for American price inflation than domestic factors such as increased money supply. Internal factors, such as the proliferation of depreciating Treasury notes and the uncontrolled banknote issues of both state and private banks, can be seen as still rising after the war. If, as Rockoff suggests, internal wholesale price inflation had been 'fuelled primarily' by Treasury and banknote issues, it is unlikely to have peaked in 1814 as shown or fallen in 1815 before any decrease in government currency and banknote issue. British commercial blockade therefore appears to have been a more important determinant of American wholesale price inflation than the continued rise in money supply. American prices fell in anticipation of peace and the end of the British commercial blockade, as well as immediately on peace becoming a certainty. As early as 5 January 1815 Maybin wrote to Ives from Philadelphia that 'after the dispatches of the *Chauncey*', raising hopes of peace 'were made publick', prices of 'Merchandize in General have been declining'.[243]

One of the clearest indications of the impact of the British commercial blockade on the American economy, particularly its international position, is provided by the United States terms of trade. Those shown as Appendix B Table 27 make a correlation between an import price index and an export price index for the United States between 1807 and 1815. The import and export price indices from which these terms of trade were calculated are shown as Appendix B Tables 25–26.[244] Because of the importance of customs duties to overall tax revenue, and the impact of trade restrictions on the incomes of the affluent, the terms of trade also throw light on the fiscal and financial position of the United States before and during its war with Britain. It is also possible, to some extent, to compare the relative impact of American legislative trade restrictions and the operation of the British commercial blockade by reference to the relevant United States terms of trade.

Having fallen by 19.2 points between 1807 and 1809 as a result of Jefferson's embargo, the United States terms of trade reflect a more favourable relationship between export and import prices after 1809, improving by 16.2 points between 1809 and 1811, recovering all but 3 points of the index for 1807. This will provide a benchmark for later changes. Between 1811 and 1812 the effects of both Madison's first 90-day embargo, which ended on 3 July, and the tentative beginnings of the British commercial blockade combine to produce a 9.7 point fall in the American terms of trade, as official export prices fall 1.5 points and the index of legitimate import prices rises by 10.6 points, reflecting their increasing scarcity. So far, the combined impact of Madison's embargo and British blockade does not match the impact on America's trading position of Jefferson's embargo.

By 1813 the effectiveness of the British commercial blockade was evidently increasing, while Madison's second embargo was widely evaded. North's index of American import prices between 1812 and 1813 rises by no less than 48 points, while the index of export prices falls by 0.6 points. American grain and flour surpluses still exported to the Iberian Peninsula, although at lower prices, absorbed one last season's output before output was reduced to levels nearer self-sufficiency. North's terms of trade are therefore 26.1 points lower in 1813 than in 1812, largely measuring the success of the British commercial blockade during the year.

In 1814, with the British commercial blockade extended to include New England, unaccompanied for the final ten months of the war by any American legal constraints on trade, the index of import prices rises by 52.6 to a remarkable 232.3 points, reflecting scarcity and exploitative speculation. The index of export prices for 1814 shows a small increase of 0.8 points. Nevertheless, the United States' terms of trade show a further decrease of 15.6 points. While protecting developing textile manufacturing, thereby producing a short-term prosperity in some areas of the United States, the worsening terms of trade reflect a lack of overseas trade, associated unemployment and falling wages in others, including New England. Altogether, North's American terms of trade fell by 41.7 index points between 1812 and 1814. In turn, the declining terms of trade caused a fall in the American national income, as measured by real GDP, for each year of the war, falling by 0.7% in 1812, almost 6% in 1813, over 9% in 1814, and 8.8% in 1815 despite the peace in February of that year.[245]

The effect on individual citizens of the deterioration in the United States' trading position is shown by the total export and import figures given as Appendix B Tables 28–29, but disguised there as *real* exports and imports per head in dollars by having had the effect of inflation subtracted from them.[246] Making allowance for changing prices, real exports per head fell between 1812 and 1814 by $3.27, and real imports per head fell by as much as $5.16 over the same period. Such a shortage of overseas export markets, and of imports for either consumption or re-export, would almost certainly have reduced incomes while raising prices. Severe inflation would be part of the economic damage expected of British commercial blockade, and to remove its impact on import and export prices is to invite misunderstanding. The decision to declare war on the world's major maritime power had indeed involved costs for ordinary American citizens.

North omitted shipping prices from his calculation of the American terms of trade and points out that, since freight rates increased more than other international prices between 1790 and 1815, and that, since for much of that time shipping prices formed a 'significant proportion' of the credit items in the American terms of trade, they would have been 'much more favourable' if the price of shipping had been included.[247] As shown in Appendix B Table 17, this would certainly have been true in 1807, in the prosperous pre-war period without embargoes. However, the wartime tonnage of American shipping engaged in diminishing United States foreign trade fell by over 94% between 1811 and 1814.[248] As the British commercial blockade continued, what remained of American foreign trade had increasingly been carried in neutral vessels. The inclusion of shipping prices in wartime American terms of trade, with a British commercial blockade in operation, would have made little difference by 1814. As shown in Appendix B Table 30, the net earnings of the American merchant marine fell by almost 94%, from $40.8m in 1811 to $2.6m in 1814.[249]

The British commercial blockade theoretically ended on the Atlantic in early March 1815, following the ratification of peace in February. Most of the year, therefore, saw a resumption of more normal overseas trade. The export price index for 1815 shows an immediate 55.6 point increase, while the import price index falls by a significant 41 points. The measured competitiveness of American foreign trade therefore improved by 40 index points immediately the British commercial blockaded ended, itself a useful reflection of its effectiveness.

Lipsey's terms of trade index for 1789–98 to 1904–13, given as Appendix B Table 31, shows that the war of 1812–15 contributed to an interruption in an overall improvement of 41 index points during that time.[250] Lipsey points out that the rise in the United States' terms of trade during most of the nineteenth century also shows that any wartime fall was not caused solely by an American dependence on exporting primary products, such as cotton and grain. The fall of six index points in the United States' terms of trade during the decade including the war more probably indicates the American wartime difficulty in exporting anything owing to British commercial blockade.

As seen in Appendix B Table 27, the greatest change in North's United States' terms of trade, during 1813, corresponds with the greatest level of operational success in British commercial blockade. Considering only the North America section of Warren's United Command, and excluding other stations, a total of 209 prizes reached Halifax in 1813, with a further nine up to 1 April 1814, when Warren relinquished command. During Cochrane's command of the North America Station alone, 136 prizes reached Halifax. Clearly, during two comparable time periods, each of almost exactly a year, Warren's North America squadrons were operationally more effective between March 1813 and the end of March 1814 than those commanded by Cochrane between April 1814 and the end of the war, probably because potential prizes became scarce.

It took time, however, for Madison's administration to realise its predicament. From the end of 1813 to 27 June 1814 the increasingly obvious destruction of American overseas trade as a source of revenue, and the unreliability of credit, had eroded the possibility of American success. Later, American isolation, with the defeat of France, and frequently unopposed British landings, the destruction of Washington, awareness of impending insolvency and growing internal dissent brought Madison to the point of serious illness and despair and of issuing instructions which limited the American Peace Commissioner's options. These constraints on their negotiating position were relieved only by American naval successes on the Lakes and British failure at Baltimore. American success at New Orleans came too late to affect the outcome of the Ghent treaty. With the effectiveness of the Royal Navy's convoys in protecting the bulk of British seaborne trade, and both its commercial and naval blockades of the United States, British maritime economic warfare had been a resounding success.

THE TREATY OF GHENT

The growing need for peace was increasingly discussed between Americans aware of the government's financial position. John Jacob Astor wrote to Gallatin on 22 December 1814: 'I have not a Doubt that unless we have a Peace there will be a great Depression.'[251] Nevertheless, rumours of peace were treated with caution even in February 1815. Ives wrote to Maybin from Rhode Island on 6 February that 'until proven information be received business of all ports of this country must be at a stand, much distress prevails in our section of the Union which will increase with the direction of the war'.[252] However, the peace treaty, already ratified by the Prince Regent, reached New York on the evening of 11 February. It arrived in Washington on 14 February and was unanimously ratified by the Senate on 16 February. Having been signed by Madison later the same day, and with ratifications duly exchanged between Monroe and Baker, it came into effect at 11p.m. on 17 February 1815.[253] On 15 February Maybin had replied to Ives from Philadelphia that bonds and 'Stocks of Every description have advanced very materially'; even Treasury notes were at par, and Government 6% stock had risen to between 90 and 92. 'Imports will not sell unless at such prices as the holders are not disposed to accept. British Manufactures I am told have fallen about One Half from what they were last week.'[254]

THE OUTCOME AND THE COST

Unsurprisingly, given the disparity in naval terms between Britain and the United States, on 1 February 1815 the Admiralty issued figures making clear its overall success against American warships during the war. The Admiralty admitted to having lost sixteen British ships of war and armed vessels at sea, with a total of 266 guns and the loss of 2,015 men and boys. It had lost another seven vessels on Lake Erie, including the unlaunched *Detroit*, and a further five on Lake Champlain and the rivers of North America, making a total of twenty-eight.[255]

On the same day, the Admiralty accounted for all the national 'Ships of War and Armed Vessels belonging to the United States of America, taken or destroyed by His Majesty's Ships since the Commencement of the War'. To thirty-four American warships and smaller vessels taken at sea, with 407 guns and 1,956 men and boys, were added eight more with 47 guns taken on the Lakes, totalling forty-two fighting vessels with 454 guns and 2,294 men and boys killed or captured. This excluded 'Privateers and other Ships and Vessels Armed and Commissioned for War', of which there had been 228 with 906 guns and 8,974 men and boys.[256]

Commercial maritime warfare had been extensive, although with different proportional effects on each economy. The highest claim of British losses to American vessels, John Russell's list of 1815, included prizes said to have been taken into foreign ports, sunk or burned, and reached an overall total of 1,613 craft.[257] Even this number represented only 7.5% of the British merchant fleet comprised in 1814 of 21,449 vessels, which, despite such losses, had grown in number by 4.7% between 1811 and 1814, as shown in Appendix B Table 32. The tonnage of the British merchant fleet had also risen by 7.4% between 1811 and 1814, as vessels increased in size.[258] The $45.5m claimed as the value of total British losses throughout the war, to the United States Navy and American privateers combined, loses much of its significance when converted to the £10.25m it then represented, and when compared to the aggregate value of British overseas trade in 1814, in that year alone worth £151.1m.[259] Compared with the impact of British commercial blockade on American overseas trade shown earlier, British maritime losses seem to have left Britain's foreign trade in 1814 relatively unaffected, its aggregate value having increased by as much as 67.3% since 1811, as seen in Appendix B Table 2. The value of British imports by 1814 increased by 59.4% since 1811; domestic exports rose in value by 38.3% in the same time. Most notably, British re-exports, of largely colonial produce, had increased in value by a remarkable 270.2% between 1811 and 1814.

By comparison, the aggregate total of 1,407 American merchant vessels captured or destroyed by the Royal Navy throughout the war constituted a much larger proportion of the American merchant navy, which was about half the size of its British counterpart.[260] The statistics issued by the Admiralty Office on 1 February were accepted by the House of Commons, which ordered their printing on 9 February 1815.[261] The Parliamentary Paper's total of American losses was conservative, excluding captures by British privateers 'not reported regularly to the Admiralty'. Nor were the Royal Navy's returns complete. If many reports resembled that of Commander Richard Coote of HMS *Borer* to his commanding officer – that he had 'captured five merchant vessels and destroyed many more' – the British total is certainly an underestimate.[262] The illegal ransoming of captured American vessels had continued throughout 1814. HMS *Nymphe*, for example, blockading New England during that summer, had ransomed at least ten, which had, naturally, not been reported.[263] No returns had been 'received from the East Indies or Cape of Good Hope Stations', while those of other stations had been received only 'in part'. American vessels detained in Irish ports were not included.[264] In addition, further legitimate British prizes would continue to reach Halifax and other North American and Caribbean ports until May 1815. The 1,407 merchant vessels reported to the Admiralty as taken or destroyed by the Royal Navy between June 1812 and February 1815 can be usefully compared with the number of American merchant craft still in use for foreign trade by 1814, estimated to have been no more than 420 vessels of average size.[265] Even the 1,407 United States merchant vessels officially taken or destroyed during the Royal Navy's wartime commercial blockade exceeded by more than three times the number still in American use for foreign trade by the war's end. It would still have represented almost 30% of those American merchant vessels engaged in foreign trade during the time of post-war recovery and booming overseas trade after February 1815, when the fleet approached 1.4m gross tons.[266]

Throughout the war the British maritime commercial blockade had captured American vessels and cargoes worth more than £500,000 in prize money, then worth about $2.2m.[267] As eventual proceeds through Vice-Admiralty prize courts, rather than through an open market at the commercially appropriate time, this also seems likely to be a conservative estimate of values and a poor measure of the damage caused to the American economy, counting only lost capital and excluding lost profits and the wages and spending power from employment. The British commercial blockade had ended America's virtual monopoly of shipping its own overseas trade. In 1811 96.6% of the net tonnage carrying American foreign trade had been American;[268] and only 6.6% of the net tonnage arriving in American ports in 1812 had been foreign. By 1813 32.5% of this tonnage was foreign and, by 1814, no less than 44.4% of arriving tonnage was non-American.[269] American merchant shipping space had been so little used that North's shipping activity index based on 100 for 1796–1800 fell to 9.0 by 1814.[270] Furthermore, the Royal Navy's captures and the deterrent effect of the proclamation of successive British blockades progressively reduced the overall number of arrivals in American ports, of whatever nationality.

The damage caused to American merchant shipping between 1812 and 1814 had significantly exceeded that caused earlier by Jefferson's embargo. The net tonnage of vessels of all nationalities entering American ports had fallen by over 51% from 1.2m in 1807 to 586,000 in 1808. By 1809, however, this had recovered by 20.3% to 705,000 net tons. The proportion of American shipping involved throughout had changed little, from 92.7% in 1807 to 91.9% in 1808. Between 1812 and 1814 entries of vessels of all nationalities to American ports had fallen 84.9%, from 715,000 to 108,000 net tons. Moreover, the proportion of American vessels had fallen from 93.4% in 1812 to only 55.6% in 1814, from 668,000 net tons in 1812 to just 60,000 in 1814. For the last ten months of the war this reduction had been due solely to British commercial blockade. The impact of the war is also shown by the peace. By the end of 1815 American imports had recovered quickly, with port entries totalling 918,000 net tons, of which 76.4% were American-owned. By 1816, entries to American ports had again reached 1.1m net tons, of which 77.2% was American.[271]

The monetary cost of the war to the United States has been variously estimated at between $105m and $158m, excluding damage to property but including veteran's pensions.[272] Between 1812 and 1814 the United States government had been deprived of $8.6m of net customs revenue, while overseas trade altogether worth $97.4m was lost; up to 1815 a nominal $80m had been borrowed, repayable over twelve years, although because of the discounts found necessary, and the depreciated Treasury and banknotes accepted in payment for loan stock, this has been estimated as having been worth only $34m in specie.[273] According to Dewey, as shown in Appendix B Table 33, more than $16.6m of interest was paid on money borrowed by the war's end.[274] Having reached a low point of $45.2m in 1813, the United States' national debt had reached $127.3m by the end of 1815.[275] As early as September 1814 Liverpool had written to Bathurst 'I confess I cannot believe that, with the prospect of bankruptcy before them, the American government would not wish to make peace, if they can make it upon terms which would not give a triumph to their enemies.'[276] In December, just such a peace had been offered at Ghent.

In human terms, the war is estimated to have cost the United States 20,000 lives in battle and disease, and the suffering of 20,961 naval prisoners.[277] As prisoners of war in Britain many American officers had been released on parole. A subsistence allowance for rent and food, paid by the Transport Board and often supplemented by unofficial earnings, had supported officers living more or less amicably among civilian populations in towns such as Reading in Berkshire and Ashburton in Devon. Other ranks had been incarcerated in prisons such as Dartmoor, where in April 1815 a riot over bread shortages and delayed repatriation led to seven fatal shootings.[278]

In the United States, with the single exception of Baltimore, the populations of the major ports dropped and, for the only time in American history to date, the urban proportion of the population decreased.[279] As American wartime export markets decreased and imports generally became more scarce and expensive, and with taxation heavier, Thomas Jefferson summarised the effect of the war on a still primarily rural population by asking 'How can people who cannot get 50 cents a bushel for their wheat, while they pay $12 a bushel for their salt, pay five times the amount of taxes they ever paid before?'[280]

During its course the war had sometimes been unjustifiably described, both within Congress and outside, as a second war of independence.[281] However, had the Ghent treaty not been ratified it seems doubtful whether Britain would have been able to sponsor the separation of New England from the Union, beyond the initially selective British blockade, because of further potential British military and financial commitments in Europe in 1815.[282] In America the apparent possibility of New England's secession, and a separate treaty with Britain, had prompted discussion of its commercial isolation, and military intervention, by the rest of the Union.[283]

The first of the 'Headings of Negotiation' which Foreign Secretary Castlereagh sent to the British Commissioners at Ghent concerned the 'Maritime rights of Great Britain, including impressment'. The future right to 'claim and enforce in war the allegiance & services' of British subjects was a prerequisite from which the Government could 'never recede'.[284] In the event, the ratified

Treaty of Ghent preserved important British naval rights. It made no mention of British impressment or provision for compensation for American mercantile property legitimately destroyed or confiscated during the war. The treaty left unresolved the issues of British navigation rights on the Mississippi and American fishing rights on the Canadian coast, as well as the ownership of several islands in Passamaquoddy Bay, between the coast of the District of Maine and Nova Scotia. The treaty established joint legal Commissions to fix the borders between Canada and the United States and to determine ownership of various islands. It specified the continued opposition of both countries to the slave trade. Less effectively, the treaty sought to protect the rights of the indigenous tribes of North America.[285] In signing it, Madison had made an expedient withdrawal from a war he had declared without adequate fiscal and financial preparation.

In writing to Monroe from Ghent on 25 December 1814 Gallatin appears to have made his own assessment of the impact of the British commercial blockade, especially that of New England. He considered its fiscal and financial consequences and their eventual political effects, both domestic and international. Gallatin thought that 'The treaty of peace we signed yesterday with the British ministers is, in my opinion, as favorable as could be expected under existing circumstances, so far as they were known to us.' New England's prosperity had been sufficiently threatened by the final phase of the British commercial blockade to make suggestions of secession appropriate to some, such that Gallatin felt it necessary to add 'The attitude taken by the State of Mass[achusetts], and ... in some of the neighbouring States, had a most unfavorable effect' on the American negotiating position.[286] As early as April 1814 he had written to fellow Peace Commissioner Henry Clay that 'above all, our own divisions and the hostile attitude of the Eastern States give room to apprehend' that the United States could not continue the war without becoming divided, or, therefore, successfully.[287]

Ironically, a month to the day before the war was to end, the Republican semi-official newspaper, the Washington *National Intelligencer*, was to summarise precisely why the Americans had in effect lost the war they had declared on Britain, probably with insufficient forethought and certainly without adequate fiscal reform or financial preparation. On 17 January 1815 an editorial reflected that

> Whilst again other nations find it difficult to provide the pecuniary
> means for commencing war, and are quickly checked by that
> difficulty in carrying it on, Great Britain is under no
> embarrassment of that sort. Such is her credit and such her capacity,
> honorable doubtless to sound maxims in her political economy ...
> such her resources and systems of revenue, that the greatest part of
> the tax is so disguised as scarcely to be known to those who pay it.
> And such finally is the superiority of her capital in trade and her

predominance on the ocean that she levies contributions on the whole commercial world, and not infrequently, more in time of war than at other times.[288]

Apart perhaps from passages owing more to hyperbole and bitterness than fact, the editorial recognises the causes of the United States' abandonment of its original war aims and its inability to continue financing the war for much longer. Had this analysis appeared in one of the more outspoken New England newspapers in 1812 it would probably have been dismissed by the *National Intelligencer* as representative of the undue pessimism, if not the unpatriotic misgivings, of the prosperous minority conducting most of the American shipping and foreign trade with what was then the world's industrial, commercial and maritime superpower. Had the influential and well-connected editor of the *National Intelligencer* arrived at his conclusion in the early months of 1812, the war itself might conceivably have been avoided. In a very real sense, the prediction made in Congress by Republican Representative Adam Seybert in January 1812 – that 'The British force in the American seas is too competent for our interest' – had proved to be true.[289]

CHAPTER 8

RESULTS AND CONCLUSIONS

It will be agreed on all sides that most operative [of causes] have been the inadequacy of our system of taxation to form a foundation for public credit ... but the public credit at this juncture is so depressed that no hope of adequate succour on moderate terms can safely rest upon it. (John Eppes, Committee of Ways and Means, to Secretary of the Treasury, Alexander Dallas, 14 October 1814)[1]

IF, IN THE EARLY NINETEENTH CENTURY, defeat in war lay in the inability to continue fighting while an opponent was able to do so, then, despite its victory at New Orleans in January 1815, the United States was defeated in the Anglo-American War of 1812. The Americans had failed to occupy Canada, either as a bargaining counter or permanently, as Jefferson, Madison and Gallatin had earlier agreed. Furthermore, the Royal Navy's economic warfare, in the form of its commercial and naval blockades, had deprived the United States of the financial means to continue fighting beyond the first few months of 1815. By depriving the United States of its imports the British commercial blockade had so reduced American customs duties, the major source of government revenue until the last year of the war, as to create major budget deficits and cause American dependence on increasingly unreliable public credit. The British naval blockade had so largely confined the American navy to port as to prevent its being able to lift the British commercial blockade or prevent British amphibious landings and major incursions into the United States at will. The unopposed landing which led to the British capture of Washington in August 1814 had had far-reaching but hitherto under-appreciated financial consequences which contributed to an outcome of the war favourable to Britain.

The British commercial blockade had, over time, so far reduced American agricultural exports that newly introduced taxes were paid from reduced incomes only with difficulty and evident reluctance. Overland transport intended to replace increasingly blockaded coastal traffic had become so expensive as to permit farmers to sell either to local markets at prices depressed by glut or to distant urban consumers at high prices, which effectively reduced demand. Speculators had made the most of real or contrived shortages. Unemployment, especially in ports and other cities had combined with rising prices to contribute to popular unrest. The proliferation of state and local banks with poorly controlled note issues contributed to severe inflation and reduced the overall acceptability of paper money. Banknotes, even those held by the government, had become far from universally acceptable, frequently refused or accepted only at a discount. Banks had eventually been forced to suspend payment in precious metals.

The proportion of the American merchant fleet actually taxed and in use had declined sharply as blockades continued during a war which damaged it more severely and for longer than Jefferson's embargo, or either of Madison's. This had further reduced the American government's income, from light and harbour dues and registration and enrolment fees. Shippers and merchants deprived of much of their business had sought alternative outlets for their financial capital and declined to lend to an administration seen as responsible for their loss of livelihood. While in 1811 96.6% of net tonnage capacity entering United States ports had been American, in 1814 it was 55.6%.[2]

Peace had brought a rapid but temporary recovery. By the end of 1815 76.4% of net tonnage capacity involved in United States foreign trade was American. Measured differently, the proportion of total gross tonnage of documented United States merchant vessels engaged in foreign trade in 1810 had been 68.8%; it then fell from 62.4% in 1815 to a low point of 44% in 1822, not rising again above 50%.[3] The American merchant fleet was never again as relatively important to the American economy as it had been before 1812. The relative diversion of investment funds from merchant shipping became permanent. The American government had declared war after seeking to secure a maritime trading advantage during Britain's prolonged war in Europe. For largely commercial reasons it had interposed itself between Britain and its French enemy, and the American merchant fleet had paid the price.

It is often argued that it was precisely the extended British commercial blockade that greatly stimulated expansion in American manufacturing industry, especially of textiles, and notably cotton.[4] However, on close examination, the war's exclusion of British imports created a temporarily protected and short-lived explosion of growth that was largely reversed when British textile exports to America resumed on a large scale in 1815. Then, almost 92% of American cotton manufacturing was concentrated in around 165 mills in New England.[5] Output having more than doubled between 1812 and 1815, the collapse of American military demand and re-exposure to cheap British imports reduced New England cotton production by almost 65% the following year. 'As a result, virtually every cotton mill in New England was closed in 1816', at least temporarily.[6]

Only those with the financial capital to re-invest in new water power-looms survived to re-open. When, after a post-war gap, growth in the American textile industry began again, especially in cotton manufacturing, it had more to do with tariff protection, initially for two years after the peace, but again in 1816, 1824 and 1828, than with a false start provided by the war.[7] The availability of high-quality American raw material was also significant. Recovery, when it came, had more to do with the application of new power-loom technology, some of it British, as well as American developments. The higher productivity of American physical capital and more expensive American labour and finance was of greater lasting significance than the temporary wartime diversion of some financial capital from shipping.[8]

When the Treaty of Ghent ended the war after thirty-two months of fighting, the Americans had gained none of the aims they had hoped for at the outset and had bankrupted themselves in the process. Between 1812 and the end of 1814 the American government had collected $35.1m in wartime taxes, at the same time spending $86.7m, creating a $51.6m shortfall. Over the same period it had sought to borrow $62.5m by selling government stock, of which it appears to have received only $42.6m, probably worth less than half that value in specie.[9] The Treasury's short-term loan notes had changed hands only at discount, and calls for loans had fallen short of their targets even when the securities were sold far below par. Before the negotiated peace of 1815 the government's creditworthiness had collapsed.

As well as learning that the Treasury had indeed needed a wider tax base before any declaration of war, members of Congress concluded from its course that the United States had, after all, needed a national bank. When in 1811 they had, for reasons of their own, refused to renew the charter of the first, thereby precluding use of its paper currency or loans, Congressmen had made a successful war against Britain all the more improbable. Creation of the Second Bank of the United States in 1816 allowed the establishment of a fiduciary currency which, in time, was to become practically universal.

Significantly, the head of the British negotiating team at Ghent had been Dr William Adams, an Admiralty lawyer rather than a diplomat or career politician. He was accompanied by the retired Admiral Lord Gambier. No part of the Ghent treaty had narrowed contraband solely to 'munitions of war', nor prohibited mid-ocean 'paper blockades' imposed far from named coasts or harbours. None of its clauses had removed or limited a belligerent's right to stop and search neutral merchant vessels in wartime, a right on which Britain would have to depend in later wars. This feature of the peace agreement reflected the Royal Navy's successful implementation of maritime economic warfare in North America, and the American's inability to withstand its fiscal and financial consequences. The treaty had not even required Britain to concede its assumed right of compulsorily impressing apparently British seamen found in neutral merchant vessels, formerly so often American. This was despite its having been the point on which Madison and Monroe had concentrated after Britain had revoked its 1806 Orders in Council restraining neutral trade as far as the United States was concerned, an earlier bone of contention. Secretary of State Monroe's answer to Warren's peace-feeler in November 1812 had required Britain's abandonment of impressment as an prerequisite of peace negotiations, ensuring that war continued. The temporary ending of the long European war which had made Britain's manpower shortage so urgent a problem as to make impressment necessary did not make the principle of Britain's future rights over its subjects any less important. Napoleon's first abdication did not mean that the potential recovery of valuable British seamen from foreign merchant vessels would not again prove crucial in the event of another prolonged nineteenth-century war.

American awareness that the currently under-employed state of their merchant fleet made it less useful for the United States to retain foreign seamen may have contributed to American preparedness to forgo insistence on a formal solution to what had earlier been seen as a 'crying enormity'. The issue of impressment had been abandoned by Madison's cabinet in late June 1814 when it became clear that nothing would come of the administration's penultimate wartime attempt to borrow even enough money to maintain current expenditure. Between June and December 1814 Madison had come to understand that, during this war with Britain, unlike the last one, no financial, material, or even diplomatic help from France would be forthcoming. Nor, despite an urgent application, would any financial help come from a country such as Holland, recently liberated from the French but unwilling to lend to a United States unable to defend its foreign trade, maintain overseas communications or keep the enemy out of its capital. Nor was Russia, itself still in receipt of British loans and subsidies, in any position to offer financial or military help to America, or repeat the offer, earlier rejected by Britain, to mediate between the United States and its enemy in the hope of winning concessions for trading neutrals in wartime.

Conversely, when ratifications were exchanged on the evening of 17 February 1815, no territory had been due to change hands. Despite the British occupation of parts of northern Maine since September 1814, news of American successes reaching London in October had caused the British Peace Commissioners to relinquish earlier territorial claims. The *status quo ante bellum* was to be resumed. This reflected the abandoned British intention to invade the United States from Canada, unrealistic without naval control of the Lakes, although costing the hoped-for overland route between Halifax and Quebec. British concern over disagreements between the victorious Allies meeting in Vienna, and the real possibility of renewed fighting in Europe, with the implied need for continued heavy taxation and borrowing in Britain, had moderated attitudes on anything less vital than the retention of British maritime rights. Comparison of the British government's unimpaired ability to borrow with their own inability to raise any appreciable loans at home or in Europe had renewed the American Peace Commissioner's search for a negotiated settlement.

Having been in a position to defend and maintain its own overseas trade, Britain had remained the world's major financial as well as maritime power, subsidising allies while withholding funds from others. While the British banker Alexander Baring advanced small sums to American envoys in Europe to avoid their immediate embarrassment, he did not, apparently, despite his close personal and business links with the United States, lend its government enough to affect the outcome of the war.

British success in maritime economic warfare in Europe and North America up to 1815 was to affect thinking on war and its legality during the rest of the nineteenth century, and the way in which it was conducted in the 20th. Britain had softened its position regarding neutrals before the Crimean War to facilitate its use of blockade against Russia, and again after the war, with the 1856 Declaration of Paris. Despite this restrictive agreement, Britain had maintained its right in wartime to seize contraband from neutral vessels and incapacitate an enemy's merchant fleet. Especially after 1900, Britain would remain heavily reliant on maritime economic warfare.[10] In both 1914 and 1939 Britain was to use what remained of its naval supremacy to blockade in turn the Central Powers and Nazi Germany, much as it had earlier blockaded the United States. At the same time, in both world wars, the Germans had adapted the strategy, using submarines to conduct efficient blockades of Britain, only countered, after serious delay, by the use once more of merchant convoys as defensive economic warfare.

Therefore, in 1914 and again in 1939 the cargoes of enemy and neutral vessels, often materials crucial to the opponent's war effort, would again be intercepted by the Royal Navy, often with punctilious care to avoid the entry of neutrals into the war on the wrong side. In an effort to avoid confrontation, before the United States joined the Allies in 1917 Britain bought some intercepted neutral cargoes and repaid the American producers of canned meat, oil and cotton.[11]

As early in Britain's war against the United States as 4 April 1813, the Russian Minister at Washington had enquired into the possibility of an armistice during a proposed Russian mediation. He concluded that 'It would be almost impossible to establish an armistice without raising the blockade, since the latter does them more harm than all the hostilities.'[12] This realisation made such an impact on succeeding United States administrations that a House of Representatives Committee on Naval Affairs referred to British commercial blockade as long after the Anglo-American war as 1842. At a time when a series of diplomatic incidents made another war with Britain a possibility, the Committee expressed concern over the defencelessness of the southern and Gulf of Mexico ports, vital not only for American international but also internal trade. Their report, dated 12 May 1842, concluded 'If you desire to measure the hazard to which a maritime war with a formidable naval Power would expose this commerce, you have but to consult the testimony of experience.'[13]

EPILOGUE

THE TERMS OF THE TREATY OF GHENT made possible British re-use of the strategy of offensive and defensive economic warfare in further wars, and memories of the Royal Navy's past commercial and naval blockades and defensive convoys remained alive. The impact of the Royal Navy's blockades of the United States between 1812 and 1815, perhaps reinforced by those of Germany between 1914 and 1919 and in 1939, was such that they were recalled by some into living memory. During a tour of America in 1942, just after the United States' entry into the Second World War, the British Broadcasting Corporation's correspondent, Alistair Cooke, met an insurance broker in Hartford, Connecticut, who told him 'Of course, some things we won't insure. Nobody in this country will insure any cargo that the British might consider contraband. The British Navy virtually controls the seas, and we can't insure against British capture.'[1]

Hard feelings in some circles had evidently taken so long to diminish that the United States War Department's *Instructions for American Servicemen in Britain*, issued in 1942, mentioned the War of 1812 and cautioned that '… there is no time today to fight old wars over again, or bring up old grievances'.[2] But there may be time enough to acknowledge that, for too long, the significance of the Royal Navy's blockades of the United States during the War of 1812 has been seriously under-estimated.

APPENDIX A

TABLE 1. Royal Naval Prizes sent into Halifax Nova Scotia between 18 June 1812 and 26 March 1815.

Date of Capture	Prize Name	Rigged	Captors
24/06/1812	Malcolm	brig	HMS *Belvidera*
25/06/1812	*Fortune*	ship	HMS Belvidera
06/07/1812	*Minerva*	brig	*HMS Africa*
07/07/1812	*Enterprise*	brig	HMS *Ring Dove*
08/07/1812	*George*	brig	HMS *Guerriere*
08/07/1812	*Mary Elizabeth*	brig	HMS *Indian*
09/07/1812	*William* (recap)	barque	HMS *Indian*
10/07/1812	Marquis de Someruelas	ship	HMS *Atalante*
11/07/1812	*Oroonoko*	ship	HMS *Shannon*
11/07/1812	*Illuminator*	brig	HMS *Emulous*
12/07/1812	*Lively*	schooner	HMS *Emulous*
12/07/1812	*Traveller*	schooner	HMS *Emulous*
13/07/1812	*Maria*	ship	HMS *Emulous*
15/07/1812	*Start* (recap)	brig	HMS *Spartan*
15/07/1812	Belleisle	brig	HMS *Emulous*
16/07/1812	*Cordelia*	brig	HMS *Emulous*
16/07/1812	*USS Nautilus*	US brig	HMS *Shannon*
16/07/1812	*Fair Trader*	brig	HMS *Indian*
16/07/1812	*Active*	schooner	HMS *Spartan*
17/07/1812	*Nimrod* (recap)	schooner	HMS *Paz*
17/07/1812	George	schooner	HMS *Emulous*
17/07/1812	*Argus*	brig	HMS *Indian*
17/07/1812	*Mary*	schooner	HMS *Spartan*
18/07/1812	*Hiram*	brig	HMS *Spartan*
18/07/1812	*Actress*	schooner	HMS *Spartan*
18/07/1812	*Magnet* (became HM prison ship)	sloop	HMS *Ring Dove*
18/07/1812	*Martha* (recap)	ship	HMS *Paz*
18/07/1812	*Eliza* (recap)	schooner	HMS *Chubb*
18/07/1812	*Ann* (recap)	schooner	HMS *Chubb*
19/07/1812	*Fanny* (recap)	brig	HMS *Colibri*
19/07/1812	*Rover* (recap)	ship	HMS *Ring Dove*

Date of Capture	Prize Name	Rigged	Captors
19/07/1812	Four Sisters	schooner	HMS *Ring Dove*
19/07/1812	*Friendship*	ship	HMS *Indian*
20/07/1812	*Hesper* (recap)	schooner	HMS *Ring Dove*
22/07/1812	*George* (recap)	brig	HMS *Maidstone*
22/07/1812	*Mariner* (recap)	brig	HMS *Colibri*
23/07/1812	*Mary-Ann* (recap)	ship	HMS *Maidstone*
23/07/1812	Gleanor	schooner	HMS *Colibri*
24/07/1812	*Curlew*	sloop	HMS *Acasta*
26/07/1812	*Catherine*	brig	HMS *Colibri*
30/07/1812	*Gossamer*	brig	HMS *Emulous*
31/07/1812	*Eleanor*	schooner	HMS *Shannon*
31/07/1812	*Prevoyante*	schooner	HMS *Emulous*
01/08/1812	*Zodiac*	ship	HMS *Alphea*
01/08/1812	*Polly*	schooner	HMS *Maidstone*
01/08/1812	Morning Star	schooner	HMS *Maidstone*
03/08/1812	*Commodore Barry*	sloop	HMS *Maidstone*
03/08/1812	*Madison*	schooner	HMS *Maidstone*
04/08/1812	*Concordia*	ship	HMS *Shannon*
07/081812	*Grace* (recap)	brig	HMS *Chubb*
08/08/1812	Buckskin	schooner	HMS *Statira*
09/08/1812	*Pythagoras*	sloop	HMS *Bream*
10/08/1812	*Bolina*	ship	HMS *Morgiana*
10/08/1812	*Union Lass* (recap)	schooner	HMS *Chubb*
10/08/1812	*Sally* (recap)	brig	HMS *Morgiana*
11/08/1812	*Henry* (recap)	ship	HMS *Emulous*
11/08/1812	Polly	schooner	HMS *Acasta*
11/08/1812	*Prudence*	brig	HMS *Morgiana*
11/08/1812	*Regulator*	schooner	HMS *Colibri*
12/08/1812	*Dolphin*	schooner	HMS *Earl of Moria*
13/08/1812	*Dolphin*	schooner	HMS *Maidstone*
13/08/1812	*John*	brig	HMS *Maidstone*
13/08/1812	*Apollo* (recap)	ship	HMS *Statira*
14/08/1812	*Union* (recap)	brig	HMS *Morgiana*
14/08/1812	Lewis	schooner	HMS *Hope*
16/08/1812	*Union*	ship	HMS *Emulous*
17/08/1812	*Bainbridge*	ship	HMS *Belvidera*
17/08/1812	*William* (recap)	snow	HMS *Statira*
17/08/1812	*Nancy* (recap)	ship	HMS *Statira*
17/08/1812	Eastern Star	ship	HMS *Africa*
18/08/1812	*Russel* (recap)	brig	HMS *Statira*
19/08/1812	*Osbourne* (recap)	ship	HMS *Emulous*
19/08/1812	Phoebe	brig	HMS *Aeolus*
21/08/1812	*Dolphin*	schooner	HMS *Colibri*

Date of Capture	Prize Name	Rigged	Captors
21/08/1812	Hare	brig	HMS Belvidera
22/08/1812	Monsoon	schooner	HMS Aeolus
23/08/1812	Adeline (recap)	ship	HMS Statira
23/08/1812	Monk	brig	HMS Colibri
24/08/1812	Honestas	ship	HMS Nymph
25/08/1812	Science	ship	HMS Emulous
25/08/1812	Henrietta (recap)	sloop	HMS Emulous
26/08/1812	Patriot	barque	HMS Acasta
27/08/1812	Jane	schooner	HMS Nymph
28/08/1812	Merchant	ship	HMS Nymph
28/08/1812	Georgiana	ship	HMS Nymph
28/08/1812	Doris	ship	HMS Nymph
29/08/1812	Merchant	ship	HMS Statira
30/08/1812	Betsy	ship	HMS Acasta
30/08/1812	Sophia	schooner	HMS Plumper
30/08/1812	Prince of Asturias (recap)	brig	HMS Statira
31/08/1812	Ceres	brig	HMS Spy storeship
02/09/1812	Stockholm	ship	HMS Maidstone
02/09/1812	Planter (recap)	schooner	HMS Shannon
03/09/1812	Argo (recap)	ship	HMS Plumper
04/09/1812	Aristomenes	snow brig	HMS Shannon
04/09/1812	Britannia (recap)	ship	HMS Junon
05/09/1812	Howe (recap)	ship	HMS Plumper
06/09/1812	Hector (recap)	snow brig	HMS Plumper
06/09/1812	Charles Faucett	brig	HMS Emulous
06/09/1812	Fabius	ship	HMS Shannon
11/09/1812	Friendship	schooner	HMS Belvidera
12/09/1812	Ambition	brig	HMS Orpheus
12/09/1812	Hiram	schooner	HMS Belvidera
16/09/1812	Sally Ann	schooner	HMS Statira
17/09/1812	Melantho	ship	HMS Spartan
17/09/1812	Federal	brig	HMS Acasta
21/09/1812	Diana (recap)	ship	HMS San Domingo
21/09/1812	Abigail (recap)	ship	HMS Poictiers
24/09/1812	Packet	ship	HMS Orpheus
01/10/1812	Elisia	brig	HMS Aeolus
05/10/1812	Pitt (recap)	brig	HMS Nymph
05/10/1812	El Rayo	brig	HMS Maidstone
11/10/1812	Wily Reynard	schooner	HMS Shannon
17/10/1812	Blonde (recap)	schooner	HMS Acasta
18/10/1812	Rapid (became HMS Nova Scotia)	brig	HMS Maidstone
19/10/1812	Union	schooner	HMS Maidstone

Date of Capture	Prize Name	Rigged	Captors
31/10/1812	*Thorn*	brig	HMS *Tenedos*
04/12/1812	*Revenge*	schooner	HMS *Paz*
" "	*Tulip*	brig	HMS *Atalante*
09/01/1813	Highflyer (became HMS *High Flyer*)	schooner	HMS *Acasta*
17/02/1813	Sarah	brig	HMS *Tenedos*
13/03/1813	*Lucy*	schooner	HMS *Rattler*
26/03/1813	*Volant*	ship	HMS *Curlew*
04/04/1813	*Cossack*	schooner	HMS *Emulous*
04/04/1813	*Traveller*	sloop	HMS *Rattler*
05/04/1813	*Favorite*	schooner	HMS *Valiant*
08/03/1813	*Specie*	schooner	HMS *Nymph*
10/04/1813	*Packet*	sloop	HMS *Valiant*
11/04/1813	*Expedition*	schooner	HMS *Rattler*
12/04/1813	*Jennet*	brig	HMS *Junon*
12/04/1813	*Flight*	schooner	HMS *Spartan*
12/04/1813	*Caroline*	brig	HMS *La Hogue*
16/04/1813	*Dispatch*	brig	HMS *La Hogue*
16/04/1813	*Plough Boy*	schooner	HMS *Orpheus*
16/04/1813	*Sally*	ship	HMS *La Hoge*
18/04/1813	*Bird*	schooner	HMS *Emulous*
19/04/1813	*Lark*	sloop	HMS *Bream*
20/04/1813	*Vivid*	brig	HMS *Nymph*
20/04/1813	*Ulysses*	brig	HMS *Orpheus*
20/04/1813	*Susannah*	sloop	HMS *Bream*
23/04/1813	*Sibae*	brig	HMS *Atalante*
23/04/1813	*Semiramis*	sloop	HMS *Bream*
23/04/1813	*Victorious*	schooner	HMS *Rattler*
24/04/1813	*Sally*	brig	HMS *Curlew*
26/04/1813	*Branch*	schooner	HMS *Bream*
28/04/1813	*Henry*	ship	HMS *La Hogue*
28/04/1813	*Aoelus* (recap)	brig	HMS *La Hogue*
30/04/1813	Hector	brig	HMS *Spartan*
01/05/1813	Juana	sloop	HMS *Spartan*
02/05/1813	*Catherine* (recap)	brig	HMS *La Hogue*
05/05/1813	Montgomery	brig	HMS *Nymph*
05/05/1813	*Ann* (recap)	schooner	HMS *Nymph*
09/05/1813	*Young Pheonix* (recap)	ship	HMS *Orpheus*
10/05/1813	Diomede	brig	HMS *Nymph*
10/05/1813	*Emperor* (recap)	schooner	HMS *Ramilies*
10/05/1813	*Juliet*	sloop	HMS *Paz*
10/05/1813	*Columbia* (recap)	schooner	HMS *Rattler*
11/05/1813	Juliana Smith	schooner	HMS *Nymph*

Date of Capture	Prize Name	Rigged	Captors
13/05/1813	Sally	schooner	HMS Bream
16/05/1813	Orion	brig	HMS La Hogue
18/05/1813	Duck (recap)	ship	HMS Bold
18/05/1813	Pilgrim	brig	HMS La Hogue
19/05/1813	Alexander	ship	HMS Rattler
19/05/1813	Dolphin	brig	HMS La Hogue
19/05/1813	Fidelia	ship	HMS Orpheus
20/05/1813	Finland	ship	HMS Chesapeake's squadron
20/05/1813	Volador	brig	HMS Statira
21/05/1813	Enterprize	schooner	HMS Tenedos
24/05/1813	Post Boy	schooner	HMS Rattler
26/05/1813	Paragon (recap)	ship	HMS Tenedos
26/05/1813	Lucy (recap)	brig	HMS Shannon
28/05/1813	Harriet	brig	HMS Victorious
28/05/1813	Nancy	schooner	HMS Victorious
30/05/1813	Plough Boy	sloop	HMS Statira
30/05/1813	Commerce	brig	HMS Spartan
31/05/1813	William	brig	HMS Shannon
01/06/1813	USS Chesapeake	US frigate	HMS Shannon
01/06/1813	Fanny	brig	HMS Statira
02/06/1813	Flor de Lisboa	brig	HMS Spartan
02/06/1813	Carlotta	brig	HMS Spartan
08/06/1813	Belle	brigantine	HMS Spartan
08/06/1813	Hetty	schooner	HMS Statira
12/06/1813	Hero (recap)	brig	HMS Martin
13/06/1813	Morning Star	brig	HMS Spartan
14/06/1813	Del Carmen	sloop	HMS Spartan
14/06/1813	Star	schooner	HMS Victorious
15/06/1813	Lark (recap)	ship	HMS Borer
16/06/1813	Christiana (recap)	schooner	HMS Borer
16/06/1813	Roscio	brig	HMS Dover
17/06/1813	Porcupine	brig	HMS Valiant
18/06/1813	Eunice	brig	HMS Wasp
18/06/1813	Protectress	schooner	HMS Victorious
22/06/1813	Gustava	ship	HMS Sylph
22/06/1813	Thomas	brig	HMS Wasp
24/06/1813	Norht Star	brig	HMS Tenedos
24/06/1813	Carl Gustaf	brig	HMS Martin
24/06/1813	H erman (recap)	ship	HMS Atalante
24/06/1813	Maria	ship	HMS Bold
26/06/1813	Carnarvon	brig	HMS Woolwich
27/06/1813	Young Teazer	brig	HMS La Hogue

Date of Capture	Prize Name	Rigged	Captors
27/06/1813	*Little Bill*	schooner	HMS *Loup Cervier*
27/06/1813	*Rebecca*	schooner	HMS *Boxer*
28/06/1813	Nancy	schooner	HMS *Boxer*
28/06/1813	*Harriet* (recap)	schooner	HMS *Dover*
30/06/1813	Minerva	brig	HMS *La Hogue*
30/06/1813	Thomas	schooner	HMS *Nymph*
30/06/1813	Liverpool Packet	ship	HMS *Dover*
30/06/1813	*Ulysses*	brig	HMS *Majestic*
06/07/1813	*Two Brothers*	schooner	HMS *Boxer*
07/07/1813	*Swift*	schooner	HMS *Curlew*
07/07/1813	*Two Brothers*	schooner	HMS *Curlew*
07/07/1813	*Ellen*	brig	HMS *La Hogue*
07/07/1813	*Prudentia*	ship	HMS *Rattler*
07/07/1813	*Eunice*	sloop	HMS *Curlew*
07/07/1813	*Friendship*	sloop	HMS *Boxer*
08/07/1813	*Fanny*	brig	HMS *La Hogue*
08/07/1813	*Sea Flower* (recap)	brig	HMS *Fantome*
09/07/1813	Pricilla	schooner	HMS *Curlew*
10/07/1813	*Roxanna*	ship	HMS *La Hogue*
11/07/1813	*Republican*	ship	HMS *Nimrod*
11/07/1813	*John Adams*	brig	HMS *Rattler*
11/07/1813	*Mentor*	sloop	HMS *La Hogue*
11/07/1813	Jerusha	sloop	HMS *La Hogue*
11/07/1813	*Friendship*	sloop	HMS *La Hogue*
12/07/1813	*Ohio*	brig	HMS *Manly*
12/07/1813	*Jefferson*	schooner	HMS *Bream*
13/07/1813	*Anna*	brigantine	HMS *Poictiers*
14/07/1813	*Betsey*	schooner	HMS *Bream*
14/07/1813	*Triton*	schooner	HMS *Bream*
14/07/1813	*Malaren*	brig	HMS *La Hogue*
17/07/1813	*YorkTown*	ship	HMS *Maidstone*
18/07/1813	*Lavinia* (recap)	ship	HMS *Recruit*
18/07/1813	*Machester* (recap)	brig	HMS *Maidstone*
20/07/1813	Lively	schooner	HMS *L'Epervier*
22/07/1813	*Isabella*	brig	HMS *Pictou*
22/07/1813	*Fanny*	brig	HMS *Statira*
25/07/1813	Fair Play	sloop	HMS *Boxer*
25/07/1813	*Providence* (recap)	schooner	HMS *Nymphe*
27/07/1813	*Stamper* (recap)	brig	HMS *Ring Dove*
29/07/1813	*Mary* (recap)	sloop	HMS *Nimrod*
31/07/1813	Flor de Tejo	brig	HMS *Manly*
31/07/1813	*Porpoise*	schooner	HMS *Rattler*
31/07/1813	*William & Ann* (recap)	sloop	HMS *Nimrod*

Date of Capture	Prize Name	Rigged	Captors
31/07/1813	Anaconda	brig	HMS *Sceptre*
02/08/1813	*Hope* (recap)	ship	HMS *Manly*
03/08/1813	Luisa	schooner	HMS *Martin*
03/08/1813	*Hannah*	schooner	HMS *Boxer*
03/08/1813	*Rebecca*	schooner	HMS *Boxer*
04/08/1813	*Four Brothers* (recap)	schooner	HMS *Emulous*
08/08/1813	Wasp	sloop	HMS *Bream*
12/08/1813	*Gannet*	schooner	HMS *Curlew*
13/08/1813	*Paragon*	schooner	HMS *Curlew*
13/08/1813	*Polly* (recap)	schooner	HMS *Statira*
16/08/1813	Flor de Mar	ship	HMS *La Hogue*
17/08/1813	*Endeavour*	sloop	HMS *Curlew*
18/08/1813	*Morning Star*	schooner	HMS *Curlew*
18/08/1813	*Chance* (recap)	brig	HMS *La Hogue*
18/08/1813	*King George* (recap)	schooner	HMS *Recruit*
24/08/1813	Espozy y Mina	schooner	HMS *Statira*
25/08/1813	*Raven*	schooner	HMS *Manly*
26/08/1813	*Elizabeth* (recap)	brig	HMS *Shelburne*
27/08/1813	Euphemia	schooner	HMS *Majestic*
28/08/1813	*Hope*	ship	HMS *Loup Cervier*
29/08/1813	*Mariner* (recap)	brig	HMS *Poictiers*
31/08/1813	Fortune	schooner	HMS *Boxer*
31/08/1813	*Divina Pastora*	ship	HMS *Statira*
02/09/1813	*Jerusalem*	ship	HMS *Majestic*
02/09/1813	*Drake*	sloop	HMS *Belvidera*
03/09/1813	*Watson* (recap)	brig	HMS*Poictiers*
11/09/1813	Torpedo	schooner	HMS *Plantagenet*
11/09/1813	*Massachusett*	ship	HMS *Canso*
11/09/1813	*Ocean* (recap)	brig	HMS *Borer*
13/09/1813	Elvira	sloop	HMS *Orpheus*
13/09/1813	*Mary* (recap)	schooner	HMS *Sylph*
14/09/1813	Santa Cecilia	ship	HMS *Wasp*
16/09/1813	*Catalana Patriota*		HMS *Shannon*
16/09/1813	*Alianza*		HMS *Shannon*
17/09/1813	*Queen Charlotte* (recap)	schooner	HMS *Shannon*
18/09/1813	Little Sisters	schooner	HMS *Belvidera*
19/09/1813	*Gamla Lodelse*	brig	HMS *High Flyer*
20/09/1813	*Active*	ship	HMS *L'Epervier*
22/09/1813	Ambition	sloop	HMS *Statira*
24/09/1813	*Venus*	ship	HMS *Borer*
25/09/1813	*Resolution*	ship	HMS *Majestic*
27/09/1813	*Shannon* (recap)	brig	HMS *Manly*
29/09/1813	*Margarett* (recap)	sloop	HMS *Martin*

Date of Capture	Prize Name	Rigged	Captors
30/09/1813	Montezuma	ship	HMS *La Hogue*
30/09/1813	*Edward* (recap)	brig	HMS *Fantome*
04/10/1813	Charles	ship	HMS *Paz*
05/10/1813	*Medel padria*	brig	HMS *Conflict*
05/10/1813	*Portsmouth Packet*	schooner	HMS *Fantome*
11/10/1813	*Charlotte*	ship	HMS *Comet*
11/10/1813	*Richard de Stanley*	schooner	HMS *Paz*
11/10/1813	*Atlantic* (recap)	brig	HMS *Maidstone*
14/10/1813	Randolph	schooner	HMS *Paz*
16/10/1813	*Baltic*	ship	HMS *La Hogue*
16/10/1813	*Sally*	schooner	HMS *Loire*
19/10/1813	*Alert*	sloop	HMS *Borer*
20/10/1813	*Dispatch* (recap)	brig	HMS *Albion*
21/10/1813	Betsey & Jane	schooner	HMS *Majestic*
25/10/1813	*Hoppett*	brig	HMS *Emulous*
25/10/1813	*Telemachus* (recap)	brig	HMS *Narcissus*
27/10/1813	William	schooner	HMS *Paz*
28/10/1813	*Paris* (recap)	bark	HMS *Ring Dove*
29/10/1813	*John & Mary* (recap)	brig	HMS *Loup Cervier*
03/11/1813	Industry	schooner	HMS *Arab*
03/11/1813	*Peggy*	sloop	HMS *L'Epervier*
04/11/1813	*Ann* (recap)	brig	HMS *Jaseur*
11/11/1813	Huntress	sloop	HMS *Boxer*
14/11/1813	*Husaren*	brig	HMS *Jaseur*
14/11/1813	Hero	schooner	HMS *Belvidera*
23/11/1813	*Franklin*	sloop	HMS *Belvidera*
24/11/1813	*Venus* (recap)	schooner	HMS *Rifleman*
27/11/1813	Dove	schooner	HMS *Martin*
01/12/1813	*General Marion*	schooner	HMS *Ramilies*
01/12/1813	*Rising Sun*	sloop	HMS *Loire*
02/12/1813	*Chili*	ship	HMS *Nimrod*
03/12/1813	*Manhattan*	sloop	HMS *Nimrod*
04/12/1813	*Gardner*	ship	HMS *Loire*
04/12/1813	*Catharine*	sloop	HMS *Majestic*
04/12/1813	*Policy* (recap)	ship	HMS *Loire*
06/12/1813	Jane	sloop	HMS *Junon*
08/12/1813	*West Indian*	schooner	HMS *Loire*
08/12/1813	*Julian*	schooner	HMS *Martin*
10/12/1813	*Rolla*	schooner	HMS *Loire*
11/12/1813	*Erie*	schooner	HMS *Sophie*
13/12/1813	*Emeline*	sloop	HMS *Boxer*
17/12/1813	*Calmar*	sloop	HMS *Curlew*
23/02/1814	Alfred	brig	HMS *L'Epervier*

Date of Capture	Prize Name	Rigged	Captors
05/03/1814	Lizard	schooner	HMS Prometheus
16/03/1814	Margaret (recap)	schooner	HMS Maidstone
23/03/1814	San Joaquin	brig	HMS Albion
28/03/1814	Holstein	schooner	HMS Belvidera
29/03/1814	Esperanza	schooner	HMS Belvidera
30/03/1814	Union (recap)	ship	HMS Curlew
09/04/1814	Plutus (recap)	ship	HMS Curlew
18/04/1814	Sarah	schooner	HMS La Hogue
21/04/1814	New Zealander (recap)	ship	HMS Belvidera
21/04/1814	Minerva	brig	HMS La Hogue
27/0401814	Pilgrim	schooner	HMS Bream
30/04/1814	Hannah (recap)	brig	HMS Martin
04/05/1814	Maria Francisca (recap)	brig	HMS Curlew
09/05/1814	Dantzig	brig	HMS Fantome
13/05/1814	Catalina	brig	HMS Superb
13/05/1813	Victor	brig	HMS La Hogue
13/05/1814	Experiment	schooner	HMS Bulwark
15/05/1814	Amelia	sloop	HMS Bulwark
15/05/1814	Tejo	ship	HMS La Hogue
19/05/1814	Candelaria	sloop	HMS Superb
22/05/1814	Dominica	schooner	HMS Majestic
23/05/1814	Quiz	schooner	HMS Nieman
23/05/1814	Model	schooner	HMS Nieman
23/05/1814	Clara	schooner	HMS Nieman
25/05/1814	Two Brothers (recap)	ship	HMS Curlew
25/05/1814	Ontario (recap)	ship	HMS Curlew
25/05/1814	Hussar	schooner	HMS Saturn
26/05/1814	Thomas & Sally (recap)	brig	HMS Curlew
28/05/1814	Diomede	schooner	HMS Rifleman
29/05/1814	Success (recap)	brig	HMS Charybdis
31/05/1814	Fame	sloop	HMS Endymion
01/06/1814	Mary (recap)	ship	HMS Martin
04/06/1814	Francisa de Paula	brig	HMS Nimrod
04/06/1814	Betsy	schooner	HMS Recruit
05/06/1814	Magdalena	schooner	HMS Martin
06/06/1814	Herculaneum	brig	HMS La Hogue
07/06/1814	Flash	sloop	HMS Nieman
11/06/1814	Orient	schooner	HMS Bulwark
14/06/1814	Tickler	sloop	HMS Saturn
16/06/1814	Voador	brig	HMS La Hogue
19/06/1814	William (recap)	schooner	HMS Wasp
22/06/1814	Delesdernier	schooner	HMS Tenedos
23/06/1814	Ex-Bashaw	sloop	HMS Bulwark

Date of Capture	Prize Name	Rigged	Captors
23/06/1814	*Commerce* (recap)	brig	HMS *Superb*
28/06/1814	Voador	brig	HMS *Nymphe*
30/06/1814	*Snap Dragon*	schooner	HMS *Martin*
30/06/1814	*Nighthawk*	schooner	HMS *Superb*
02/07/1814	*Morning Star*	sloop	HMS *Dragon*
02/07/1814	*Robust*	sloop	HMS *Dragon*
02/07/1814	*Eclipse*	sloop	HMS *Dragon*
01/07/1814	*Eliza*	schooner	HMS *Armide*
03/07/1814	*Eliza*	schooner	HMS *Rifleman*
03/07/1814	*Bee*	schooner	HMS *Nymphe*
10/07/1814	*Nelly* (recap)	schooner	HMS *Bulwark*
10/07/1814	Prudence	schooner	HMS *Acasta*
11/07/1814	Rattlesnake	brig	HMS *Leander*
11/07/1814	*Thorn*	schooner	HMS *Bulwark*
12/07/1814	*Henry Gilder*	brig	HMS *Nieman*
13/07/1814	*Governor Shelby*	schooner	HMS *Narcissus*
13/07/1814	*Ranger*	schooner	HMS *Superb*
13/07/1814	*Union*	schooner	HMS *Rifleman*
14/07/1814	*Maria Frederica*	ship	HMS *Seahorse*
15/07/1814	*Sir Alexander Ball* (recap)	ship	HMS *Nieman*
16/07/1814	Stephanie	schooner	HMS *Acasta*
18/07/1814	*Antelope*	schooner	HMS *Tenedos*
19/07/1814	*Diana*	sloop	HMS *Acasta*
19/07/1814	*Brizi*	schooner	HMS *Dragon*
21/07/1814	*Tyger*	brig	HMS *Bulwark*
23/07/1814	*Fame*	sloop	HMS *Spencer*
23/07/1814	*Unity*	sloop	HMS *Asia*
24/07/1814	*Hazard*	schooner	HMS *Acasta*
26/07/1814	*Cidade de Leira*	brig	HMS *Fantome*
31/07/1814	*Defiance*	sloop	HMS *Superb*
02/08/1814	*Delaware*	schooner	HMS *Acasta*
02/08/1814	*Jane*	sloop	HMS *Acasta*
03/08/1814	*Victory*	schooner	HMS *Leander*
03/08/1814	*Hibernia*	schooner	HMS *Nieman*
05/08/1814	*Dalkarlen*	brig	HMS *Leander*
06/08/1814	*Julian*	schooner	HMS *Borer*
07/08/1814	*Old Carpenter*	schooner	HMS *Spencer*
07/08/1814	*Enigheton*	brig	HMS *Nieman*
09/08/1814	*Anita*	brig	HMS *Leander*
09/08/1814	*Ida*	brig	HMS *Newcastle*
15/08/1814	*Herald*	schooner	HMS *Armide*
16/08/1814	*Invincible* (recap)	ship	HMS *Armide*
16/08/1814	*Helen* (recap)	ship	HMS *Wasp*

Date of Capture	Prize Name	Rigged	Captors
19/08/1814	Wanderer	snow	HMS *Tenedos*
20/08/1814	*Conde dos Arcos*	ship	HMS *Superb*
21/08/1814	*Judith*	sloop	HMS *L'Espoir*
24/08/1814	*Landrail* (recap)	sloop	HMS *Wasp*
28/08/1814	Bee	schooner	HMS *Rifleman*
30/08/1814	*Enterprize*	schooner	HMS *Nieman*
31/08/1814	*Charlotte* (recap)	brig	HMS *Wasp*
02/09/1814	*Favorite* (recap)	brig	HMS *Albion*
03/09/1814	William	schooner	HMS *Albion*
03/09/1814	*Caledonian* (recap)	ship	HMS *Nymph*
04/09/1814	Two Brothers	schooner	HMS *Nieman*
04/09/1814	*Maria*	schooner	HMS *Nimrod*
05/09/1814	*James*	schooner	HMS *Nieman*
06/09/1814	*Alexander* (recap)	brig	HMS *Wasp*
07/09/1814	*Betsy* (recap)	ship	HMS *Pylades*
08/09/1814	Fox	schooner	HMS *Bacchante*
10/09/1814	Betsy	schooner	HMS *Albion*
13/09/1814	*Nancy* (recap)	brig	HMS *Pylades*
15/09/1814	Vestal	ship	HMS *Dragon*
18/09/1814	*Daedalus*	schooner	HMS *Nieman*
18/09/1814	*Perserverance*	sloop	HMS *Bacchante*
21/09/1814	*Albion* (recap)	brig	HMS *Jaseur*
26/09/1814	Good Hope	schooner	HMS *Loire*
28/09/1814	*Sarah* (recap)	schooner	HMS *Maidstone*
30/09/1814	*Cod Hook* (recap)	ship	HMS *Spencer*
04/10/1814	Tickler	schooner	HMS *Neiman*
06/10/1814	*Mary* (recap)	schooner	HMS *Wasp*
11/10/1814	*William* (recap)	brig	HMS *Armide*
20/10/1814	Saucy Jack	schooner	HMS *Saracen*
22/10/1814	*Amazon* (recap)	ship	HMS *Bulwark*
23/10/1814	Eagle	schooner	HMS *Narcissus*
23/10/1814	*Harlequin*	schooner	HMS *Bulwark*
24/10/1814	*Black Swan*	brig	HMS *Maidstone*
26/10/1814	*Lively*	sloop	HMS *St Lawrence*
27/10/1814	*Mentor* (recap)	ship	HMS *Maidstone*
30/10/1814	*Halifax Packet* (recap)	brig	HMS *Bulwark*
01/11/1814	Macdonough	brig	HMS *Bacchante*
05/11/1814	*Charles* (recap)	brig	HMS *Saturn*
05/11/1814	Theodore	brig	HMS *Saturn*
08/11/1814	*General Putnam*	schooner	HMS *Leander*
09/11/1814	*Jane* (recap)	brig	HMS *Maidstone*
19/11/1814	*Hero*	sloop	HMS *Tenedos*
23/11/1814	*Fermina*	ship	HMS *Maidstone*

Date of Capture	Prize Name	Rigged	Captors
24/11/1814	*Superb*	brig	HMS *Spencer*
01/12/1814	Three Williams (recap)	brig	HMS *Arab*
08/12/1814	*Lady Prevost* (recap)	brig	HMS *Nimrod*
24/12/1814	Armistice	schooner	HMS *Junon*
03/01/1815	Guerriere	brig	HMS *Junon*
22/01/1815	*Tomahawk*	schooner	HMS *Bulwark*
24/01/1815	*Joseph & Mary*	brig	HMS *Bulwark*
23/02/1815	*Margaret* (recap)	brig	HMS *Bulwark*
26/02/1815	Rhoda	schooner	HMS *Bulwark*
07/03/1815	*Legal Tender* (recap)	brig	HMS *Spencer*
19/03/1815	*Thistle* (recap)	schooner	HMS *Cossack*
26/03/1815	*Louisa* (recap)	brig	HMS *Maidstone*

Source: F. Kert; adapted from *Prize and Prejudice: Privateering and Naval Prize in Atlantic Canada in the War of 1812*, Research in Maritime History 11, International Maritime Economic History Association, St John's, Newfoundland, 1997, Appendix 1, pp. 160–203.

TABLE 2. Named United States navy vessels blockaded, taken or destroyed by February 1815.

Adams	24	Sloop, blockaded July 1813, burned at Hampden, Sept 1814
Argus	16	Brig, captured 14 August 1813, by HMS Pelican
Argus	-	Sloop, burned in Washington Navy Yard, 24 August 1814
Asp	-	Schooner, burned by British boats, 14 July 1814
Boston	-	Decayed beyond repair, burned Washington N Yd, Aug 1814
Chesapeake	38	Captured 1 June 1813 by HMS Shannon
Columbia	53	Burned while under construction in Washington Navy Yard
Constellation	38	Blockaded from 4 February 1813 in Norfolk & Elizabeth River
Constitution	44	Blockaded – Boston, July 1813
Congress	38	Blockaded from December 1813, Portsmouth New Hampshire
Erie	22	Ship-sloop, blockaded at Annapolis, March 1814
Essex	32	Destroyed off Valparaiso, 28 March 1814
Frolic	22	Sloop, captured 20 April 1814 by HMS's Orpheus & Shelburne
Hornet	18	Blockaded in New London, 1 June 1813 – January 1814

Independence	74	Launched at Charlestown 4 July 1814, incomplete at war's end
John Adams	22	Major refit, guns and crew sent to Great Lakes, July 1813
Macedonian	38	Blockaded in New London from 1 June 1813
Nautilus	14	Captured by HMS Shannon on 16 July 1812
New York	-	Decayed beyond repair, burned in Washington N Yd, Aug 1814
Ohio	1	Schooner, captured Lake Erie, 12 August 1814
Ontario	22	Ship-sloop, blockaded at Baltimore for duration of war
President	44	Captured by HMS Endymion & others, 15 January 1815
Rattlesnake	14	Brig, captured by HMS Leander off Cape Sable, June 1814
Scorpion	5	Schooner, captured on Lake Huron on 6 September 1814
Siren	-	Blockaded in Boston from 17 June 1813
Syren	16	Brig, captured 1814
Tigress	1	Schooner, captured on Lake Huron on 3 September 1814
United States	44	Blockaded in New London from 1 June 1813
Viper	12	Captured by HMS Narcissus on 17 January 1813
Vixen	14	Captured HMS Southampton, 22 November, lost 27 Nov 1812
Vixen	18	Captured by HMS Belvidera on 25 December 1812
Wasp	18	Sloop, captured by HMS Poictiers on 18 October 1812
Wasp	22	Sloop, lost at sea in October 1814

TABLE 3. Admiralty Office 7 August 1812: a list of Ships and Vessels on the West Indian and American stations

Rate	Name	No. guns	Commander
ON THE NORTH AMERICAN STATION			
3	*St Domingo*	74	Capt. Gill, Charles
3	*Africa*	64	Capt. Bastard, John
5	*Acasta*	44	Capt. Kerrs, Th Robert
5	*Guerriere*	38	Capt. Dacres, Jas R.
5	*Spartan*	38	Capt. Brenton, Ed'd Pelham
5	*Shannon*	38	Capt. Broke, J B Vere
5	*Nymphe*	38	Capt. Epworth, T Pr
5	*Junon*	38	Capt. Sanders, James
5	*Belvidera*	36	Capt. Byron, Rich'd
5	*Maidstone*	36	Capt. Burdett, Geo.

Rate	Name	No. guns	Commander
5	*Rolus*	32	Capt. Townsend, Lord Jas.6
5	*Tartarus*	20	Capt. Pasco, John
Sloop	*Indian*	16	Capt. Jane, Henry
Sloop	*Emulous*	16	Capt. Godfrey, Wm Howe
Sloop	*Atalante*	16	Capt. Hickey, Fred'k
Sloop	*Rattler*	16	Capt. Gordon, Alex'r
Sloop	*Goree*	16	Capt. Byng, H'n Dilkes
Sloop	*Recruit*	16	Capt. Senhouse, Humph F.
Sloop	*Morgiana*	16	Capt. Scott, David
Sloop	*Sylph*	16	Lieut. Enedy
Sloop	*Magnet*	14	Recommended to be employed in the West Indies as not being fit for the American Seas
Sloop	*Martin*	16	Capt. Evans, John
Sloop	*Coquette*	18	Capt. Simpson, John
Sloop	*Colibre*	14	Capt. Thompson, John
Sloop	*Martine*	16	Capt. Debourcy, Nerion
Gunbrig	*Plumper*	12	Lieut. Dray, J.
Gunbrig	*Paz*	12	Lieut. Dumaresq, Perry
Gunbrig	*Juniper*	10	Lieut. Napal Nath'l
Gunbrig	*Cuttle*	4	Lieut. Saunders K.
Gunbrig	*Chub*	4	Lieut. Nisb ett Sam'l
Gunbrig	*Bream*	4	Lieut. Simpson
Stre Vess	*Ruby*	18	Commodore Evans A. J.
Stre Vess	*Centurion*	14	Lieut. Kinsman

LEEWARD ISLANDS

Rate	Name	No. guns	Commander
3	*Dragon*	74	Capt. J. A. Collier
5	*Statira*	38	Capt. Stackpole H
5	*Tribune*	36	Capt. Reynolds, George
5	*Orpheus*	36	Capt. Pigot, Hugh
6	*Cherub*	20	Capt. Tucker, Tho's Tudor
6	*Lightning*	20	Capt. Doyle B. C.
Sloops	*Demarara*	16	Capt. Smith Wm H.
Sloops	*Amaranthe*	16	Capt. Pringle Geo.
Sloops	*Surinam*	16	Capt. Hath S. E.
Sloops	*Scorpion*	16	Capt. Giles, Robert
Sloops	*Peruvian*	16	Capt. Dickinson
Sloops	*Ringdove*	16	Capt. Dowes William
Sloops	*Charybdis*	16	Capt. Dephane Jas
Sloops	*Arachne*	16	Capt. Chambers, Samuel
Sloops	*Spider*	14	Capt. Willock, Tim'y Geo.
Sloops	*Dominica*	14	Capt. Hocking, Robert

Rate	Name	No. guns	Commander
Sloops	Opossum	10	Capt. Holrige, Thos
Schooner	Swaggerer	14	Lieut. Evelyn, George J.
Schooner	Elizabeth	12	Lieut. Dwyer, Edw. J.
Schooner	Netley	12	Lieut. Jackson
Schooner	Laura	10	Lieut. Hunter Chas Newton
Schooner	Morning	10	Lieut. Steele J.
Schooner	Maria	10	Lieut. Kippen
Schooner	Subtle	10	Lieut. Browne Chas.
Schooner	Dallahoo	4	Lieut. King, Norfolk
Guards'p	Liberty	-	Lieut. Guise G.
Troop-	Vestal	14	Capt. Decker
Ships	Mercury	16	Capt. Milbrand

JAMAICA

Rate	Name	No. guns	Commander
3	Polyphemus	64 ordered home	Capt. Douglas
5	Thetis	38	Capt. Byam Wm Hon.
5	Arethusa	38 expected	Capt. Coffin
5	Southampton	32	Capt. Yeo, Sir J. L.
6	Barbados	28	Capt. Rushbrook Edw'd
6	Garland	22	Capt. Huskisson, Tho's
6	Cyane	22	Capt. Forrest, Thomas
6	Herald	20	Capt. Jackson, Geo.
6	Fawn	20	Capt. Fellowes Tho.
Sloops	Moselle	16	Capt. Mowbray, Geo.
Sloops	Sappho	16	Capt. O'Grady, Hayes
Sloops	Brazen	18	Capt. Davies R. Plummer
Sloops	Saphire	16	Capt. Haynes Hon. J.
Sloops	Frolic	16	Capt. Whingates Thos
Sloops	Rhodian	10	Capt. Ross, John
Schooner	Decouveste	12	Lieut. Williams R'd
Schooner	Variable	8	Lieut. Yates R. B.
Rec'g Ship	Shark	16 (deleted)	Capt. Roberts

Totals

Total at Halifax	33
Leeward Islands	28
Jamaica	18
Grand total	79

Source: NMM, HUL/18.

TABLE 4. Description of the ships on the North American station on 26 July 1814.

WITH THE FLAG

Tonnant	74
Dragon	74
Ramillies	74
Royal Oak	74
Armide	38
Surprize	38
Menelaus	38
Espoir	18
Wolverine	18
Carron	18
Rover	18
Devastation	bomb
Action	
Erebus	

HALIFAX TO NANTUCKET

Bulwark	74
Spencer	74
Leander	50
Majestic	50
Junon	38
Nymph	38
Tenedos	38*
Maidstone	36
Dauntless	18
Curlew	18
Wasp	18
Martin	18*
Arab	18
Fantome	18
Rifleman	18
Ratler	18
Recruit	18
Alban	14
Indian	14*
Alder	14
Pelter	14
Bream	4
Terror	bomb
Pictou	
Florida	[frigate]
Dominica	Sch

SHIPS EXPECTED

New Castle	50
Seahorse	38
Bachante	38
Fureuse	38
Orlando	36
Rapo[h]anock	36
Iphegenia	36
Cossack	22
Ganamede	24
Cyprus	20
Pandora	18
Pylades	18
Taracin	18

NANTUCKET TO DELAWARE

Superb	74
Ventura	50
Forth	40
Endyminion	40
Acasta	40 deleted
Pactolus	38
Pomone	38
Loire	38 deleted
Varussus	38
Tenedos	38*
Despatch	18
Nimrod	18
Sylph	18
Telegraph schooner &	
2 Sloops to be added	

CHESAPEAKE

Albion	74
Asia	74
Severn	40
Hebrus	36
Iasire	18
Manly	14
Thistle	14
Borer	[12]
Etna	bomb

CAPE HATTERAS

Lacedemonian	[38]
Peacock	18
Morgeana	18
Primrose	18
Doteral	18
1 frigate	
2 sloops to be added	

BAHAMAS & GULF OF MEXICO

Chesapeake	38
Hermes	20
Sophie	18
Childers	18
Shelburne	12
Cockchafer	4

QUEBEC

Indian	[14]*
le Corne	to Halifax

TO GO HOME

La Hogue	[74]
Orpheus	[38]
Martin	[14]

HALIFAX FOR REPAIR

ST LAWRENCE

Source: BJL, DDHO/7/4, IV. Spelling of original retained. * indicates double counting, each included once. No entries were made under the headings 'Halifax for Repair' or 'St Lawrence'.

APPENDIX B

TABLE 1. United States imports 1800–1815 in $

1800	93,252,768	1808	58,101,023
1801	113,363,511	1809	61,029,726
1802	78,333,333	1810	89,366,069
1803	65,666,666	1811	57,887,952
1804	87,000,000	1812	78,788,540
1805	125,525,175	1813	22,177,812
1806	136,561,730	1814	12,967,859
1807	144,740,342	1815	85,356,680

Source: D. North, 'United States Balance of Payments 1790–1860', *Trends in the American Economy in the Nineteenth Century*, Studies in Income and Wealth 24, National Bureau of Economic Research, Princeton, Princeton Univ. Press, 1960; repr. New York, Arno Press, 1975, pp. 591–2, Table A-2, Appendix A.

GRAPH 1. United States imports 1800–1815 in $

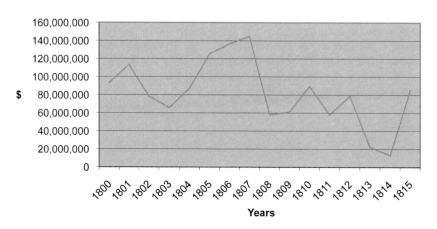

Source: see Table 1.

Availability of United States Import Statistics

No complete import figures were compiled in the United States before 1821. No value figures, only quantities, were kept on imports subject to specific rates of duty ranging from 2.5 to 40%, nor was information gathered on duty free imports. Value figures were gathered only on imports subject to *ad valorem* rates of duty, such as wines, spirits, tea, coffee, sugar and cocoa. Allen and Ely describe total figures for 1802–1820 as 'although apparently accurate … estimated many years later'[1] North notes that total import figures for 1789–1820 were officially overhauled and published in the Secretary of the Treasury's Report on Finance in 1835, although apparently unseen by Pitkin.[2] Not until 1854 did De Bow tabulate complete import figures, still published by the United States Bureau of the Census in 1975, reduced to one decimal place, probably to avoid charges of spurious accuracy, and puzzlingly described there as 'revealing, and despite their deficiencies, reliable'.[3] Variations notwithstanding, import figures indicate the pace and change in America's foreign trade during the war of 1812–15, and invite causal analysis. North's definitive American import statistics for 1812–14 crucially show that British maritime commercial blockade, protected by British naval blockade and intermittently compounded by poorly enforced and widely evaded American legislative trade restrictions, deprived Madison's administration of crucial customs duties, almost its sole source of revenue until January 1814.[4]

1. G. Allen and J. Ely, *International Trade Statistics*, New York, John Wiley and Sons, 1953, p. 269.
2. North, 'United States Balance of Payments 1790–1860', p. 588.
3. J. De Bow, *Statistical View of the United States*, Washington DC, A. Nicholson, 1854, Table CCV, p. 185.
4. North, 'United States Balance of Payments 1790–1860', pp. 591–2, Table A-2
Note: This appendix is based on Appendix 4.1, p. ii, in B. Arthur, 'The Role of Blockade in the Anglo-American Naval War of 1812–14', unpublished MA dissertation, Greenwich Maritime Institute, Univ. of Greenwich, 2002, p. 94.

TABLE 2. Computed or declared values of United Kingdom overseas trade 1796–1814, in £m.

	Imports	Domestic exports	+	Re-exports	=	Total exports
1796	39.6	30.1		8.5		38.6
1800	62.3	37.7		14.7		52.4
1806	53.3	40.9		9.2		50.1
1807	53.8	37.2		8.3		45.5
1808	51.5	37.3		6.5		43.8
1809	73.7	47.4		14.3		61.7
1810	88.5	48.4		12.5		60.9
1811	50.7	32.9		6.7		39.6
1812	56.0	41.7		9.1		50.8
1813	n/a	n/a		n/a		n/a
1814	80.8	45.5		24.8		70.3

Source: B. Mitchell and P. Deane, *Abstract of British Historical Statistics*, Cambridge, Cambridge Univ. Press, 1962, Table: Overseas Trade 2, Current Prices of Overseas Trade UK 1796–1853.

GRAPH 2. Computed or declared values of United Kingdom overseas trade 1796–1814.

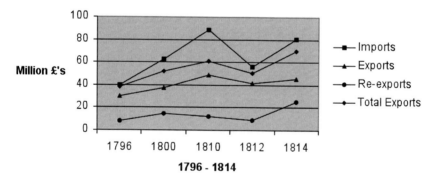

Source: see Table 2.

TABLE 3. United States net customs revenue in $ 1809–1814 to 31 December annually.

1809	6,852,577
1810	12,722,920
1811	8,223,715
1812	13,331,467
1813	6,892,925
1814	4,694,318

Source: A. Seybert, *Statistical Annals*, Philadelphia, T. Dobson, 1818, part of 'A Statement Exhibiting the gross and net amount of ad valorem and specific duties on Goods, Wares and Merchandise imported into the United States from 1st January 1794 to 31st December 1814', p. 494.

Note: when allowance is made for the doubled rate of duty after I July 1812, the net customs revenue figures of both Pitkin and North follow closely those of Seybert.

GRAPH 3. United States net customs revenue in $ 1809–1814 to 31 December annually.

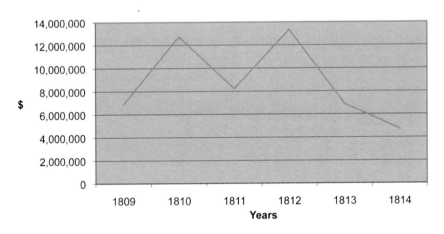

Source: see Table 3.
Note: see Table 3.

TABLE 4. United States national debt 1805–1815 in $.

1805	86,400,000
1806	82,300,000
1807	75,700,000
1808	69,200,000
1809	65,100,000
1810	57,000,000
1811	53,000,000
1812	48,000,000
1813	45,200,000
1814	63,545,831[1] Estimated by Jos Peason NC to be $105m by end of 1814
1815	119,635,000[2]

Source: D. Dewey, *Financial History of the United States*, 12th edn, New York, Kelly, 1934, repr. 1968, pp. 113, 125.

1. Calculated from additions since 1813: Seybert, *Statistical Annals*, p. 772.
2. $127,334,000 by end of calendar year: US Bureau of the Census, *Historical Statistics of the United States*, Washington DC, 1975, vol. 2, p. 1140.

GRAPH 4. United States national debt 1805–1815 in $.

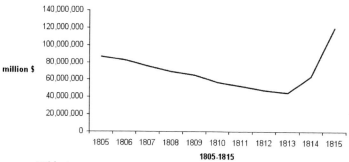

Source: see Table 4.

TABLE 5. United States total receipts and expenditure 1812–1813 in $m.

	Customs revenue	Internal revenue	Total tax revenue	Misc. receipts	Total receipts[1]	Expenditure	Deficit
1812	8.9	-	8.9	0.8	9.7	20.3	10.6[2]
1813	13.2	-	13.2	1.1	14.3	31.6	17.3

Source: Dewey, *Financial History of the United States*, pp. 141–2.

1. Excluding borrowing.
2. Clearly $10.6m by subtraction, although given by Dewey as $10.4m.

TABLE 6. Boston sugar prices 1813–1815 in $ per cwt of 100lbs.

Date	Price	
FIRST PERIOD: NEW ENGLAND SUBJECT TO EMBARGO BUT NOT BRITISH COMMERCIAL BLOCKADE		
5 August 1813	31.00	
7 August 1813	31.00	
15 December 1813	24.50	
17 December 1813		Madison's Second Embargo endorsed by Congress
29 January 1814	18.00	
2 February 1814	19.50	
7 March 1814	18.50	
15 March 1814	18.50	40.3% price fall since introduction of Second Embargo
19 March 1814	22.50	
30 March 1814		Madison calls in Congress for suspension of Embargo
SECOND PERIOD: NEW ENGLAND SUBJECT TO NEITHER EMBARGO NOR BRITISH COMMERCIAL BLOCKADE		
2 April 1814		Suspension of Embargo learned of in Boston
14 April 1814		Repeal by Congress of Embargo and Non Importation Acts
16 April 1814	15.32	31.9 % price fall since 19 March 1814
25 April 1814		British commercial blockade extended to New England
26 April 1814	15.75	
THIRD PERIOD: NEW ENGLAND SUBJECT TO BRITISH COMMERCIAL BLOCKADE ONLY		
5 May 1814		British commercial blockade of NE known of in Boston
9 May 1814	15.50	
16 May 1814	16.00	
14 July 1814	17.50	Credit sale price still available
16 August 1814	18.00	Cash price
22 August 1814	18.00	
23 August 1814	18.00	
6 October 1814	19.50	Cash price only quoted from this point
19 October 1814	19.50	
20 October 1814	20.00	
22 October 1814	20.00	
27 October 1814	22.50	45.2% price rise since commercial blockade known of in NE
17 February 1815		Treaty of Ghent ratified in Washington
24 February 1815	15.00	

Source: JCBL, Brown & Ives Corr: Box 160, ff. 9–10, from Charles Greene, Brown & Ives Boston agent to Thomas Poynton Ives, of Brown & Ives, Providence, RI, on dates given.

TABLE 7. Boston molasses prices 1813–1814 in $ per gallon.

Date	Price	
FIRST PERIOD: NEW ENGLAND SUBJECT TO EMBARGO BUT NOT		
BRITISH COMMERCIAL BLOCKADE		
20 November 1813	1.20	
13 December 1813	1.24	
17 December 1813		Madison's Second Embargo endorsed by Congress
23 December 1813	1.47	
29 January 1814	1.30	
2 February 1814	0.96	
3 March 1814	0.86.5	
12 March 1814	0.92.5	
19 March 1814	0.94.5	
25 March 1814	0.98	
30 March 1814		Madison calls in Congress for suspension of Embargo

SECOND PERIOD: NEW ENGLAND SUBJECT TO NEITHER EMBARGO
NOR BRITISH COMMERCIAL BLOCKADE

Date	Price	
2 April 1814		Suspension of Embargo learned of in Boston
14 April 1814		Repeal of Embargo and Non Importation Acts by Congress
16 April 1814	0.77	47.6% price fall since 2nd Embargo passed in Congress
25 April 1814	0.63.5	British commercial blockade extended to New England
26 April 1814	0.60.5	

THIRD PERIOD: NEW ENGLAND SUBJECT TO BRITISH
COMMERCIAL BLOCKADE ONLY

Date	Price	
5 May 1814	0.68	Cash price, British commercial blockade known of in Boston
21 May 1814	0.74.5	
9 July 1814	0.89	
14 July 1814	0.95	Cash price only quoted from this point
12 August 1814	0.91.25	
1 September 1814	1.00	
14 November 1814	1.43	110.3% price rise since commercial blockade of NE applied
22 November 1814	1.40.5	
29 November 1814	1.40	
19 December 1814	1.28	
29 December 1814	1.32	94.1 % price rise since commercial blockade of NE

Source: JCBL, Brown & Ives Corr: Box 160, ff. 9–10, from Charles Greene, Brown & Ives Boston agent to Thomas Poynton Ives, of Brown & Ives, Providence, RI, on dates given.

TABLE 8. Boston muscovado sugar prices 1813–1814, in $ per cwt of 100lbs.

Date	Price	
Date	*Price*	

FIRST PERIOD: NEW ENGLAND SUBJECT TO EMBARGO BUT NOT
BRITISH COMMERCIAL BLOCKADE

17 December 1813		Madison's Second Embargo endorsed by Congress
23 December 1813	28.50	Credit sales available
1 March 1814	16.88	
25 March 1814	18.82	34% price fall since Embargo ratified in Congress
30 March 1814		Madison calls in Congress for suspension of Embargo

SECOND PERIOD: NEW ENGLAND SUBJECT TO NEITHER EMBARGO
NOR BRITISH COMMERCIAL BLOCKADE

2 April 1814		Suspension of Embargo learned of in Boston
14 April 1814		Repeal by Congress of Embargo and Non Importation Acts
25 April 1814		British commercial blockade extended to New England

THIRD PERIOD: NEW ENGLAND SUBJECT TO BRITISH
COMMERCIAL BLOCKADE ONLY

5 May 1814		British commercial blockade of NE known of in Boston
19 May 1814	16.13	43.4 % price fall since Embargo ratified in Congress
21 May 1814	15.75	
9 July 1814	17.00	
19 August 1814	18.00	
17 October 1814	26.50	64.3% price rise since British commercial blockade of NE
20 October 1814	19.94	
3 November 1814	18.00	
9 November 1814	19.63	
15 November 1814	22.44	39.1% price rise since British commercial blockade of NE
16 November 1814	20.00	
22 November 1814	19.38	
23 November 1814	19.00	Cash sales available only
29 November 1814	16.63	
29 December 1814	18.13	

Source: JCBL, Brown & Ives Corr: Box 160, ff.9 –10, from Charles Greene, Brown & Ives Boston agent to Thomas Poynton Ives, of Brown & Ives, Providence, RI, on dates given.

TABLE 9. Boston average coffee prices 1813–1814 in cents per lb.

Date	Price	
29 July 1813		Embargo imposed by executive order
11 November 1813	0.25	
20 November 1813	0.27	
15 December 1813	0.31	
17 December 1813		Embargo passed in Congress
23 December 1813	0.33	Average prices raised 32% by embargo
27 January 1814	0.28	
29 January 1814	0.23	
2 February 1814	0.25	
25 March 1814	0.23	Average prices fall 30.3% before suspension.
30 March 1814		Embargo suspended
14 April 1814		Embargo repealed
16 April 1814	0.22	
26 April 1814	0.21	
29 April 1814	0.19	
3 May 1814		British blockade of New England known in Boston
26 May 1814	0.21	
9 July 1814	0.23	
3 August 1814	0.25	
1 September 1814	0.24	
29 September 1814	0.23	
6 October 1814	0.26	Average prices raised 36.8% by British blockade
16 November 1814	0.22	Cash prices after this date
23 November 1814	0.20	
29 November 1814	0.20	
19 December 1814	0.20	
29 December 1814	0.21	

Source: JCBL, Brown & Ives Corr: Box 160, ff. 9–10, from Charles Greene, Brown & Ives Boston agent to Thomas Poynton Ives, Providence, RI, on dates given.

TABLE 10. Boston average hyson tea prices 1812–1814 in $.

Date	Price	
20 November 1812		
26 November 1812		
8 January 1813		
14 May 1813	1.74	
26 May 1813		
29 May 1813		
29 July 1813		Embargo by executive order
7 October 1813		
17 November 1813		
30 November 1813		
8 December 1813	1.80	
15 December 1813	2.00	15% price rise since embargo imposed
17 December 1813		Congress passed embargo
4 January 1814		
1 February 1814		
2 February 1814		
30 March 1814		Embargo suspended
14 April 1814		Embargo repealed
16 April 1814		
29 April 1814	1.60	20% price fall since embargo suspended
3 May 1814		British blockade of New England known in Boston
1 September 1814		
29 September 1814	2.25	
6 October 1814	2.15	
20 October 1814	2.27	
1 November 1814	2.26	
8 November 1814	2.20	
9 November 1814	2.80	75% price rise under blockade of NE
16 November 1814	2.06	Cash prices only after this date
23 November 1814	2.00	
29 November 1814	2.16	
1 December 1814		

Source: JCBL, Brown & Ives Corr: Box 160, ff. 9–10, from Charles Greene, Brown & Ives Boston agent to Thomas Poynton Ives, Providence, RI, on dates given.

TABLE 11. Boston average souchon tea prices 1812–1814 in $.

Date	Price	
20 November 1812	0.88	
26 November 1812		
8 January 1813		
14 May 1813	1.15	
26 May 1813	1.13	
29 May 1813	1.15	
29 July 1813		Embargo imposed by executive order
7 October 1813	1.50	
17 November 1813	1.50	
30 November 1813	1.50	
8 December 1813	1.50	
15 December 1813		
17 December 1813		Embargo passed by Congress. Av prices raised 42.6% by embargo
4 January 1814	1.64	
1 February 1814		
2 February 1814		
30 March 1814		Embargo suspended
14 April 1814		Embargo & Non-Importation Act repealed
16 April 1814	1.06	
29 April 1814	1.07	Av. Prices fall 34.8% as embargo lifted
3 May 1814		British blockade of New England known in Boston
1 September 1814	1.60	
29 September 1814		
6 October 1814	1.60	
20 October 1814		
1 November 1814		
8 November 1814	1.60	Blockade raises av. prices by 49.5%
9 November 1814	1.50	Cash price only after this date
16 November 1814		
23 November 1814		
29 November 1814		
1 December 1814		

Source: JCBL, Brown & Ives Corr: Box 160, ff. 9–10, from Charles Greene, Brown & Ives Boston agent to Thomas Poynton Ives, Providence, RI, on dates given.

TABLE 12. Boston average other tea prices 1812–1813 in $.

Date	Price	
20 November 1812		
26 November 1812	0.75	
8 January 1813	0.83	
14 May 1813	1.14	
26 May 1813		
29 May 1813		
29 July 1813		Embargo
7 October 1813		
17 November 1813		
30 November 1813		
8 December 1813		
15 December 1813		
17 December 1813		Congress passed embargo
4 January 1814	1.71	
1 February 1814	1.32	
2 February 1814	1.40	
30 March 1814		Embargo suspended
14 April 1814		Embargo repealed
16 April 1814		
29 April 1814		27.5% fall since embargo suspended
3 May 1814		British blockade of New England known in Boston
1 September 1814		
29 September 1814	1.28	
6 October 1814		
20 October 1814		
1 November 1814		
8 November 1814	1.60	
9 November 1814	1.59	Cash price only after this date
16 November 1814		
23 November 1814		
29 November 1814	2.00	61% price rise under blockade of NE
1 December 1814	1.47	

Source: JCBL, Brown & Ives Corr: Box 160, ff. 9–10, from Charles Greene, Brown & Ives Boston agent to Thomas Poynton Ives, Providence, RI, on dates given.

TABLE 13. Index numbers of 116 United States monthly wholesale commodity prices, 1807–1819 (1910 = 100).

Year	Jan	Feb	Mar	Apr	May	June	July	Aug	Sept	Oct	Nov	Dec
1807	131	133	132	130	131	130	129	129	128	127	126	
1808	124	119	115	112	112	112	112	113	113	113	117	121
1809	124	126	135	133	132	132	129	129	130	127	129	128
1810	128	130	128	129	131	130	133	132	134	133	133	131
1811	132	128	127	127	128	124	124	126	124	125	124	122
1812	127	129	128	126	122	125	128	133	135	137	142	144
1813	150	152	153	157	160	158	159	**161**	**164**	**171**	**178**	**186**
1814	**186**	**184**	**182**	**182**	**179**	**179**	**178**	177	177	183	187	193
1815	**193**	**185**	**176**	**166**	**164**	165	163	165	166	166	168	163
1816	160	160	158	151	150	150	150	149	148	144	145	149
1817	152	155	156	156	157	154	149	153	147	145	144	146
1818	149	151	149	144	142	144	142	147	146	151	149	145
1819	141	137	134	130	125	124	121	119	119	120	117	114

Source: G. Warren and F. Pearson, *Wholesale Prices for 213 Years, 1720 to 1932, Part 1, Wholesale Prices in the United States for 135 Years from 1797 to 1932*, Ithaca NY, Cornell Univ., Agricultural Experimental Station, 1932, Table 2, p. 8, Monthly Index Numbers of the Wholesale Prices of all Commodities.

GRAPH 13. Index numbers of 116 United States monthly wholesale commodity prices, 1807–1819 (1910 = 100).

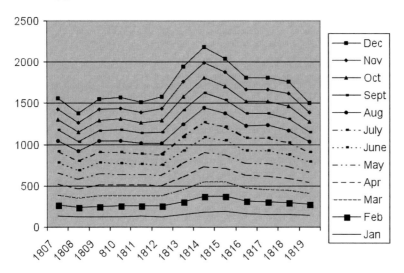

Source: see Table 13.

TABLE 14. Index numbers of United States wholesale prices of all commodities with variable group weights (1910 = 100).

1800	129	1811	126
1801	142	1812	131
1802	117	1813	162
1803	118	1814	182
1804	126	1815	170
1805	141	1816	151
1806	134	1817	151
1807	130	1818	147
1808	115	1819	125
1809	130	1820	106
1810	131		

Source: Warren and Pearson, *Wholesale Prices for 213 Years*, Table 1, p. 6.

GRAPH 14. Index numbers of United States wholesale prices of all commodities with variable group weights (1910 = 100).

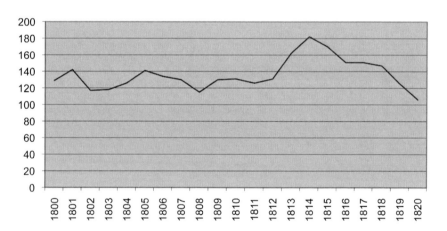

Source: see Table 14.

TABLE 15. United States exports 1805–1815 in $, from 1st October to 30th September annually.

	Total exports	Re-exports
1805	95,566,021	53,179,000
1806	101,536,963	60,283,000
1807	108,343,150	108,343,150
1808	22,430,960	12,997,000
1809	52,203,233	20,797,000
1810	66,757,970	24,391,000
1811	61,316,833	16,022,000
1812	38,527,236	8,495, 000
1813	27,855,997	2,847,000
1814	6,927,441	145,000
1815	52,557,753	6,583,000

Source: Seybert, *Statistical Annals*, p. 93

TABLE 16. Total foreign trade: United States imports and exports combined, 1805–1815, in $.

	Imports[1]	+ Exports[2]	= Total
1805	125,525,000	95,566,021	221,091,021
1806	136,562,000	101,536,963	238,098,963
1807	144,740,000	108,343,150	253,083,150
1808	58,101,000	22,430,960	80,531,960
1809	61,030,000	52,203,233	113,233,233
1810	89,366,000	66,757,970	156,123,970
1811	57,888,000	61,316,833	119,204,833
1812	78,789,000	38,527,000	117,316,236
1813	22,178,000	27,855,997	50,033,997
1814	12,968,000	6,927,441	19,895,441
1815	85,357,000	52,557,753	137,914,753

Sources:
1. North, 'United States Balance of Payments 1790–1860', pp. 591–2.
2. Seybert, *Statistical Annals*, p. 93. North's export figures are almost identical to those of Seybert.

TABLE 17. Merchant shipping tonnage in United States foreign trade 1807–1815.

	Total tonnage in US foreign trade[1]	Tonnage of US vessels in US foreign trade[2]	%age of US vessels
1807	1,176,198	1,089,876	92.7
1809		910,059[3]	
1810	986,750	906,434	91.9
1811	981,450	948,247	96.6
1812	715,098	667,999	93.4
1813	351,175	237,348	67.6
1814	107,928	56,626	53.3
1815	917,227	700,500	76.4

Sources:
1. Seybert, *Statistical Annals*, p. 318.
2. T. Pitkin, *A Statistical View of the Commerce of the United States of America*, 1st edn, Hartford, Charles Hosmer, 1816; 2nd edn, New York, James Eastburn & Co, 1817; 2nd edn, New Haven, Durrie & Peck, 1835, p. 363. Pitkin's figures are clearly based on duty paid tonnage.
3. ASP: C&N, vol. I , p. 897.

TABLE 18. Tonnage of United States merchant shipping, registered, enrolled and employed on 31 December annually 1813–1814.

	Registered tonnage	Reg. Tons duty paid	%age	Enrolled tonnage	Enrolled tons duty paid	%age	Fishing vessels duty paid
1813	674,853	233,966	37.4	471,109	252,440	53.6	18,522
1814	674,632	58,756	8.7	466,159	189,662	41.7	16,453

Source: ASP: C&N, vol. 1, p. 1017, and vol. II, p. 12.

TABLE 19. United States tax revenue, miscellaneous receipts and expenditure 1812–1815 in $m.

	Customs revenue	Internal revenue	Direct tax	Total tax revenue	Misc. receipts	Total receipts	Expenditure	Deficit
1812	8.9	-	-	8.9	0.8	9.7[1]	20.3	10.6[2]
1813	13.2	-	-	13.2	1.1	14.3	31.6	17.3
1814	6.0	1.6	2.2	9.8	1.3	11.1	34.7	23.6
1815	7.3	4.7	2.1	14.1	1.5	15.6	32.9	17.3

Source: Dewey, *Financial History of the United States*, pp. 141–2.
1. Excluding borrowing.
2. Clearly $10.6m by subtraction, although given by Dewey as $10.4m.

TABLE 20. Yields of United States direct tax and internal excise duties 1814–1815 in $ and %ages.

	Direct tax imposed	Collected	%age	Internal excise duties accrued	Collected	%age
1814	3m	2,219,497	73.98	3,262,197	1,910,995	58.57
1815	6m	2,162,673	36.04	6,242,504	4,976,530	79.76
Totals	**9m**	**4,382,170**	**ave 55.01**	**9,504,701**	**8,798,520**	**ave. 69.1**

Source: adapted from Dewey, *Financial History of the United States*, p. 140, citing Ways & Means Comm. Rpt. 9 December 1817.

TABLE 21. United States total revenue and total receipts as %age of total expenditure 1812–1815.

	Total tax revenue as %age of expenditure	Total receipts as %age of expenditure
1812	43.84	47.78
1813	41.77	45.25
1814	28.24	31.99
1815	42.86	47.42

Source: calculated from data in Dewey, *Financial History of the United States*, p. 142.

TABLE 22. Prices of United States new and old 6% stock in Philadelphia, 1812–1815, as %ages.

		New 6% Stock	Old 6% Stock
1813	July	91 to 92	95 to 96
1814	January	92.5 to 93	95 to 96
1814	July	85 to 88.5	88 to 90
1815	January	76 to 77	78 to 80
1815	July	97.5	98.5

Source: Seybert, *Statistical Annals*, p. 749, 'A Statement of the Prices quoted in Philadelphia for the evidence of the Public Debt'.

TABLE 23. Composite consumer price index 1800–1820 (1860 = 100).

1800	151	1807	139	1814	211
1801	153	1808	151	1815	185
1802	129	1809	148	1816	169
1803	136	1810	148	1817	160
1804	142	1811	158	1818	153
1805	141	1812	160	1819	153
1806	147	1813	192	1820	141

Source: J. McCusker, *How Much is That in Real Money? A historical price index for use as a deflator of money values in the economy of the United States*, Worcester MA, American Antiquarian Society, 1992, p. 326. Reprinted from *Proceedings of the American Antiquarian Society*, 101 (2), 1991.

GRAPH 23. Composite consumer price index 1800–1820 (1860 = 100).

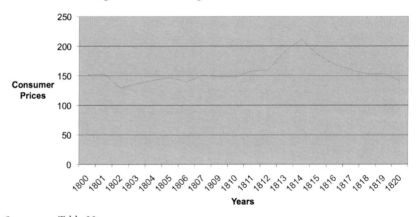

Source: see Table 23.

TABLE 24. Money supply and prices 1811–1817

	Govt. current issues (in $m)[1]	Banknote issue (in $m)	Index of wholesale prices (1811 = 100)
1811	0.0	32.5	100
1812	2.8	36.8	104
1813	4.9	41.2	129
1814	10.6	45.5	145
1815	17.6	68.0	135
1816	3.4	62.6	120
1817	0.0	56.4	120

Source: H. Rockoff, 'Banking and Finance 1789–1914', in *The Cambridge Economic History of the United States, vol. II: The Long Nineteenth Century*, eds S. Engerman and R. Gallman, Cambridge, Cambridge Univ. Press, 2000, vol. II, p. 655, Table 14.1, 'Money and Prices in the War of 1812'.

1. Treasury notes outstanding at year's end.

TABLE 25. United States import price index 1807–1815 (1790 = 100).

1807	124.7	1810	129.8	1813	179.7
1808	124.3	1811	121.1	1814	232.3
1809	129.1	1812	131.7	1815	191.3

Source: D. North, *The Economic Growth of the United States 1790–1860*, New York, Prentice Hall Inc., 1961; repr. New York, W. Norton & Co, 1966, Import Price Index, p. 229, Table F-III.

TABLE 26. United States export price index 1807–1815 (1790 = 100).

1807	136.2	1810	128.6	1813	126.5
1808	115.3	1811	128.6 also	1814	127.3
1809	116.2	1812	127.1	1815	182.9

Source: North, *Economic Growth of the United States*, Export Price Index, p. 221, Table CIII.

Note: Index for 1810 and 1811 is identical.

TABLE 27. United States terms of trade 1807–1815 (1790 = 100).

1807	109.2	1810	99.1	1813	70.4
1808	92.8	1811	106.2	1814	54.8
1809	90.0	1812	96.5	1815	95.6

Source: North, *Economic Growth of the United States*, Export Price Index, p. 221, Table CIII; Import Price Index, p. 229, Table F-III; Terms of Trade, p. 229, Table G-III.

TABLE 28. Aspects of American exports 1811–1815.

	Export price index	Real exports $m	Real domestic exports $m	Real exports per head $m	Real domestic exports per head $m
1811	61.3	47.7	35.2	6.39	4.27
1812	38.5	30.3	23.6	3.94	3.07
1813	27.9	22.0	19.8	2.77	2.49
1814	6.9	5.4	5.3	0.67	0.65
1815	52.6	28.7	25.2	3.41	2.97

Source: L. Davis and S. Engerman, *Naval Blockades in Peace and War: An Economic History since 1750*, Cambridge, Cambridge Univ. Press, 2006, pp. 80–81, Tables 3.6 and 3.7, citing D. Adams, 'American Neutrality and Prosperity 1793–1808: A Reconsideration', *Journal of Economic History*, 40, 1980, p. 736.

TABLE 29. Aspects of American imports 1811–1815.

	Total $m	Import price index	Real imports in $m	Real domestic imports in $m	Real imports per head in $m	Real domestic imports per head in $m
1811	57.9	121.1	47.8	27.0	5.00	3.62
1812	78.8	131.7	59.8	39.8	5.80	5.18
1813	22.2	179.7	12.4	9.3	1.34	1.17
1814	13.0	232.3	5.6	5.2	0.64	0.63
1815	85.4	191.3	44.6	37.0	4.89	4.51

Source: Davis and Engerman, *Naval Blockades in Peace and War*, pp. 80–81, Tables 3.6 and 3.7, citing Adams, 'American Neutrality and Prosperity', p. 736.

TABLE 30. Net freight earnings of the United States carrying trade 1807–1815, in $m.

1807	42.1	1810	39.5	1813	10.2
1808	23.0	1811	40.8	1814	2.6
1809	26.2	1812	29.0	1815	20.6

Source: North, *Economic Growth of the United States*, Table A III, p. 249.

TABLE 31. Terms of trade of the United States 1789–1913 (1913= 100).[1]

Period	Terms of Trade index
1789–1798	58
1799–1808	66
1809–1818	60
1819–1828	65
1829–1838	79
1839–1848	77
1849–1858	90
1859–1868	80
1869–1878	87
1879–1888	97
1889–1898	90
1899–1908	97
1904–1913	99

Source: R. Lipsey, 'U.S. Trade and Balance of Payments 1800–1913', in *The Cambridge Economic History of the United States, vol. II, The Long Nineteenth Century*, eds S. Engerman and R. Gallman, 3 vols, Cambridge Univ. Press, 2000, Table 15.21, p. 718.

1. Export Price Index divided by Import Price Index.

TABLE 32. British merchant marine 1811–1814, in numbers and tonnage.

	Number	Tonnage
1811	20,478	2,247,000
1812	20,637	2,263,000
1813	20,951	2,349,000
1814	21,449	2,414,000

Source: Mitchell and Deane, *Abstract of British Historical Statistics*, p. 217, Table: 'Transport 1, Shipping Registered in the United Kingdom 1788–1938'.

GRAPH 32. British merchant marine 1811–1814, in numbers and tonnage.

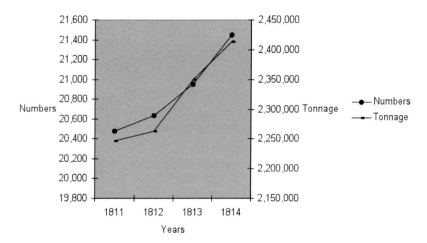

Source: see Table 32.

TABLE 33. Loan interest paid by US government 1812–1815 in $.

1812	2,451,000
1813	3,599,000
1814	4,593,000
1815	5,990,000
Total	**16,633,000**

Source: Dewey, *Financial History of the United States*, p. 141, citing Ways and Means Committee Report, Washington, 9 December 1817.

GRAPH 33. Loan interest paid by US government 1812–1815 in $.

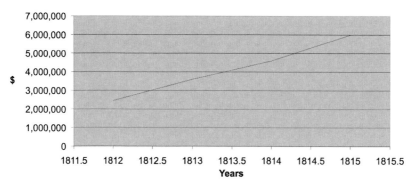

Source: see Table 33.

TABLE 34. Treasury note debt, December 1814, in $.

Where payable	When payable	Principal	Interest	Total
Philadelphia	1 November 1814	269,000	14,526	**238,526**
Philadelphia	1 December 1814	366,200	19,774	**385,974**
New York	1 December 1814	570,000	30,780	**600,780**
Boston	1 December 1814	600,000	32,400	**632,400**
Totals		**1,805,200**	**97,480**	**1,902,680**

Source: ASP: F, vol. II, p. 879, 'Schedule of Treasury Notes which have already fallen due, & remain unpaid this 2nd day of December 1814'.

TABLE 35. United Kingdom tax revenues 1812–15, in £m, and averaged for 1812–1815.

	Total gross income	Customs	Excise	Stamp duty	Land	Property & inc	Post office
1812	71.0	13.0	27.9	6.0	7.4	13.2	1.9
1813	70.3	14.0	25.9	6.0	7.5	13.1	2.0
1814	74.3	14.4	27.5	6.3	7.9	14.3	2.1
1815	77.9	14.8	29.5	6.5	8.0	14.5	2.2
Ave. 1812–							
1815	73.5	14.1	27.7	6.2	7.7	14.0	2.1
% age	100.0	19.2	37.7	8.4	10.5	19.1	2.9

Source: Mitchell and Deane, *Abstract of British Historical Statistics*, Table 3, 'Public Finance 3, Gross Public Income – United Kingdom 1801–1939, Principal Constituent Items'; average 1812–1815 calculated to one decimal place.

NOTES TO THE CHAPTERS

INTRODUCTION

1. R. Albion and J. Pope, *Sea Lanes in Wartime: The American Experience 1775-1945,* 2nd edn, New York, Archon Books, 1968, p. 118, with undetailed citing of Alfred T. Mahan; see *The Influence of Sea Power in the War of the French Revolution,* London, Samson Low, Marston & Co, 1893, vol. II, p. 118.
2. W. James, *A Full and Correct Account of the Chief Naval Occurrences of the Late War between Great Britain and the United States of America,* London, T. Egerton, 1817; see also *Warden Refuted, being a defence of the British navy against the misrepresentations of a work recently published at Edinburgh: A letter to D. B. Warden Esq., late Consul to the United States at Paris,* London, J. M. Richardson, 1819.
3. A. Mahan, *Sea Power in Its Relation to the War of 1812,* Boston MA, Little Brown, and London, Samson Low, Marston & Co, 1905, vol. I, p. 402-4.
4. Ibid., vol. II, p. 208, quoting from Niles' *Weekly Register,* Baltimore, 17 June 1815.
5. Ibid., vol. II, p. 207. The italics are my own.
6. T. Roosevelt, 'The Naval War of 1812', in *The Royal Navy: A History from the Earliest Times to the Present,* W. Clowes, 7 vols, London, Sampson Low, Marston & Co, 1897–1903, vol. VI, 1901, p. 65.
7. Ibid., p. 177.
8. Ibid., p. 156.
9. R. Horsman, *The War of 1812,* New York, Knopf, 1969, pp. 166–7, 210, citing A. Balinky, *Albert Gallatin: Fiscal Theories and Policies,* New Brunswick NJ, Rutgers Univ. Press, 1958, and H. Adams, *History of the United States during the Administrations of Jefferson and Madison,* New York, Charles Scribner's Sons, 1889–96, vols 5–9.
10. J. Stagg, *Mr Madison's War: Politics, Diplomacy and Warfare in the Early American Republic, 1783–1830,* Princeton, Princeton Univ. Press, 1983, p. 505.
11. Ibid., p. 500.
12. I. Toll, *Six Frigates: How Piracy, War and British Supremacy at Sea gave Birth to the World's Most Powerful Navy,* London, Penguin/Michael Joseph, 2006.
13. J. Latimer, *1812 War with America,* Cambridge MA, and London, Belknap Press/Harvard Univ. Press, 2007, pp. 150–73, p. 163.
14. W. Dudley, 'Without Some Risk: A Reassessment of the British Blockade of the United States, 1812–1815,' PhD dissertation, Tuscaloosa, University of Alabama, 1999, pp. 276–86, since published as *Splintering the Wooden Wall: The British Blockade of the United States, 1812–1815,* Annapolis MD, Naval Institute Press, 2003.
15. Dudley, 'Without some Risk' p. 276–7; and N. Rodger, *The Command of the Ocean: A Naval History of Britain, 1649–1815,* London, Penguin/Allen Lane/NMM, 2004, p. 569.
16. N. Tracy, *Attack on Maritime Trade,* Toronto, Univ. of Toronto Press, 1991, p. 78.
17. Imported sugar prices are an excellent indicator, readily affected by, for example, the successive interruptions in New England's supply at different times in the Spring of 1814, by Madison's second embargo and British blockade, and regularly included in lists of current prices. American attempts to produce sugar from 1795 were relatively unsuccessful; since Caribbean productivity was then at least four times that of Louisiana, almost all sugar was imported, especially from Cuba. See C. Nettels, *The Emergence of a National Economy 1775-1815, The Economic History of the United*

States vol. II, New York and London, Harper & Row, 1969, pp. 196–7. Similarly, Treasury note prices indicate government credit-worthiness over time.

18. C. Gray, *The Leverage of Sea Power: The Strategic Advantage of Navies in War*, New York, Macmillan, 1992, p. 13. The italics are my own.

CHAPTER 1. CONVOYS AND BLOCKADES: THE EVOLUTION OF MARITIME ECONOMIC WARFARE

1. Wm. Eden MP, Under Secretary of State 1772–8, Commissioner for Conciliation with America, 1778–9, in 1779, quoted by J. Black in 'Naval Power, Strategy and Foreign Policy 1775–1791', in *Parameters of British Naval Power 1650–1850*, ed. M. Duffy, Exeter, Univ. of Exeter Press, 1992, p. 93.

2. Some writers distinguish between privateers and letters of marque, trading vessels primarily carrying cargoes, but also licensed to take prizes in wartime, although admitting the distinction to be 'often blurred in practice'; see, for example, W. Dudley, *The Naval War of 1812: A Documentary History*, Washington, Naval Historical Center, vol. I, 1985, p. 166, vol. II, 1992, p. 18.

3. F. Kert, *Prize and Prejudice: Privateering and Naval Prize in Atlantic Canada in the War of 1812*, Research in Maritime History 11, International Maritime Economic History Association, St John's, Newfoundland, 1997, p. 154, table 6.1, 'A Comparison of Prize Tonnages Captured by Privateer and Royal Naval Vessels, 1812–15'.

4. *London Gazette*, June 1808. See also R. Hill, *The Prizes of War: The Naval Prize System in the Napoleonic Wars 1793–1815*, Stroud, Sutton/Royal Naval Museum Publications, 1998, pp. 201–10.

5. J. Hattendorf, *The Boundless Deep: The European Conquest of the Oceans, 1450–1840*, Providence RI, JCBL, 2003. pp. 154–5.

6. Ibid.

7. Ibid.

8. R. Harding, *The Evolution of the Sailing Navy, 1509–1815*, New York, St. Martin's Press, 1995, pp. 72–3.

9. The word 'strategy' as used here is an anachronism, not appearing in its modern sense in the OED until 1810. 'Stratagem' is still used by D. Fenning in *A New Spelling Dictionary and Grammar of the English Language*, 2nd edn, London, S. Crowther, 1773, to mean 'an artifice, a trick'.

10. N. Rodger, *The Command of the Ocean: A Naval History of Britain 1649–1815*, London, Allen Lane/Penguin/NMM, 2004, p. 76.

11. Harding, *Evolution of the Sailing Navy*, pp. 95–7.

12. Ibid., p. 97–9.

13. J. Hattendorf, 'The Struggle with France, 1689–1815', in *The Oxford History of the Royal Navy*, ed. J. Hill, 2nd edn, Oxford, OUP/BAC, 1995, p. 87.

14. S. Roskill, *The Strategy of Sea Power: Its Development and Application*, Aylesbury, John Goodchild, 1986, pp. 38 and 44.

15. D. Baugh, 'The Eighteenth Century Navy as a National Institution, 1690–1815', in *The Oxford History of the Royal Navy*, ed. J. Hill, 2nd edn, Oxford, OUP/BAC, 1995, p. 158. The development of the Royal Dockyards at Portsmouth and Plymouth was particularly rapid and important between 1711 and 1770, ibid., p. 127. See also D. Baugh, 'Naval power: what gave the British Navy superiority?' in *Exceptionalism and Industrialisation: Britain and its European Rivals, 1688–1815*, ed. L. Escosura, Cambridge, Cambridge Univ. Press, 2004, pp. 235–57, which includes Rear Admiral George Anson's advocacy of sea-keeping in the evolving blockade of France.

16. M. Duffy, ed., 'Devon and the Naval Strategy of the French Wars, 1689–1815', in *The New Maritime History of Devon*, ed. M. Duffy et al., Exeter, Conway/Univ. of Exeter, 1992, vol. I, p. 186, citing TNA ADM 2/1331, Admiralty to Martin, 17 August 1745.

17. Ibid.

18. BL Add Mss 3464, ff. 28–31, Leeds Papers, vol. CXLI, Egerton Papers, Walter Titley, English Minister to Copenhagen, to Robert D'Arcy, Lord Holdernesse, Secretary of

State for the Northern Department, Copenhagen, 19 February 1757. The Earl of Holdernesse became Sect. of State for the Southern Department in April 1757. I am grateful to Jeremy Michell of NMM, London, for directing me to this reference.

19. F. Anderson, *The Crucible of War: The Seven Years War and the Fate of Empire in British North America, 1754-1766*, London, Faber and Faber, 2000, pp. 237, 417-18.

20. R. Harding, *Seapower and Naval Warfare 1650 -1830*, London, UCL Press, 1999, p. 51. For Hawke's close blockade of Brest, see Rodger, *The Command of the Ocean*, p. 281.

21. J. Michell, 'Vexing your Neighbours for a Little Muck, British Prize-taking during the Seven Years War, 1756-63', Staff Seminar Lecture, NMM, London, 16 May 2007, Table 1. 794 enemy vessels were condemned between 1755-62, comprising 82.79% of those captured.

22. P. Kennedy, *The Rise and Fall of British Naval Mastery*, London, Allen Lane, 1976, p. 114, citing G. Graham, 'Considerations on the War of American Independence', *Bulletin of the Institute of Historical Research*, 22, 1949, p. 23, quoted in full in H. Richmond, *Statesmen and Seapower*, Oxford, Clarendon Press, 1946.

23. G. Barnes and J. Owen, eds, *The Private Papers of John Montague Earl of Sandwich, First Lord of the Admiralty 1771-1782*, Memorandum in 'Sandwich Papers, North America 1773-7', London, Navy Records Society, vol. I, 1932, pp. 64-5. [In Adm Palliser's writing: unsigned and undated, but evidently written in July 1775]; and Grave's List Book, 1 June 1775.

24. Barnes and Owen, *Private Papers of John Montague*, vol. I, p. 328, Lord Sandwich to Lord North, 7 December 1777.

25. Kennedy, *British Naval Mastery*, p. 114.

26. O. Stephenson calculates 'nine-tenths' in *American History Review*, 30, cited by P. Mackesy, *The War for America 1775-1783*, London, Longman, 1964, p. 99.

27. Rodger, *The Command of the Ocean*, p. 331. For North Atlantic currents and prevailing winds, see also Maps, 'The North Atlantic', pp. lvii-lix.

28. Graham, 'Considerations on the American War of Independence'.

29. Harding, *Seapower and Naval Warfare*, p. 292, citing J. Glete, *Navies and Nations: Warships, Navies and Statebuilding in Europe and America 1500-1860*, Stockholm, Almqvist & Wiksell, 1993, vol. 2, table A3, 'The changing structure of selected sailing navies 1770-1850'.

30. J. Plumb, *England in the Eighteenth Century 1714-1815*, Harmondsworth, Pelican, 1950, p. 129.

31. D. Syrett, *The Royal Navy in American Waters, 1775-1783*, Aldershot, Scolar, 1989, pp. 56-7.

32. R. Buel, *In Irons: Britain's Naval Supremacy and the American Revolutionary Economy*, New Haven, Yale Univ. Press, 1998, p. 86. See also D. Baugh, 'The Politics of British Naval Failure, 1775-7', *American Neptune*, 52, 1992, pp. 221-46.

33. Buel, *In Irons*, p. 229.

34. Duffy, 'Devon', p. 187, table 27.1, citing R. Merriman, ed., *Queen Anne's Navy: Documents concerning the Administration of the Navy of Queen Anne, 1702-14*, London, Navy Records Society publications 103, 1961, p. 373; and R. Knight, 'The Royal Dockyards in England at the Time of the American War of Independence', App. IV, pp. 397-8, London, PhD thesis, 1972. The actual increase is 70.18%.

35. D. O'Connell, *The Influence of Law on Sea Power*, Manchester, Manchester Univ. Press, 1975, p. 20.

36. NMM HUL/14. Copies of 1793 and 1798 Acts for reference of George Hulbert, Warren's Flag Secretary and Prize Agent.

37. J. Black, *Britain as a Military Power 1688-1815*, London, UCL Press, 1999, pp. 235-6.

38. Duffy M. op. cit. p. 187, and Rodger N. op. cit. p. 465.

39. Richmond, *Statesmen and Seapower*, Appendix 1, 'Dundas and Castlereagh on the Principles of British War, 1801-15', pp. 338-9, citing *Parliamentary History*, 36, p. 1071.

40. E. Evans, *The Forging of the Modern State: Early Industrial Britain 1783–1870*, 2nd edn, London, Longman, 1996, p. 89.

41. F. Crouzet, 'War, Blockade and Economic Change in Europe 1792–1815', *Journal of Economic History*, 24, 1964, pp. 568, 571–4.

42. A. Mahan, *The Influence of Sea Power upon the French Revolution and Empire*, London, Samson Low, Marston & Co, 1892, vol. II, p. 219.

43. D. Davies, *A Brief History of Fighting Ships*, London, Constable, 1996, republ. Robinson, 2002, p. 58. See also W. Dunne, 'The Inglorious First of June: Commodore Stephen Decatur on Long Island Sound, 1813', *The Long Island Historical Journal*, 2, Spring 1990, pp. 1–32.

44. Repair facilities existed at Chatham, Portsmouth, Torbay and Plymouth, and from 1728, in the Caribbean at English Harbour, Antigua. Victualling was also from Deptford and Devonport.

45. P. O'Brienm *War and Economic Progress in Britain and America*, Milton Keynes, Open Univ. Press, 1997, p. 182.

46. Evans, *The Forging of the Modern State*, pp. 415–16, citing R. Davis, *The Industrial Revolution and British Overseas Trade*, 2nd edn, London, Pinter, 1979, pp. 94–101. Britain is estimated to have imported 43% of its food by 1804–6. Trade percentages calculated from data in B. Mitchell and P. Deane, *Abstract of British Historical Statistics*, Cambridge, Cambridge Univ. Press, 1962, p. 281, table 1B, 'Official Values, Overseas Trade, Great Britain, 1772–1804', merchant tonnage, p. 217, 'Shipping Registered in UK 1738–1938'.

47. Evans, *The Forging of the Modern State*, p. 439; and D. French, *The British Way in Warfare 1688–2000*, London, Unwin/Hyman, 1990, pp. 106–7.

48. T. Pitkin, *A Statistical View of the Commerce of the United States of America*, 2nd edn, New Haven, Durrie & Peck, 1835, p. 363. British registered tonnage in 1807 had reached almost 2.1m tons: Mitchell and Deane, *Abstract of British Historical Statistics*, p. 217.

49. Hill, *The Prizes of War*, p. 10, citing M. Marsden, ed., *The Law and Custom of the Sea*, London, Navy Records Society, 1915–16, vol. II, p. 348.

50. Hattendorf, *The Boundless Deep*, p. 155. Robinson's work was originally published in London in 1799. See also Robinson's translation of chapters 273 and 277 of *Consolato del Mare relating to Prize Law*, London, White & Butterworth, 1800.

51. C. Robinson, *Reports of Cases heard in the High Court of Admiralty under Sir William Scott*, 6 vols, London, 1798–1808, vol. 3, 1800, pp. 157–8, quoted by Hill, *The Prizes of War*, p. 37, citing L. Townley, 'Sir William Scott, Lord Stowell, and the Development of the Prize Law in the High Courts of Admiralty, 1798–1828, with Particular Reference to the Rights of Belligerents', unpublished thesis, University of Birmingham, 1994, p. 341.

52. A. Seybert, *Statistical Annals*, Philadelphia, T. Dobson, 1818, p. 93. For concerns of West India Committee growers and merchants on American re-export of sugar and views of Spencer Percival and Castlereagh see T. Hansard, *Parliamentary Debates: House of Commons*, London, Longman, 1812–1829, vol. VIII, 630–32 and 641–4; and F. Crouzet, 'America and the crisis of the British imperial economy, 1803–1807' in *The Early Modern Atlantic Economy*, eds J. McCusker and K. Morgan, Cambridge, Cambridge Univ. Press, 2000, pp. 278–315, pp. 311–12.

53. *American State Papers: Documents, Legislative and Executive, of the Congress of the United States*, Washington DC, Gales and Seaton, 1832–61 (hereafter, *ASP*): FR, vol. III, p. 267 for text of 'Fox Blockade'. Outside the Seine to Ostend coastline, only direct trade between 'ports hostile to Britain' was to be blockaded, implying that trade to Europe from American ports carried neutral goods.

54. Richmond, *Statesmen and Seapower*, Appendix III, p. 344–5, citing *Cobbett's Parliamentary Debates*, London, Bagshaw, 1812–13, vol. 21, p. 1152.

55. *Annals of Congress* (hereafter *AC*): 9–1, 1259–62, Non-Importation Act, 14 December 1807. Although passed by Congress in December 1806, America's first

Non-Importation Act was suspended, not to come into effect until December 1807. Macon's No. 2 Bill of April 1810 became what is referred to as the Non-Importation Act of 1811.

56. R. Hope, *A New History of British Shipping*, London, Murray, 1990, p. 254, citing J. Hutchison, *The Press-Gang Afloat and Ashore*, London, G. Bell & Sons, 1913, p. 327. One in three pressed men deserted; 42,000 during the French Revolutionary War before 1803.

57. W. James, *A full and correct account of the military occurrences of the late war between Great Britain and the United States of America*, London, J. Richardson, 1818, vol. I, p. 36, quoting part of the Prince Regent's 'manifesto' of 9 January 1813, 'in reply to Mr Madison's', see also p. 16.

58. Gwyn J. *Frigates and Foremasts: The North America Squadron in Nova Scotia Waters 1745–1815*, Vancouver and Toronto, Univ. of British Columbia Press, 2003, p. 131, citing S. Jackson, 'Impressment and Anglo-American Discord 1787–1818', unpublished PhD dissertation, Univ. of Michigan, 1976, p. 52.

59. *AC*: 12–1, 818, Langdon Cheves in House of Representatives, 17 January 1812. See also H. Adams, ed., *The Writings of Albert Gallatin*, Philadelphia, J. P. Lippincott, 1879, vol. I, p. 336, Gallatin to Jefferson, 16 April 1807. Gallatin calculates that between a half and two-thirds of the 8,400 increase in American merchant seamen in the previous two years, i.e. between 4,200 and 5,600 men, will have been British.

60. Niles' *Weekly Register*, Baltimore, vol. II, p. 119.

61. James, *Military occurrences*, vol. I, pp. 41–2, citing Federalist Representative Timothy Pickering of Massachusetts, March 1814, subtracting duplicates, volunteers, and those with 'fraudulent' or 'insufficient documents', quoting *The Massachusetts' Manual; or Burdick's Political and Historical Register*, Boston, 1814. Perhaps significantly, R. Buel, in *America on the Brink: How the Political Struggle over the War of 1812 Almost Destroyed the Young Republic*, New York and Basingstoke, Palgrave/Macmillan, 2005, p. 23, asserts that Pickering's father, John, also a Federalist Representative, was 'clearly insane'.

62. Dudley, *The Naval War of 1812*, vol. I, p. 62.

63. TNA FO: 115/22, no. 7, Letter to Foreign Secretary the Marquis Wellesley, from the Collector of Customs, Richmond, Virginia, dated 12 January 1812, seeking the repatriation of impressed seaman P. Randolph Page, currently serving in HM sloop *L'Eclair*, a minute description of whom proved him to be a native-born American.

64. James, *Military occurrences*, vol. I, p. 36.

65. *ASP*: FR: vol. III, pp. 140–63, corr. re: Monroe-Pinkney treaty.

66. BL C *Morning Post*, London, 6 August 1807.

67. Adams, *Writings of Albert Gallatin*, vol. 1, p. 343, Gallatin to President Thomas Jefferson, 'Memorandum of Preparatory Measures', Washington, 25 July 1807.

68. I. Toll, *Six Frigates: How Piracy, War and British Supremacy at Sea gave Birth to the World's Most Powerful Navy*, London, Penguin/Michael Joseph, 2006, p. 285.

69. Adams, *Writings of Albert Gallatin*, p. 343.

70. Ibid., p. 248–9.

71. D. Dewey, *Financial History of the United States*, 1st edn published 1903; 12th edn, New York, Kelly, 1934, repr. 1968, p. 126.

72. Adams, *Writings of Albert Gallatin*, p. 350.

73. Ibid.

74. *AC*: 10–1, 2814–15.

75. P. Johnson, *A History of the American People*, London, Weidenfeld & Nicolson, 1997, p. 214, citing I. Brandt, *James Madison, Commander in Chief 1812–36*, New York, Bobbs-Merrill & Co Inc., 1961, vol. IV, p. 306.

76. *AC*: 10–2, 1824.

77. *ASP*: FR, vol. III, p. 386, letter from J. B. Champagny, Duc de Cadore, French Minister for Foreign Affairs to John Armstrong, American Minister in Paris, apparently dated 5 August 1810. Appearing to revoke the Berlin and Milan decrees from 1 November 1810,

it was ambiguously worded, but published in March 1811. It was apparently accepted by Madison at its face value, but dismissed in Britain as fraudulent, as in the Prince Regent's speech of 1 January 1813. See also, James, *Military occurrences*, vol. I, p. 24.

78. *Naval Chronicle*, vol. 25, 'Naval History of the Present Year', May–June 1811, p. 502.
79. N. Tracy, ed., *The Naval Chronicle: The Contemporary Record of the Royal Navy at War*, consolidated edn, London, Chatham Publishing, 1999, vol. 5, *1811: Naval News*, p. 1.
80. *Naval Chronicle*, vol. 27, 'State Papers: Message of the President of the United States, James Madison, to Congress, 5 November 1811', pp. 28–32.
81. Ibid.
82. James, *Military occurrences*, vol. I, pp. 2–4. 'President's message to both houses of congress'.
83. Buel, *America on the Brink*, p. 125. The Royal Navy had added four vessels to its North America squadron.
84. TNA CO 43/49, p. 153/266, Henry Goulburn to George Harrison, Second Secretary at the Admiralty, 're Upper & Lower Canada', Downing Street, dated 27 November 1812.
85. *AC*: 12–1, 815, Langdon Cheves, House of Representatives, 17 January 1812.
86. Thomas Jefferson to James Madison, 1812, quoted in Johnson, *A History of the American People*, p. 217, citing A. Lipscomb and A. Bergh, eds, *Thomas Jefferson's Writings*, New York, 1903, vol. IX, p. 366.
87. A. Lambert, 'Introduction', in *The Naval War of 1812*, ed. R. Gardiner, London, Caxton Editions/NMM, 2001, p. 10.
88. TNA FO: 115/22, letter 2, John Morier, British chargé d'affaires in Washington, to Foreign Office, London, dated Washington, 12 January 1811.
89. Ibid., letter 8, Morier to Foreign Office, 24 January 1811. Robert Smith was replaced as Secretary of State on 11 April 1811, by James Monroe.
90. TNA FO: 115/23, letter 9, p. 107, Foreign Secretary Lord Castlereagh to Augustus Foster, British Minister in Washington, dated Foreign Office, 10 April 1812.
91. Ibid.; in the contemporary Foreign Office copy, an expletive was apparently dictated, but subsequently expunged, although precisely when the offensive word was removed, and by whom, is unfortunately unknown.
92. *AC*: 12–1, 2322–3. Voting on Declaration of war, in the House of Representatives, 4 June 1812, voted for: 79, against: 49; in the Senate, 17 June 1812, voted for: 19, against: 13.
93. NMM KEI/37/9, 'Private' letter, Ld. Melville to Admiral Ld. Keith, dated, Admiralty, 11 June 1812.
94. TNA ADM 1/4220: Letter from Foreign Secretary, Marquis Wellesley, Foreign Office, to Lords Commissioners of the Admiralty, 21 January 1812.
95. TNA CO 43/49, pp. 266–7, Lord Bathurst to Lords Commissioners of the Admiralty, dated Downing Street, 21 November 1812.
96. Dudley, *The Naval War of 1812*, vol. I, p. 633, citing ADM 2/1375, Secret Letters and Orders, pp. 337–8, Lords of Admiralty Rbt Melville, Wm Domett and Geo. Hope to Warren, 26 December 1812, refers to earlier order of 27 November 1812.
97. *The Edinburgh Review*, for 1813, vol. 6, p. 112.
98. TNA ADM 1/4222, p. 169, Confidential letter from Lord Castlereagh to Admiralty, dated Foreign Office, 12 August 1812.
99. Huntington Library, Melville Papers: reel 1, April 1812.
100. Dudley, *The Naval War of 1812*, vol. II, pp. 11–14, 'Private' letter from Admiral Sir Henry Stanhope to Melville, dated Stanwell House, Staines, 5 January 1813.

CHAPTER 2. CONSTRAINTS AND SOLUTIONS: THE PRACTICALITIES OF MARITIME BLOCKADE

1. George Hulbert to his brother John Hulbert, 2 January 1813, quoted by A. Gutridge in 'Prize Agency 1800–1815 with special reference to the career and work of George Redmond Hulbert', unpublished MPhil dissertation, Univ. of Portsmouth, 1989, p. 83, citing Portsmouth City Records Office, 626A1/1/21.

2. *Naval Chronicle*, vol. 28, p. 159. Warren left Portsmouth on 14 August 1812 and reached Halifax, Nova Scotia, on 26 September 1812.

3. NMM LBK/2, Warren to Robert Dundas, Lord Melville, First Lord of the Admiralty, dated Bermuda, 30 December 1813.

4. TNA ADM 1/502, Vice-Admiral Sawyer to First Secretary of the Admiralty John Croker, dated Halifax, NS, 5 July 1812, via the packet *Julia*. A letter sent by Warren in Halifax on 26 October 1813 reached the Admiralty on 17 November, in an extraordinarily fast 22 days.

5. TNA ADM 1/4221, Letter form Foreign Secretary, Lord Castlereagh to the Lords Commissioners of the Admiralty, dated Foreign Office, 9 May 1812.

6. TNA FO: 115/22 July 1812. In October 1810, Madison revealed a letter from the Duc de Cadore, French Minister for Foreign Affairs, apparently dated 5 August 1810, ambiguously claiming revocation of the Berlin and Milan decrees and restrictions on neutral American shipping if Britain withdrew its Orders in Council. Failing this, an American Non-Importation law would apply solely to Britain, adding to Anglo-American hostility while French detentions of American vessels continued. The St Cloud decree published in May 1812, apparently dated 28 April 1811, sought to confirm French revocation, and although a transparent fraud, made British revocation of the Orders in Council expedient.

7. NMM KEI/37/9, 'Private' letter from Admiral George Hope to Admiral Lord Keith, Admiralty, 17 June 1812. Had Madison got early warning of French naval intentions, either through diplomatic or intelligence channels, and planned his inflammatory 'Message to Congress' of 1 June 1812 to coincide with these new British difficulties?

8. *AC*: 12–1, 815, 17 January 1812.

9. *AC*: 12–1, 830–31, 18 January 1812. Republican Representative Adam Seybert told Congress that, according to Steel's list, in July 1811, the Royal Navy had 3 ships of the line among 29 vessels in Halifax and Newfoundland. In the West Indies, comprising the Leeward Islands and Jamaica, it had 2 battleships in a total of 69, while in South America it had 2 ships of the line and 7 frigates in a total of 13 vessels, making a total of 111 in his broadly defined 'American seas'. Seybert referred to D. Steel, *Original and Correct List of the Royal Navy*, published monthly between 1793 and 1815.

10. B. Lohnes, 'British Naval Problems at Halifax During the War of 1812', in *Mariner's Mirror*, 59, 1973, p. 317, citing R. Albion, *Forests and Sea Power*, p. 365–6.

11. W. Clowes, *The Royal Navy: A History from the Earliest Times to the Present*, London, Sampson Low, Marston & Co, 1900, vol. V, p. 10. 'The Active List of the Ships of the Royal Navy 1803–1815', which had been 'compiled chiefly from Appendices in James, checked against Steel, official lists and the *Naval Chronicle*'. Modern scholarship would greatly reduce the British Nay of 1810. R. Harding, in *Seapower and Naval Warfare 1650–1830*, London, UCL Press, 1999, pp. 294–5, cites J. Glete, *Navies and Nations: Warships, Navies and Statebuilding in Europe and America, 1500–1860*, Stockholm, Almqvist & Wiksell, 1993, vol. II, table A4: 'The changing structure of selected sailing navies:1805–30', in suggesting that in 1810, Britain had 152 'battleships', 183 'cruisers', equivalent to frigates, and 63 'small ships', making a total of 398 warships available. Also for 1810, Glete calculates that the United States had no battleships, 9 cruisers, and 3 small ships, giving a total of 12 warships. However calculated, the disparity in naval strength between Britain and the United States is inescapable.

12. W. Dudley, ed., *The Naval War of 1812: A Documentary History*, Washington, Naval Historical Center, vol. II, 1992, pp. 16–18, 'Secret', Croker to Warren, 10 February 1813, citing ADM 2/1376, pp. 73–87.

13. NMM WAR/82 p. 20, letter from Melville to Warren, 3 December 1812.

14. Dudley, *The Naval War of 1812*, vol. II, p. 78, Croker to Warren 20 March 1813, citing TNA ADM 2/1376, pp. 341–67.

15. NMM LBK/2, Melville to Warren, 4 June 1813.

16. Dudley, *The Naval War of 1812*, vol. I, pp. 218, 508–9, and vol. II, p. 11.

17. D. Skaggs and G. Altoff, *Signal Victory: The Lake Erie Campaign 1812–13*, Annapolis, MD, Naval Institute Press, 1997, p. 148. The British squadron comprised 2 ships, 2 brigs, a schooner and a sloop. See also C. Stacey, 'Another Look at the Battle of Lake Erie', *Canadian Historical Review*, 39, 1958, pp. 41–51, suggesting that, at the end of a supply line, the British were poorly equipped.

18. Dudley, *The Naval War of 1812*, vol. II, p. 59, citing Brynmor Jones Library, Univ. of Hull, DDHO 7/98.

19. Dudley, *The Naval War of 1812*, vol. II, pp. 59–60, Warren's Standing Orders on the North American Station, 'Genl. Order', Bermuda, 6 March 1813, citing Brynmor Jones Lib., Hotham Papers, DDHO 7/45.

20. Dudley, *The Naval War of 1812*, vol. II, p. 60, note 1. Admiralty circular order 23 March 1813.

21. Ibid., vol. I, pp. 181, 509.

22. Ibid., pp. 594–5.

23. Ibid., vol. II, p. 11, and Lohnes, 'British Naval Problems', p. 319.

24. Clowes, *The Royal Navy*, vol. V, p. 9.

25. Ibid.; actually 66.33%.

26. N. Rodger, *The Command of the Ocean: A Naval History of Britain 1649–1815*, London, Allen Lane/Penguin/NMM, 2004, Appendix VI, 'Manpower', p. 639.

27. Clowes, *The Royal Navy*, p. 9.

28. TNA ADM 8/100 Ships in Sea Pay 1 July 1812; see also NMM HUL/18 shown as Appendix A Table 3: Flag Secretary George Hulbert's 'List of Ships & Vessels on the West Indies & American Stations' dated 7 August 1812. When figures for Newfoundland are added to the latter, both arrive at a total of 83, including 3 receiving ships.

29. TNA ADM 1/503, Pt 1, pp. 99–102, Warren to Melville, 29 December 1812.

30. B. Lavery, *Nelson's Navy: The Ships, Men and Organisation 1793–1815*, London, Conway Maritime Press/Brassey's, 1989, p. 50, citing HMS *Triton* of 1796 as an example.

31. Dudley, *The Naval War of 1812*, vol. I, p. 53–60, Secretary of the Navy Hamilton to Langdon Cheves, Chairman of the Naval Committee, Washington Navy Yard, 3 December 1811. For use of 'live' oak in American naval shipbuilding see: I. Toll, *Six Frigates: How Piracy, War and British Supremacy at Sea gave Birth to the World's Most Powerful Navy*, London, Penguin/Michael Joseph, 2006, pp. 58–61.

32. Dudley, *The Naval War of 1812*, vol. I, p. 132n.

33. A. De Conde, *The Quasi War: The Politics and Diplomacy of the Undeclared War with France 1797–1801*, New York, Charles Scribner's Sons, 1966.

34. Clowes, *The Royal Navy*, vol. V, p. 567. Named losses of the US Navy to December 1812, excluding gunboats.

35. R. Knight, 'The Introduction of Copper Sheathing into the Royal Navy, 1779–86', *Mariners' Mirror*, 59, 1973, pp. 229–309; see also D. Baugh, 'The Eighteenth Century Navy as a National Institution, 1690–1815', in *The Oxford History of the Royal Navy*, ed. J. Hill, 2nd edn, Oxford, OUP/BAC, 1995, p. 132.

36. Dudley, *The Naval War of 1812*, vol. II, p. 261, citing TNA ADM 1/504, pp. 417–20, Warren to Croker 16 October 1813, lists *Victorious* 74 and *Nymphe* 38 as refitting, *Orpheus* and *Statira* 38's going for heavy repair, and *Narcissus* 38, on passage, 5 of 25 vessels being unavailable. Melville had earlier written that 50% of a blockading force might be absent in transit or repair.

37. D. Baugh, 'Naval power: what gave the British Navy superiority?' in *Exceptionalism and Industrialisation: Britain and its European Rivals, 1688–1815*, ed. L. Escosura, Cambridge, Cambridge Univ. Press, 2004, pp. 235–57, p. 256

38. Ibid.

39. Lavery, *Nelson's Navy*, p. 242, citing NMM HAL/E3.

40. NMM LBK/2, Warren to Melville, HMS *San Domingo* off Kent Island, Chesapeake, 24 August 1813. See enclosed un-named newspaper cutting dated 29 July 1813, 'Copy

of Secretary Wm. Jones Naval General Order', describing the need for Madison's second Embargo, to be rejected by Congress, and imposed by Executive Order on 29 July 1813. Since Warren refers to 'the small Extracts from Official Sources ... enclosed from the Enemies papers', it was probably taken from the Washington semi-official *National Intelligencer*. See also W. Whitehill, ed., *The Journal of Lieutenant Henry Napier in HMS Nymphe: New England Blockaded – 1814*, Salem MA, Peabody Museum, 1939, pp. 21 and 23; on 5 June 1814, *Nymphe* had taken a cargo of potatoes from the American schooner *Maria*, and on 9 June, 'received vegetables and stock of all kinds from Boston'.

41. Dudley, *The Naval War of 1812*, vol. II, p. 272, Capt. John Hayes to Warren, undated but included in TNA ADM 1/504, pp. 733–6, dated HMS *Majestic* 25 October 1813.
42. NMM LBK/2, Intelligence report forwarded by Warren to Melville, 16 March 1813.
43. S. Bonnett, *The Price of Admiralty: An Indictment of the Royal Navy 1805–1960*, London, Hale, 1968, p. 16.
44. NMM LBK/2, Melville to Warren, 'Private', Admiralty, 4 June 1813.
45. NMM WAR/49, Letter 12, Warren to Melville; Halifax, 5 October 1812; TNA ADM 1/502, Sawyer to Croker, 5 July 1812. Sawyer's proclamation to pardon deserters in the Maritime Provinces was dated 3 July 1812, and Warren's, 5 October 1812. See also NMM LBK/2, Warren to Melville, Halifax 7 October 1812.
46. NMM LBK/2, Warren to Melville, Halifax, 5 November 1812.
47. R. Hill, *The Prizes of War: The Naval Prize System in the Napoleonic Wars 1793–1815*, Stroud, Sutton/Royal Naval Museum publications, 1998, pp. 218, 241.
48. NMM WAR/37, reverse of p. 37, 'Vessels Captured and Detained 2 June–13 September 1813'. Agents were obliged to advertise distributions of prize money and were supposed to meet provable claims by the dead's dependents. See Hill, *The Prizes of War*, p. 236.
49. *Naval Chronicle*, vol. 30, p. 42, Broke of the *Shannon* burned prizes 'to his own severe loss'; see also Whitehill, *Journal of Lieutenant Henry Napier*, p. 18; between 6 and 7 June 1814, Capt. Epworth of HMS *Nymphe* had burned five prizes in two days.
50. Niles' *Weekly Register*, Baltimore, vol. V, pp. 184 and 316, 8 January and 5 February 1814. See also ibid., vol. VI, p. 344; A British 'cockswain' and 10 seamen deserting at Accomack, Virginia, on the Chesapeake, received £50 for their barge, and with certificates of naturalisation, 'set off for Baltimore'.
51. M. Crawford, ed., *The Naval War of 1812: A Documentary History*, Washington DC, Naval Historical Center, vol. III, 2002, p. 116. Rear-Adm George Cockburn to Vice-Adm. Alexander Cochrane, HMS *Albion*, Tangier Island, 25 June 1814.
52. Dudley, *The Naval War of 1812*, vol. II, p. 274, citing ADM 1/504, pp. 509–10, Warren to Croker, Halifax, 27 October 1813.
53. Lohnes, 'British Naval Problems', p. 328, note 13. Vice-Adm. Sawyer, for example, is described as lacking energy. No evidence of preparation for war is said to be found in Sawyer's correspondence with his captains in TNA ADM 1/502. See also J. Goldenburg, 'The Royal Navy's Blockade in New England Waters, 1812–1815', *International History Review*, 6, 1984, p. 425, for Admiralty criticism of Sawyer, citing TNA ADM 2/1375. See also W. James, *Naval History of Britain 1793–1820*, London, 1837, vol. VI, p. 224. James thought Warren 'a superannuated admiral, whose services, such as they were, bore a very old date'.
54. Huntington Library, Melville Papers: reel 1, Cochrane to Melville, Government House, Guadaloupe, 27 April 1812.
55. Rodger, *The Command of the Ocean*, pp. 432–3.
56. Markham, Sir C., *Selections of the Correspondence of Admiral John Markham*, London, Navy Records Society, 1904, p. 60, St Vincent to Adm. Markham, HMS *Hibernia*, Cawsand Bay, 26 October 1806.
57. Ibid., p. 49, St Vincent to Adm. Markham, HMS *Hibernia* near Ushant 16 May 1806. By 'puisne', St Vincent apparently meant any junior officer in his own fleet, superior to Warren's detached squadron. See *The Concise Oxford Dictionary*, Oxford, Oxford Univ. Press, 1964.

58. Grenville T., to his brother the Marquis of Buckingham, Huntington Lib, STG 37(32), 8 November 1806. Grenville had been First Lord of the Admiralty since September 1806. See J. Sainty, *Admiralty Officials 1660–1870*, London, Athelone Press, 1975, p. 33.

59. NMM WAR/27 p. 66: Castlereagh to Warren, Foreign Office, 17 June 1812, 'Most Secret re the Declaration of His Maj's Ministers'. See also NMM WAR/82, p. 2, Melville to Warren, Admiralty, 30 July 1812. On 30 July 1812 Warren was required by Melville, First Lord since 25 March 1812, to 'come up to Town forthwith' to meet Castlereagh. By 8 August 1812 Warren had sought Melville's clarification of some of 'the Instructions that Lord Castlereagh did me the Honour of explaining to me the other day'. NMM LBK/2, Warren to Melville, Upper Gros'or Street, 8 August 1812.

60. TNA ADM 2/1376, pp. 73–87, Croker to Warren, 'Secret', Admiralty, 10 February 1813.

61. NMM LBK/2, Warren to Melville, Halifax, 7 October 1812. Warren was not, however, to learn of Sawyer's replacement as his second in command by Rear Adm. George Cockburn until 3 December 1812. Sawyer was recalled, and given command of Cork, in Ireland.

62. Hulbert to his brother John, 26 January 1813, quoted in Gutridge 'Prize Agency 1800–1815', p. 83, citing Portsmouth City Records Office, 626A1/1/3/21.

63. NMM LBK/2, Warren to Melville, Lynhaven Bay, 6 September 1813. Yellow fever was endemic on the Chesapeake; see Lohnes, 'British Naval Problems', p. 73, citing TNA ADM 1/504 14 August 1813.

64. Crawford, *The Naval War of 1812*, vol. III, p. 339, Capt. Robt. Barrie to his mother, dated *Dragon* off Tangier Isle, Chesapeake Bay, 11 November 1814.

65. TNA ADM 1/4222, SS vol. 3, No. 165: 52.25. Foreign Office, August 6 1812, 'Instructions to be given to Admiral Sir John Warren on the Subject of the Relations between this Country & the United States.' These replicated Foreign Office instructions were originally intended for the British Minister in Washington, Augustus Foster, or chargé d'affaires Anthony Baker, and dated 8th July 1812, unless a declaration of war had caused their prior departure from the United States.

66. *Naval Chronicle*, vol. 28, pp. 138–9.

67. C. Vane, *Correspondence, Despatches and other Papers of Viscount Castlereagh*, 3rd Series, London, Henry Colburn, 1848–53, vol. 8, p. 289, Castlereagh to Admiralty, 6 and 12 August 1812.

68. NMM WAR/49.

69. NMM WAR/43, Warren to John Baker, British chargé d'affaires, dated Halifax, 16 November 1812. Monroe's letter, dated 27 October 1812 is in *ASP*: FR, vol. I, pp. 595–7

70. F. Kert, *Prize and Prejudice: Privateering and Naval Prize in Atlantic Canada in the War of 1812*, Research in Maritime History 11, International Maritime Economic History Association, St John's, Newfoundland, 1997. Calculated from Appendix 1, pp. 160–203.

71. R. Guernsey, *New York City and Vicinity during the War of 1812–15, being a Military, Civic and Financial Local History of that Period*, New York, Charles Woodward, 1889–95, vol. I, p. 387.

72. NMM LBK/2, Warren to Melville Halifax, 7 October 1812; see also TNA ADM 1/4222, Foreign Office to Admiralty, Hamilton to Croker, 26 August 1812, for Letters of Protection for neutral vessels sailing with American grain and flour for Spain and Portugal, left by Augustus Foster before leaving Washington. Sawyer and Allen's issue of so many licences caused a British agent to complain on 13 March 1813 that dishonoured licences were a breach of faith, causing the ruin of hitherto pro-British 'respectable Merchants'. Warren forwarded the report to Melville on 16 March 1813, see NMM LBK/2.

73. NMM LBK/2, Warren to Melville, 'Private', HMS *San Domingo*, Bermuda, 19 February 1813.

74. *Naval Chronicle*, vol. 28, pp. 48–51, 12 August 1812. The annual average of British licences issued between 1807–1811 was actually 9,740. The number issued is often given incorrectly, although in 'An Account of the Number of Commercial Licences

Granted during the Last Ten Years', *British Sessional Papers: House of Commons*, 13 February 1812, p. 343, and quoted in A. Seybert, *Statistical Annals*, Philadelphia, T. Dobson, 1818, p. 70, and W. Galpin, 'The American Grain Trade to the Spanish Peninsula 1810–14', *American Historical Review*, 28, 1922, p. 25.

75.   D. Hickey, *The War of 1812: A Forgotten Conflict*, Urbana IL, Univ. of Illinois Press, 1989, p. 117.

76.   JCBL Box 236, f.2, John Maybin to Brown and Ives, Providence, RI, dated Philadelphia, 11 September 1812.

77.   NMM LBK/2, Warren to Melville, Halifax, 24 August 1813.

78.   Ibid., 7 October 1812.

79.   Ibid., postscript to above.

80.   BL C *The Times*, London, 20 March 1813.

81.   Dudley, *The Naval War of 1812*, vol. II, p. 18, citing ADM 2/1376 pp. 73–87, Croker to Warren, Admiralty, 10 February 1813. Most licences to sail without convoy were revoked on 31 July 1812, as published in the *London Gazette*.

82.   Dudley, *The Naval War of 1812*, vol. II, p. 79, 'Private' Melville to Warren, Admiralty, 26 March 1813.

83.   NMM LBK/2, 'Private', Warren to Melville, Halifax, 27 September 1813 and 30 November 1813.

84.   Dudley, *The Naval War of 1812*, vol. II, p. 18, TNA ADM 2/1376, pp. 73–87, Croker to Warren, Admiralty, 10 February 1813.

85.   P. Padfield, *Broke and the Shannon*, London, Hodder & Stoughton, 1968, p. 114–15, Capt to Mrs Broke, HMS *Shannon*, 14 December 1812.

86.   NMM WAR/82, pp. 5–7, 'Secret & Confidential', Melville to Warren, Admiralty, 4 June 1813, and copy marked 'Private' in NMM LBK/2.

87.   NMM LBK/2, Halifax, 7 October 1812. In a later NMM LBK/2 letter to Melville on 29 March 1813, Warren thought that 'Madison is alarmed from not obtaining Cash & being so ill-supported by the French'; the possibility of French intervention clearly continued to cause concern both to Warren and in London.

88.   NMM WAR/28: 'Papers Relating to Convoys, Transports & Trade', 1813–14, vol. 2, pp. 204–5.

89.   Library of Congress (hereafter LC): Royal Navy Logbooks, Log 205, HMS *Spartan*, 38; Record Book of James Dunn, 1808–18, including Commonplace Book kept between 1811–13; 'Blockade – Book of Regulations and Instructions'. Dunn was later to become a Purser and, in 1819, an Admiral's private secretary. *Spartan* made nine major captures and one re-capture while on the North America station in 1813, for which see Dudley, *The Naval War of 1812*, vol. II, pp. 171, 771.

90.   Hill, *The Prizes of War*, p. 56, citing *Naval Chronicle*, vol. 30, p. 255 for capture. £4,000 would then have been worth about $17,760.

91.   Whitehill, *Journal of Lieutenant Henry Napier*, p. 59, citing *Boston Patriot*, 18 May 1814. Three female passengers from the burned American brig *Three Sisters* were put ashore 'with all their trunks, baggage and many presents'. 'The ladies tendered their grateful acknowledgments to the captain and officers of the *Nymph* for the gentlemanly & polite treatment they received while on board their ship.' Similarly, on 2 July 1814, Capt. Thomas Hopkins, 'late a prisoner' recorded 'his most grateful thanks … for the very polite treatment he received' while aboard *Nymphe*, in Boston's *Columbian Centinel*.

92.   R. Horsman, *The War of 1812*, New York, A. Knopf, 1969, p. 264.

93.   NMM LBK/2, Warren to Melville, *San Domingo*, Bermuda, 1 June 1813.

94.   TNA ADM 1/502, 22 February 1813.

95.   R. Knight, Review in *Journal of Imperial and Commonwealth History*, 32 (3), 2004, pp. 132–3. Knight notes that Halifax had only a careening wharf and, although capable of re-fitting the West Indies squadron in both 1802 and 1807, still sent larger ships back to England for major maintenance and repair.

96.   Rodger, *The Command of the Ocean*, p. 570, citing A. Broadley and R. Bartelot, *Nelson's Hardy: His Life, Letters and Friends*, London, J. Murray, 1909, p. 162, letter

to Hardy's brother Joseph, 1 May 1813. See also Dudley, *The Naval War of 1812*, vol. II. p. 272, Capt. Hayes to Warren, encl., 25 October 1813.

97. NMM LBK/2, Warren to Melville, 1 June 1813.

98. Dudley, *The Naval War of 1812*, vol. II, p. 137, citing TNA ADM 1/504, pp. 223–6, Oliver to Warren, *Valiant* at Sea, 13 June 1813.

99. NMM LBK/2, Warren to Melville, Hampton Roads, Chesapeake, 6 July 1813. See also ibid., Warren to Melville, *San Domingo*, River Potomac, 22 July 1813.

100. Ibid., Warren to Melville, *San Domingo*, Bermuda 1 June 1813.

101. Ibid., Warren to Melville, 29 November 1813.

102. TNA ADM 1/505, pp. 87–90.

103. NMM LBK/2, Warren to Melville, 19 February 1813.

104. Padfield, *Broke and the Shannon*, p. 130.

105. Dudley, *The Naval War of 1812*, vol. II, pp. 284, citing TNA ADM 1/504, pp. 713–15. Warren to Croker, Halifax, 13 November 1813. Later local accounts recalled 'nearly 100 sail of vessels were drove onshore and not one escaped some damage', adding that 'a number of lives were lost … the following day never was witnessed in Halifax such a scene of destruction and devastation'. C. Fergusson, ed., *Glimpses of Nova Scotia 1807–24*, Public Archives of NS Bulletin 12, Halifax, Nova Scotia, 1957, pp. 22–3, quoted in Lohnes, 'British Naval Problems', p. 326.

106. Dudley, *The Naval War of 1812*, vol. II, pp. 284.

107. NMM LBK/2, Warren to Melville, *San Domingo*, River Potomac, 22 July 1813.

108. Whitehill, *Journal of Lieutenant Henry Napier*, pp. 29–31. On 3 July 1814, *Nymphe* 'Lost sight of the *Bulwark* in a fog, continuance of which we have had in whatever point of compass the wind blows. Temperature 60 to 62 degrees Fahrenheit.'

109. Hodge, G., *George Hodge his Book Consisting of Difrint ports & ships that I have sailed in since the year 1790. Aged 13 years.* London, The Times, 15 August 2008, for which extract I am indebted to Mr R. Stafford-Smith.

110. IHR: J. Bioran, W. Duane and R. Weightman, *Laws of the United States of America from 4th March 1789 to 4th March 1815*, Philadelphia and Washington DC, 2nd edn, 1816, vol. IV, p. 650.

111. Dudley, *The Naval War of 1812*, vol. II, p. 354, citing Elijah Mix to Madison, 8 April 1813.

112. NMM WAR/82, p. 60, Melville to Warren, 23 April 1813.

113. Dudley, *The Naval War of 1812*, vol. II, pp. 355–6, Cockburn to Warren, 16 June 1813, and pp. 162–3, Warren to Croker, 26 June 1813.

114. Ibid., p. 355, Cockburn to Warren, 16 June 1813. Boats from HMS *Victorious* picked up one of Fulton's 'infernal machines'.

CHAPTER 3. FROM BUSINESS PARTNERS TO ENEMIES: BRITAIN AND THE UNITED STATES BEFORE 1812

1. *ASP*: F, vol. II, p. 854, Chairman of Ways and Means Committee John Eppes' report on 'State of the Finances', to House of Representatives, 10 October 1814.

2. *The London Gazette*, 2 July 1783.

3. J. Holroyd, first Earl of Sheffield, *Observations on the Commerce of the American States*, London, 1783, republ. J. Debrett, 1784.

4. V. Harlow and F. Madden, *British Colonial Developments 1774–1834: Select Documents*, Oxford, Clarendon Press, 1953, p. 256, footnote 2.

5. F. Thistlethwaite, *America and the Atlantic Community: Anglo-American Aspects, 1790–1850*, Philadelphia, Univ. of Pennsylvania Press, 1959, p. 5.

6. J. Killick, 'The Atlantic Economy and Anglo-American Industrialization, 1783–1865', in *Liberal Capitalism: Political and Economic Aspects*, Milton Keynes, Open Univ. Press, 1997, p. 87.

7. US Bureau of the Census, *Historical Statistics of the United States from Colonial Times to 1970*, Washington DC, 1975, p. 8, giving an actual average annual increase for 1770–90 of 4.95% and for 1790–1800, of 3.59%.

8. Ibid., and B. Mitchell and P. Deane, *Abstract of British Historical Statistics*, Cambridge, Cambridge Univ. Press, 1962, p. 8. United States figure from 1810 census. Mitchell and Deane's figure for Ireland, politically incorporated in 1801, is included in the UK total.
9. Killick, 'The Atlantic Economy', p. 88.
10. Ibid., p. 94.
11. Ibid., p. 93.
12. A. Seybert, *Statistical Annals*, Philadelphia, T. Dobson, 1818, p. 255.
13. Ibid. American visible imports from Britain 1802–4 of $35,737,030, minus visible exports to Britain of $23,707,988, produces a visible trade deficit for the United States of minus $12,029,042.
14. Seybert, *Statistical Annals*, p. 92, actually 67.8%.
15. Ibid., p. 287–8, quoting 'the Report of the Inspector General of Exports and Imports to the House of Commons 1812.'
16. Ibid., p. 282, footnote 90.
17. Ibid., p. 288.
18. Ibid.
19. Ibid., p. 89.
20. C. Nettels, *The Emergence of a National Economy 1775–1815*, The Economic History of the United States vol. II, New York and London, Harper & Row, 1962, p. 232, citing E. Johnson, *The History of the Domestic and Foreign Commerce of the United States*, Washington DC, Columbia, Carnegie Institute, 1915, vol. II, p. 20.
21. Nettels, *National Economy*, p. 399, table 21, 'Shipping Engaged in the Carrying Trade of the United States 1789–1815', citing Johnson, *Domestic and Foreign Commerce*, vol. II, p. 28.
22. J. Hedges, *The Browns of Providence Plantations: vol. II, The Nineteenth Century*, 2nd edn, Providence RI, Brown Univ. Press, 1968, vol. II, p. 133.
23. To avoid an over-optimistic evaluation of a country's overseas trading position, it later became customary to calculate 'visible' exports as 'f.o.b.' ('free on board'), valued at their price before export, without shipping costs or insurance premiums, on the assumption that each would be 'invisible' imports. Conversely, imports would be calculated as 'c.i.f.' ('cost, insurance, freight'), on the assumption that the buyer bore the cost of the product and also paid both shipping and insurance costs. This became regarded as the safest method, with exports probably under-estimated and imports over-estimated, although Britain, for example, often supplied goods, shipping and insurance to overseas buyers.
24. Nettels, *National Economy*, p. 399, table 21.
25. JCBL Box 160, f.11; see also Nettels, *National Economy*, p. 314.
26. Nettels, *National Economy*, p. 396, table 17, 'Total Foreign Trade of the United States 1790–1815', citing Johnson, *Domestic and Foreign Commerce*, vol. II, p. 20.
27. Calculated from Nettels, *National Economy*, table 17, actually averaging an adverse annual balance of $19,846,400.
28. Ibid., p. 236, citing E. Bogart, *Economic History of the American People*, 2nd edn, New York, Longmans Green and Company, 1939, pp. 233–4.
29. Nettels, *National Economy*, p. 236.
30. Seybert, *Statistical Annals*, p. 282, footnote 91, quoting 'Baring's Inquiry Concerning the Orders in Council', i.e. A. Baring, *An Inquiry into the causes and consequences of the Orders in Council and an Examination of the Conduct of Great Britain towards the Neutral Commerce of America*, London, J. M. Richardson and J. Ridgway, 1808.
31. D. Warden, *A Statistical, Political and Historical Account of the United States of North America from the Period of Their First Colonization to the Present Day*, Edinburgh, Archibald Constable & Co, 1819, vol. III, p. 286.
32. ASP: C&N, vol. I, p. 897.
33. Warden, *Statistical, Political and Historical Account*, p. 286.
34. D. Hickey, *The War of 1812: A Forgotten Conflict*, Urbana IL, Univ. of Illinois Press,

1989, pp. 12–13, quoting Republican Representative Barnabas Bidwell, 8 March 1806, citing *AC*: 9–1, 653.

35. *ASP*: FR, vol. I, p. 520.
36. Nettels, *National Economy*, p. 396, table 17, 'Total Foreign Trade of the United States'.
37. Harlow and Madden, *British Colonial Developments*, p. 275, note 1, and p. 273, note 3. The authors note that the treaty was concluded on 19 November 1794, but not ratified in London until 28 October 1795, nor proclaimed until 27 February 1796.
38. Ibid.
39. Ibid., citing BL Add MSS 38,310, f. 148, to Charles Bond, 4 January 1796.
40. J. Stephen, *War in Disguise: Or the Frauds of Neutral Flags*, London, October 1805, quoted by Harlow and Madden, *British Colonial Developments*, p. 284.
41. Ibid.; BL W48/6609, 4th edn, p. 250. Although customarily referred to as a 'pamphlet', Stephen's work is a substantial booklet of 250 pages. It was republished twice more by February 1806, and for a fourth time later that year. The 2nd edition was read in the United States, and by December 1807, by Spencer Perceval in Britain. In the United States, by the time Stephen wrote, the succeeding Republican government had repealed the Federalist's interior taxes.
42. J. Marryat, *Concessions to America the Bane of Britain; or the Cause of the Present Distressed Situation of the British Colonial and Shipping Interests explained, and the Proper Remedy suggested*, London, 1807, pp. 5–10 and 36–41, reprinted in Harlow and Madden, *British Colonial Developments*, pp. 280–83, quotation p. 282.
43. Marryat, *Concessions*, reprinted in part in Harlow and Madden, *British Colonial Developments*, quotation p. 281. In fact, $28m was actually £6.31m at the official exchange rate: see Lord Hawkesbury to Anthony Merry, British Minister at Washington, 16 September 1803, in B. Mayo, ed., *Instructions to the British Ministers to the United States 1791–1812*, Washington DC, Annual Report of the American Historical Association, 1936, vol. III, p. 200.
44. Marryat, *Concessions*, as reprinted in Harlow and Madden, *British Colonial Developments*, quotation p. 282.
45. Baring, *An Inquiry*, reprinted in part in Harlow and Madden, *British Colonial Developments*, pp. 283–4. Napoleon's Berlin decree dated from 21 November 1806, and the Milan decree from 17 December 1807.
46. Baring, *An Inquiry*, reprinted in Harlow and Madden, *British Colonial Developments*, p. 284, citing *Bosanquet's Letter on the Causes of the Depression of West Indian Property*, London, 1807, p. 42.
47. Baring, *An Inquiry*, reprinted in Harlow and Madden, *British Colonial Developments*, p. 285.
48. Hickey, *The War of 1812*, p. 18.
49. *The Declaration of Independence & the Constitution of the United States*, with an introduction by P. Maier, New York, Bantam Dell, 1998, republ. 2008, Article II, section 9, p. 66.
50. Seybert, *Statistical Annals*, p. 157.
51. A. Smith, *An Enquiry into the Nature and Causes of the Wealth of Nations*, first publ. London, W. Strahan & T. Cadell, 1776; see Everyman edn, London, Dent, 1966, vol. II, Book V, Chapter II, Part II, pp. 306–9. The first American edition was published by Th. Dobson of Philadelphia in 1789, although copies of earlier British editions may also have been available in the United States, in the view of the LC's Rare Books & Special Coll. Div. It was also republished in Leipzig in 1778, and in Basle by 1791 (BL online catalogue) Both Madison and the Swiss-educated Albert Gallatin may therefore have been familiar with it.
52. D. Dewey, *Financial History of the United States*, 12th edn, New York, Kelly, 1934, repr. 1968, pp. 113–25. According to J. Bristed, *The Resources of the United States of America; or a View of the agricultural, commercial … moral and religious capacity and character of the American people*, New York, J. Eastburn & Co, 1818, p. 77, such repayments were customarily made a year in arrears.

53. Nettels, *National Economy*, p. 396, table 17, 'Total Foreign Trade of the United States'.
54. D. North, 'United States Balance of Payments 1790–1860', in *Trends in the American Economy in the Nineteenth Century*, Studies in Income and Wealth 24, National Bureau of Economic Research, Princeton, Princeton Univ. Press, 1960; repr. New York, Arno Press, 1975, pp. 591–2, table A-2, Appendix A.
55. Hickey, *The War of 1812*, p. 20, quoting Randolph's speech of 14 April 1808, citing *AC*: 10–1, 2136.
56. *AC*: 11–3, 1338–9.
57. C. Challis, ed., *A New History of the Royal Mint*, Cambridge, Cambridge Univ. Press, 1992, Appendix 1, pp. 693–4; see also E. Kelly, *Spanish Dollars and Silver Tokens: An Account of the Issues of the Bank of England 1797–1816*, London, Spink & Son, 1976, Appendix A, table IV, p. 123. No ordinary silver currency had been minted since 1787, and gold struck annually had not exceeded £0.5m since 1804. Countermarked Spanish dollars, Bank of England and private tokens circulated internally beside worn regal currency.
58. A. Balinky, 'Gallatin's Theory of War Finance', *William & Mary Historical Quarterly*, 3rd series, 1959, pp. 73–82.
59. F. Crouzet, 'Wars, Blockade, and Economic Change in Europe, 1792–1815', *Journal of Economic History*, 24, 1964, pp. 568, 571–4.
60. *ASP*: F, vol. II, p. 497, Secretary of the Treasury Gallatin's report to the Senate on the 'State of the Finances' dated 22 November and presented 25 November 1811.
61. JHL Jonathan Russell Correspondence A30002, Reuben Beasley to Jonathan Russell, London, 16 June 1812. Beasley remained in London as consul to deal with the affairs of detained American seamen and, later, of prisoners of war.
62. *ASP*: F, vol. II, pp. 495–7.
63. Ibid., p. 497.
64. Ibid.
65. Ibid., pp. 524–5.
66. Ibid., p. 527.
67. *AC*: 12–1, 1099.
68. *Ibid.*, 1100.
69. *ASP*: F, vol. II, p. 539.
70. Warden, *Statistical, Political and Historical Account*, p. 299, for net customs revenue, and J. De Bow, *Statistical View of the United States*, Washington DC, A. Nicholson, 1854, p. 185, for total government receipts.
71. Dewey, *Financial History*, p. 142.
72. Mitchell and Deane, *Abstract of British Historical Statistics*, p. 487. 'Prices 9, Wheat', contd.
73. W. Galpin, 'The American Grain Trade to the Spanish Peninsula 1810–14', *American Historical Review*, 28, 1922, p. 24.
74. Mitchell and Deane, *Abstract of British Historical Statistics*, p. 498, calculated from 'Prices 14, Average Price of Bread in London (in pence per 4lb loaf)', contd.
75. E. Evans, *The Forging of the Modern State: Early Industrial Britain 1783–1870*, 2nd edn, London, Longman, 1996, p. 89.
76. Mitchell and Deane, *Abstract of British Historical Statistics*, p. 311, 'Overseas Trade 10, Official Values of Imports and of Exports and Re-exports combined, according to Regional Direction – Great Britain 1755–1822', contd.; percentage actually 381.3%.
77. Ibid., p. 313, 'Overseas Trade 12, Values at Current Prices of Overseas Trade According to Principal Countries – UK 1805–1938'.
78. D. French, *The British Way in Warfare 1688–2000*, London, Hyman/Unwin, 1990, pp. 106–7, and P. Kennedy, *The Rise and Fall of British Naval Mastery*, London, Allen Lane, 1976, p. 147.
79. Evans, *The Forging of the Modern State*, p. 416, citing R. Davis, *The Industrial Revolution and British Overseas Trade*, 1st edn, Leicester Univ. Press, 1979, pp. 96–7, 104–5, 114–17.

80. Evans, *The Forging of the Modern State*, p. 415, citing Davis, *The Industrial Revolution*, pp. 104–5.
81. Mitchell and Deane, *Abstract of British Historical Statistics*, p. 410, 'Public Finance 7. Produce of the Poor Rates and Expenditure on Relief of the Poor – England and Wales 1748–1885'.
82. T. Hansard, *The Parliamentary Debates from 1803 to the Present Time*, London, Longman 1st series, 1803–20, vol. 23, Brougham to House of Lords, p. 486.
83. Ibid., vol. XXIII, p. 715.
84. Mitchell and Deane, *Abstract of British Historical Statistics*, p. 392, 'Public Finance 3. Gross Public Income-United Kingdom 1801–1939, Principal Constituent Items'.
85. Ibid., calculated from data in table above.
86. Ibid., calculated from table above. Income Tax was re-imposed in 1803 as 'the property tax', being 10% of incomes greater than £60 per annum, mainly from property. The value of property was assessed, rather than personal incomes. See P. Deane and W. Cole, *British Economic Growth 1688–1957*, 2nd edn, Cambridge, Cambridge Univ. Press, 1969, Appendix II, p. 323.
87. P. Hudson, *The Industrial Revolution*, London, Arnold, 1993, p. 59, citing P. O'Brien, 'The Impact of the Revolutionary and Napoleonic Wars on the Long-run Growth of the British Economy', *Fernand Braudel Centre Review*, 12, 1989.
88. P. O'Brien, *War and Economic Progress in Britain and America*, Milton Keynes, Open Univ. Press, 1997, p. 182.
89. Hudson, *The Industrial Revolution*, p. 59, citing O'Brien, 'The Impact of the Revolutionary and Napoleonic Wars', p. 347.
90. Mitchell and Deane, *Abstract of British Historical Statistics*, pp. 355, 'Wages and Standard of Living 6'; and 'Prices 14' p. 498; actually, 32.94%. The British duty on sugar had doubled between 1794–6 and 1814, but consumption per head had increased, see Davis, *The Industrial Revolution*, p. 45.
91. Mitchell and Deane, *Abstract of British Historical Statistics*, p. 349, 'Wages and Standard of Living Table 3'.
92. Rockoff, H., Banking and Finance 1789–1914, in the *Cambridge Economic History of the United States*; vol. II, *The Long Nineteenth Century*, Engermans and Gallman, R. eds., Cambridge Univ. Press, 2000, p. 655, Table 14.1 'Money and Price in the War of 1812'.
93. Kennedy, *British Naval Mastery*, p. 141, citing E. Schumpeter, 'English Prices and Public Finance 1660–1822', *Review of Economic Statistics*, 20 (1), 1938, p. 27; N. Silberling, 'The financial and monetary policy of Great Britain during the Napoleonic Wars', *Quarterly Journal of Economics*, 38, 1924, pp. 217–18.
94. Kennedy, *British Naval Mastery*, p. 141.
95. Kennedy, *British Naval Mastery*, p. 141, citing B. Murphy, *A History of the British Economy 1086–1970*, London, Longman, 1973, p. 490.
96. BL C *The National Intelligencer*, Washington, 28 March 1814. Some had argued that 70% of stockholders had been foreign, including prominent British politicians: see R. Buel, *America on the Brink: How the Political Struggle Over the War of 1812 Almost Destroyed the Young Republic*, New York and Basingstoke, Palgrave/Macmillan, 2006, p. 111.
97. W. James, *A full and correct account of the military occurrences of the late war between Great Britain and the United States of America*, London, James Richardson, 1818, vol. I, pp. 1–2.
98. Hedges, *The Browns of Providence Plantations*, p. 131.
99. W. Galpin, 'The American Grain Trade', p. 25, citing T. Pitkin, *A Statistical View of the Commerce of the United States*, 2nd edn, New Haven, Durrie & Peck, 1835, pp. 119–20.
100. Kelly, *Spanish Dollars and Silver Tokens*, pp. 96–8, 100. Shipments of specie had arrived in HMS *Galatea* in November 1812, and in *Foudroyant* and *Brazen* from India, in January 1813. However, as shown by Mitchell and Deane, *Abstract of British Historical Statistics*, p. 442, Bank of England bullion reserves never fell below £2m.

101. T. Jefferson, quoted in R. Albion and J. Pope, *Sea Lanes in Wartime: The American Experience 1775–1942*, 2nd edn, New York and Portland ME, Norton & Co/Archon Books, 1968, p. 116.
102. Hedges, *The Browns of Providence Plantations*, p. 133.
103. Ibid. p. 134.
104. Mitchell and Deane, *Abstract of British Historical Statistics*, p. 313, 'Overseas Trade 12, Values at Current Prices of Overseas Trade According to Regions and Principal Countries'.
105. J. Croker, *A key to the orders in council respecting trade with French ports, etc. 7 Jan. 1807–21 April 1812*, London, Murray, 1812. BL 8135.e.34.
106. J. Madison, 'Address to Congress', 1 June 1812, in James, *Military occurrences*, vol. I, pp. 4–5.
107. *AC*: 12–1, Supplement 1637–8, 2322–3. Voted for: 79 to 49 in House of Representatives on 4 June, and 19 to 13 in Senate on 17 June 1812.
108. *AC*: 12–1, 1511.
109. BL Add MSS 38249, f.7, letter from James Abernethy to Lord Liverpool, dated Francis Street, Bedford Square, 2nd August 1812.
110. Ibid.
111. BL Add MSS 38250, f.42, letter to Lord Liverpool from Lord Bathurst, dated Brighton, 3 October 1812.
112. *Naval Chronicle*, vol. 28, pp. 304–6. In the event, General Reprisals would not be fully implemented until Warren's receipt, on 16 November 1812, of Monroe's negative reply, dated 27 October, to his armistice proposal of 30 September 1812.
113. *The Annual Register*, 1812, London, vol. 5, Pt 2, pp. 166.
114. Hedges, *The Browns of Providence Plantations*, p. 131.
115. C. Lyne, *A Letter to Lord Castlereagh on the North American Export Trade During the War and during any time the Import and Use of our Manufactures are interdicted in the United States*, London, J. Richardson, 1813, p. 5.
116. Ibid., pp. 9–10, 12.
117. Ibid., p. 40.
118. Ibid., p. 45.

CHAPTER 4. THE UNITED STATES BLOCKADED: ADMIRAL WARREN'S 'UNITED COMMAND', AUGUST 1812–APRIL 1814

1. JHL: A30433, Letter from Rueben Beasley to Jonathan Russell, London, 26 December 1812.
2. R. Gardiner, ed., *The Naval War of 1812*, London. Caxton Editions/NMM, 2001, p. 34. *President's* main armament was 30 × 24 pdrs, with an upper deck armament of 2× 24 pdrs, 1 × 18 pdr and 24 × 42 pdr carronades, a total of 55 guns.
3. W. Dudley, *The Naval War of 1812: A Documentary History*, Washington DC, Naval Historical Center, vol. I, 1985, p. 138, Rodgers to Sect. of Navy Paul Hamilton, USS *President*, New York, 19 June 1812.
4. Dudley, *The Naval War of 1812*, vol. I, p. 262. Letter: Rodgers to Hamilton, Boston 1 Sept. 1812. See also BL Add MSS 38248, p. 310. Letter from Alexander Howe to his son, dated Halifax, 21 August 1812. See also W. James, *A Full and Correct Account of the Chief Naval Occurrences of the Late War between Great Britain and the United States of America*, London, T. Egerton, 1817, republ. as *Naval Ocurrences of the War of 1812: A Full and Correct Account of the Naval War between Great Britain and the United States of America, 1812–1815*, London, Conway Maritime Press, 2004, p. 37. The 85-ship convoy was said to be worth £12m, then about $57.6m.
5. Dudley, *The Naval War of 1812*, vol. I, p. 634, citing I. Brandt, *James Madison, Commander in Chief 1812–36*, New York, Bobbs-Merrill & Co Inc., 1961, p. 125.
6. Dudley, *The Naval War of 1812*, vol. I, p. 138.
7. Ibid.
8. Ibid., p. 157, Capt. Byron to Vice-Adm. Sawyer, HMS *Belvidera* Halifax Harbour, 27 June 1812.

9. Ibid., p. 154, Extract from Rodger's Journal, 23 June 1812.
10. Ibid., p. 157.
11. Ibid., p. 157–60 citing TNA ADM 1/502, Pt 1, pp. 299–302; and *Naval Chronicle*, vol. 28, 'Naval History of the Present Year June–July 1812', p. 73. Rodgers opened fire 'without previous communication with the Belvidera'.
12. TNA ADM 1/4221 9 May 1812.
13. Dudley, *The Naval War of 1812*, vol. I, p. 138.
14. *Naval Chronicle*, vol. 28, p. 73–4.
15. Ibid.
16. Ibid., p. 426, Letter, Halifax 15 October 1812. Sawyer had intended his blockade to include Boston, New York, Norfolk and Charleston.
17. D. Hickey, *The War of 1812: A Forgotten Conflict*, Urbana IL, Univ. of Illinois Press, 1989, p. 93, citing Governor Tompkins to NY legislature, 3 November 1812.
18. See, for example, C. Forester, *The Naval War of 1812*, London, Michael Joseph, 1957, p. 30.
19. A. Mahan, *Sea Power in its Relations to the War of 1812*, Boston MA and London, Little Brown/Sampson, Marston Low and Company, 1905, vol. II, p. 21–3.
20. Sawyer to Croker, Halifax, 5 July 1812, cited in B. Lohnes, 'British Naval Problems at Halifax', *Mariner's Mirror*, 59, 1973, p. 330.
21. T. Hansard, *The Parliamentary Debates from 1803 to the Present Time*, London, 1st series, 1803–20, vol. 23, pp. 715–21. See also *ASP: FR*, vol. III, pp. 593, 594–5.
22. NMM WAR/82, p. 2, letter from Melville to Warren, 30 July 1812. Warren had served in North American waters in 1777–8, and as an ambassador-extraordinary in Russia 1801–4, and then as Vice-Admiral, C in C North America, 1808–10. In the draft of an undated letter to Melville, Warren wrote 'having considered the Orders and Instructions Lord Castlereagh read to me the other Day, I am anxious to have … further Information as well as the Determination of His Majesty's Government'. NMM WAR/82 p. 3. See TNA ADM 2/1375, pp. 62–3, dated 12 August 1812.
23. NMM WAR/82, p. 3.
24. TNA ADM 2/1375, pp. 62–3, and ADM 1/4222, p. 168, Castlereagh to Admiralty, Foreign Office, 12 August 1812.
25. *Naval Chronicle*, vol. 28, 'Naval History of the Present Year', July–August 1812, p. 157.
26. *London Gazette*, no. 16629, 1–4 August 1812, p. 1483.
27. *Naval Chronicle*, vol. 28, p. 138, pp. 158–9.
28. R. Albion and J. Pope, *Sea Lanes in Wartime: The American Experience 1775–1945*, 2nd edn, New York and Portland ME, Norton & Co/Archon Books, 1968, p. 115. Libelled ships and brigs alone represent 10.2%, while all vessels detained by 17 September 1812 are less than 13% of Halifax's wartime total.
29. *London Gazette*, no. 16630, p. 1503.
30. Ibid., as reprinted in *Naval Chronicle*, vol. 28, p. 139.
31. *Naval Chronicle*, vol. 31, p. 165.
32. TNA ADM 2/1375, p. 33.
33. TNA ADM 1/4222, p. 165. 52.25 'Instructions to be given to Sir John Borlase Warren on the subject of the Relations between this Country & the United States. SS vol. 3, No: 165'; 'Mr Foster our Envoy left Washington 14th July in *Atalanta* sloop of war', not reaching Portsmouth until 19 August 1812. *Naval Chronicle*, vol. 28, p. 157.
34. C. Vane, *Correspondence, Despatches and other Papers of Viscount Castlereagh*, 3rd Series, London, Henry Colburn, 1848–53, vol. 8, pp. 289–90.
35. TNA ADM 2/1375, pp. 48–9, 'Draft Letter' provided by Foreign Office to Admiralty for 'Sir J B Warren to Mr Monroe' 7 August 1812.
36. NMM LBK/2, Warren to Melville, London, 8 August 1812.
37. TNA ADM 1/502, letter, Warren to Croker, dated 11 August 1812.
38. *Naval Chronicle*, vol. 28, p. 173, 'Admiralty Office 12 August 1812'.

39. Ibid., p. 159.
40. Ibid.
41. Dudley, *The Naval War of 1812*, vol. I, p. 263, letter from Rodgers to Hamilton, USS *President*, Boston, 24 September 1812.
42. Ibid. See also letter of Sawyer to Croker 17 September 1812, TNA ADM 1/502, Pt 3, pp. 581–6, cited in Dudley, *The Naval War of 1812*, vol. I, pp. 497–8; and James, *Chief Naval Occurrences*, p. 39, for reference to scurvy.
43. D. Lyons, *The Sailing Navy List*, London, Conway Maritime Press, 1993, p. 279. 'Brig sloop *Magnet* lost in Atlantic 10.9.1812'. See also NMM HUL/18. On a 'list of Ships and Vessels on the West Indies and American stations', dated 7 August 1812, *Magnet* is prophetically annotated 'Recommended to be employed in the West Indies as not being fit for the American Seas', shown as Appendix A Table 3.
44. *ASP*: FR, vol. III, p. 595, letter from Warren to Sect. of State James Monroe, Halifax, Nova Scotia, 30 Sept. 1812.
45. NMM LBK/2, Warren to Melville, Halifax, 7 October 1812.
46. TNA ADM 8/100, 'Ships in Sea Pay – 1st July 1812', cited in Dudley, *The Naval War of 1812*, vol. I, pp. 180–82. See also Appendix of NMM HUL/18 for 'List of Ships and Vessels on the West Indies and American Stations', dated 7 August 1812, naming 33 on the North American station, 28 for the Leeward Islands, and 18 for Jamaica, totalling 79. Inclusion of figures for Newfoundland gives a total of 83 vessels from both sources.
47. NMM WAR/49, Letter 13, Warren to Croker, Halifax, 5 October 1812. See also TNA ADM 1/502, Pt 3, pp. 613–15, cited in Dudley, *The Naval War of 1812*, vol. I, pp. 508–9.
48. TNA ADM 1/502, Pt 4, pp. 541–5, Capt. J. Dacres to Vice Ad. Sawyer, Boston, 7 September 1812, and TNA ADM 1/502, Pt 3, pp. 613–15, Warren to Croker, Halifax, 5 October 1812.
49. *Naval Chronicle*, vol. 28, p. 420, Warren's Proclamation, 5 October 1812. Warren's offer of pardon for returning deserters appears to have been no more productive than Sawyer's earlier attempt of 3 July 1812.
50. NMM LBK/2, Warren to Melville, Halifax, 7 October 1812; see also J. Gwyn, *Frigates and Foremasts: The North American Squadron in Nova Scotia Waters, 1745–1815*, Vancouver, Univ. of British Columbia Press, 2003, p. 138, citing TNA ADM 1/502, p. 343.
51. Dudley, *The Naval War of 1812*, vol. I, p. 492, citing TNA ADM 1/502, Pt 3, p. 419, letter: Sawyer to Andrew Allen, HMS *Centurion* at Halifax, 5 Aug. 1812.
52. TNA ADM 1/503, Pt 1, pp. 51–2, Warren to Melville, 11 November 1812. See also Hickey, *The War of 1812*, p. 117, for British licences apparently on open sale in American cities for $5,000, citing *Morning Chronicle* 12 August and 18 September 1812, and Baker to Castlereagh, 22 March 1813, TNA FO 5/88.
53. D. Hickey, 'Trade Restrictions during the War of 1812', *Journal of American History*, 68 (3), 1981, p. 527. Given an annual average between 1807–11 of 9,740, Hickey's estimate for two and a half months does not seem excessive.
54. JCBL Box 236, f.2, letter from John Maybin of Philadelphia to Brown & Ives of Providence, RI, dated 11 September 1812.
55. NMM LBK/2, Warren to Melville, Halifax, 7 October 1812.
56. BL Add MSS 38250, f.197, Letter from Capt. Robt. Barrie to Rear Ad. George Cockburn, 6 Nov. 1812, and f.198, from Lord Clancarty to Prime Minister, Lord Liverpool, 24 Nov. alleging Allen's improper issue of Protections, also f.193, Liverpool to Castlereagh: 25 Nov. asking for 'answer by return', and f.194, Croker to Lord Chetwynd: 25 Nov., marked 'Immediate' in which the Admiralty seeks the Privy Council's opinion on the issue.
57. TNA ADM 1/503 Pt 1, pp. 52–8, enclosures from Allen dated 21 October, in letter from Warren to Melville, dated Halifax, 11 November 1812.
58. TNA ADM 1/502 Pt 4, p. 455, Sawyer to Croker. HMS *Centurion*, Halifax, 2 August 1812, cited in Dudley, *The Naval War of 1812*, vol. I, 216.

59. NMM WAR/49, Letter 12, Warren to Croker, dated Halifax 5 October 1812.
60. Gwyn, *Frigates and Foremasts*, p. 182, citing TNA ADM 1/502, p. 249.
61. NMM LBK/2, Warren to Melville, Halifax, 7 October 1812.
62. Mahan, *Sea Power*, vol. I, p. 395, summarising Niles' *Weekly Register*, Baltimore, 1811–49.
63. *Naval Chronicle*, vol. 29, p. 198, Letter of 'Faber'; *Morning Chronicle*, 17–18 September 1812, and *Times*, 30 December 1812.
64. NMM HUL/1, Warren's Order Book, order No. 1 to Capt. John Bastard of HMS *Africa*, 4 October 1812.
65. NNM WAR/49, Letter 12, Warren to Croker, dated Halifax 5 October 1812.
66. NMM HUL/1, Warren's Order Book, order No. 2, Warren to Capt. Sir John Beresford of HMS *Poictiers*, Halifax, 10 October 1812.
67. Ibid.
68. Dudley, *The Naval War of 1812*, vol. I, vol. II, pp. 80–81, citing TNA ADM 1/4359, enclosed with Warren's letter to Croker of 28 March 1813.
69. *London Gazette*, 13 October 1812, and reprinted in *Naval Chronicle*, vol. 28, p. 409.
70. *London Gazette*, no. 16663, p. 2183, for 31 October–3 November 1812.
71. NMM WAR/11, 'Schedule of Orders in Council, Circular Orders, Letters etc delivered by Ad Rt: Hon:ble Sir J B Warren Bart KB to Vice Ad the Hon:ble Sir Alexander Cochrane KB at Bermuda the first day of April 1814', reverse of p. 139.
72. Ibid. This spelling of Foster's name probably indicates its current pronunciation. See also R. Morriss, *Cockburn and the British Navy in Transition: Admiral Sir George Cockburn 1772–1853*, Exeter, Exeter Univ. Press 1997, p. 86, citing NMM Folder 4, Troubridge Papers.
73. NMM HUL/1, Warren's Order Book, order No. 3, 14 October 1812. Burning or sinking small prizes had been practised by both sides almost from the outset. P. Padfield calculates that Broke's squadron burned forty American prizes between 5 and 19 July 1812 (*Broke and the Shannon*, London, Hodder and Stoughton, 1968, p. 90).
74. *London Gazette*, no. 16658, p. 2079.
75. NMM HUL/4, Bermuda. 'Copy of Vice-Admiralty Court Records, 25 November 1812–2 July 1814'.
76. NMM WAR/43, Warren to Anthony Baker, British chargé d'affaires, Halifax, 16 November 1812.
77. NMM LBK/2, Warren to Melville, Bermuda, 5 November 1812.
78. Albion and Pope, *Sea Lanes in Wartime*, p. 115.
79. NMM LBK/2, Warren to Melville, Bermuda, 5 November 1812.
80. TNA ADM 1/503, Pt 1, pp. 117–19.
81. NMM HUL/1, Warren's Order Book, order No. 2, 10 October 1812. Warren was later ordered to make Bermuda his permanent headquarters. NMM WAR/82, 23rd March 1813. Quotation from E. Brenton, *The Naval History of Great Britain*, London, 1837, vol. 1, pp. 9–10.
82. NMM LBK/2, Warren to Melville, 18 November 1812.
83. Ibid., Warren to Melville, 9 November 1812.
84. Dudley, *The Naval War of 1812*, vol. I, p. 561, letter from Commodore Tingey to Sec. of Navy Hamilton, Washington Navy Yard, 7 November 1812.
85. TNA CO 43/49, Bathurst to Lords Commissioners of Admiralty, Downing Street, 21 November 1812, printed, pp. 153–4, i.e. handwritten, pp. 266–7.
86. TNA ADM 2/1375, 'Secret Letters and Orders', Admiralty to Warren, Secret, 26 December 1812, pp. 337–8; enclosing TNA CO 43/49, Bathurst to Lords Commissioners of Admiralty, 25 December 1812, pp. 280–83.
87. TNA CO 43/49, pp. 280–83.
88. Ibid.
89. *London Gazette*, no. 166684, p. 2567. Proclamation of 'Foreign Office, 26 December 1812'.

90. Specifically, Macon's No. 2 Bill of 1 May 1810, in *AC*: 10–2, 2582–3, applied to Britain only after 2 March 1811. The American Enemy Trade Act of 6 July 1812 prohibited seaborne trade with the British Empire; see *AC*: 12–1, 2354.

91. G. Oddie, 'The Circulation of Silver, 1697–1817', Lecture to London Numismatic Club, Warburg Institute, 6 July 2004. The Bank of England had suspended payment of specie on 27 February 1797 and, by 1815, 60% of silver in circulation in Britain was accounted for by the official tokens of the Banks of England and Ireland and the unofficial, and technically illegal, tokens of individuals. Britain spent £400,000 in gold between 1809 and 1813 on American grain and flour used in Spain and Portugal.

92. *AC*: 12–2, pp. 1264–7, and Gallatin to Cheves, Treasury Dept. 18 November 1812, in *AC*: 12–2, pp. 1251–2.

93. TNA FO 5/88. Baker to Castlereagh, 18 December 1812.

94. *AC*: 12–2, p. 1252. Gallatin to Cheves.

95. Ibid.

96. *AC*: 12–2, pp. 1252–4. Technically, based on comparative gold content, the £/$ exchange rate should have been $4.8665 to £1; see *Maps and Statistical Tables*, Milton Keynes, Open Univ. Press, 1997, p. 31, despite which, on 16 September 1803, the British and American governments agreed on an exchange rate of $4.44 to £1. B. Mayo, ed., *Instructions to British Ministers to the United States 1791–1812*, Washington DC, Annual Report of American History Association, 1936, vol. III, p. 200, Lord Hawkesbury to Anthony Merry. However, for convenient conversion, $4.80 was sometimes adopted; see B. Perkins, *Castlereagh and Adams: England and the United States 1812–23*, Berkeley CA, Univ. of California Press, 1964, p. 229, citing G. Taylor, *Economic History of US*, New York, 1951, p. 447n.

97. *AC*: 12–2, pp. 33–4, 100, 315, 450–51.

98. TNA ADM 1/503, Pt 1, pp. 99–102, Warren to Croker, Bermuda, 29 December 1812.

99. NMM LBK/2, 'Private & Confidential' letter from Warren to Melville, dated *San Domingo*, Bermuda, 25 February 1813. Warren's estimation of Stirling was vindicated when, later in 1813, Stirling was recalled on a Court Martial charge of having accepted a bribe of $2,000 to provide convoy protection for a merchantman, found 'partly proved' in May 1814. Stirling was retired on half-pay without the possibility of further promotion. See R. Morriss, *Dictionary of National Biography* entry, vol. 51, pp. 801–2, Oxford University Press, 1982.

100. NMM LBK/2, Warren to Melville, 25 February 1813.

101. TNA ADM 1/503, Pt 1, pp. 99–102, Warren to Croker, dated Bermuda, 29 December 1812. Theoretically reduced from 74 to 58 guns, razees are often recorded as carrying more. *Majestic*'s armament is given as 28 × 42 pdr carronades, 28 × 32 pdrs and 2 × 12 pdrs. J. Colledge, *Ships of the Royal Navy*, revised edn, London, Greenhill, 1987, p. 204.

102. TNA ADM 1/503, p. 221.

103. NMM WAR/82, Melville to Warren, 3 December 1812.

104. Ibid., p. 19.

105. NMM COC/11. Cockburn's memoirs, pp. 100–101.

106. NMM LBK/2, Warren to Melville, *San Domingo*, Bermuda, 19 February 1813.

107. NMM LBK/2, Warren to Croker, 21 February 1813. Until 3 March 1813 only *Junon* 38, *Maidstone* and *Belvidera*, each 36, and the 6th Rate *Laurestinus* 26, were on station.

108. Dudley, *The Naval War of 1812*, vol. II, 1992, p. 313. Letter from Secretary of the Navy Jones to Capt. J. Cassin, Commandant of Navy Yard Gosport, dated 'Feb:16. 1813'.

109. NMM HUL/18, 'Narcissus's List of Ships who composed the Blockading Squadron in the Chesapeake'. This list is annotated in red ink, presumably by Hulbert himself, with 'This list kept by Capt. Lumley is the most correct account I have been able to obtain between 4 March and July 1813.'

110. Dudley, *The Naval War of 1812*, vol. II, p. 320, Capt. G. Burdett to Warren, *Maidstone*, Lyn Haven Bay Chesapeake, 9 February 1813. Logwood provided a red dye.

111. NMM HUL/18, 'Narcissus's List of Ships'.
112. Dudley, *The Naval War of 1812*, vol. II, pp. 326–7, Cockburn to Warren, *Marlborough*, Hampton Roads, 23 March 1813.
113. Ibid.
114. Ibid., p. 328.
115. Ibid.
116. Ibid., pp. 329–30.
117. Ibid., p. 330.
118. Ibid.
119. Ibid., p. 331.
120. NMM HUL/18, 'Narcissus's List of Ships'.
121. Niles' *Weekly Register*, Baltimore, vol. III, p. 383, 13 February 1813.
122. NMM HUL/18, 'List of Captures 19 December 1812–12 June 1813'. Many of these prizes were not condemned or 'paid out' until February 1816.
123. Ibid.
124. NMM HUL/1, Warren's Order Book, orders for 27 November 1812 and 8 March 1813.
125. Ibid., Warren's Order Book, order dated 2 December 1812. This order also appears to have been given to Broke's squadron, although that would seem to require him to be in two places at once. The mistake may have been in Warren's dictation, or perhaps the clerk misunderstood who the order was for, or even dated it wrongly. Nonetheless, it forms significant evidence of the Royal Navy's role in protecting Britain's economically and strategically vital trade.
126. Dudley, *The Naval War of 1812*, vol. II, pp. 15–16, citing a letter marked 'private' and dated '*San Domingo* Off N. York. Janry. 25th 1813'.
127. NMM HUL/1, Warren's Order Book, orders to Richard Byron of *Belvidera*, dated 'Bermuda 2nd Jan'y 1813'.
128. Niles' *Weekly Register*, Baltimore, vol. III, 20 February 1813. Niles suggests that the *Emily* was sent back on 5 February, but Warren's reference to 'yesterday's' proclamation suggests 7 February 1813.
129. Dudley, *The Naval War of 1812*, vol. II, pp. 15–16, Warren to Croker 25 January 1813.
130. Ibid.
131. Albion and Pope, *Sea Lanes in Wartime*, p. 120.
132. NMM LBK/2, Warren to Melville, *San Domingo*, Bermuda, 19 February 1813.
133. NMM WAR/27, 'Papers Relating to Convoys Transports, Commerce and Trade, 1797–1813', vol. I, p. 152. Copied in a letter from Andrew Allen, former British Consul in Boston, to Warren, dated 20 November 1812.
134. NMM WAR/28, 'Papers Relating to Convoys, Transports, Commerce and Trade, 1797–1813', vol. II, pp. 204–5. Letter from John and Samuel Musson on behalf of Boston merchants, dated 22 December 1812, and not forwarded by Warren until 22 December 1813.
135. TNA ADM 2/1375, p. 252, Croker to Warren, 18 November 1812.
136. NMM WAR/82, p. 18, Melville to Warren, 3 December 1812.
137. Dudley, *The Naval War of 1812*, vol. II, p. 14, Croker to Warren, 9 January 1813.
138. Ibid.
139. BJL DDHO 7/1, Melville to Capt. Henry Hotham, 1 January 1813.
140. BJL DDHO 7/3, Second Secretary to the Admiralty John Barrow to Capt Henry Hotham in Bermuda, e.g. Admiralty Office, 9 July 1813, 8 November 1813, 7 March 1814, 16 April 1814, 7 March 1814, some in duplicate.
141. Dudley, Wade, 'Without some Risk', pp. 134, 167, citing Hotham Papers, BJL Univ. of Hull.
142. BJL DDHO 7/1, Croker to Hotham, Confidential, dated Admiralty Office 9 January 1813.
143. NMM LBK/2, private letter, Warren to Melville, *San Domingo*, Bermuda, 19 February 1813.
144. Dudley, *The Naval War of 1812*, vol. II, p. 14, Croker to Warren, 9 January 1813, citing TNA ADM 2/1375, pp. 365–73.

145. NMM LBK/2, Warren to Melville, 19 February 1813.
146. Dudley, *The Naval War of 1812*, vol. II, pp. 80–81, citing TNA ADM 1/4359, Warren to Croker, enclosed with letter dated 28 March 1813.
147. Ibid.
148. Hickey, *The War of 1812*, p. 169, citing report to Gallatin in Treasury Dept, National Archives, Washington (M175, reel 2).
149. Dudley, *The Naval War of 1812*, vol. II, pp. 80–81, Warren to Croker, citing TNA ADM 1/4359.
150. Dudley, *The Naval War of 1812*, vol. II, p. 19, Croker to Warren, citing ADM 2/1376, pp. 73–87, 10 Feb. 1813.
151. NMM HUL/1, Warren's Order Book, Warren to Broke 3 March 1813.
152. Dudley, *The Naval War of 1812*, vol. II, p. 76, Croker to Warren 20 March 1813.
153. Ibid. Clearly, the 'disposal' of Warren's forces of which the Admiralty approved on 20 March, must have been an earlier version than that Dudley notes as enclosed with Warren's letter of 28 March 1813.
154. Ibid.
155. Dudley, *The Naval War of 1812*, vol. II, p. 19, Croker to Warren, 10 February 1813. Warren's proposal had been dated 29 December 1812.
156. NMM WAR/82, pp. 62–3, dated 23 March 1813. See also Colledge, *Ships of the Royal Navy*, p. 152. Launched as early as 1781, as a 74-gun 3rd rate three-decker, the now obsolescent *Goliath* was among those razed between 1812 and 1813, cut down to 58-gun two-deckers but retaining their line-of-battle ship scantlings, matching those of the massively built American heavy frigates, and, with their reduced draught, potentially useful in blockading ports and estuaries. Others included the *Majestic*, launched in 1785, and *Saturn*, of 1786; pp. 204, 289.
157. NMM WAR/82, pp. 62–3, dated 23 March 1813.
158. Dudley, *The Naval War of 1812*, vol. II, p. 78–9, Melville to Warren, 'Private, 26 March 1813', citing War of 1812 MSS. Lilley Library. Univ. of Indiana.
159. Dudley, *The Naval War of 1812*, vol. II, p. 79, citing Admiralty to Warren, 26 March 1813, Nat. Lib. of Scotland. Alex. Cochrane Papers, MS2340, fols 49–50. The order refers to Port Royal, South Carolina.
160. *London Gazette*, no. 16715, 625. Notification to Neutrals, 30 March 1813.
161. Dudley, *The Naval War of 1812*, vol. II, p. 57, Letter from Capt. John Dent to Secretary of the Navy William Jones, Charleston, North Carolina, 1 March 1813. Jones had succeeded Hamilton as Sect. of the Navy in December 1812.
162. NMM LBK/2, Warren to Melville, HMS *San Domingo*, Lynnhaven Bay, 29 March 1813.
163. Dudley, *The Naval War of 1812*, vol. II, p. 347, Secretary of the Navy Jones, to Capt. Charles Stewart, Commanding Naval Officer, Norfolk Harbour, April 8. 1813.
164. NMM LBK/2, Warren to Melville, HMS *San Domingo*, 19 April 1813.
165. NMM LBK/2, Warren to Melville, 1 June 1813.
166. NMM WAR/82, p. 63, 23 March 1813.
167. Dudley, *The Naval War of 1812*, vol. II, pp. 359–60, Warren to Croker, *San Domingo*, Hampton Roads, 24 June 1813.
168. Ibid., pp. 362–4, Colonel T. Beckwith to Warren, *San Domingo*, Hampton Roads, 28 June, and July 5 1813.
169. Ibid., p. 97, Capt. J. Dent to Sect. of the Navy Jones, May 8 1813.
170. Ibid., p. 114, letter from Capt. Hugh Pigot, HMS *Orpheus* Off Block Island, April 29 1813, to Capt. Sir Thomas Hardy, citing TNA ADM 1/503, pp. 629–31.
171. R. Guernsey, *New York and its Vicinity during the War of 1812–15, being a Military, Civil and Financial Local History of that Period*, New York, Charles Woodward, 1889–95, vol. I, p. 393. Letter to John Bogert, Russian vice-consul in New York, from Thomas Barclay, former British consul, 2 July 1813.
172. Dudley, *The Naval War of 1812*, vol. II, p. 184, Cockburn to Warren, *Sceptre* off Ocracoke Bar, 12 July 1813.

173. Ibid., pp. 364–5, Cockburn to Warren, *Sceptre*, 19 July 1813. Dudley notes that Cockburn had transferred his flag from *Marlborough* to *Sceptre*, 74.

174. NMM HUL/18, Copy of Warren's Bermuda proclamation of the blockade of 'New York, Charleston, Port Royal, Savannah and of the River Mississippi', dated 26 May 1813, with extension from 1 September 1813. 'To the Respective Flag Officers' from 'HMS *San Domingo*, Chesapeake, 1st Sept. 1813', and sent to 'John Dougan Esq. Re: Agent to the Commissioners for American Property Condemned as Droits to the Crown'.

175. D. Minor, *World Canals 1810–1819*, New York, Facts on File, 1986, citing Nashville, Tennessee Archives Library. Among the 'Original Stockholders of the Dismal Swamp Canal', James Madison 'of Williamsburg, Virginia' had contributed $500 for two shares.

176. J. Lambert, *Travels through Canada, and the United States of North America in the Years 1806, 1807 and 1808*, 3rd edn, vol. II, London, Baldwin Cradock and Joy, 1816, as quoted in *New York from Harper's Magazine*, New York, Gallery Books, 1991, p. 221.

177. Dudley, *The Naval War of 1812*, vol. II, pp. 80–81, citing TNA ADM 1/4359, Warren to Croker, enclosed with letter of 28 March 1813.

178. *Naval Chronicle*, vol. 30, pp. 250–55. *List of Captures made by the Squadron under the Orders of ... Sir John Borlase Warren ... between 30th March and 22nd July, 1813.*

179. NMM WAR/37, passim.

180. Calculated from data in *Naval Chronicle*, vol. 30, pp. 250–55, covering 30 March to 22 July 1813. The destinations to which 38 captures were sent, mainly those of *Statira*, *Spartan* and *Martin*, but including some taken by *Marlborough*, *Victorious*, *Ramillies* and *Narcissus*, are not recorded in *Naval Chronicle*.

181. Ibid., p. 254. Cassia was a valuable sweet spice, similar to cinnamon bark.

182. Ibid., p. 255, and TNA ADM1/504, p. 703–11, Warren to Croker, 11 November 1813. Details of lists vary; *Naval Chronicle* gives Star as from Norfolk, Virginia, at which it possibly called after leaving Alexandria. Similarly, Warren lists *Protectress* as bound for Halifax rather than Lisbon.

183. *Naval Chronicle*, vol. 30, p. 252, and NMM WAR/37, p. 3.

184. NMM WAR/37.

185. Ibid., p. 3.

186. Ibid., p. 33.

187. *Naval Chronicle*, vol. 30, p. 251.

188. Ibid., p. 252.

189. NMM WAR/37, p. 22.

190. Ibid.

191. Ibid. Warren's pencilled note on inside cover.

192. TNA ADM 1/504, pp. 703–11. 'Captures, 20th April to 20th September 1813'. This list was sent to London enclosed with ADM 1/504, p. 699, Warren to Croker, dated 11 November 1813, reproduced in Dudley, *The Naval War of 1812*, vol. II, p. 277. Warren's apparent delay in reporting to London may be that, since duplicate copies were often sent in different vessels, this may not have been the first dispatched to, or indeed received at, the Admiralty.

193. NMM HUL/18, 'List of Captures', pp. 3, 4.

194. W. Dunne, 'The Inglorious First of June: Commodore Stephen Decatur on Long Island Sound, 1813', *Long Island Sound Historical Journal*, 2, Spring 1990, excerpt published New York, Naval Scribe Inc., p. 24, citing Decatur to Sect. of Navy Jones, 3 June 1813, Washington, Nat. Archives, M125, roll 29.

195. Dudley, *The Naval War of 1812*, vol. II, pp. 137–8, citing TNA ADM 1/504, pp. 179–81, 223–6, Capt. Robt. Oliver to Warren, *Valiant* at Sea, 13 June 1813.

196. NMM LBK/2, Warren to Melville, 1 June 1813.

197. Ibid., Melville to Warren, 4 June 1813.

198. Ibid. Referring to such 'fir frigates' as *Leander* and *Newcastle*, Melville remarked in the same letter, 'I am unwilling at present to introduce a new & cumbersome Description of Ships into our Navy to any considerable extent; simply because the

Americans have three of them. We may more easily supply Line of Battle Ships.' Perhaps surprisingly, this seems to overlook the frigates' relative advantages in draught and manoeuvrability as well as cost.

199. Ibid., Warren to Melville, 1 June, and 22 July 1813.
200. Ibid., Warren to Melville, Halifax, 27 September 1813.
201. Ibid. Annotated press cutting forwarded by Warren to Melville, headed 'Naval General Order of Wm Jones, Navy Dept, July 29 1813. Warren's annotation reads 'Now this has been adopted and several small [American] vessels have been chased.'
202. Ibid.
203. FCO: Brannan J. Letter of Cmdr. Stephen Decatur to Sect. of Navy Jones, 20 December 1813, *Official Letters of Military and Naval Officers of the United States during the War with Great Britain 1812–14, Collected and Arranged by John Brannan*, Washington City, 1823, p. 287.
204. NMM LBK/2, Warren to Melville, '*San Domingo*, In the River Potomac 40 miles below Washington. 22nd July, 1813'; side 6.
205. Dudley, *The Naval War of 1812*, vol. II, pp. 168–78, citing TNA: ADM 8/100, Extract of 'Ships in Sea Pay – The present disposition of His Majesty's Ships and Vessels in Sea Pay. Admiralty Office, 1st July 1813'.
206. Dudley, *The Naval War of 1812*, vol. II, p. 178, 'General Abstract'. Warren's United Command was part of what the General Abstract for the Royal Navy gave as 624 ships and 135,889 men on 1 July 1813, not the '1,000 ship navy' so often referred to in, for example, A. Friendly, *Beaufort of the Admiralty*, London, Hutchinson, 1977, citing letter of Francis Beaufort to his bother-in-law Richard, 9 December 1809, 'There are 1000 King's Ships'. See also C. Lloyd, 'Armed Forces and the Art of War: Navies', in *The New Cambridge Modern History, Volume IX: War and Peace in an Age of Upheaval 1793–1815*, ed. C. Crawley, Cambridge Cambridge Univ. Press, 1974, p. 90. By 1815, '1168 warships, 240 of them ships of the line'.
207. NMM LBK/2, Warren to Melville, *San Domingo*, Potomac, 22 July 1813.
208. Ibid., Warren to Melville, *San Domingo*, River Potomac, 22 July 1813. As a postscript, Warren added: 'the following ships are in Port & blockaded viz: In the Chesapeake *Constellation* 36 & *Adams* 36 New London *United States* 44 *Macedonian* 38 & *Hornet* 18 Boston *Constitution* 44 At Sea *President* 44 *Congress* 36 having escaped our Squadron off Boston in a fog Brazil stated to be Blockaded St Salvador *Essex* 36 Halifax Harbour *Chesapeake* 36 guns'. By December 1813 at least 18 named American vessels, 10 of more than 20 guns, had been blockaded, captured or destroyed, as shown in Appendix A as Table 2.
209. Dudley, *The Naval War of 1812*, vol. II, p. 270–71, citing TNA ADM 1/504, p. 523, 25 October 1813.
210. NMM LBK/2, Warren to Melville, 'Private' dated *San Domingo*, Lynnhaven Bay, Chesapeake, 6 September 1813.
211. Ibid.
212. Ibid., Warren to Melville, 27 September 1813.
213. Dudley, *The Naval War of 1812*, vol. II, p. 250; p. 261, citing TNA ADM 1/504, pp. 417–20. USS's *President* and *Congress* had escaped from Boston on 30 April 1813.
214. NMM LBK/2, Warren to Melville, 26th October 1813. In another, less well-written, copy of this letter, Warren says 'not by 30 sail as many as proposed in your Lordship's former letter'. This letter is noted as being received at the Admiralty on 17 November 1813, in a remarkable 22 days.
215. Dudley, *The Naval War of 1812*, vol. II, pp. 262–3, citing TNA ADM 1/504, pp. 551–3.
216. Ibid.
217. Ibid.
218. Niles' *Weekly Register*, Baltimore, vol. V, pp. 264–5, 18 December 1813.
219. Guernsey, *New York and its Vicinity*, p. 393.
220. Ibid., quoting letter from Capt. Robert Oliver to Don Thomas Stoughton, Spanish consul in New York, dated 'HMS *Valiant*, Off New London, December 2 1813'.

221. NMM LBK/2, Warren to Melville, 9 November 1813.
222. Ibid., Warren to Melville, 30 November 1813.
223. TNA ADM 1/505, Warren to Croker, Bermuda, 30 December 1813, pp. 44–5.
224. NMM LBK/2, Warren to Melville, 30 December 1813.
225. Ibid.
226. TNA ADM 8/100, 1 July 1813, and ADM 1/505, pp. 320–22.
227. See Appendix A, Table 2, p. 478, but excluding *Congress* and *President*, which had escaped in July 1813.
228. NMM LBK/2, Warren to Melville, 30 December 1813.
229. Mahan, *Sea Power*, vol. II, p. 330.
230. NMM LBK/2, Copy letter Melville to Warren, 'Private', dated Admiralty, 24 November 1813, referring to letter Croker to Warren, dated 4 November 1813, TNA ADM 2/1378, pp. 146–51.
231. Ibid.
232. TNA ADM 1/505, Warren to Croker, Bermuda, 30 December 1813, pp. 87–90.
233. NMM LBK/2, Melville to Warren, dated Admiralty, 24 November 1813.
234. Ibid.
235. Ibid., Warren to Melville, 'Private' dated Bermuda, 3 February 1814.
236. Ibid.
237. TNA ADM 2/1378, pp. 58 and 146, Croker to Warren 4 November 1813.
238. E. Hume, ed., 'Letters Written During the War of 1812 by the British Naval Commander in American Waters – Admiral Sir David Milne', *William & Mary Historical Quarterly*, 2nd series, 10 (4), 1930, p. 290. Letter from Capt. David Milne to George Hume, HM Ship *Bulwark*, Portsmouth, 2 January 1814. The title of the edited letters is disingenuous since Milne was not appointed C in C North America, nor knighted, until 1816, post-war, not taking up his appointment until 1817. 'The Prince' referred to is the Prince Regent, to become George IV in 1820.
239. Ibid.
240. NMM WAR/37, note in Warren's hand on the back of p. 37. Although pencilled on the cover of a record of prizes between March and 13 September 1813, the totals appear to be for the whole term of his command up to 1 April 1814, when Warren would have ceased to share in new prize money. The figure of '60' prizes for Jamaica is puzzling since Warren had noted that 70 cases there were 'unaccounted for' in September 1813. Some had possibly arrived there before Warren's appointment on 3 August 1812. Warren appears to have taken a close interest in the entries of captures and detentions, and the adjudication of prizes, even after his recall and retirement.
241. *The Annual Register*, 1822, London, pp. 272–3.
242. J. Marshall, *Royal Naval Biography*, London, Longman et al., 1823, vol. I. Warren had died on 27 February 1822 while visiting Sir Richard Keats, former commander on the Newfoundland station and Governor of the Royal Naval Hospital at Greenwich.

CHAPTER 5. BLOCKADES AND BLUNDERS: VICE-ADMIRAL COCHRANE'S COMMAND, APRIL 1814–FEBRUARY 1815

1. H. Adams, ed., *The Writings of Albert Gallatin*, Philadelphia, J. P. Lippincott, 1879, vol. 1, p. 627, Gallatin to Monroe, 13 June 1814.
2. TNA ADM 1/505, p. 434, 1 April 1814. Letter of appointment from Lords of Admiralty to Cochrane, dated 25 January 1814, TNA ADM 2/933, pp. 91–5.
3. C. Markham, ed., *Selections from Correspondence of Adm. John Markham During the Years 1801–4 and 1806–7*, London, Navy Records Society, 1904, vol. 28, p. 153, Lord Keith to Adm. Markham, 23 February 1804.
4. D. Cordingly, *Cochrane the Dauntless: The Life and Adventures of Thomas Cochrane*, London, Bloomsbury, 2008, pp. 82, 384.
5. *The Oxford Dictionary of National Biography*, Oxford, Oxford Univ. Press, 2004, vol. 12, p. 301.
6. Cordingly, *Cochrane the Dauntless*, p. 13. Colonel Charles Cochrane, second son of

the eighth earl, was killed at Yorktown in the autumn of 1781 while serving as aide-de-camp to General Cornwallis. Clearly a close family, Vice-Adm. Sir Alexander had invited his nephew Capt. Lord Thomas RN, to be his flag captain, and to prepare HMS *Tonnant*, 80, for sea as his flagship while it was moored at Chatham. See Cordingly, *Cochrane the Dauntless*, p. 237.

7. BJL DDHO 7/4, on a letter dated 25 July 1814.
8. TNA ADM 1/506 p. 46, Cochrane to Croker, 27 April 1814.
9. E. Hume, ed., 'Letters Written During the War of 1812 by the British Naval Commander in American Waters – Admiral Sir David Milne', *William & Mary Historical Quarterly*, 2nd series, 10 (4), 1930, p. 291. Letter from Capt David Milne to George Hume, Portsmouth, 30 January 1814. Milne was not in fact appointed C in C North America, nor knighted, until 1816.
10. Ibid., p. 292. Letter to George Hume, HMS *Bulwark*, Bermuda, 26 April 1814. Milne was most concerned over USS *Independence*, 74, to be launched in 1814.
11. Ibid.
12. M. Crawford, ed., *The Naval War of 1812: A Documentary History*, Washington DC, Naval Historical Center, vol. III, 2002, p. 17, Capt. Robt. Barrie to his mother, from 'HMS *Dragon* off Mockjack Bay the Chesapeak. Feby. 4th 1814'. Crawford notes that the Bay is now known as Mobjack Bay.
13. Crawford, *The Naval War of 1812*, vol. III, p. 18, Capt. Robt. Barrie to his half-sister, dated *Dragon* Hampton Roads, March 14 [1814].
14. Crawford, *The Naval War of 1812*, vol. III, p. 36–7, Act. Master Commandant Joshua Barney to Secretary of the Navy Jones, Baltimore, 25 March 1814.
15. *Naval Chronicle*, vol. 32, p. 256, 'vessels captured, recaptured, detained or destroyed by Squadron commanded by Sir A. Cochrane … return received at Bermuda June 17th 1814'.
16. TNA ADM 1/506, pp. 273–7 and 280, and *Naval Chronicle*, vol. 32, p. 171.
17. TNA ADM 1/506, pp. 47–8, 27 April 1814, and p. 203, 10 May 1814.
18. Crawford, *The Naval War of 1812*, vol. III, pp. 46–7, Cockburn to Warren, HMS *Albion*, Tangier Bay, Chesapeake, 13 April 1814. Despite having written to congratulate Cochrane on his appointment on 2 April 1814, Cockburn addressed this to Warren, who had already left Bermuda for England. Cockburn was later to insist that he did not know of Cochrane's command until 28 April 1814.
19. Crawford, *The Naval War of 1812*, vol. III, pp. 60 and 340 re: training on Tangier Island, Chesapeake.
20. National Library of Scotland, MS 2333 f.59. Letter to Vice-Adm. Cochrane to Rear Adm. Cockburn, dated *Albion* in Tangier Bay Chesapeake, 9 May 1814.
21. D. Hickey, *The War of 1812: A Forgotten Conflict*, Urbana IL, Univ. of Illinois Press, 1989, p. 124, citing General Order of the Secretary of the Navy July 29 1813, in Navy Department (M149) reel 11.
22. *AC*: 13–1, 98–101, 500–504; and *AC*: 13–2, 741.
23. TNA ADM 1/506, p. 42. See also Crawford, *The Naval War of 1812*, vol. III, p. 134, Cochrane to Melville, *Tonnant*, Bermuda, 17 July 1814.
24. TNA ADM 1/506, pp. 40–41, Cochrane to Croker, 25 April 1814.
25. Ibid.
26. Ibid.
27. NMM WAR/11, reverse p. 139.
28. TNA ADM 2/1376, pp. 320–22, Croker to Warren, 'Secret'. Admiralty, 28 April 1813.
29. TNA ADM 1/506, p. 44, 25th April 1814.
30. *London Gazette*, 31st May 1814.
31. *Naval Chronicle*, vol. 31, p. 5, footnote.
32. TNA ADM 2/1380, p. 98, Croker, 30th April 1814.
33. *Naval Chronicle*, vol. 31, p. 475. 'State Papers', reprint of *London Gazette*'s Foreign Office notification to neutrals, published Tuesday, 31 May 1814, referring to Cochrane's Proclamation of 25 April 1814.

34. *London Gazette*, 31 May 1814.
35. E. Whitehill, ed., *The Journal of Lieutenant Henry Napier in HMS Nymphe: New England Blockaded - 1814*, Salem MA, Peabody Museum, 1939, p. 17.
36. Crawford, *The Naval War of 1812*, vol. III, p. 67, Cochrane to Cockburn, Bermuda, 26 May 1814.
37. Ibid., p. 69, *Disposition of His Majestys Ships upon the Coast of America*, enclosed in the above letter from Cochrane to Cockburn, 26 May 1814.
38. TNA ADM 2/1380, p. 178, Croker to James Buller, Council Officer, 31 May 1814. Warren had reached Spithead on 22 May 1814, see Crawford, *The Naval War of 1812*, vol. III, p. 135, note 1. Captain Broke was still recovering from the head wound received in concluding his capture of USS Chesapeake off Boston on 1 June 1813.
39. TNA ADM 1/506, pp. 478–88, 5 July 1814.
40. Niles' *Weekly Register*, Baltimore, vol. VI, p. 317, 9 July 1814.
41. R. Albion and J. Pope, *Sea Lanes in Wartime: The American Experience 1775–1945*, 2nd edn, New York and Portland ME, Norton & Co/Archon Books, 1968, p. 121. Albion and Pope calculated that the average tonnage of prizes taken into Halifax fell from 139 tons between 1812 and 1813 to only 73 tons during the last year of the war, but this disguises a more complete analysis of the type and size of Halifax prizes more fully discussed in Chapter 7, p. 19.
42. Whitehill, *Journal of Lieutenant Henry Napier*, pp. 17, 29–30. *Nymphe* had been undergoing repair in Halifax since 'the violent storm' of 12 November 1813, delayed by shortage of dockyard resources.
43. Ibid. p. 17.
44. Ibid., p. 20.
45. Ibid., pp. 22, 31, June–July 1814.
46. Ibid., p. 18. Napier's opinions on the American character include; 'Begin with a dollar and proceed to any amount; you can always buy a Yankee in almost any rank and station.'
47. Ibid., p. 21. By 'notions', contemporary Americans meant vegetables.
48. Ibid., pp. 15–28.
49. Ibid., p. 26
50. Ibid., p. 23 and p. 26.
51. Ibid., p. 24.
52. Ibid.
53. Ibid.
54. BJL DDHO 7/4, 'Description of the Ships on the North American Station 26th July 1814', shown as Appendix A, Table 4. The totals do not include *La Hogue*, 74, *Orpheus*, 38, or *Martin*, 18, 'to go home', and avoids some double-counting, and pencil notes of potential re-distributions. 'Ships in Sea Pay' for 1 July 1814, comparable to those for 1812 and 1813, does not seem to have survived.
55. Crawford, *The Naval War of 1812*, vol. III, p. 40, note 1, and p. 69, enclosure in Cochrane to Cockburn, Bermuda, 26th May 1814, 'Disposition of HM Ships upon the Coast of America'; also p. 115, note 1, citing Cochrane to Troubridge, 24 May 1814, Washington. Lib. of Congress, Cockburn Papers, vol. 38, pp. 311–12.
56. H. Hall, *American Navigation*, New York, Appletons, 1880, p. 46; Crawford, *The Naval War of 1812*, vol. III, p. 97, note 6, citing Washington. Nat. Archives and Records, Gordon to Jones, 21 July 1814, M125 Roll 38.
57. BJL DDHO 7/4, No. 6, Cochrane to Hotham, Bermuda, 28 July 1814. Hotham was promoted to flag rank on 4 June 1814, to Rear Admiral of the White, but news of his promotion was delayed.
58. Ibid.
59. One of three enclosures in above letter, dated 'Nantucket 11th April 1814'.
60. TNA ADM 1/507, 12–13 August 1814.
61. R. Morriss, *Guide to British naval papers in North America*, London and New York,

NMM/Mansell, 1994, p. 181, citing letter in Nantucket Hist. Ass's Peter Foulger Museum, Nantucket MA.

62. BJL DDHO 7/4 30, August 1814 to *Surprise* on Patuxent.
63. Hickey, *The War of 1812*, p. 214, citing E. Byers, *The Nation of Nantucket: Society and Politics in an Early American Commercial Center 1660-1820*, Boston, Northeastern Univ. Press, 1987, pp. 277–89. See also TNA ADM 1/507, pp. 24–8, 12 –13 August 1814, 249–61, 453–9, 464; WO 1/142, pp. 415, 419–21, 427–9.
64. TNA ADM 1/506, pp. 242, 244–7, Cochrane to Sherbroke, 30 May 1814.
65. Hickey, *The War of 1812*, p. 194, citing B. Lohnes, 'A New Look at the Invasion of Eastern Maine, 1814', *Maine Historical Society Quarterly* 15, 1975, p. 9.
66. TNA ADM 1/506, pp. 539–40; ADM 1 507, pp. 128–37, 304–7; ADM 1/508, pp. 28–32, Griffith to Croker, 27 September 1814.
67. E. and L. Hertslet, eds, *British and Foreign State Papers: Compiled by the Librarian and Keeper of Papers for the Foreign Office*, London, J. Ridgway & Sons Ltd, 1841, vol. I, 1812–14, part II, pp. 1369–71. See also Niles' *Weekly Register*, Baltimore, vol. VII pp. 117–18, 29 October 1814.
68. Niles' *Weekly Register*, Baltimore, vol. VII, p. 270, and vol. VIII, Supplement, p. 149.
69. Crawford, *The Naval War of 1812*, vol. III, p. 131, Cochrane to Earl Bathurst, Secretary of State for War and the Colonies, HMS *Tonnant*, Bermuda, 14 July 1814.
70. Ibid., p. 133, Cochrane to Melville, First Lord of the Admiralty, HMS *Tonnant*, Bermuda, 17 July 1814.
71. NMM COC 11, pp. 105–6. This undertaking had first been made during Cockburn's first raids in the Chesapeake in 1813, but still applied.
72. Crawford, *The Naval War of 1812*, vol. III, pp. 229–30, Stock prices authorised by Rr Adm. Sir Ed. Codrington Capt of the Fleet. *Iphigenia*, 22 August 1814, citing NMM COD 6/4.
73. Crawford, *The Naval War of 1812*, vol. III, p. 131, Cochrane to Bathurst, *Tonnant*, 14 July 1814.
74. Ibid.
75. Ibid., p. 133, Cochrane to Melville, *Tonnant*, 17 July 1814.
76. This number of American warships counted as hors d'combat excludes the *Hornet*, which escaped in January 1814. See Appendix A, Table 2.
77. Crawford, *The Naval War of 1812*, vol. III, p. 786.
78. Ibid., p. 196, Cockburn to Cochrane, 22 August 1814. Barney's flotilla had comprised one large sloop and sixteen gunboats; all were destroyed but for one gunboat captured by Cockburn's boats.
79. Ibid., pp. 222–3, Cockburn to Cochrane, HM Sloop *Manly*, Nottingham, Patuxent, 27 August 1814. Crawford's note on p. 223 identifies the vessels. See also ibid., pp. 226–8, Cochrane to Croker, *Tonnant*, in the Patuxent 2 September 1814. The American frigates *Boston* and *New York*, decayed beyond economical repair, were also burned.
80. Ibid., p. 786, Appendix, Enclosure E, 'Report on the State of the US Navy', Secretary of the Navy Jones to President James Madison, Navy Department, 6 June 1814. *Columbia* was intended 'to mount 53 guns to be launched in August', and *Argus* was 'ready to receive a Crew'.
81. JCBL Box 160, f.10, Charles Greene to B & I, 12 March and 3 August 1814; *The National Intelligencer*, Washington, 22 July 1814; Niles' *Weekly Register*, Baltimore, vol. VI, p. 353; Hickey, *The War of 1812*, p. 224.
82. Crawford, *The Naval War of 1812*, vol. III, pp. 237–42, citing TNA ADM 1/507, pp. 160–68, Capt. James Gordon to Cochrane, *Seahorse*, Chesapeake, 9 September 1814.
83. Ibid., p. 289, Cochrane to Melville, 'Private', *Tonnant*, off Baltimore, 17 September 1814.
84. Ibid., p. 269, Cochrane to Melville, *Tonnant*, Patuxent River, 3 September 1814
85. Ibid., p. 270, Cochrane to Melville, *Tonnant*, Patuxent River 3 September 1814.
86. Ibid., p. 277–8, Cochrane to Cockburn, *Tonnant*, off Baltimore, 13 September 1814.

87. Ibid., p. 279, Colonel Brooke to Cochrane, 14 September 1814. Brooke had assumed command of British land forces at Baltimore on Ross's death.

88. Ibid., p. 287, citing TNA ADM 1/507, pp. 171–5, Cochrane to Croker, *Tonnant*, Chesapeake, 17 September 1814.

89. Ibid., p. 289, Cochrane to Melville, 'Private', *Tonnant*, off Baltimore, 17 September 1814.

90. Ibid., pp. 269–70. Cochrane to Melville, *Tonnant*, Patuxent River, 3 September 1814.

91. Ibid., p. 71. Croker to Cochrane, Admiralty Office, 4 April 1814, and 19 May 1814, latter referring to Croker to Warren, 20 March 1813, giving him discretion on objectives for land forces under his command. See also ibid., p. 72, Bathurst to Major General E. Barnes, 'Copy, Secret, Downing Street, 20 May 1814', enclosed in Croker to Cochrane, 21 May 1814.

92. Ibid., p. 132, citing TNA ADM 1/506, pp. 390–93, Cochrane to Croker, 20 June 1814.

93. Ibid., p. 131, citing TNA WO 1/141, pp. 7–14, Cochrane to Bathurst, HMS *Tonnant*, Bermuda 14 July 1814.

94. Ibid., p. 269–70, Cochrane to Melville, *Tonnant*, Patuxent River, 3 September 1814, and p. 140, Cochrane to Commanding Officers of the North American Station, 18 July 1814. Sir George Prevost, Governor-General of British North America, had reported to Cochrane on 2 June 1814 that 'the American troops in Upper Canada have committed the most wanton and unjustifiable outrages on the unoffending inhabitants' of Dover on Lake Erie in May 1814. See also ibid., p. 489.

95. Ibid., pp. 286–91, and p. 329–30, note 2 citing Melville to Cochrane, 29 July 1814 in National Library of Scotland MS 2574, p. 146–8.

96. Crawford, *The Naval War of 1812*, vol. III, p. 330, note 3, Cochrane to Melville, 17 September 1814, citing Lilley Library, University of Indiana, War of 1812 MS.

97. Crawford, *The Naval War of 1812*, vol. III, p. 335, note 1, and p. 339, note 5.

98. Ibid., p. 335, note 2, citing Cochrane to Cockburn, 1 October 1814, National Library of Scotland MS 2346 pp. 13–14 and 350, note 1.

99. Crawford, *The Naval War of 1812*, vol. III, p. 340, Barrie to his half-sister, from '*Dragon*, off Tangier Isle, Chesapeak Bay, Novr. 11th 1814'.

100. Ibid., pp. 344–5, Cockburn to Capt. John Clavell, 13 Dec. 1814.

101. *Naval Chronicle*, vol. 33, pp. 258–9, calculated from: 'A List of Vessels captured, burnt, and destroyed by the Squadron under the Orders of Rear Admiral the Honourable Henry Hotham, as reported to him between the 6th August and 9th October 1814'.

102. J. Colledge, *Ships of the Royal Navy*, revised edn, London, Greenhill, 1987, p. HMS *Forth* was one of the 'fir-frigates' built for North American waters in 1813, which proved satisfactory, although expected to last only six or seven years. The *Forth* was to be broken up in 1819.

103. *Naval Chronicle*, vol. 33, p. 258. 'From Captain Pym of HMS *Niemen*, off the River Delaware, 30th September 1814' and from Captain Lumley of HMS *Narcissus*, 'off Negro Head, 13th October 1814'.

104. *Naval Chronicle*, vol. 33, pp. 345–6.

105. *Historical Statistics of the United States from Colonial Times to 1957*, Washington, Bureau of the Census, 1960, Series Q, 178–82, 'Merchant Vessels Built & Documented by Type: 1797–1957, p. 448.

106. A. Mahan, *Sea Power in its Relation to the War of 1812*, Boston MA and London, Little Brown/Sampson, Marston Low and Company, 1905, vol. II, p. 388.

107. Crawford, *The Naval War of 1812*, vol. III, p. 331, note 3.

108. Mahan, *Sea Power*, vol. II, p. 386. Mahan adds that *Hermes*' Capt. Percy was exonerated at Court Martial, citing *Naval Chronicle*, vol. 33, p. 429.

109. Mahan, *Sea Power*, p. 388.

110. *Naval Chronicle*, vol. 33, p. 337–41; and Crawford, *The Naval War of 1812*, vol. III, p. 134, Cochrane to Melville, HMS *Tonnant*, Bermuda, 17 July 1814. 'Send me flat bottomed Vessels that will act as Gun Vessels to cover landings and carry at least 100 Soldiers for a short distance, this Coast requires them.'

111. *Naval Chronicle*, vol. 33, p. 341, Cochrane's Report.

112. Crawford, *The Naval War of 1812*, vol. III, p. 786, 'State and Stations of Vessels of War', 6 June 1814; and Mahan, *Sea Power*, pp. 391–2. Mahan mistakenly refers to the schooner as the *Caroline*.

113. D. Hickey, 'American Trade Restrictions During the War of 1812', *The Journal of American History*, 68 (3), 1981, p. 520, citing R. Walters, *Albert Gallatin: Jeffersonian Financier and Diplomat*, New York, Macmillan, 1957, p. 259. Albert Gallatin had resigned in March 1813 and left for Europe as a Peace Commissioner on 9 May 1813.

114. National Library of Scotland MS 2343, Admiralty Letters 1813–15, 30 December 1814; and Niles' *Weekly Register*, Baltimore, vol. VII, p. 361, Cochrane to Croker 14 February 1815.

115. NMM HUL/5B, Hulbert to Fraser, 14 March 1815, quoted by A. Gutridge, 'Prize Agency 1800–1815 with special reference to the career and work of George Redmond Hulbert', unpublished MPhil dissertation, Univ. of Portsmouth, 1989, p. 85.

116. TNA ADM 2/1381, pp. 96–7, and *Senate Journal* 2: 618–20.

CHAPTER 6. TRADE AND WAR: THE EFFECTS OF WARREN'S BLOCKADES, AUGUST 1812–APRIL 1814

1. C. Davenant, *An essay upon the ways and means of supplying the war*, London, 1695, quoted in D. French, *The British Way in Warfare 1688-2000*, London, Unwin/Hyman, 1990, p. 24, citing H. Dickinson, *Liberty and Property: Political Ideology in Eighteenth Century Britain*, London, Methuen, 1977, p. 85.

2. R. Morriss, *Cockburn and the British Navy in Transition: Admiral Sir George Cockburn 1772-1853*, Exeter, Univ. of Exeter Press, 1997, p. 87; and W. Dudley, 'Without Some Risk: A Reassessment of the British Blockade of the United States 1812-15', PhD dissertation, Univ. of Alabama, 1999, e.g. p. 106. See also esp. pp. 111, 119, 125, 131–2.

3. T. Hansard, *The Parliamentary Debates from 1803 to the Present Time*, London, 1st series 1803–20, vol. 23, pp. 21, 71–5 for British revocation of Orders in Council, 23 June 1812. For British hopes, see *ASP*: FR, vol. III, pp. 593–5, Jonathan Russell to Monroe.

4. I. Toll, *Six Frigates: How Piracy, War and British Supremacy at Sea gave Birth to the World's Most Powerful Navy*, London, Penguin/Michael Joseph, 2006, p. 372. Canning quoted from H. Adams, *History of the United States during the Administration of James Madison*, Library of America edn, Washington, 1986. p. 627.

5. Hansard, *The Parliamentary Debates*, vol. 24, p. 70, Canning to House of Commons.

6. Ibid., p. 72.

7. Ibid., p. 74.

8. D. Hickey, *The War of 1812: A Forgotten Conflict*, Urbana IL, Univ. of Illinois Press, 1989, p. 93, quoting Governor Tompkins to New York legislature, 3 November 1812. The American ports Sawyer had intended to blockade included Boston, New York, Norfolk and Charleston.

9. BL Add Mss 38250, f.42, letters to Prime Minister Lord Liverpool from Secretary of State for War and Colonies, Lord Bathurst, dated 3 October 1812; and Add Mss 8299 cc 20(4) from Mr C. Lyne, to Ld. Liverpool, representing cotton manufactures outlining stocks held and blockading possibilities, dated 2 March 1813.

10. R. Albion and J. Pope, *Sea Lanes in Wartime: The American Experience 1775-1945*, 2nd edn, Portland ME, Archon Books, 1968, p. 115. These 46 vessels represented no less than 57% of the full-rigged ships and 26.5% of the brigs detained in Halifax during the war.

11. *Naval Chronicle*, vol. 28, p. 494, 'American Memorial against the War by 1500 Inhabitants of the County of Rockingham in New Hampshire, 5th August 1812.'

12. JCBL Box 236, f2, letter from Thomas Poynton Ives of Providence, Rhode Island, to John Maybin of Philadelphia, 12 November 1812.

13. F. Kert, *Prize and Prejudice: Privateering and Naval Prize in Atlantic Canada in the War of 1812*, Research in Maritime History 11, International Maritime Economic History Association, St John's, Newfoundland, 1997, pp. 159–69.

14. JCBL Box 236, f3, letter, Ives to Maybin, Providence Rhode Island, 15 January 1813.
15. B. Arthur, 'The Role of Blockade in the Anglo-American Naval War of 1812–14', unpublished MA dissertation, Greenwich Maritime Institute, Univ. of Greenwich, 2002, Appendix 4.1, page ii, p. 94.
16. Actually 59.86%.
17. *AC*: 9–1, 1259–62, and *AC*: 10–1, 2814–15.
18. *AC*: 10–1, 2582–3 for Macon's No. 2 Bill. In a document allegedly dated 5 August 1810, Napoleon's foreign minister, the Duc de Cadore, had reworded Napoleon's ambiguously written instructions and implied that French detention of American vessels would end when the American government 'caused their rights to be respected by the English'. Madison's apparent acceptance of French manipulation on 2 November 1810 resulted in the implementation of Macon's No. 2 Bill and caused heated debate in Congress. See A. Mahan, *Sea Power in its Relation to the War of 1812*, Boston MA and London, Little Brown/Sampson, Marston Low and Company, vol. I, p. 237, for translation.
19. Actually 35.2%.
20. A. Seybert, *Statistical Annals*, Philadelphia, T. Dodson, 1818, p. 454, part of 'A Statement Exhibiting the gross and net amount of ad valorem and specific duties on Goods, Wares and Merchandise imported into the United States from 1st January 1794 to 31st December 1814'. The evident time-lag between one year's net customs revenue and the following year's government income is explained by J. Bristed, *Resources of the United States of America; or a View of the agricultural, commercial …moral and religious capacity and character of the American people*, New York, J. Eastburn & Co, 1818, p. 77: 'The amount is secured to government by bonds payable at different periods according to the term of credit given to the importer', often a year.
21. Actually 21.58%.
22. D. Hickey, 'American Trade Restrictions during the War of 1812', *The Journal of American History*, 38 (3), 1981, p. 525. The goods were worth $30m on the American market.
23. *AC*: 12–1, p. 2046, 25 November 1811.
24. *The Annual Register*, 1813, London, vol. 5, part 2, pp. 317–18, Madison to Congress, 4 November 1812, and in *State papers and publick documents of the United States, from the accession of George Washington to the presidency: exhibiting a complete view of our foreign relations since that time*, 12 vols, 3rd edn, Boston, Thomas Wait, 1819, vol. IX 1812, p. 54. Although not to be repealed until 14 April 1814, until then, the number of laden American merchant ships attempting to reach American ports suggests that the Non-Importation Act was widely evaded, see: *AC*: 13–2, pp. 1946–8, 2830.
25. Ibid. Madison had included in his revenues to 30 September 1812 the $5.8m so far lent to the government as part of the $11m loan authorised in March, and anticipated that the remainder would follow. Only $6m of the $11m was lent.
26. W. Dudley, *The Naval War of 1812: A Documentary History*, Washington DC, Naval Historical Center, vol. 1, 1985, p. 561, Commodore Tingey to Sect. of Navy Hamilton, 7 November 1812; and TNA CO 43/49, pp. 153–4, Earl Bathurst to Lords Commissioners of Admiralty, dated Downing Street, 21 November 1812.
27. D. North, 'United States Balance of Payments 1790–1860', in *Trends in the American Economy in the Nineteenth Century*, Studies in Income and Wealth 24, National Bureau of Economic Research, Princeton, Princeton Univ. Press, 1960; repr. New York, Arno Press, 1975, pp. 591–2, table A-2, Appendix A. North's figures produce 36.1%. Earlier, uncorrected figures, such as those in J. De Bow (*Statistical View of the United States*, Washington DC, A. Nicholson, 1854, table CCV, p. 185); suggest a larger increase, of 43.25%. Madison and Congress may have been led to believe the increase to be larger than it now appears.
28. *ASP*: F, vol. II, p. 539, Gallatin to Bacon, 24 June 1812. Only $6.5m of this $11m had

been subscribed by June 1812, and, eventually, only $8.1m was. The immediate shortfall was met by the first issue of Treasury notes.

29. T. Pitkin, *A Statistical View of the Commerce of the United States of America*, 2nd edn, New Haven, Durrie & Peck, 1835, p. 307; see also Bristed, *Resources of the United States of America*, p. 77. The total 'accrued' net customs revenue includes some becoming due in 1812, but, according to Bristed, not necessarily collected until up to a year later. As well as doubling customs duties, a 10% surcharge on goods imported in foreign vessels was imposed, and the tonnage duty on foreign ships of 50 cents per ton was raised to $2 per ton. Even adjusted figures are therefore still too high.

30. In the absence of actual net customs revenue figures for the six months of January–July 1812, assuming a constant rate of imports during 1812, and *ceteris paribus*, a halved raw accrued total gives an adjusted first-half yield of $6,665,733, to which 50% for July December is added, producing an overall adjusted annual total at the original rates of duty of $9,998,600, i.e.>25% less than the raw data.

31. Some imports were duty free. This could explain the disparity between the 36.1% increase in imports and the 21.6% rise in net customs revenue adjusted for the changed rates of duty between 1811 and 1812.

32. *AC*: 12–1, imports: 186–7, 189, 1598, 1612–14, 2262–4; exports: *AC*: 12–1, 203.

33. Speech of John Cahoun, 24 June 1812, in *AC*: 12–1, 1541.

34. *AC*: 12–1, 1543–6. Speaker Clay refused to resolve a tied vote to end restrictions.

35. See Appendix A, Table 2.

36. See, for example, Niles' *Weekly Register*, Baltimore, vol. II, p. 101–4, 12 April 1812.

37. Seybert, *Statistical Annals*, p. 454.

38. D. Dewey, *Financial History of the United States*, 1903; 12th edn New York, A. Kelly, 1934, repr. 1968, p. 142.

39. Dewey, *Financial History*, p. 141.

40. *ASP*: F, vol. II, p. 539. Loan originally proposed by the Ways and Means Committee on 17 February 1812, Bacon's Report to the House; see also Gallatin to Bacon, 24 June 1812.

41. *ASP*: F, vol. II, p. 839. 'Revised Statement of the Public Debt, 14th April 1814'; also 'Receipts and Expenditures from March 1789 to 15th December 1815', p. 920.

42. *ASP*: F, vol. II, Gallatin on 'State of the Finances', 7 December 1812, p. 580. Gallatin had first suggested the careful use of Treasury notes in wartime as early as February 1810, and advocated them again in a letter to Bacon on 10 January 1812; see *ASP*: F, II, pp. 512–16.

43. Seybert, *Statistical Annals*, p. 454.

44. D. Warden, *A Statistical Political and Historical Account of the United States of North America from the Period of their First Colonization to the Present Day*, Edinburgh, Archibald Constable & Co, 1819, vol. III, p. 309.

45. Seybert, *Statistical Annals*, p. 93. American total exports fell 1811–12 by 37.17%. North's corrected export and re-export figures are almost identical.

46. North, 'United States Balance of Payments', pp. 591–2. American re-exports between 1811 and 1812 actually fell 46.979% when calculated from North's figures.

47. Ibid.

48. Mahan, *Sea Power*, vol. II. p. 12, letter from Isaac Hull, USS *Constitution*, New York, 29 October 1812.

49. NMM WAR/43, pages unnumbered; Warren's entry for 16 November 1812.

50. TNA CO 43/49, Bathurst to Admiralty, Downing Street, London, 21 November 1812; TNA ADM 2/1375, Secret Orders and Letters to Warren 25 November 1812. A month later Warren was sent a duplicate of the orders and a copy of Bathurst's letter.

51. *London Gazette*, 26 December 1812.

52. TNA ADM 1/503, p. 221.

53. NMM LBK/2 Private letter from Warren to Melville, 19 February 1813, and officially, Warren to Croker, First Secretary of Admiralty, 21 February 1813, referred to TNA ADM 2/1376 pp. 341–67. 20 March 1813.

54. C. Hall, *British Strategy in the Napoleonic Wars 1803–1815*, Manchester, Manchester Univ. Press, 1992, p. 61, citing TNA ADM 109/105. American grain and flour sent to the British Peninsula Army comprised 835,000 barrels of a total 1,385,000 exported in 1811, equal to 60.28%.

55. TNA FO 5/88, Ld. Castlereagh to Anthony Baker, 3 February 1813.

56. 2nd Duke of Wellington, *Despatches, Correspondence and Memoranda...edited by his son, A. R. Wellington*, London, John Murray, 1867–80, vol. X, pp. 371–3, Wellington to Bathurst, 11th May 1813. Bathurst had earlier sought supplies from Morocco, Algiers, Tunis and Tripoli. N. Thompson, *Earl Bathurst and the British Empire*, Barnsley, Pen and Sword, 1999, p. 61, Bathurst to Thomas A'Court, 27 March 1813, citing BL Add Mss 41512. Nevertheless, while American grain exports to Britain fell 90.5% between 1812 and 1813 and those to Portugal in the same period fell by 2.7%, those to Spain actually rose by 12.7%. W. F. Galpin, 'The American Grain Trade to the Spanish Peninsula 1810–14', *American Historical Review*, 28, 1922, pp. 24–44; citing *British Parliamentary Papers 1825–6*, No. 227, and Pitkin, *A Statistical View*, pp. 119–20.

57. Mahan, *Sea Power*, vol. I, p. 411.

58. Extending from Charleston to St Mary's, Georgia, including Savannah, this blockade was complained of by Commodore Tingey to Sect. of Navy Hamilton, 7 November 1812, reproduced in Dudley, op.cit., p. 561.

59. Dudley, *The Naval War of 1812*, vol. II, pp. 15–16, Warren to First Secretary of the Admiralty John Croker, 25 January 1813.

60. TNA ADM 1/4359. Warren included his detailed 'Coast of America, Proposed Division of Ships and Their Stations' with letter 104 to Croker, dated 28 March 1813, naming vessels to be stationed 'Off New York, Charleston, Savannah and St Augustine', before he could have received either Melville's letter or Admiralty orders to this effect. Niles maintains that it was already happening. Warren's earlier outline proposals had gained Admiralty approval on 20 March 1813.

61. Niles' *Weekly Register*, Baltimore, vol. III, 20 February 1813.

62. Dudley, *The Naval War of 1812*, vol. II, pp. 78–9, private letter, Melville to Warren 26 March 1813.

63. National Library of Scotland MS 2340, pp. 49–50, First Sect. of Admiralty Croker to Warren, 26 March 1813.

64. *London Gazette*, no. 16715, p. 625, 'Notification to Neutrals', 30 March 1813.

65. Niles' *Weekly Register*, Baltimore, vol. III, p. 383, vol. IV, p. 159, and vol. V, pp. 76, 264.

66. NMM LBK/2, Copy of an intercepted American letter dated 'Good Friday [April] 1813', forwarded by Warren to Melville, 5 June 1813.

67. JCBL Box 172, f.9. Letter from Thomas Poynton Ives of Providence, Rhode Island, New England, to Joseph Head of Boston, dated Providence, April 5 1813.

68. JCBL Box 160, f.9. letter from Thomas Ives, to Charles Greene, B & I's commission agent in Boston, 15 June 1813. Greene's reply, dated 'Tuesday afternoon 15th June 1813', appears in Box 160, f.11.

69. NMM LBK/2 Copy of a letter dated 'Good Friday 1813', forwarded by Warren with others to Melville, 5 June 1813.

70. NMM LBK/2 'From a Federalist'; letter enclosed with others, by Warren to Melville, 5 June 1813.

71. Warden, *Statistical Political and Historical Account*, p. 299.

72. Seybert, *Statistical Annals*, pp. 697–80.

73. Ibid., p. 680.

74. E. Johnson, *The History of the Domestic and Foreign Commerce of the United States*, Washington DC, Columbia, Carnegie Institute, 1915, vol. 1, p. 335.

75. Ibid., p. 210.

76. Ibid., calculated from data in vol. 1, pp. 204 and 210, citing J. McMaster, *A History of the People of the United States*, New York, D. Appleton & Co, 1902, vol. III, pp. 463–4.

77. NMM LBK/2, Warren to Melville 5 June 1813.
78. Seybert, *Statistical Annals*, pp. 144–5, 680.
79. NMM HUL/18, Copy of Warren's Bermuda Proclamation dated May 1813, sent to John Dougan, Agent for Commissioners for American Property Condemned as Droits of the Crown, adding interdiction of ports linked with inland navigation to be effective from 1 September 1813, *San Domingo*, Chesapeake, 26 May 1813.
80. TNA ADM 1/504, pp. 551–3, and ADM 1/505, pp. 277–8, Warren to Croker, enclosing a copy of Warren's Proclamation of 16 November 1813.
81. Niles' *Weekly Register*, Baltimore, vol. 5, p. 264, December 1813.
82. Kert, *Prize and Prejudice*, p. 151, citing Public Archives of Canada, RG 8, IV, vol. 118, *Pilgrim*, Vincent Nolte to Alexander Baring, 6 April 1813.
83. Ibid., p. 150, citing *Nova Scotia Royal Gazette*, 19 May 1813.
84. Dudley, *The Naval War of 1812*, vol. II, pp. 341–4, citing Cockburn to Warren, 3 May 1813, TNA ADM 1/503, pp. 334–8.
85. C. Nettels, *The Emergence of a National Economy 1775-1815, The Economic History of the United States vol. II*, New York and London, Harper & Row, 1969, pp. 339–40; see also Hickey, *The War of 1812*, p. 80, citing *ASP: MA*, vol. 1, p. 303.
86. Hickey, *The War of 1812*, pp. 202–3, citing Smith Papers, Lib of Congress, reels 2 & 3.
87. Seybert, *Statistical Annals*, pp. 11–12.
88. J. Lambert, *Travels through Canada, and the United States of North America in the years 1806, 1807 and 1808*, 3rd edn, London, Baldock, Craddock & Joy, 1816, vol. II; calculated from data, pp. 86–7. New York city's population in 1810 of 96,373 had increased 15.4% since 1808. J. De Bow, *Compendium of 7th Census*, Washington, US Bureau of the Census, Senate Printer, 1854, p. 192.
89. Ibid., pp. 74–5. Lambert notes that in 1806 New York had collected $6.5m and paid in $4.5m net.
90. JCBL Box 236, f.3, John Maybin to B & I, Providence RI, Dated Philadelphia, 5 May 1813; and B & I to Maybin, 13 May 1813.
91. JCBL Box 236, f.3, Thomas Ives to John Maybin, dated Providence, 16 June 1813.
92. JCBL Box 236, f.3, John Maybin to B& I, dated Philadelphia, 21 June 1813, and Box 236, f.4, B & I to Maybin, 14 September 1813, and Maybin to B & I, 18 September 1813.
93. *ASP*: C&N, vol. I, pp. 998, 1018.
94. R. Guernsey, *New York City and its Vicinity during the War of 1812-15, being a Military, Civic and Financial Local History of that Period*, New York, Charles Woodward, 1889, vol. I, p. 383.
95. *AC*: 13–1, 166, House of Representatives, Maritime Defence. June 1813.
96. Seybert, *Statistical Annals*, 'Statement of the Gross and Net amount of the Customs contd., 1st January to 31st December annually', pp. 434–7. Actually, 34.73% and 52.56% respectively.
97. Actually 68.38%, 1812 adjusted to $2,163,826.5 and 1813 to $684,309.
98. A. Cole, *Wholesale Commodity Prices in the United States 1700-1861*, Cambridge MA, Harvard Univ. Press, 1938, Appendix B, table 45, p. 135. All Commodity Index of Wholesale Prices with Variable Group Weights at New York, Monthly 1797–1861.
99. Ibid., Appendix B, table 46, p. 136, 30 Basic Commodity Index of Wholesale Prices with Constant Weights at New York, Monthly 1797–1861. The 30 basic commodities included were: beef, butter, coal, codfish, coffee, copper, corn, cotton, hemp, hides, indigo, iron (bar and pig), lard, lead, leather, linseed oil, molasses, pork, salt, cotton sheeting, sugar, tallow, tar, tin, tobacco, turpentine, whale oil, wheat, white lead.
100. Guernsey, *New York City and its Vicinity*, vol. I, Appendix note 1, p. 417. The Census of 1 June 1810 gave New York city's population as 96,373, inferred by Guernsey as 98,000 for 1812; it had fallen by December 1813 to 92,448.
101. Dudley, *The Naval War of 1812*, vol. II, pp. 384–5. Letter from Capt. Robt. Barrie to his mother, Mrs George Clayton, dated HMS *Dragon*, 14 September 1813, Chesapeake Bay. Barrie's underlining of '<u>any</u> trade whatever' seems significant.

102. TNA ADM 1/505, pp. 139–43, cited in Crawford, *The Naval War of 1812*, vol. III, p. 15; *Naval Chronicle*, vol. 31, pp. 246–9. Since 22% of this list omits tonnage, the total probably approaches 5,000 tons. Several of the prizes are privateers.

103. Dudley, *The Naval War of 1812*, vol. II, pp. 85–6, letter from Master Commandant James Biddle to Sect. of the Navy Jones, Philadelphia, 28 April 1813.

104. JCBL Box 236, f.3, John Maybin, Philadelphia, to Thomas Ives of B & I, Providence RI, 5 May 1813.

105. Ibid., Ives to Maybin, 16 June 1813. The italics are mine.

106. Ibid., f.4. John Maybin to Thomas Ives, dated Philadelphia, 21 June 1813.

107. C. Wright, *Economic History of the United States*, 2nd edn, New York, McGraw-Hill, 1949, p. 221, fig. 11. 'Index numbers of wholesale prices of domestic and imported commodities in Philadelphia, 1784–1820, 100 = average 1821–25. Based on Bezanson, Gray and Hussey, 'Wholesale Prices in Philadelphia, 1784–1861'. See also graph on frontispiece.

108. Nettels, *National Economy*, p. 389, table 9 'Wages of Farm Labor and Prices of Farm Products 1801–1816', citing Bidwell and Falconer, 'History of Agriculture in the Northern United States', p. 495.

109. Seybert, *Statistical Annals*, pp. 434–7.

110. Ibid.

111. H. Adams, *History of the United States during the Administrations of Jefferson and Madison*, New York, Charles Scribner's Sons, 1889–96, vol. VII, p. 264. Adams does not appear to have made any allowance for the change in the rate of custom duties in July 1812. His citation of T. Pitkin, *A Statistical View*, for customs revenue is incorrect – the data appears in neither edition of Pitkin – but can be found in Seybert, *Statistical Annals*, pp. 434–7.

112. Dewey, *Financial History*, p. 142.

113. *ASP*: F, vol. II, pp. 580–81, 1 December 1812; see also Dewey, *Financial History*, p. 132. Until now, government stock had been sold only at par, at its face value.

114. *AC*: 12–2, 32–4, 100, 198–9, 450–51, 855, 1126, 1251–5, 1316, 1321–2, 1334–5.

115. *ASP*: C&N, vol. I, p. 931, Gallatin to Langdon Cheves, 10th June 1812, and *AC*: 12–2, 1063, 9 February 1813.

116. *AC*: 12–2, 870, 23 January 1813.

117. LC Papers of James Madison, reel 15, Gallatin to Madison, 5 March 1813.

118. *AC*: 12–2; 75, 97, 907–8, 919–20, 1062–5, 1091–1100, 1105–9, 1111–13, 1326–8, 1330–33.

119. *ASP*: F, vol. II. pp. 625–6.

120. JCBL Box 236, f.3, Thomas Ives to John Maybin of Philadelphia, dated Providence, 19 March 1813.

121. R. Walters, *Albert Gallatin: Jeffersonian Financier and Diplomat*, New York, Macmillan, 1957, p. 258, citing LC Papers of James Madison, April 19 1816. After an apparent personal approach by Gallatin, David Parish and Stephen Girard together lent $7,055,800, and John Jacob Astor $2,056,000, for 6% stock at 88; 'that amount ... did much to embarrass' the latter. US Accounts for 1814 show that Parish and Girard between them received $17,639 50c in commission, Astor $5,140 at 1/8th of 1%. See also *ASP*: F, vol. II, pp. 646–7, Report of Sect. of Treasury, 28 July 1813.

122. *ASP*: FR, vol. III, pp. 623–7. In return for mediation, which Britain rejected, the Russians sought a commercial treaty with the United States. Despite declaring his intention to leave the Treasury Gallatin was apparently still attending there on 22 March 1813 to oppose the payment of $200,000 in prize money to Decatur and his crew for the capture of HMS *Macedonian* on 25 October 1812. J. de Kay, *Chronicles of the Frigate* Macedonian *1809-1922*, New York, W. Norton & Co, 1995, pp. 100–108.

123. G. Dangerfield, *The Era of Good Feelings*, London, Methuen, 1953, p. 54, citing H. Adams, *The Writings of Albert Gallatin*, Philadelphia, J. P. Lippincott, 1879, p. 493.

124. *ASP*: M, vol. II, p. 206. In *ASP*: F, vol. II, p. 264, Jones is first described as Acting

Secretary of the Treasury on 2 June 1813. See also *AC*: 13–1, 85–6, Executive Proceedings. Gallatin's successors in office were to be either as pre-occupied as Jones, aware of being out of their depth, like Campbell, or, like Dallas, very able, but appointed too late to avert financial disaster.

125. *ASP*: M, vol. II, p. 240, and Senate Journal 2, 355.
126. H. Adams, *The Education of Henry Adams*, first publ. New York, 1907; rev. and ed. N. Saveth, London, New English Library, 1966, p. 1. According to Adams, Gallatin's 'combination of ability, integrity, knowledge, unselfishness and social fitness … has no equal'.
127. *AC*: 13–1, 499–500. Madison was to call on Congress to enact another embargo on 20 July and, when unsuccessful, was to issue an Executive Order to that effect on 29 July 1813.
128. Hickey, *The War of 1812*, p. 171. Gallatin, as a favour to John Jacob Astor, had earlier recommended the easing of restrictions on fur trading with Canada.
129. *ASP*: C&N, vol. I, p. 931, Gallatin to Langdon Chieves 10 June 1812. Gallatin suggested the repeal of the Non-Importation Act, increased tonnage duties and decreased draw-backs as alternatives to internal excise duties and 'direct' taxes, for which, however, Congress passed legislation in July and August 1813, but not to be implemented before January 1814.
130. NMM LBK/2, letter from Warren to Melville, HMS *San Domingo*, Bermuda, 9 March 1813.
131. Ibid., Confidential letter from Warren to Melville dated HMS *San Domingo*, Lynhaven Bay, 29 March 1813.
132. Ibid., Copy of a letter to Warren, dated 24 February 1813, forwarded to Ld. Melville on 5 June 1813. The well-informed letter writer may have been the former British Consul to Boston, Andrew Allen, one of Warren's earlier correspondents, still apparently resident in America despite a threat in 1812 to prosecute him for selling trading licences to Americans, later reduced to an order to leave the country. On 28 June 1813, a British Mr Allen, 'an unruly man', was ordered to be removed to Worcester. Listed under 'Dispositions of requests for indulgence by suspected persons' in K. Scott, *British Aliens in the United States during the War of 1812*, Baltimore MD, Genealogical Publishing, 1979, p. 384. Allen is not reported to have left America until 4 September 1813 in Niles' *Weekly Register*, Baltimore, vol. V, p. 4.
133. *AC*: 13–1, 17.
134. NMM LBK/2, 24 February 1813.
135. Actually 71.85%.
136. Actually 48.29%.
137. Actually 65.53%.
138. *AC*: 13–1, 46. Senate Proceedings, 9 July 1813.
139. *AC*: 13–1, 149–50. Report of Ways and Means Committee, 10 June 1813. Banks could choose either a stamp duty on their notes or a 1.5% tax on their dividends. The House approved laws for internal excise duties between 24 and 29 July, and those for 'direct' taxes by 2 August 1813.
140. *AC*: 13–1, 2717–73.
141. *AC*: 13–1, 63–4, Senate debate of Jones' Treasury letter of 19 July 1813.
142. Ibid.
143. *ASP*: F, vol. II, p. 644.
144. See n. 136 for Chapter 7.
145. NMM LBK/2, Warren to Melville, 26 October 1813. Although almost certainly mistaken in believing that Baring had found large-scale finance for the wartime American government, Warren's fears were not entirely groundless. In 1808, Baring had written *An Inquiry into the Causes and Consequences of the Orders in Council*, and supported Brougham's calls for the repeal of the Orders in the Commons. Baring had certainly helped the Americans borrow more than $11m for the Louisiana Purchase in 1803, and as a Whig, would not have been admired by Warren. See

R. Hidy, *The House of Baring in American Trade and Finance*, New York, Russell & Russell, 1949, repr. 1970, pp. 33–4, 46.

146. BL Add Mss 38255, ff.43–4, Liverpool Papers, Warren to Prime Minister Lord Liverpool, 'Private', Halifax Nova Scotia, 16 November 1813.

147. Adams, *Albert Gallatin*, vol. 1, pp. 551–2, Baring to Gallatin, London 22 July 1813. Gallatin was waiting in St Petersburg for a British reply to the Russian offer of mediation. He later left the Russian capital for London via Amsterdam.

148. Ibid.

149. Ibid. No evidence has so far been found that Baring lent the American government any money in this war until 1814, as will be seen in Chapter 7, and then only the relatively small amount of $133,300 to meet the overlooked $128,000 interest due on the Louisiana Loan Stock held by their Dutch bankers, due on 1 January 1815, together with the American Peace Commissioner's incidental expenses. A letter recalling Warren, having already been written by the Admiralty on 4 November 1813, although not yet received, may partly explain why no Prime Ministerial reply to Warren's letter has yet been found.

150. Actually 27.69%, calculated from data of Seybert, *Statistical Annals*, p. 93.

151. North, 'United States Balance of Payments', pp. 591–2, table A-2, Appendix A.

152. Domestic exports alone had fallen by only 16.7% during 1812–13, compared with 34% between 1811 and 1812. Calculated from Nettels, *National Economy*, vol. II, p. 396, Table 17, citing Johnson, *Domestic and Foreign Commerce*, vol. II, p. 20, which cites Seybert, *Statistical Annals*, p. 93.

153. F. Crouzet, 'America and the Crisis of the British Imperial Economy 1803–1807', in *The Early Modern Atlantic Economy*, eds J. McCusker and K. Morgan, Cambridge, Cambridge Univ. Press, 2000, p. 283.

154. Seybert, *Statistical Annals*, p. 93.

155. *ASP*: C&N, vol. I p. 992. For the year ending 30 September 1813, American grain and flour worth $15.5m was exported to the Peninsula alone.

156. *AC*: 13–1, 499–500, Madison to Congress, 20 July 1813.

157. Dudley, *The Naval War of 1812*, vol. II, p. 272, undated report to Warren from Capt. Hayes, HMS *Majestic*, enclosed with letter dated 25 October 1813. Water, firewood, fish, fruit and vegetables supplied 'on reasonable terms'. See also Hickey, *The War of 1812*, p. 171: 'some sixty [American] vessels were reportedly engaged in this traffic in Long Island Sound alone'.

158. *AC*: 13–2, 554–5, 2053, 2781–8.

159. Dudley, *The Naval War of 1812*, vol. II, p. 244, letter to Sect. of Navy Jones from District Attorney's Office, Newport, Rhode Island, 14 September 1813; and Mahan, *Sea Power*, vol. II, p. 197.

160. Hickey, *The War of 1812*, pp. 167–71; and Dudley, *The Naval War of 1812*, p. 272, undated report to Warren from Capt. J Haynes of HMS *Majestic* enclosed in his letter dated 25 October 1813, 'I have given a note to several Owners of Schooners going for a Cargo stating the assistance afforded the *Majestic* and recommending their being permitted to pass.'

161. H. Adams, *History of the United States during the Administration of Jefferson and Madison*, New York, Charles Scribner's Sons, 1889–96, vol. VII, pp. 262–4.

162. *Columbian Central*, Boston, 7 September 1813.

163. Ibid., 25 September 1813.

164. Ibid., 18 December 1813.

165. *AC*: 13–1, 48–9.

166. Niles' *Weekly Register*, Baltimore, vol. V, p. 41, 18 September 1813, 'Prices Current'.

167. Adams, op. cit., vol. VII, p. 263.

168. Mahan, *Sea Power*, vol. II, p. 179

169. Ibid.

170. Actually 44.74%.

171. Ibid.

172. *ASP*: C&N, vol. I. p. 969. Sheldon presumably included Madison's second embargo, imposed by Executive Order on 29 July, banning American exports, ratified by Congress only five days earlier on 17 December 1813, suspended on 30 March 1814 and repealed on 14 April 1814.

173. J. Brannan, ed., *Official Letters of the Military and Naval Officers of the United States during the War with Great Britain in the Years 1812, 13, 14 and 15*, Washington DC, 1823, p. 287, Cmdr Stephen Decatur to Wm. Jones, Sect. of the Navy, 20 December 1813.

174. Dudley, *The Naval War of 1812*, vol. II, p. 710–11, citing TNA ADM 2/1380, pp. 370–75, Admiralty to Capt. J. Hillyar, 12 March 1813.

175. Dudley, *The Naval War of 1812*, vol. II, pp. 155–7, Astor to Secretary of the Navy Jones, New York, 17 June 1813; and Jones to Astor, Navy Dept. 22 June 1813. Astor had first written to Jones on 6 June 1813, but Jones' reply was probably delayed by Madison's illness.

176. Ibid., p. 711, Rear-Admiral Manley Dixon to Croker, dated HM Ship *Montagu*, Rio de Janeiro, 21 June 1813.

177. J. Latimer, *1812: War with America*, Cambridge MA, and London, Belknap Press/Harvard Univ. Press, 2007, p. 240. North West's partner was Donald McTavish.

178. Dudley, *The Naval War of 1812*, vol. II, p. 714, citing TNA ADM 1/21, p. 464.

179. US Works Progress Administration, *Boston Looks Seaward*, Boston MA, 1941, republ. London, MacDonald and Jane's, 1974, p. 89.

180. Calculated from data in Mahan, *Sea Power*, vol. II. p. 181. From $5,944,121 in 1811, New England's re-exports had fallen to $302,781 by 1813.

181. Ibid., p. 182, citing *The Columbian Centinel* for 7 September and 15 December 1813.

182. Mahan, *Sea Power*, vol. II. p. 181, citing Niles' *Weekly Register*, Baltimore, vol. V, p. 311.

183. TNA ADM 1/506, pp. 40–41, Cochrane to Croker, 25 April 1814.

184. A. Gutridge, 'Prize Agency 1800–1815 with special reference to the career and work of George Redmond Hulbert', unpublished MPhil dissertation, Univ. of Portsmouth, 1989, pp. 78 and 137, and in personal correspondence. Warren seems to have gained about £97,500. See also R. Hill, *The Prizes of War: The Naval Prize System in the Napoleonic Wars 1793–1815*, Stroud, Sutton/Royal Naval Museum Publications, 1998, pp. 151 and 207, citing Gutridge while comparing Warren's earning to those of others. Hill estimated £100,000 in 1815 to be equivalent to approximately £20m in 1998.

185. Gutridge, 'Prize Agency', pp. 86–7, citing Portsmouth City Record Office, 626A1/1/3/21, Hulbert to his brother John, 11 November 1813, and p. 161.

186. JCBL Box 236, f.3, John Maybin to Thomas Ives, Providence RI, dated Philadelphia, 21 June 1813.

187. W. James, *The Naval History of Great Britain, from…1793 to…1820, with an Account of the Origin and Increase of the British Navy*, new edn, London, Harding, Lepard, and Co, 1826, vol. 6, p. 437, repr. Milton Keynes, Nabu Public Domain Reprints, 2010. On p. 325 James had mentioned Warren's earlier successes on the French and Irish coasts, now disparagingly calling him 'a superannuated admiral, whose services, such as they were, bore a very old date …'.

CHAPTER 7. CAPITAL AND CREDIT: THE IMPACT OF THE FINAL PHASE

1. H. Adams and H Agar, ed., *The History of the United States during the Administrations of Jefferson and Madison: The Formative Years*, London, Collins, 1948, vol. II, p. 860, Mrs D. Madison to Mrs H. Gallatin, Washington, 7 January 1814.

2. *AC*: 13–1, 149.

3. *AC*: 13–1, 63–4.

4. *AC*: 13–2, 1453.

5. D. Dewey, *Financial History of the United States*, 1903; 12th edn, New York, A. Kelly, 1934, repr. 1968, pp. 111, 124, 141.

6. Ibid., p. 125, and *AC*: 13–2, 1453.

7. Ibid.

8. *AC*: 13–2, 1451.
9. Ibid.
10. *AC*: 13–2, 1451–2.
11. *AC*: 13–2, 1452.
12. D. Hickey, *The War of 1812: A Forgotten Conflict*, Urbana IL, Univ. of Illinois Press, 1989, p. 160, citing Klein, *Memoirs of John Roberts*, p. 366. This opinion of Campbell, voiced by Republican Jonathan Roberts of Pennsylvania, seems to have been widely held.
13. Hickey, *The War of 1812*, p. 165, citing *ASP*: F, vol. II, pp. 651–3, Report of the Secretary of the Treasury, 8 January 1814.
14. Hickey, *The War of 1812*, p. 166, citing *AC*: 13–2, 1374, 14 February 1814.
15. *AC*: 13–2, p. 1689, House of Representatives, Loan Bill, 25 February 1814, John Calhoun.
16. Hickey, *The War of 1812*, p. 166, quoting *The National Intelligencer*, Washington, 12 March 1814.
17. M. Crawford, ed., *The Naval War of 1812: A Documentary History*, Washington DC, Naval Historical Center, vol. III, 2002, p. 7, Secretary of the Navy, Wm. Jones to Capt. Gordon, USS *Constellation*, Washington, 5 January 1814.
18. W. Dudley, ed., *The Naval War of 1812: A Documentary History*, Washington DC, Naval Historical Center, vol. II, 1992, pp. 294–5, Jones to G. Parker, o/c USS Siren, Navy Dept. 8 Dec 1813. Jones was also concerned that allocating prize crews would dangerously deplete American manning levels.
19. Crawford, *The Naval War of 1812*, vol. III, pp. 412, 515.
20. J. Russell, *The history of the war between the United States and Great-Britain To which is added … a list of vessels taken from Great-Britain during the war*, 2nd edn, Hartford CT, B. & J. Russell, 1815, pp. 377–402.
21. R. Horsman, *The War of 1812*, New York, A. Knopf, 1969, p. 142.
22. Russell, *The history of the war*, 'List of Vessels taken from Great Britain …', pp. 401–2. Captures 1520–21, and 1581–2. On these occasions, the *Constitution* appears to have taken two brigs, one burnt and the other successfully sent into New York. The *President* appears to have succeeded in sending a brig and a schooner into French ports.
23. A. Mahan, *Sea Power in its Relation to the War of 1812*, Boston MA and London, Little Brown/Sampson, Marston Low and Company, 1905, vol. II, p. 232, citing Niles' *Weekly Register*, Baltimore, vol. VI, pp. 69–71.
24. F. Kert, *Prize and Prejudice: Privateering and Naval Prize in Atlantic Canada in the War of 1812*, Research in Maritime History 11, International Maritime Economic History Association, St John's, Newfoundland, 1997. Calculated from data in Appendix 1: 'Prize Cases Appearing in the Vice-Admiralty Court of Halifax from June 1812 to May 1815', pp. 159–203. For Halifax alone, when recaptures by British and Canadian privateers are included, the recovery rate falls to 18.8%. For figures supplied by Lloyd's to the House of Commons, see F. Kert, 'The Fortunes of War: Commercial Warfare and Maritime Risk in the War of 1812', *Northern Mariner*, 8 (4), 1998, pp. 1–16, p. 2. The recovery rate is actually 31.74%.
25. Hickey, *The War of 1812*, p. 124, citing National Archives, Washington, M149, reel 11. Similar orders for the army from the Secretary of War were published in Niles' *Weekly Register*, Baltimore, vol. IV, p. 386.
26. Boston commodity prices at auction are taken from the Brown & Ives correspondence, JCBL Box 160 ff.9–10 onwards; sugar fell from 31c. per lb on 5 August 1813, to 18c. per lb on 29 January 1814, actually 41.94%.
27. *AC*: 13–2, 2781–8.
28. JCBL Box 160, f.9, from Charles Greene, Brown & Ives Boston agent, to B & I, Providence, RI, 23 December 1813.
29. Ibid., f.10, Charles Greene, Boston to B & I, Providence, 29 January 1814.
30. Ibid., ff.9–10 onwards. See Appendix B, tables 10–13. Coffee fell 30.3% from a

maximum 33c. per lb on 23 December 1813, six days after Congressional ratification, to 23c. per lb on 27 January 1814. Molasses fell 11.6% from $1.47 on 23 December 1813 to $1.30 on 29 January 1814.

31. BL C *The National Intelligencer*, Washington, 1 April 1814 (A204) Despite his having complained to Madison on 24 July 1813 that being Secretary of both Treasury and Navy was 'absolutely impracticable', Jones had only 'declared his seat at the Treasury vacant' on 9 February 1814 and been replaced as Secretary of the Treasury by George Campbell on that day, although remaining Sect. of the Navy until December 1814.

32. NYHS *The American & Commercial Daily Advertiser – Extra* for 31 March 1814 reported that Madison's decision 'was yesterday transmitted to both Houses of Congress'. AC: 13–2, 1986–2001; see also *Journal of the House*, p. 410, for Thurs. 14 April 1814.

33. JCBL Box 160, f.10, letters from Charles Greene, 29 January and 12 March 1814. 'Your letter for London will be forwarded in a day or two by a private opportunity, & I shall frequently be enabled to send your letters without inspection.' The earlier letter confirms the sending of a letter via Lisbon in the Swedish brig *Hadjen*.

34. Ibid., Thomas Ives of Providence to Charles Greene, Boston, 25 April 1814.

35. Ibid., p. 671, Charles Greene of Boston, to Thomas Ives in Providence, Rhode Island. American 'short' hundredweights were of 100lbs, unlike British cwts of 112lbs.

36. Calculated from 'current prices' in B & I correspondence, and actually 30.96%.

37. See Appendix B, Tables 7–13, up to and including Boston sale of 16 May 1814.

38. JCBL Box 160, Charles Greene to Thomas Ives, dated Boston, 15 March 1814.

39. TNA ADM 1/506, pp. 40–44, 25 April 1814.

40. JCBL Box 160, letter 6, Ives to Greene, Providence 4 May 1814.

41. Actually 45.16%.

42. JCBL Box 160, letter 7, Greene to Ives, Boston, 5 May 1814. Always more expensive than other sugars, from an average $16.12 on 5 May 1814 Havannah brown sugar rose to $23.00 on 29 September 1814, a rise of 42.68%. Average Boston coffee prices were briefly higher under Embargo than blockade, but had fallen so far on the Embargo's suspension that the proportional increase was then greater under the British blockade.

43. Hickey, *The War of 1812*, pp. 170–71, citing National Archives, Washington, 'Letters Received by Sect. of War' (M222 r.10), 'Marcellus' to Armstrong, 'early 1814'.

44. W. Whitehill, *The Journal of Lieutenant Henry Napier in HMS Nymphe: New England Blockaded – 1814*, Salem MA, Peabody Museum, 1939, pp. 22, 31 for June and July 1814. NMM 355.49.

45. JCBL Box 160, f.11, letter 14, Thomas Ives to Charles Greene, Boston, 24 May 1814. Ives actually meant Capt. David Milne of HMS *Bulwark*.

46. Ibid., letter 15, Charles Greene, Boston to B & I, Providence, 26 May 1814. It seems probable that a cargo of cotton from Amelia Island would be taken directly to Liverpool for the Lancashire mills, rather than to Gothenburg for possible re-export.

47. Ibid., Charles Greene Boston, to B & I Providence, 18 July 1814. While the privateer *Shannon* took the sloop *John*, sailing in ballast from Salem to Wells, MA, on 18 May 1814, all of the *Bulwark*'s captures for this period carried cargoes and it is therefore reasonable to assume that the *Nicholas Paulowitch* was not, in fact, in ballast. By August 1814, the British blockading squadrons were routinely taking prizes in ballast, including the *Anita* and *Fermina* from Boston to Havana and Amelia Island respectively. See Kert, *Prize and Prejudice*, p. 189–94, 200.

48. *London Gazette*, 31 May 1814, reprinted in *Naval Chronicle*, vol. 31, p. 475.

49. Niles' *Weekly Register*, Baltimore, vol. VI, p. 182–3, 14 May 1814.

50. Ibid., p. 317, 9 July 1814.

51. JCBL Box 160, f.11, letter 18, Charles Greene, Boston to B & I, Providence, 20 July 1814.

52. Kert, *Prize and Prejudice*, Appendix 1, pp. 189–203. The foreign ports included Amsterdam, Bahia, Demarera, Haiti, Halifax, Nova Scotia, Havana, Lisbon, San

Domingo, San Salvador and St Iago de Cuba. Cargoes included coffee, hides, meats, metals, molasses, sugar and textiles.

53. Crawford, *The Naval War of 1812*, vol. III, p. 69, Cockburn to Cochrane, 26 May 1814. E. Hume, ed., 'Letters Written During the War of 1812 by the British Commander in American Waters – Admiral Sir David Milne', *William & Mary Historical Quarterly*, 2nd series, 10, 1930, p. 293, Capt. David Milne to George Hume, HM Ship *Bulwark*, 30 May 1814. The article's title is disingenuous since Milne was neither knighted nor C in C during the war. He was appointed C in C North America in May 1816 and knighted in September 1816 for services off Algeria.

54. G. Warren and F. Pearson, *Wholesale Prices for 213 Years, 1720 to 1932, Part 1, Wholesale Prices in the United States for 135 Years from 1797 to 1932*, Ithaca NY, Cornell Univ., Agricultural Experimental Station, 1932, p. 8, table 2 'Index Numbers of the Wholesale Prices of All Commodities with Variable Group Weights 1720 to 1932. Monthly, 1800–1820. (1910=100)'.

55. Niles' *Weekly Register*, Baltimore, vol. V, pp. 228–9, 4 December 1813.

56. D. North, 'United States Balance of Payments 1790–1860', in *Trends in the American Economy in the Nineteenth Century*, Studies in Income and Wealth 24, National Bureau of Economic Research, Princeton, Princeton Univ. Press, 1960; repr. New York, Arno Press, 1975, pp. 591–2, table A-2, Appendix A. Calculated from this data, the figure is actually 71.85%.

57. Ibid. Actually 41.53%.

58. Ibid. Actually 83.54%.

59. A. Seybert, *Statistical Annals*, Philadelphia, T. Dobson, 1818, p. 454, part of 'A Statement Exhibiting the gross and net amount of ad valorem and specific duties on Goods Wares and Merchandise imported into the United States from 1st January 1794 to 31st December 1814'. The decrease in net customs revenue adjusted for the doubling of rate from 1 July 1812 calculated from this data is actually 65.53%. For a summary of the method of adjustment, see nn. 29 and 30 for Chapter 6.

60. Actually 31.90%.

61. Actually 76.53%

62. B. Arthur, 'The Role of Blockade in the Anglo-American Naval War of 1812–14', unpublished MA dissertation, Greenwich Maritime Institute, Univ. of Greenwich, 2002, p. 52.

63. S. Ratner, *American Taxation*, cited by C. Nettels, *The Emergence of a National Economy 1775–1815, The Economic History of the United States, vol. II*, New York and London, Harper & Row, 1969, for Gallatin's surplus. Revenue decrease calculated from data actually 54.39%.

64. Madison's first 90-Day Embargo, between 4 April and 3 July 1812, and second Embargo, from 29 July 1813 to repeal on 14 April 1814 (260 days), together comprise a total of 350 days of American embargo, of which only 275 were in force during wartime after 18 June 1812 concurrently with British maritime commercial blockades, i.e. 27.75% of 991 days of war, significantly less than one-third.

65. Seybert, *Statistical Annals*, pp. 301, 381.

66. Ibid., p. 93; decrease actually 75.13%.

67. Kert, *Prize and Prejudice*, extracted from Appendix 1, pp. 157–201.

68. T. Pitkin, *A Statistical View of the Commerce of the United States of America*, 1st edn, Hartford, Charles Hosmer, 1816, BL 1391g 6., and 2nd edn, New Haven, Durrie & Peck, 1835, BL 1137 k 22. Inclusion of exports of the last three months of 1814, and continuation until 31 December 1815, may account for Congressman Pitkin's exaggerated figure for the American post-war recovery of exports in 1815.

69. Hickey, *The War of 1812*, p. 117.

70. W. Galpin, 'The American Grain Trade to the Spanish Peninsula 1810–14', *American Historical Review*, 28, 1922, pp. 24–44. Early in 1812 Augustus Foster, British Minister in Washington, had been given over £304,000, then worth $1,337,600, to spend on American corn and flour for Wellington's Peninsular Army.

71. Niles' *Weekly Register*, Baltimore, vol. IV, p. 168, 8 May 1813: 'It is said that 300,000 barrels of flour remain unsold at Cadiz March 23rd'; also p. 280: 'At Cadiz 7th May, afloat & in store 160,000 bls of American flour, 20,000 tierces of rice &c'. Once the market had been flooded Congress' License Act, at the third attempt on 29 July 1813, prohibited the use of British licences for export to the Peninsula, previous Bills having been blocked by the 'agriculturalists'. See House Journal, 16–29 July 1813.

72. Pitkin, *A Statistical View*, pp. 119–20: 'American exports of flour in barrels to Spain and Portugal', combined. If Pitkin's figure for 1813 is accepted, a decrease of 99.55% is found. Since prices there began to fall in March 1813 his total for sales of American flour to the Peninsula may have been exaggerated to minimise the apparent impact of the British commercial blockade. The *Providence Gazette* for 29 June 1813 notes a 'decided decrease from the previous year' in American vessels at Lisbon in 'the first half of 1813'. Galpin, 'The American Grain Trade', p. 44, note 81.

73. Nettels, *National Economy*, p. 393, table 13, citing Bidwell and Falconer *History of Agriculture in the United States*, p. 493, actually 85.41%; and Pitkin, *A Statistical View*, p. 102, actually 90.75%

74. Nettels, *National Economy*, table 13, p. 393.

75. Actually 94.91%.

76. Calculated from data in D. Warden, *A Statistical Political and Historical Account of the United States of North America from the Period of their First Colonization to the Present Day*, Edinburgh, Archibald Constable & Co, 1819, p. 309.

77. Calculated from data in Seybert, *Statistical Annals*, p. 149, actually 93.57%.

78. Actually 68.1%.

79. Actually 40.6%.

80. North, 'United States Balance of Payments', pp. 591–2 for imports, and Seybert, *Statistical Annals*, p. 93 for exports, then combined.

81. Actually 57.4%.

82. Actually 60.2%.

83. Actually 83.04%.

84. R. Gardiner, *The Naval War of 1812*, London, Caxton Editions/NMM, 2001, p. 76.

85. Ibid., p. 28.

86. I. Toll, *Six Frigates: How Piracy, War and British Supremacy at Sea gave Birth to the World's Most Powerful Navy*, London, Penguin/Michael Joseph, 2006, pp. 271–2, citing S. P. Tucker and F. T. Reuter, *Injured Honor: The Chesapeake–Leopard Affair, June 22, 1807*, Annapolis MD, Naval Institute Press, 1996, pp. 62–6.

87. Pitkin, *A Statistical View*, p. 363.

88. Ibid. Actually 29.55%.

89. Ibid. Actually 64.47%.

90. Hickey, *The War of 1812*, pp. 169–71.

91. Actually 74.47%.

92. Pitkin, *A Statistical View*, pp. 387–91. Coastal vessels under 20 tons, 'licensed' separately before 1811, were then included in 'enrolled and licensed tonnage'.

93. *ASP*: C&N, vol. I, p. 1017, and vol. II, p. 12; calculated as 37.4% of 674,853 registered tonnage.

94. Mahan, *Sea Power*, vol. II, p. 205.

95. Calculated from data in *ASP* as 8.7% of 674,632 registered tons.

96. *ASP*: C&N, vol. I, p. 1017; actually 39.3%.

97. Ibid. Actually 53.6% and 41.7% respectively.

98. *ASP*: C & N, vol. II. p. 12, 354. and Mahan, *Sea Power*, vol. II, p. 205.

99. W. Marvin, 'Tonnage in Whaling Fisheries', in his *Registered & Enrolled Tonnage, 1800-1901*, US Bureau of Navigation, New York, Charles Scribner's Sons, 1902, p. 172. The actual decrease is 80.9%.

100. Kert, *Prize and Prejudice*. Calculated from Kert's figures, augmented by reference to other contemporary sources, these average sizes differ from those found by Albion and Pope using the prize totals of Essex Institute, *American Vessels Captured by the*

British during the Revolution and War of 1812: The Records of the Vice-Admiralty Court at Halifax, Nova Scotia, Salem MA, 1911.

101. C. Wright, *Economic History of the United States*, 2nd edn, New York, McGraw-Hill, 1949, pp. 314–15. Among such alternative investments was Francis Lowell's initially water-powered cotton carding, spinning and weaving mill at Waltham, Massachusetts, opened in 1814: the first integrated textile mass-production in America. The 'Waltham Plan' was to be widely imitated in New England and elsewhere.

102. Kert, *Prize and Prejudice*, calculated from augmented Halifax Vice Adm. Court records. In addition to that of Halifax, Nova Scotia, Vice Adm. Courts were also operated in St George's Bermuda, Nassau in the Bahamas, Port Royal Jamaica and in Antigua, for all of which complete records appear to be unavailable. The Bahamian *Royal Gazette* for 14 January and 17 March 1814 asserts that 246 vessels, not all American, had been condemned during the war so far.

103. Dewey, *Financial History*, p. 142; and J. Bristed, *The Resources of the United States of America; or a View of the agricultural, commercial ...moral and religious capacity and character of the American people*, New York, J. Eastburn & Co, 1818, p. 77. Bristed explains that 'the amount is secured to government by bonds payable at different periods according to the term of credit given to the importer', often a year, and that therefore Seybert's accrued net customs revenue for each year became the government's cash-flow revenue for the following year, successively between 1811 and 1815. Dewey's customs revenue figure for 1812 slightly exceeds Seybert's net customs revenue for 1811, probably because of costs and late payments. Seybert's net customs revenue, accrued in 1812, becomes Dewey's government income for 1813, a pattern followed by net customs revenues for 1813 and 1814. The apparent discrepancy for 1814–15 could be explained by a later end to the government's income accounting year.

104. Bristed, *The Resources of the United States of America*, p. 82, using figures from the Ways & Means Committee Report dated 9 December 1817. Using Bristed's figures, the cost is actually 8.46% of net receipts in 1814 and 5.94% in 1815. Dewey calculated the cost as between 4.8% and 7.8% of *gross* receipts. For comparison, collection costs of customs duties in 1812 are calculated as 3.62% of net receipts and 3.49% of gross receipts.

105. Total US tax revenue as a proportion of expenditure is actually: 1812, 43.84%; 1813, 41.77%; 1814, 28.24%; 1815, 42.86%.

106. Federalist Congressman Timothy Pitkin appears to have sought to demonstrate the damage of both embargoes and the war to his constituent's interests by emphasising the post-war recovery of American overseas trade, particularly exports, and to have included trade figures up to 31 December for 1815, when previous accounting years ended on 30 September.

107. North, 'United States Balance of Payments', pp. 591–2, and Seybert, *Statistical Annals*, p. 93. The US Balance of *Trade* (as distinct from its Balance of *Payments*) compared only 'visible' imports with 'visible' exports, excluding earnings from 'invisible' services such as shipping and insurance.

108. Nettels, *National Economy*, p. 334, citing E. Johnson, *The History of the Domestic and Foreign Commerce of the United States*, Washington DC, Columbia, Carnegie Institute, 1915, vol. II, p. 20. By 1815, New England's specie holdings had been reduced to $3,915,000.

109. Niles' *Weekly Register*, Baltimore, vol. VII, p. 195.

110. JCBL Box 160, f.10, Charles Greene of Boston to Brown & Ives Providence RI, 12 March 1814.

111. P. Jones, *An Economic History of the United States*, London, Routledge and Kegan Paul, 1956, repr. 1969, pp. 36–7. Lowell's textile mill at Waltham, Massachusetts, was financed by the new Boston Manufacturing Company with an initial paid-up capital of $300,000, to be doubled within a decade. Many of the financial surpluses described in Greene's letter seem likely to have been contributed.

112. JCBL Box 160, f.10, Charles Greene of Boston, to Brown & Ives, Providence RI, 12 March 1814.
113. Ibid.
114. *AC*: 13–2, 2012–13.
115. JCBL Box 160, f.10, Charles Greene of Boston to Brown & Ives, Providence RI, 12 March 1814. 5% would yield £750.00 net p.a., then worth about $3,300. This correspondence appears to refute the claim that references to a drain of American specie 'lack provenance or even logical support, quite probably because no such drain of specie existed'. See W. Dudley, 'Without Some Risk: A Reassessment of the British Blockade of the United States, 1812–1815', PhD dissertation, Tuscaloosa, Univ. of Alabama, 1999, p. 240.
116. *AC*: 13–2, 1526; 1534–6. John Jackson was Madison's step-son in law.
117. JCBL Box 161, f.1, Charles Greene, Boston, to Brown & Ives, Providence RI, 3 August 1814.
118. Hickey, *The War of 1812*, p. 224. See Hickey's note 40, p. 409.
119. Crawford, *The Naval War of 1812*, vol. III, p. 786–7; p. 321, *Columbia*, 53 guns, was ready for launch, *Argus* had received its crew in June. Net costs after reclamation operations, citing National Archives, Washington, M125/40, Commodore Tingey to Secretary of the Navy Jones, 9 Nov. 1814.
120. Niles' *Weekly Register*, Baltimore, vol. VII, Supplement, p. 176. 'Proclamation to the Public, Philadelphia, August 31 1814', signed by the Presidents of the Pennsylvania, North America, Philadelphia, Farmer's and Mechanic's, Commercial and Merchant's banks.
121. TNA ADM 1/507, pp. 160–68, Capt. James Gordon's squadron escaped downriver.
122. JCBL Box 161, f.2, Charles Greene to Brown & Ives, Boston, 6 and 12 September 1814.
123. *AC*: 13–3, 1, and Appendix, 'State of the Finances', pp. 1486–7. G. Campbell, Treasury Department, 23 September 1814.
124. JCBL Box 236, f.6, T. P. Ives of Providence to J. Maybin of Philadelphia, 5 October 1814.
125. JCBL Box 236, f.6, J. Maybin to T. Ives, 12 October 1814.
126. Nettels, *National Economy*, pp. 333, and 338.
127. A. Gallatin, H. Adams, ed., *The Writings of Albert Gallatin*, Philadelphia, J. P. Lippincott, 1879, vol. III, p. 283, 285–6; and G. Campbell *AC*: 13–3, 1486–7, 23 September 1814.
128. *ASP*: F, vol. II, p. 878.
129. Seybert, *Statistical Annals*, p. 749; and Niles' *Weekly Register*, Baltimore, vol. VII, Supplement, p. 176.
130. JCBL OS/04577. *An Account of the Receipts and Expenditures of the United States for the Year 1813*, Washington DC, A. & G. Way, 1814.
131. The government accounts total the nominal value of stock issued at $18,109,377, possibly net of commission.
132. *ASP*: F, II, pp. 644, 661–2.
133. JCBL Box 236, f.6, John Maybin to B & I in Providence RI, dated Philadelphia, 26 April 1814. Maybin previously mentions a shipowner's failure, and 'losses made on sugar, and no sales in Tea'.
134. JCBL Box 236, f.6, Thomas Ives to John Maybin, dated Providence RI 4 May 1814.
135. *AC*: 13–3 Appendix. 'State of the Finances', p. 1493; Jones to Madison, dated Navy Department, 6 May 1814, Crawford, *The Naval War of 1812*, vol. III, p. 462; and D. Gilchrist, ed., *The Growth of the Seaport Cities, 1790–1825*, Charlottesville VA, Univ. of Virginia Press, 1967, pp. 106–7. Jacob Barker's New York Exchange Bank was to fail in 1819; his petitions for loan commissions at a quarter of 1% continued until 1821; see also *ASP*: C, p. 828, 21 December 1821.
136. JCBL, *An Account of the Receipts and Expenditures of the United States for the Year 1814*, Washington DC, A. & G. Way, 1815. These accounts also show that the February 1813

issue of $5m of Treasury notes brought in only $1,070,000; and of the $7.5m Loan sought on 2 August 1813 only $3,907,335 had been received by 1815, no mention being made of the still outstanding balance. This contradicts earlier and subsequent claims that the $7.5m loan was met, although at a discount. See also *ASP*: F, vol. II, p. 845. Of the first $10m of the $25m sought in March 1814, the Treasury only ever received $7,935,581. By November 1815, loan subscriptions may have been recorded in specie values only, excluding discounted paper money, although this is not specified.

137. Crawford, *The Naval War of 1812*, vol. III, p. 462, Sect. of Navy Jones to Madison, dated Navy Dept., 6 May 1814. Jones had also been Secretary of the Treasury until 9 February 1814.

138. R. Guernsey, *New York City & Vicinity during the War of 1812-15, being a Military, Civic and Financial Local History of that Period*, New York, Charles Woodward, 1889-95, vol. II, p. 270, Jacob Barker to General John Armstrong, Sect. of War, 17 May 1814.

139. I. Brandt, *James Madison, Commander in Chief 1812-36*, New York, Bobbs-Merrill & Co Inc., 1961, vol. 6, p. 259, Madison to Campbell, 25 May 1814.

140. JCBL, *An Account of the Receipts and Expenditures for the Year 1814*. Of $6m, subscribers actually offered only $3,452,300 and paid only $2,520,300. For the $6m call see also: *AC*: 13-3, 1484-6.

141. Dewey, *Financial History*, p. 134.

142. *ASP*: F, vol. II, pp. 845-7.

143. JCBL, *An Account of the Receipts and Expenditures for the Year 1814*. The 4 March issue of $10m of Treasury notes actually brought in only $7,227,280.

144. National Library of Scotland MS 2333, ff.54-9, Rear-Adm. Cockburn to Vice-Adm. Cochrane, dated *Albion* in Tangier Bay, Chesapeake, 9 May 1814.

145. Brandt, *James Madison*, p. 268, quoting Louis Serurier, French Minister at Washington, to Leforest, 27 June 1814.

146. LC Papers of James Madison online. 'James Madison to Cabinet, June 23, 1814. Includes note from June 27, 1814', p. 94.

147. LC Papers of James Madison online. 'James Madison to Cabinet, June 23, 1814. Includes note from June 27, 1814', pp. 94-5, 141. See also G. Hunt, ed., *The Writings of James Madison comprising his public and private papers and his private correspondence*, New York, G. Putnam's Sons, vol. 8: 1808-19, 1908, p. 281.

148. LC Papers of James Madison online. 'James Madison to Cabinet, June 23, 1814. Includes note from June 27, 1814', pp. 94-5; 141. On 23 June the Cabinet was also asked 'Shall a treaty be authorised comprising an article referring the subject of impressment along with that of commerce to a separate negotiation?' 'Monroe, Campbell, Armstrong & Jones aye – Rush for awaiting further information from Europe.' Monroe wrote to the US PCs on 25 June 1814 with this proposal, to be superceded by that of 27 June. See JHL Jonathan Russell Corr: Sect of State Monroe to PCs. Richard Rush was the newly appointed Attorney General.

149. JHL A30901 Jonathan Russell Corr; Secretary of State Monroe to Peace Commissioner Jonathan Russell, Washington, 27 June 1814, annotated as received 10 August 1814; also *ASP*: FR, vol. III, p. 704, letter from Sect. of State Monroe to American Peace Commissioners, 27 June 1814.

150. National Library of Scotland MS 2333 f.54, Letter No. 3, from Rear-Adm. Cockburn to Vice-Adm. Cochrane dated Tangier Bay, Chesapeake, 9 May 1814.

151. Hunt, *The Writings of James Madison*, pp. 244-7, 'Madison's Message to a Special Session of Congress, Washington, 25 May 1813'.

152. Ibid., p. 278. Letter from Madison to Campbell, 'Private, Montpelier, 25 May 1814'. Campbell had succeeded Jones as Secretary of the Treasury on 9 February 1814.

153. NYHS Gallatin Papers I, reel 9, letter 115, p. 1, Campbell to Wilhelm and Jan Willink of Amsterdam, dated August 1, 1814. This letter does not specify the amount sought, but authorises Gallatin, Adams and Crawford, 'ministers of the United States in Europe or either of them', to 'negociate' a loan, for which 6% stock worth $6m 'has been constituted', and made out to the Willinks. Crawford claimed, in a post-script to his

letter to Gallatin in Ghent, dated Paris, 26 September 1814, that he had checked the stock, and found it 'substantially correct', but by 16 November Gallatin complained that only $3m worth of US stock had reached Europe, and no funds to pay either the interest on Louisiana stock, due on January 1, or 'diplomatic advances' on which to live. Both of the last two difficulties were later resolved by the British banker Alexander Baring, via the Willinks. See also NYHS GP II, letters 161/1–2, 168/4, and 175/1.

154. BL Add MSS 38259, ff.91–3, Liverpool Papers, Memorandum to Prime Minister, Treasury Chambers, 2nd September 1814.

155. Ibid.

156. *AC*: 13–3, 1.

157. J. Bioran, W. Duane and R. Weightman, *Laws of the United States of America from 4th March 1789 to 4th March 1815*, Philadelphia and Washington DC, 2nd edn, 1816, vol. IV, p. 761.

158. *AC*: 13–3, 14, Madison's Presidential Message to Congress, 20 September 1814.

159. Hickey, *The War of 1812*, p. 222, Jones to Dallas, 15 September 1814.

160. *AC*: 13–3, 1479, Appendix, 'State of the Finances', September 23 1814.

161. *AC*: 13–3, 14.

162. *AC*: 13–3, 1482–6.

163. *AC*: 13–3, 1486; and *ASP*: F, vol. II, p. 842.

164. *AC*: 13–3, 1488.

165. *AC*: 13–3, 1487.

166. NYHS Gallatin Papers I, reel 9, 141/1, Gallatin to W. and J. Willink, dated Ghent, 3 October 1814.

167. NYHS Gallatin Papers I, reel 9, 144/1, Crawford to Gallatin, in Ghent, dated Paris, 6 October 1814; and 144/3, referring to a comment, presumably made in either Paris or Vienna, by 'the Prince of Benevent', once Bishop of Autun, better known as Talleyrand. The name is here practically indecipherable.

168. NYHS Gallatin Papers I, reel 9, 146/1, Wilhelm Willink and Nicholas van Staphorst, dated 'Amsterdam 11 October 1814' to Gallatin and Adams in Ghent. Some, e.g. R. Walters, *Albert Gallatin: Jeffersonian Financier and Diplomat*, New York, Macmillan, 1957, cite this letter as dated 14 October 1814. In comparison with the 5% interest rate charged on British loans to Russia and Prussia, 4% to Denmark and 2.5% on 25m guilders for the Dutch government, the 6% offered by the US was high, especially in view of Russia's failure to pay either interest or principal since 1812. See NYHS Gallatin Papers I, reel 9, 146/3.

169. NYHS Gallatin Papers I, reel 9, 146/3. For the date of the Anglo-Dutch peace treaty see C. Crawley, ed., *The New Cambridge Modern History Volume IX War and Peace in an Age of Upheaval 1793–1830*, Cambridge, Cambridge Univ. Press, 1974, p. 672n.

170. NYHS Gallatin Papers I, reel 9, 152/1, Crawford, dated Paris 25 October 1814, to Gallatin and Adams in Ghent. The letter is partially decoded, other parts respond to scrutiny.

171. NYHS Gallatin Papers I, reel 9, 153, Gallatin and Adams, dated Ghent 26 October 1814, to Campbell, Secretary of the Treasury, Washington.

172. NYHS Gallatin Papers I, reel 9, 154/1–3, Gallatin, dated Ghent, 26 October 1814, to Campbell, Secretary of the Treasury, Washington.

173. NYHS Gallatin Papers II, Letterbook II, pp. 215–19, p. 218, Gallatin, dated Ghent, 26 October 1814, to Monroe, Sect. of State.

174. J. Stagg, *Mr Madison's War: Politics, Diplomacy, and Warfare in the Early American Republic 1783–1830*, Princeton, Princeton Univ. Press, 1983, p. 432, citing Campbell to Madison, September 28 1814, LC Papers of James Madison.

175. *ASP*: F, vol. II, p. 868.

176. JCBL Box 161, f.3, Greene to Ives, dated Boston, 29 October 1814. On 16 October 1814 Jones had written to Madison 'Seamen unpaid & not a dollar to move them'. See Brandt, *James Madison*, vol. 6, p. 345.

177. *ASP*: F, vol. II, p. 866.

178. Technically, insolvency, rather than bankruptcy, which applies only to individuals actually declared so. For political reasons, domestic and international, few administrations would actually admit to being unable to pay their creditors, preferring an apparently short-term explanation such as Dallas's alleged shortage of available specie.

179. Niles' *Weekly Register*, Baltimore, vol. VII, p. 270, 24 December 1814.

180. *ASP: F*, vol. II, p. 872, Dallas to Lowndes, 27 November 1814.

181. NYHS Gallatin Papers I, reel 9, 168/4 and 175/1, Baring to Gallatin, dated London, 29 November 1814; and Gallatin to W. & J. Willink, and N., J. & R. van Staphorst, dated Ghent, 9 December 1814. Baring provided, via the Willinks, 300,000 guilders, then about £30,000 or $132,000, for the Louisiana loan stock interest, and another 100,000 guilders, then about £10,000 or $44,000, for 'diplomatic advances' for the envoy's living costs. See also Adams, *Writings of Albert Gallatin*, vol. I, p. 644, Gallatin to Dallas, Ghent, 24 December 1814.

182. *ASP: F*, vol. II, p. 878.

183. *AC*: 13–3, Appendix, 1501–2, 'Statement of A. J. Dallas Sect. of Treas. Feb. 6 1815', Hertslet L. and E., London, J. Ridgway & Sons, 1841, British and Foreign State Papers 1816–17, p. 512; see also *An Account of the Receipts and Expenditures for the Year 1814*. Boston State Bank was not to be repaid until 30 September 1816, and then only $130,000 were drafts for cash, the remaining $370,000 was in interest-bearing Treasury notes.

184. Ibid.

185. JCBL Box 161, f.4, Greene to Ives, Boston, 14 December 1814.

186. JCBL Box 161, f.4, Greene to Ives, Boston, 29 December 1814.

187. NYHS Gallatin Papers I, reel 9, 182/1–2, W. Willink and N. van Staphorst to A. Gallatin and J. Bayard at Ghent, dated Amsterdam 14 December 1814. A note under the address reads 'should be Gallatin & Adams'. The exchange rate was fixed at 50 stuivers to the dollar; there appear to have been 20 stuivers to the guilder in 1814/15. The £ was officially $4.44 to the $. Speculation on the buyer's identity centres on the family firm of Parish of Hamburg, and its associates; see E. Perkins, *American Public Finance and Public Services 1700–1815*, Columbus OH, Ohio State Univ. Press, 1994, pp. 334–5, cited below.

188. Dudley Wade., op. cit., p. 229, footnote 25; see also Perkins, *American Public Finance*, pp. 334–5.

189. NYHS Gallatin Papers I, reel 9, 189, Gallatin and Adams to A. J. Dallas, Secretary of the Treasury, dated Ghent, 25 December 1814.

190. Hickey, *The War of 1812*, p. 194, citing B. Lohnes, 'A New Look at the Invasion of Eastern Maine, 1814', *Maine Historical Society Quarterly* 15, 1975. Sir John Sherbrooke had been ordered in June 1814 to occupy 'that part of the District of Maine which at present intercepts the communication between Halifax and Quebec'.

191. L. and E. Hertslet, *British & Foreign State Papers: Compiled by the Librarian and Keeper of Papers for the Foreign Office*, London, J. Ridgway & Sons Ltd, 1841, vol. I, 1812–14, part II, 1841, pp. 1396–71, 'Proclamation of C in C British Military and Naval Forces, North America, 21 September 1814'.

192. Niles' *Weekly Register*, Baltimore, vol. 7, pp. 117–18.

193. B. Mitchell and P. Deane, *Abstract of British Historical Statistics*, Cambridge, Cambridge Univ. Press, 1962, table 12, 'Values at Current Prices of UK Overseas Trade According to Region', p. 313. Sadly, the figure for 1813, for comparison, is unavailable.

194. Hickey, *The War of 1812*, p. 227.

195. Crawford, *The Naval War of 1812*, vol. III, p. 66, Rear-Adm. Cockburn to Vice-Adm. Cochrane, dated *Albion* in Tangier Bay, Chesapeake, 10 May 1814.

196. Ibid., p. 136, Cockburn to Cochrane, dated *Albion* off Jerome's Point Patuxent 17 July 1814.

197. Ibid., p. 351, note; Joshua Barney to Secretary of the Navy Jones, Baltimore, 10 and 26 October 1814.

198. Ibid., p. 668, Secretary of the Navy Jones to Navy Agent John Bullus, dated Navy Department, 20 November 1814.
199. Ibid., pp. 686–7 note; Adam and Noah Brown to Secretary of the Navy Benjamin Crowningshield, dated New York, 15 January 1815. Requisitions of Navy agents, going back over three months, totalling $800,000, had had to be 'laid over again'. See Brandt, *James Madison*, vol. 6, p. 345.
200. JCBL, *An Account of the Receipts and Expenditures for the Year 1814*, p. 61.
201. Seybert, *Statistical Annals*, p. 549. The US Mint struck $3,578 30c in cents in 1814, and none in 1815; see also P. Smith, *America's Copper Coinage 1783–1857*, pp. 149–74.
202. JCBL Box 236, f.6, B & I to John Maybin, 6 July 1814.
203. *ASP*: C&N, vol. 1, p. 1018; Mahan, *Sea Power*, vol. II, pp. 179–83.
204. Hickey, *The War of 1812*, p. 230, citing *Synopsis of Debates in the Massachusetts Legislature*, Boston, 11 October 1814.
205. JCBL Box 236, f.6, John Maybin of Philadelphia to B & I in Providence, RI, 12 October 1814.
206. Ibid., B & I to John Maybin, 6 July 1814.
207. Ibid., John Maybin to Thomas Ives, of Providence RI, dated Philadelphia, 22 August, 5 September and 12 October 1814.
208. Hickey, *The War of 1812*, p. 269, quoting Salem *Gazette*, 23 September 1814.
209. H. Adams, *History of the United States during the Administration of Jefferson and Madison*, New York, Charles Scribner's Sons, 1889–96, vol. VIII, p. 225.
210. BL C *Columbian Centinel*, Boston, 9 November 1814.
211. *AC*: 13–3, 612, 17 November 1814.
212. Adams, op. cit., p. 1070, 1986 ed., citing Kennedy's *Life of Wirt*, vol. 1, p. 339, Wirt to Mrs Wirt, dated 14 October 1814; Hickey, *The War of 1812*, p. 231, citing Wm. Wirt Papers Maryland Historical Society, r.2, dated October 25 1814, reading 'revolt' in place of 'sedition'.
213. NYHS Gallatin Papers II, Letterbook II, Gallatin to Monroe, June 14 1814. Gallatin warns of a British intention to attack coastal towns; see also Stagg, *Mr Madison's War*, p. 473.
214. JCBL Box 236, f.7, Thomas Ives to John Maybin, 20 January 1815. The Convention had ended on 5 January 1815.
215. *AC*: 13–3, H of R, pp. 381–3, 393; Senate, pp. 24, 28. Madison first mentioned the Cabinet instructions to the Peace Commissioners of 25 and 27 June and in messages to Congress, on 10 October as to be 'the subject of another communication'. They were read to a closed session of the Senate on 13 October 1814. On 14 October copies were read to a House emptied of strangers and, with certain omissions, ordered to be printed for 'transmission to Congress', and recorded in *ASP*: FR, vol. III, p. 695. The suggestion that Congress was first told of them on 1 December 1814 (e.g. Stagg, *Mr Madison's War*, p. 462), is mistaken, since they were discussed by the House Ways and Means Committee during October 1814. See *AC*: 13–3, pp. 429–38.
216. *AC*: 13–3, p. 383.
217. JHL A30899 Jonathan Russell Corr., Monroe to American Peace Commissioners at Ghent, Washington, 25 June 1814.
218. JHL A30899(i) Jonathan Russell Corr., Monroe to Peace Commissioners, postscript to above.
219. Adams, *Writings of Albert Gallatin*, vol. I, p. 602, Gallatin to Crawford, American Minister at Paris, London, 21 April 1814.
220. Ibid., vol. I, pp. 606–7, Gallatin to Clay, dated London, 22 April 1814.
221. Brandt, *James Madison*, p. 267, citing LC Papers of James Madison, Beasley to Jones, dated London, 18 May 1814. Reuben Beasley was the London agent for American prisoners of war held in Britain.
222. Adams, *Writings of Albert Gallatin*, p. 612, Gallatin and Bayard to Monroe, dated London, 6 May 1814.
223. *ODNB*, vol. 21, pp. 352–4. Gambier had been C-in-C Newfoundland, and commanded at Copenhagen in 1807.

224. Brandt, *James Madison*, p. 267.
225. JHL A30901 Jonathan Russell Corr., Monroe to Peace Commissioners, Washington, 27 June 1814.
226. Adams, *Writings of Albert Gallatin*, pp. 627–8, Gallatin to Monroe, London, 13 June 1814.
227. *AC*: 13–3, p. 383, 10 October 1814.
228. *AC*: 13–3, 877–81, Appendix, p. 1481, actually $47,270,172; *ASP*: F, vol. II p. 885, actual expenditure $57,694,590, receipts $40,007,661; Dewey's figure for 1814's expenditure is that for only the 9 months ending 30 June 1814; for proposed income tax, see *ASP*: F, vol. II, p. 873.
229. Seybert, *Statistical Annals*, p. 464.
230. *ASP*: F, vol. II, p. 879, 'Schedule of Treasury Notes, which have already fallen due & remain unpaid, this 2nd day of December 1814'. See Appendix B 34 (p. 249), Treasury notes outstanding at year's end, 1811–17.
231. Hickey, *The War of 1812*, p. 247–8, citing *ASP*: F, vol. III, p. 121.
232. JCBL Box 236, f.6, Ives to Maybin, 29 November 1814. A second United States Bank had been proposed to the Ways and Means Committee on 10 October 1814 by its chairman, John Eppes of Virginia, a son-in-law of Jefferson's.
233. *ASP*: F, vol. II, p. 867. Congress had failed to renew the first US Bank's charter in 1811.
234. Niles' *Weekly Register*, Baltimore, vol. VII, Supplement p. 176; and Seybert, *Statistical Annals*, p. 749, 'A Statement of the Prices quoted in Philadelphia for the evidence of the public Debt', prices of new and old US 6% stock during 1813–15.
235. JCBL Box 236, f.7, Ives to Maybin, 21 January 1815.
236. *ASP*: F, vol. II, pp. 885–9.
237. Hickey, *The War of 1812*, p. 247, quoting George Ticknor to Edward Channing, 22 January 1815, in S. Hillard et al., eds, *Life, Letters, and Journals of George Ticknor*, Boston, James R. Osgood and Co., 1876, vol. 1, pp. 30–31.
238. Dewey, *Financial History*, p. 136.
239. Adams and Agar, *The History of the United States*, vol. II, p. 943.
240. TNA ADM 1/506, 30 December 1814.
241. J. McCusker, *How Much is That in Real Money? A historical price index for use as a deflator of money values in the economy of the United States*, Worcester MA, American Antiquarian Society, 1992, p. 326. Reprinted from *Proceedings of the American Antiquarian Society*, 101 (2), 1991.
242. H. Rockoff, 'Banking and Finance 1789–1914', in *The Cambridge Economic History of the United States, vol. II: The Long Nineteenth Century*, eds S. Engerman and R. Gallman, Cambridge, Cambridge Univ. Press, 2000, pp. 654–5, including table 14.1, 'Money and Prices in the War of 1812'.
243. JCBL Box 236, f.7, Maybin to Ives, 5 January 1815.
244. D. North, *The Economic Growth of the United States 1790–1860*, New York, Prentice Hall Inc., 1961; repr. New York, W. Norton & Co Inc., 1966: Export Price Index, p. 221, Table C-III; Import Price Index, p. 229, Table F-III; Terms of Trade, p. 229, Table G-III. The terms of trade shown in the 1966 edition use the method of calculation generally adopted after 1963, i.e. an index of export prices divided by a comparable index of import prices, multiplied, for the convenience of whole numbers, by 100, which gives a *rising* favourable index, and *falling* adverse terms of trade.
245. L. Davis and S. Engerman, *Naval Blockades in Peace and War: An Economic History since 1750*, Cambridge, Cambridge Univ. Press, 2006, p. 91, citing D. Adams, 'American Neutrality and Prosperity 1793–1808: A Reconsideration', *Journal of Economic History*, 40, 1980, p. 718.
246. Davis and Engerman, *Naval Blockades*, pp. 80–81, citing Adams, 'American Neutrality and Prosperity', p. 736–7.
247. North, *Economic Growth of the United States*, p. 31.
248. Pitkin, *A Statistical View*, p. 363. The actual fall between 1811 and 1814 is 94.03%.

249. North, *Economic Growth of the United States*, p. 249, an actual fall of 93.6%.
250. R. Lipsey, 'U.S. Trade and Balance of Payments 1800–1913', in *The Cambridge Economic History of the United States, vol. II, The Long Nineteenth Century*, eds S. Engerman and R. Gallman, 3 vols, Cambridge Univ. Press, 2000, table 15.21, p. 718.
251. G. Dangerfield, *The Era of Good Feelings*, London, Methuen, 1953, p. 12.
252. JCBL Box 236, f.7, 6 February 1815.
253. Hickey, *The War of 1812*, p. 298. Ratifications were exchanged between Secretary of State James Monroe and Anthony Baker, newly arrived in Washington, citing T. Hansard *The Parliamentary Debates from 1803 to the Present Time*, London, vol. 30, p. 218.
254. JCBL Box 236, f.7, 15 February 1815.
255. BL *Parliamentary Papers*, vol. IX, pp. 481–8, Nos 3 & 4, 'Papers Relating to War with America, Admiralty Office, Ordered by the House of Commons to be Printed 9 & 10 February 1815'.
256. BL *Parliamentary Papers*, vol. IX, p. 489, No. 5, Admiralty Office, 1 February 1815.
257. Russell, *The history of the war*, pp. 377–402, in US Coast Guard Academy Lib. New London, Conn. A copy of Russell's list in the John Hay Library, Providence, RI, gives 1,607 British prizes; the extra five may have been added to later editions. However, Lloyd's of London calculated British wartime losses as 1,175 vessels, of which 373, i.e. 31.74%, were later recaptured. Many of the captures recorded in Russell's list were probably uninsured by owners deterred by high insurance premiums, although apparently no higher between 1812 and 1814 than in 1810–11. See N. Rodger, *The Command of the Ocean: A Naval History of Britain 1649–1815*, London, Penguin/Allen Lane/NMM, 2004, p. 569.
258. Mitchell and Deane, *Abstract of British Historical Statistics*, calculated from table: Transport 1, 'Shipping Registered in the United Kingdom 1788–1938', p. 217.
259. Kert, 'The Fortunes of War', p. 2, citing E. Maclay; and Mitchell and Deane, *Abstract of British Historical Statistics*, calculated from table: Overseas Trade 2, 'Official Values and Values at Current Prices of Overseas Trade United Kingdom 1796–1853, Computed or Declared Values', p. 282. Conversion at the then official $4.44 to £1.
260. W. James, *Warden Refuted, being a defence of the British Navy against the misrepresentations of a work recently published at Edinburgh: a letter to D. B. Warden Esq., late Consul to the United States at Paris*, London, J. M. Richardson, 1819, p. 42, see also Colonial Papers, House of Commons, London, FCO: No. 4, 1813–15, and No. 7, Admiralty Office, 1 February 1815.
261. BL *Parliamentary Papers*, vol. IX, p. 490, No. 7, Adm. Office, 1 February 1815.
262. TNA ADM 1/504, p. 341, Cmdr. Rich. Coote, HMS *Borer*, 12, off Martha's Vineyard, 22 October 1813, to Capt. Robt. Oliver, HMS *Valiant*, 74.
263. Whitehill, *Journal of Lieutenant Henry Napier*, pp. 22–36, June–July 1814. The American *Welcome Return*, for example, had been ransomed by HMS *Nymphe* in June 1814 for $3,500.
264. BL *Parliamentary Papers*, vol. IX, p. 490, No. 7, Adm. Office, 1 February 1815.
265. Calculated from data in BL *Parliamentary Papers*, vol. IX, p. 490, and Nettels, *National Economy*, table 21, p. 399. The Royal Navy had taken or destroyed 546 American merchant vessels of known tonnage, totalling 77,625 tons, giving an average of 142.17 tons. Therefore, the 59,626 tons of American merchant shipping still engaged in the foreign trade of the US by 1814, according to Nettels, represents only 419 vessels of average size.
266. Ibid. Actually 28.56%.
267. A. Gutridge, 'Prize Agency 1800–1815 with special reference to the career and work of George Redmond Hulbert', unpublished MPhil dissertation, Univ. of Portsmouth, 1989, p. 137. Warren had gained personally just over £51,400, less than the £100,000 earned by Pellew and Keith in other theatres. Another £46,000 had been shared by Warren's junior flag officers. I am grateful to Tony Gutridge for his very helpful correspondence in 2008.

268. Nettels, *National Economy*, table 21, p. 399.
269. US Bureau of the Census, supplement to *Historical Statistics of the United States: Colonial Times to 1957*, Washington 1960, Series Q192–4, p. 415.
270. North, *Economic Growth of the United States*, Chart III-IV, p. 42, and Appendix I, Table C-IV, p. 231, originally North, 'United States Balance of Payments', Appendix A, Table A3.
271. US Bureau of the Census, supplement to *Historical Statistics of the United States: Colonial Times to 1957*, Washington, 1960, Series Q192–4, p. 415.
272. J. Mahon, *The War of 1812*, Gainesville FL, Univ. of Florida Press, 1972, republ. De Capo Press, 1991, p. 385; and Hickey, *The War of 1812*, p. 303.
273. Hickey, *The War of 1812*, p. 303, citing US Bureau of the Census, *Historical Statistics of the United States*, vol. 2, p. 1140; and US Dept. of the Treasury, *Report of the Secretary of the Treasury for 1866*, p. 304; Report of the Ways and Means Committee, 13 April 1830 in *Register of Debates in Congress*, 29 vols, 1825–37, 21–1, Appendix 115.
274. Dewey, *Financial History*, p. 141.
275. US Bureau of the Census, *Historical Statistics of the United States*, Washington, 1975, vol. 2, p. 1140.
276. Wellington, 2nd Duke, ed., *Supplementary Despatches, Correspondence and Memoranda of Field Marshall Arthur Duke of Wellington*, London, John Murray, 1858–72, vol. IX, p. 240, Liverpool to Bathurst, 11 September 1814.
277. Hickey, *The War of 1812*, p. 303; and BL *British Parliamentary Papers*, vol. IX, p. 490, No. 6.
278. T. James, *Prisoners of War in Dartmoor Towns: French and American Officers on Parole, 1803–1815*, Newton Abbot, Orchard Publications, 2000, pp. 3, 22–3, 45, and Horsman, *The War of 1812*, p. 264.
279. M. Haines, 'The Population of the United States, 1790–1920', in *The Cambridge Economic History of the United States, Volume II – The Long Nineteenth Century*, eds S. Engerman and R. Gallman, 3 vols, Cambridge, Cambridge Univ. Press, 2000, table 4.2, p. 156; see also North, *Economic Growth of the United States*, pp. 48 and 62. Both estimate that, in 1810, the US population was 7.3% urban and, by 1820, only 7.2%.
280. Adams, op. cit., vol. VIII, p. 1087, Jefferson to Short, 28 November 1814, citing *Works of Thomas Jefferson*, vol. VI, p. 398.
281. AC: 13–2, 1442, 1497; and *National Advocate*, New York, 20 February 1815, quoted by Hickey, *The War of 1812*, p. 437.
282. J. Gurwood, ed., *The Dispatches of Field Marshall the Duke of Wellington, 1799–1818*, London, 1834–9, vol. 9, p. 495, Liverpool to Castlereagh, 23 December 1814.
283. Stagg, *Mr Madison's War*, pp. 481–2. Apparently believing that New England was in a position to defy the Union, Monroe briefly allocated volunteers and funds towards resisting its possible secession.
284. C. Vane, ed., *Correspondence, Despatches and other Papers of Viscount Castlereagh*, 3rd Series, London, H. Colburn, 1848–53, vol. 10, pp. 67–9, 'Headings of Negotiation to Commissioners at Ghent'.
285. W. James, *A full and correct account of the military occurrences of the late war between Great Britain and the United States of America*, London, James Richardson, 1818, vol. 2, includes the complete text of the Treaty of Ghent. It is also included in J. Russell, *The history of the war*.
286. NYHS Gallatin Papers II, Letterbook II, pp. 215–19, Letter 10, Gallatin to Monroe, Ghent, 25 December 1814.
287. Adams, *Writings of Albert Gallatin*, vol. I, pp. 606–7, Gallatin to Clay, 22 April 1814.
288. BL C *National Intelligencer*, Washington, 17 January 1815, probably written by Joseph Gales, co-proprietor and editor.
289. AC: 12–1, 831, Adam Seybert, Republican Representative for Philadelphia, to Congress, 18 January 1812.

RESULTS AND CONCLUSIONS

1. *ASP*: F, vol. II, p. 867.
2. US Bureau of the Census, supplement to *Historical Statistics of the United States: Colonial Times to 1957*, Washington, n.d., Series Q192–4, p. 415.
3. L. Davis and S. Engerman, *Naval Blockades in Peace and War: An Economic History Since 1750*, Cambridge, Cambridge Univ. Press, 2006, p. 79, table 3.5, citing US Bureau of the Census, *Historical Statistics of the United States from Colonial Times to 1970*, Washington, Government Printing Office, 2 vols, 1975. Series Q 425–432, p. 750.
4. J. Mahon, *The War of 1812*, Gainesville FL, Univ. of Florida Press, 1972, republ. Da Capo Press, 1991, p. 385.
5. M. Hammond, *The Cotton Culture and the Cotton Trade*, New York, Macmillan, 1897, p. 242; actually 91.78%.
6. R. Zevin, *The Growth of Manufacturing in Early Nineteenth Century New England*, New York, Arno, 1975, table 1, 'Cotton Industry Output 1805–1860', p. 8. Output actually fell by 64.38% in 1816. For lost military demand see Mahon, *The War of 1812*, p. 227. Before around 1820, power-looms were generally water driven.
7. C. Wright, *Economic History of the United States*, 2nd edn, New York, McGraw-Hill, 1949, pp. 320–21.
8. H. Habakkuk, 'Britain and America: the economic effects of labour scarcity', in *Britain and America: Studies in Comparative History 1760–1970*, ed. D. Englander, New York and Milton Keynes, Yale Univ. Press/Open Univ. Press, 1997, p. 62.
9. *ASP*: F, vol. II, 'Revised Statement of the Public Debt', p. 839, and 'Receipts and Expenditure', p. 920; and *AC*: 12–3, 1493, and A. Seybert, *Statistical Annals*, Philadelphia, T. Dobson, 1818, 'A Statement of Loans Authorised by Acts of Congress', p. 535; and D. Dewey, *Financial History of the United States*, 12th edn, New York, Kelly, 1934, pp. 141–2. Only $0.6m of $3m authorised on 15 November 1814 was raised. *ASP*: F, vol. III, p. 121. Tax revenue and expenditure for 1815, including a loan of $18.5m authorised by Congress on 3 March 1815, is omitted here as being called for after the Treaty of Ghent was ratified on 17 February 1815.
10. E. Osborne, *Britain's Economic Blockade of Germany 1914–1919*, London, Frank Cass, 2004, pp. 8–9. Osborne notes that in March 1854 Britain eased its policy towards enemy property in neutral vessels, and in 1856 signed the Declaration of Paris which protected neutral goods (except contraband), under an enemy flag, and enemy goods (except contraband) under a neutral flag and banned privateering. Osborne argues that the British Foreign Office advocated its acceptance, seeing Britain as a trading neutral in future major wars. The US did not sign the Declaration which was, by the early 20th century, largely discredited; blockade remained as Britain's strongest potential weapon.
11. E. Keble-Chatterton, *The Big Blockade*, 3rd edn, London, Hurst & Blackett Ltd, 1938, p. 148–9.
12. NMM LBK/2, Report of Col. Barclay dated April 1813 in Warren to Melville, 5 June 1813.
13. R. Berens Matzke, 'Britain Gets Its Way: Power and Peace in Anglo-American Relations, 1838–1846', *War in History*, 8 (1), 2001, pp. 24–5, citing 'Defenceless Condition of the Southern Coast of the United States and Gulf of Mexico: Statement Submitted by the Chairman of the Committee on Naval Affairs to the House of Representatives, 27th Congress, 2nd session, 12th May 1842', published in B. Cooling, ed., *The New American State Papers: Military Affairs*, Wilmington DE, Scholarly Resources, 1979, vol. II, pp. 180–85.

EPILOGUE

1. A. Cooke, *Alistair Cooke's American Journey*, London, Allen Lane/Penguin, 2006, p. 256.
2. US War Department, *Instructions for American Servicemen in Britain*, Washington, 1942, republ. Oxford, Bodleian Library, Univ. of Oxford, 2004, p. 4.

BIBLIOGRAPHY

PRIMARY SOURCES

Manuscript sources

British Library
Add MSS 3464, ff. 28–31, Leeds Papers, English Minister at Copenhagen to Ld Holdernesse, Sect. of State for Northern Dept, February 1757, vol. CXLI, Egerton Papers
Add MSS 38248-9, Official Correspondence of 2nd Earl
Add MSS 38250, ff.193–8, Correspondence of Ld. Castlereagh
Add MSS 38255, ff. 43–4, Liverpool Papers, Warren to Prime Minister 16 November 1813
Add MSS 38259, ff. 91–3, Liverpool Papers, Memorandum to Prime Minister 2 Sept. 1814
Add MSS 38299, cc 20(4), Letter to Prime Minister from Mr C. Lyne 2 March 1813
Add MSS 38365, ff.153–4, Liverpool Papers, 'Headings of Negotiation to Commissioners at Ghent'
Add MSS 38572, Liverpool Papers

Brynmor Jones Library: University of Hull
Hotham Papers: Correspondence of Rear Adm. Hotham with Lords Commissioners of Admiralty and others, 1812–14
DDHO 7/1: Melville and Croker to Hotham, January 1813
DDHO 7/3: 2nd Sect. Barrow to Hotham, 1813–14
DDHO 7/4: Letter head, Bermuda, April 1814. 'Description of the Ships on the North American Station 26 July 1814'. Cochrane to Hotham, 28 July 1814, and routine orders
DDHO 7/45: Warren's Standing Orders North America Station, General Order, Bermuda, March 1813
DDHO 7/98

Huntington Library: San Marino, California
Melville Papers: reels 1 and 2, April 1812

John Carter Brown Library: Brown University, Providence RI
Brown & Ives Correspondence
Box 160: ff.6–7, ff.9–11, Correspondence of Thomas Poyton Ives of Providence, with Charles Greene, B & I agent in Boston
Box 161: ff.1–4, Greene to T. P. Ives, of B & I, Providence
Box 172: f.9, T. P. Ives to Joseph Head, of Boston, June 1813
Box 236: ff.2–3, 6–7, Correspondence of T. P. Ives with John Maybin of Philadelphia

John Hay Library: Providence RI
A30002: Jonathan Russell Correspondence
A30433: Jonathan Russell Correspondence

A30899: (1) Jonathan Russell Correspondence
A30901: Jonathan Russell Correspondence

Library of Congress, Washington DC
Papers of James Madison: reel 15, Gallatin to Madison, 5 March 1813, and online: to Cabinet, 23–27 June 1814
Record Book and Commonplace Book of James Dunn, 1811–13
'Blockade – Book of Regulations and Instructions'
Royal Navy Logbooks – HMS *Spartan*, 38

National Library of Scotland, Edinburgh
Alexander F. I. Cochrane Papers:
MS 2333, ff.54–9, Rear-Adm.Cockburn to Vice Adm. Cochrane, May 1814
MS 2343, Admiralty Letters 1813–1815, to Cochrane 30 December 1814

National Maritime Museum, London: Caird Library
Hulbert Papers: Correspondence of George Redmond Hulbert, Secretary and Prize Agent of Adm. Sir J.B. Warren, 1807–14:
HUL/1: Warren's Order Book
HUL/4: 'Copy of Vice-Admiralty Court Records, 25 November 1812–2 July 1814'
HUL/5B: Hulbert to Fraser, 14 March 1815
HUL/14
HUL/18: Appendix: 'List of Ships & Vessels on West Indies and American Stations, 7 August 1812'
Keith Papers: Private Correspondence of Adm. Lord Keith:
KEI/37/9: from Adm. George Hope, June 1812
Warren Papers:
LBK/2 Correspondence of Adm. John Borlase Warren, C in C North America and West India Stations 1812–14 to Robert Saunders
Dundas, 2nd Viscount, Lord Melville, First Lord of the Admiralty, 1812–27
WAR/11: 'Schedule of Orders in Council, Circular Orders, Letters etc delivered by Ad Rt: Hon:ble Sir J B Warren Bart KB to Vice Ad the Hon:ble Sir Alexander Cochrane KB at Bermuda the first day of April 1814'
WAR/27: 'Papers Relating to Convoys, Transports, Commerce & Trade, vol. 1, 1797–1813', inc. Castlereagh, and Andrew Allen to Warren, 1812
WAR/28: 'Papers Relating to Convoys, Transports & Trade, vol. 2, 1813–14'
WAR/37: 'Vessels captured & detained 2 June–13 Sept 1813'
WAR/43: Warren to Anthony Baker, British chargé d'affaire, Halifax
WAR/49
WAR/82: Melville/Warren correspondence, December 1812

The National Archives (TNA), Kew
ADM 1/501: January 1811
ADM 1/502: Routine Letters and Orders, Vice Adm. Sawyer to First Sect of the Adm. John Croker 5 July, 18 July, 5, 11 August, 16 September, 5 October, 4 November 1812
ADM 1/503
ADM 1/504
ADM 1/505
ADM 1/506: 2, 25, 28 April 1814, 30 May 1814
ADM 1/507: 12, 13 August 1812

ADM 1/1374: 26 December 1812

ADM 1/4220: Foreign Secretary Marquis Wellesley to Lords Commissioners of the Admiralty, January 1812

ADM 1/4221: Foreign Secretary Castlereagh to Lords Commissioners of the Admiralty, May 1812

ADM 1/4222: Foreign Secretary Castlereagh to Admiralty, August 1812

ADM 1/4359: 26–28 March 1813

ADM 2/933

ADM 2/1375: Secret Orders and Letters, 3 & 12 August, 18 November, 26 December 1812, and 9 January 1812

ADM 2/1376: 20, 26 March 1813

ADM 2/1378 4 November 1814

ADM 2/1380 20 March 1813, 30 April 1814, 31 May 1814

ADM 2/1381

ADM 8/100: Ships in Sea Pay, 1 July 1814

ADM 12/154: Digest, 12 August 1812, 25 November 1814

CO 43/49: Secretary of State for War Lord Bathurst to Admiralty November 1812

COC 11: Cockburn's Memoirs

FO 115/22: British Minister or chargé d'affaire, Washington, January–April 1811 to Foreign Office or Foreign Secretary Wellesley, January–March 1812

FO 115/23: Foreign Secretary Castlereagh to British Minister Washington, April 1812

FO 5/88: Baker to Castlereagh 18 December 1812, 3 February 1813

WO1/142: Vice Adm. Cochrane to Sect. of State for War, Ld Bathurst 12 August 1814

New York Historical Society
Gallatin Papers I, reel 9, April 1813–January 1815
Gallatin Papers II, Letterbook II, 1814–1815

Printed primary sources

Adams, H., *History of the United States during the Administrations of Jefferson and Madison*, 9 vols, New York, Charles Scribner's Sons, 1889–96

—, ed., *Memoirs of John Quincy Adams*, 4 vols, Philadelphia, J. P. Lippincott, 1874

—, ed., *The Writings of Albert Gallatin*, 3 vols, Philadelphia, J. P. Lippincott, 1879

— and Agar, H., ed., *The History of the United States during the Administrations of Jefferson and Madison: The Formative Years*, 2 vols, London, Collins, 1948

American State Papers: Documents, Legislative and Executive, of the Congress of the United States, 38 vols, Washington DC, Gales and Seaton, 1832–61: ASP: Part I: Foreign Relations, vols 1–3, Part III: Finance, vols 1–2, Part IV: Commerce & Navigation, vols 1–2 Part VI: Naval Affairs, Part IX: Claims, Part X: Miscellaneous. Online at http://memory.loc.gov/ammem/amlaw/lwsp.html

Allen, G. and Ely, J., *International Trade Statistics*, New York, John Wiley and Sons, 1953

An Account of the Receipts and Expenditures of the United States for the Year 1813, Washington DC, A. & G. Way, 1814

An Account of the Receipts and Expenditures of the United States for the Year 1814, Washington DC, A. & G. Way, 1815

Annals of Congress: formally *The Debates and Proceedings in the Congress of the United States*, New York, ed. D. Appleton, 1857–61: e.g. 12th Congress, 1st session, column 2354 cited as *AC*: 12–1, 2354. Online at http://memory.loc.gov/ammem/amlaw/lwac.html

Baring, A., *An Inquiry into the causes and consequences of the Orders in Council and an Examination of the Conduct of Great Britain towards the Neutral Commerce of America*, London, J. M. Richardson and J. Ridgway, 1808

Bioran, J., Duane W. and Weightman, R., *Laws of the United States of America from 4th March 1789 to 4th March 1815*, 5 vols, Philadelphia and Washington DC, 1st edn, 1815; 2nd edn, 1816

Brannan, J., *Official Letters of the Military & Naval Officers of the United States during the War with Great Britain in the years 1812,13,14 and 15*, Washington DC, 1823

Bristed, J., *The Resources of the United States of America; or a View of the agricultural, commercial ...moral and religious capacity and character of the American people*, New York, J. Eastburn & Co, 1818

British Parliamentary Papers: Parliamentary Reports: Diplomatic Correspondence between the American and British governments: 1810–1812, 4 parts; 1815, 3 parts. London, J. Ridgway & Sons Ltd, 1838–41

Cobbett's Parliamentary Debates/Hansard: vol. 21 January 1812–March 1812; London, Bagshaw, 1812–1813, vol. 22 March 1812–May 1812; vol. 23 May 1812–30 July 1812

Colonial Papers, House of Commons, London, FCO: vol. 3, 1809–1812; no. 4, 1813–1815, nos. 6 and 7

Cope, T., *Diary of a Philadelphia Merchant, 1800 –1820*, ed. Eliza Cope Harrison, South Bend IN, Gateway Editions, 1978

Crawford, M., ed., *The Naval War of 1812: A Documentary History*, Washington DC, Naval Historical Center, vol. III, 2002

Croker, J. W., *The Correspondence and Diaries of the late Right Hon. John Wilson Croker, Secretary to the Admiralty 1809–1830*, 2nd revised edn, 3 vols, London, John Murray, 1885

—, *A key to the orders in council respecting trade with French ports, etc. 7 Jan. 1807–21 April 1812*, London, John Murray, 1812

Davenant, C., *An essay upon the ways and means of supplying the war*, London, 1695

De Bow, J., *Compendium of 7th Census*, Washington DC, US Bureau of the Census, Senate Printer, 1854

—, *Statistical View of the United States*, Washington DC, A. Nicholson, 1854

The Declaration of Independence & the Constitution of the United States, with an introduction by P. Maier, New York, Bantam Dell, 1998, republ. 2008

Dudley, W., ed., *The Naval War of 1812: A Documentary History*, Washington DC, Naval Historical Center, vol. I, 1985, vol. II, 1992, vol. III, 2002

Essex Institute, *American Vessels Captured by the British during the Revolution and War of 1812: The Records of the Vice-Admiralty Court at Halifax, Nova Scotia*, Salem MA, 1911

Fenning, D., *A New Spelling Dictionary and Grammar of the English Language*, 2nd edn, London, S. Crowther, 1773

Gurwood, J., ed., *The Dispatches of Field Marshall the Duke of Wellington, 1799–1818*, London, 1834–9, 12 vols

Hansard, T., *The Parliamentary Debates from 1803 to the Present Time*, London, Longman 1st series 1803–20, vols 21–29, 1812–14/15

Hertslet, E. and L., eds, *British and Foreign State Papers: Compiled by the Librarian and Keeper of Papers for the Foreign Office*, London, J. Ridgway & Sons Ltd, 1841, vol. I, 1812–14, vol II, 1814–16

Holroyd, J., first Earl of Sheffield, *Observations on the Commerce of the American States*, London, 1783, republ. J. Debrett, 1784

Hopkins, J., ed., *The Papers of Henry Clay*, 10 vols, Lexington KT, Univ. of Kentucky Press, 1959, vol. I, *The Rising Statesman, 1794–1814*

Hunt, G., *The Writings of James Madison comprising his public and private papers and his private correspondence*, 9 vols, New York, G. Putnam's Sons, 1900–1910

James, W., *A Full and Correct Account of the Chief Naval Occurrences of the Late War between Great Britain and the United States of America*, London, T. Egerton, 1817

—, *A full and correct account of the military occurrences of the late war between Great Britain and the United States of America*, 2 vols, London, J. Richardson, 1818

—, *Naval Ocurrences of the War of 1812: A Full and Correct Account of the Naval War between Great Britain and the United States of America, 1812–1815*, with an introduction by Andrew Lambert, London, Conway Maritime Press, 2004

—, *The Naval History of Great Britain, from... 1793, to... 1820, with an Account of the Origin and Increase of the British Navy*, in 6 vols, vol. 6, new edn, London, Harding, Lepard, and Co, 1826, repr. Milton Keynes, Nabu Public Domain Reprints, 2010

—, *Warden Refuted: being a defence of the British Navy against the misrepresentations of a work recently published at Edinburgh: a letter to D. B. Warden Esq., late Consul to the United States at Paris*, London, J. M. Richardson, 1819

Lambert, J., *Travels through Canada, and the United States of North America in the years 1806, 1807 and 1808*, 3rd edn, London, Baldock, Craddock & Joy, 1816

Londonderry, Marquis, ed., *Memoirs and Correspondence of Viscount Castlereagh*, London, 1848–53 in 12 vols, vols IX–XI

Lyne, C., *A Letter to Lord Castlereagh on the North American Export Trade During the War and during any time the Import and Use of our Manufactures are interdicted in the United States*, London, J. Richardson, 1813

Marryat, J., *Concessions to America the Bane of Britain; or the Cause of the Present Distressed Situation of the British Colonial and Shipping Interests explained, and the Proper Remedy suggested*, London, 1807

Marshall, J., *Royal Naval Biography*, London, Longman et al., 1823, vol. 1

Mayo, B., ed., *Instructions to British Ministers to the United States 1791–1812*, 3 vols, Washington DC, Annual Report of the American History Association, 1936

Naval Chronicle vol. XXV January–June 1811; vol. XXVII January–June 1812; vol. XXVIII July–December 1812; vol. XXIX January–June 1813; vol. XXX July–December 1813; vol. XXXI January–June 1814; vol. XXXII July–December 1814; vol. XXXIII January–June 1815

Parliamentary Papers, vol. IX, 'Papers Relating to War with America, Ordered by the House of Commons to be Printed, 9 & 10 February 1815'

Parliamentary Papers of Interest to the Foreign Office 4, 1810–1815, Nos 1–31, London, Foreign Office

Peters, R., ed., *The Public Statutes at Large of the United States from the Origin of the Government in 1789 to March 3rd 1845*, 8 vols, Boston MA, Little & Brown, 1846–67

Pitkin, T., *A Statistical View of the Commerce of the United States of America*, 1st edn, Hartford, Charles Hosmer, 1816; 2nd edn, New York, James Eastburn & Co, 1817; 2nd edn, New Haven, Durrie & Peck, 1835

Richardson, J., *A Compilation of the Messages and Papers of the Presidents of the United States, 1789–1897*, Washington DC, Govt. Printing Office, 1896, vol. I

Robinson, C., *Reports of Cases heard in the High Court of Admiralty under Sir William Scott*, 6 vols, London, 1798–1808

—, *A translation of the chapters CCLXXIII and CCLXXXVII of the Consolato del mare, relating to prize law*, London, White & Butterworth, 1800

Russell, J., *The history of the war between the United States and Great-Britain To which is added ... a list of vessels taken from Great-Britain during the war*, 2nd edn, Hartford CT, B. & J. Russell, 1815

Seybert, A., *Statistical Annals*, Philadelphia, T. Dobson, 1818. BL: 579 i 24

Smith, A., *An Enquiry into the Nature and Causes of the Wealth of Nations*, first publ. London, W. Strahan & T. Cadell, 1776; see Everyman edn, London, Dent, 1966

State papers and publick documents of the United States, from the accession of George Washington to the presidency: exhibiting a complete view of our foreign relations since that time, 12 vols, 3rd edn, Boston, Thomas Wait, 1819

Stephen, J., *War in Disguise; Or the Frauds of Neutral Flags*, London, 1806

Vane, C., ed., *Correspondence, Despatches and other Papers of Viscount Castlereagh*, 12 vols, London, Henry Colburn, 1848–53

Warden, D., *A Statistical, Political and Historical Account of the United States of North America, from the Period of their first Colonization to the Present Day*, 3 vols, Edinburgh, Archibald Constable & Co, 1819

Wellington, 2nd Duke, ed., *Supplementary Despatches, Correspondence and Memoranda of Field Marshall Arthur Duke of Wellington*, 15 vols, London, John Murray, 1858–72, vol. III

Whitehill, W., ed., *The Journal of Lieutenant Henry Napier in HMS Nymphe: New England Blockaded - 1814*, Salem MA, Peabody Museum, 1939

Newspapers and Periodicals

British Library Newspaper Collection, Colindale, London, Institute of Historical Research, University of London and New York Historical Society

The American & Commercial Daily Advertiser

The Boston Gazette, Boston, 1812–15, BL:A263

The Columbian Centinel, Boston, 1812–15, BL:A259

The Hampshire Chronicle, Winchester, 1812

The London Gazette, 1807–1815

The Morning Post, London, 6 August 1807

The National Intelligencer, Washington, 1812–15, BL:A204

The Times, London, 1812–15

British Library, Euston, London, and Institute of Historical Research, University of London

The Annual Register, London 1812–15

The Edinburgh Review, 1813

The Weekly Register, H. Niles, Baltimore, vols II to VIII, 1812–15; vol. II, 1811–12; vols III & IV, 1812–13; vols V & VI, 1813–14; vols VII & VIII, 1814–15

SECONDARY SOURCES

Abramson, L., 'State Taxation of Exports: The Stream of Constitutionality', *North Carolina Law Review*, vol. 54, no. 59, 1975, pp. 59–82

Albion, R. and Pope, J., *Sea Lanes in Wartime: The American Experience 1775–1945*, 2nd edn, New York and Portland ME, Norton & Co/Archon Books, 1968

Adams, D., 'American Neutrality and Prosperity 1793–1808: A Reconsideration', *Journal of Economic History*, 40, 1980, pp. 713–37

Adams, H., *The Education of Henry Adams*, first publ. New York, 1907, rev. and ed. N. Saveth, London, New English Library, 1966

Anderson, F., *The Crucible of War: The Seven Years War and the Fate of Empire in British North America, 1754–1766*, London, Faber and Faber, 2000

Arthur, B., 'The Role of Blockade in the Anglo-American Naval War of 1812–14', unpublished MA dissertation, Greenwich Maritime Institute, Univ. of Greenwich, 2002

Balinky, A., *Albert Gallatin: Fiscal Theories and Policies*, New Brunswick NJ, Rutgers Univ. Press, 1958

—, 'Gallatin's Theory of War Finance', *William & Mary Historical Quarterly*, 3rd series, 1959, pp. 73–82

Barnes, G. and Owen, J., eds, *The Private Papers of John Montague Earl of Sandwich, First Lord of the Admiralty 1771–1782*, 4 vols, London, Navy Records Society, 1932, vol. I

Baugh, D., 'The Eighteenth Century Navy as a National Institution, 1690–1815', in *The Oxford History of the Royal Navy*, ed. J. Hill, 2nd edn, Oxford, OUP/BAC, 1995, pp. 120–160

—, 'Naval power: what gave the British Navy superiority?' in *Exceptionalism and Industrialisation: Britain and its European Rivals, 1688–1815*, ed. L. Escosura, Cambridge, Cambridge Univ. Press, 2004, pp. 235–57

—, 'The Politics of British Naval Failure, 1775–7', *American Neptune*, 52, Fall 1992, pp. 221–46

Baumber, M., *General at Sea: Robert Blake and the Revolution in Naval Warfare*, London, John Murray, 1989

Berens Matzke, R., 'Britain Gets its Way: Power and Peace in Anglo-American Relations, 1838–1846', *War in History*, 8 (1), 2001, pp. 19–46

Black, J., *Britain as a Military Power 1688–1815*, London, UCL Press, 1999

—, 'Naval Power, Strategy and Foreign Policy 1775–1791', in *Parameters of British Naval Power 1650–1850*, ed. M. Duffy, Exeter, Univ. of Exeter Press, 1992, pp. 93–120

Blaug, M., *Economic Theory in Retrospect*, 2nd edn, London, Heinemann, 1970

Bogart, E., *Economic History of the American People*, 2nd edn, New York, Longmans Green and Company, 1939

Bonnett, S., *The Price of Admiralty: An Indictment of the Royal Navy 1805–1960*, London, Hale, 1968

Borden, M., *Parties and Politics in the Early Republic 1789–1815*, London, Routledge & Kegan Paul, 1968

Brandt, I., *James Madison, Commander in Chief 1812–36*, 6 vols, New York, Bobbs-Merrill & Co Inc., 1961

Brenton, E., *The Naval History of Great Britain*, 2 vols, London, 1837

Broadley, A. and Bartelot, R., *Nelson's Hardy: His Life, Letters and Friends*, London, J. Murray, 1909

Buel, R., *America on the Brink: How the Political Struggle Over the War of 1812 Almost Destroyed the Young Republic*, New York and Basingstoke, Palgrave/Macmillan, 2005

—, *In Irons: Britain's Naval Supremacy and the American Revolutionary Economy*, New Haven, Yale Univ. Press, 1998

Burt, A., *The United States, Great Britain and British North America from the Revolution to the Establishment of Peace after the War of 1812*, New Haven, Yale Univ. Press, 1940

Byers, E., *The Nation of Nantucket: Society and Politics in an Early American Commercial Center 1660–1820*, Boston, Northeastern Univ. Press, 1987

Challis, C., *A New History of the Royal Mint*, Cambridge, Cambridge Univ. Press, 1992

Cipolla, C., *Between History and Economics: An Introduction to Economic History*, London, Blackwell, 1991

Clark, G., 'War Trade and Trade War 1701–1713', *Economic History Review*, 1, 1929, pp. 262–80

Clowes, W., *The Royal Navy: A History from the Earliest Times to the Present*, 6 vols, London, Sampson Low, Marston & Co, 1900

Cockton, P., *Subject Index of the House of Commons Parliamentary Papers 1801–1900*, Cambridge, Cambridge Univ. Press, 1988

Cole, A., *Wholesale Commodity Prices in the United States 1700–1861*, 2 vols, Cambridge MA, Harvard Univ. Press, 1938

Colledge, J., *Ships of the Royal Navy*, revised edn, London, Greenhill, 1987

The Concise Oxford Dictionary, Oxford, Oxford Univ. Press, 1964

Cooke, A., *Alistair Cooke's American Journey*, London, Allen Lane/Penguin, 2006

Corbett, J., *Some Principles of Maritime Strategy*, London, Longman, Green, 1911

Cordingly, D., *Cochrane the Dauntless: The Life and Adventures of Thomas Cochrane*, London, Bloomsbury, 2008

Crawley, C., ed., *The New Cambridge Modern History Volume IX War and Peace in the Age of Upheaval 1793–1830*, Cambridge, Cambridge Univ. Press, 1974

Crouzet, F., 'America and the crisis of the British imperial economy, 1803–1807' in *The Early Modern Atlantic Economy*, eds J. McCusker and K. Morgan, Cambridge, Cambridge Univ. Press, 2002, pp. 278–315

—, 'War, Blockade and Economic Change in Europe 1792–1815', *Journal of Economic History*, 24, 1964, pp. 567–90

Dangerfield, G., *The Era of Good Feelings*, London, Methuen, 1953

Davies, D., *A Brief History of Fighting Ships*, London, Constable, 1996; republ. Robinson, 2002

Davis, L. and Engerman, S., *Naval Blockades in Peace and War: An Economic History since 1750*, Cambridge, Cambridge Univ. Press, 2006

Davis, R., *The Industrial Revolution and British Overseas Trade*, 1st edn, Leicester Univ. Press, 1979; 2nd edn, London, Pinter, 1979

Deane, P. and Cole, W., *British Economic Growth 1688–1959*, 2nd edn, Cambridge, Cambridge Univ. Press, 1969

Decker, L. and Seager, R., eds, *America's Major Wars: Crusaders, Critics and Scholars 1775–1972*, 2 vols, Reading MA, Addison-Wesley, 1973, vol. 1 1775–1865

De Conde, A., *The Quasi War: The Politics and Diplomacy of the Undeclared War with France 1797–1801*, New York, Charles Scribner's Sons, 1966

Dewey, D., *Financial History of the United States*, 1st edn published 1903; 12th edn, New York, Kelly, 1934, repr. 1968

Dickinson, H., *Liberty and Property: Political Ideology in Eighteenth Century Britain*, London, Methuen, 1977

Dudley, W., 'Without Some Risk: A Reassessment of the British Blockade of the United States, 1812–1815', PhD dissertation, Tuscaloosa, Univ. of Alabama, 1999, published as *Splintering the Wooden Wall: The British Blockade of the United States, 1812–1815*, Annapolis MD, Naval Institute Press, 2003

Duffy, M., ed., 'Devon and the Naval Strategy of the French Wars, 1689–1815', in *The New Maritime History of Devon*, ed. M. Duffy et al., Exeter, Conway/Univ. of Exeter, 1992, vol. I, pp. 183–191

—, 'The Establishment of the Western Squadron as the Linchpin of British Naval Strategy', in *Parameters of British Naval Power 1650–1850*, ed. M. Duffy, Exeter, Univ. of Exeter Press, 1992, pp. 60–81

Dunne, W., 'The Inglorious First of June: Commodore Stephen Decatur in Long Island Sound, 1813', *The Long Island Historical Journal*, 2, Spring 1990, pp. 1–32

Ellerman, B. and Paine, S., *Naval Blockades and Seapower: strategies and counter-strategies 1805–2005*, London, Routledge, 2006

Engerman, S. and Gallman, R., eds, *The Cambridge Economic History of the United States, vol.II, The Long Nineteenth Century*, 3 vols, Cambridge, Cambridge Univ. Press, 2000

Escosura, L., ed., *Exceptionalism and Industrialisation, Britain and its European Rivals, 1688–1815*, Cambridge, Cambridge Univ. Press, 2004

Evans, E., *The Forging of the Modern State: Early Industrial Britain 1783–1870*, 2nd edn, London, Longman, 1996

Fergusson, C., ed., *Glimpses of Nova Scotia 1807–24*, Public Archives of Nova Scotia Bulletin 12, Halifax NS, 1957

Forester, C., *The Naval War of 1812*, London, Michael Joseph, 1957; republ. as *The Age of Fighting Sail*, London, New English Library, 1968

French, D., *The British Way in Warfare 1688–2000*, London, Hyman/Unwin, 1990

Friendly, A., *Beaufort of the Admiralty*, London, Hutchinson, 1977

Galpin, W., 'The American Grain Trade to the Spanish Peninsula 1810–14', *American Historical Review*, 28, 1922, pp. 24–44

—, *The Grain Supply of England during the Napoleonic period*, New York, 1925; repr. 1977

Gardiner, R., ed., *The Naval War of 1812*, London, Caxton Editions/NMM, 2001

Gilchrist, D., ed., *The Growth of the Seaport Cities, 1790–1825*, Charlottesville VA, Univ. of Virginia Press, 1967

Glete, J., *Navies and Nations: Warships, Navies and Statebuilding in Europe and America 1500–1860*, Stockholm, Almqvist & Wiksell, 1993, vol. 2

Goldenburg, J., 'Blue Lights and Infernal Machines – The British Blockade of New London', *Mariners' Mirror* 61, 1975, p. 385

—, 'The Royal Navy's Blockade in New England Waters 1812–1815', *International History Review*, 6, 1984, pp. 424–39

Graham, G., 'Considerations on the American War of Independence', *Bulletin of the Institute of Historical Research*, 22, 1949, p. 23

Gray, C., *The Leverage of Sea Power: The Strategic Advantage of Navies in War*, New York, Macmillan, 1992

Guernsey, R., *New York City & Vicinity during the War of 1812–15, being a Military, Civic and Financial Local History of that Period*, 2 vols, New York, Charles Woodward, 1889–95

Gutridge, A., 'Prize Agency 1800–1815 with special reference to the career and work of George Redmond Hulbert', unpublished MPhil dissertation, Univ. of Portsmouth, 1989

Gwyn, J., *Ashore and Afloat: the British Navy and the Halifax Naval Yard before 1820*, Ottowa, Univ. of Ottawa Press, 2004

—, *Frigates and Foremasts: The North America Squadron in Nova Scotia Waters 1745–1815*, Vancouver and Toronto, Univ. of British Columbia Press, 2003

Habakkuk, H., 'Britain and America: the economic effects of labour scarcity', in *Britain and America: Studies in Comparative History 1760–1970*, ed. D. Englander, New York and Milton Keynes, Yale Univ. Press/Open Univ. Press, 1997, pp. 51–81

Haines, M., 'The Population of the United States, 1790–1920', in *The Cambridge Economic History of the United States, Volume II – The Long Nineteenth Century*, eds S. Engerman and R. Gallman, 3 vols, Cambridge, Cambridge Univ. Press, 2000

Hall, C., *British Strategy in the Napoleonic Wars 1803–1815*, Manchester, Manchester Univ. Press, 1992

Hall, H., *American Navigation*, New York, Appletons, 1880

Hammond, M., *The Cotton Culture and the Cotton Trade*, New York, Macmillan, 1897

Harding, R., *The Evolution of the Sailing Navy, 1509–1815*, New York, St. Martin's Press, 1995

—, *Seapower and Naval Warfare 1650–1830*, London, UCL Press, 1999

Harlow, V. and Madden, F., eds, *British Colonial Developments 1774–1834: Select Documents*, Oxford, Clarendon Press, 1953

Hattendorf, J., *The Boundless Deep: The European Conquest of the Oceans, 1450–1840*, Providence RI, John Carter Brown Library, 2003

—, 'The Struggle with France, 1689–1815', in *The Oxford History of the Royal Navy*, ed. J. Hill, 2nd edn, Oxford, OUP/BAC, 1995, pp. 80–119

Hawkins, N., *The Starvation Blockades: Naval Blockades of WWI*, Barnsley, Leo Cooper, 2002

Hedges, J., *The Browns of Providence Plantations: vol. I, The Colonial Years*, and *vol. II, The Nineteenth Century*, 2 vols, Cambridge MA, Harvard Univ. Press, 1952; 2nd edn Providence RI, Brown Univ. Press, 1968

Hickey, D., 'American Trade Restrictions during the War of 1812', *The Journal of American History*, 68 (3), 1981, pp. 517–38

—, *The War of 1812: A Forgotten Conflict*, Urbana IL, Univ. of Illinois Press, 1989

Hidy, R., *The House of Baring in American Trade and Finance*, Cambridge MA, Harvard Univ. Press, 1949, and New York, Russell & Russell, 1949, reprinted 1970

Hill, R., *The Prizes of War: The Naval Prize System in the Napoleonic Wars 1793–1815*, Stroud, Sutton/Royal Naval Museum Publications, 1998

Hillard, S., et al., eds, *Life, Letters, and Journals of George Ticknor*, 2 vols, Boston, James R. Osgood and Co., 1876

Hodges, H. and Hughes, E., *Select Naval Documents*, Cambridge, Cambridge Univ. Press, 1922

Hope, R., *A New History of British Shipping*, London, Murray, 1990

Horsman, R., *The War of 1812*, London, Eyre & Spottiswood, 1969, New York, A. Knopf, 1969

Hudson, P., *The Industrial Revolution*, London, Arnold, 1993

Hume, E., ed. 'Letters Written During the War of 1812 by the British Commander in American Waters – Admiral Sir David Milne', *William & Mary Historical Quarterly*, 2nd series, 10 (4), 1930, pp. 279–96

Hutchins, J., *The American Maritime Industries and Public Policy 1789–1914: An Economic History*, Cambridge MA, Harvard Univ. Press, 1941

Hutchison, J., *The Press-Gang Afloat and Ashore*, London, G. Bell & Sons, 1913

Jackson, J., ed., *The Oxford Book of Money*, Oxford, Oxford Univ. Press, 1995

Jackson, S., 'Impressment and Anglo-American Discord 1787–1818', unpublished PhD dissertation, Univ. of Michigan, 1976

James, T., *Prisoners of War in Dartmoor Towns: French and American Officers on Parole, 1803–1815*, Newton Abbot, Orchard Publications, 2000

Johnson, E., *The History of the Domestic and Foreign Commerce of the United States*, 2 vols, Washington DC, Columbia, Carnegie Institute, 1915

Johnson, P., *A History of the American People*, London, Weidenfeld & Nicolson, 1997

Jones, P., *An Economic History of the United States*, London, Routledge and Kegan Paul, 1956, repr. 1969

Kay, de J., *Chronicles of the Frigate* Macedonian *1809–1922*, New York, W. Norton & Co, 1995

Keble-Chatterton, E., *The Big Blockade*, 3rd edn, London, Hurst & Blackett Ltd, 1938

Kelly, E., *Spanish Dollars and Silver Tokens: An Account of the Issues of the Bank of England 1797–1816*, London, Spink & Son, 1976

Kennedy, P., *The Rise and Fall of British Naval Mastery*, London, Allen Lane, 1976

Kert, F., 'Cruising in Colonial Waters: The Organisation of North American Privateering in the War of 1812', in *Pirates & Privateers: New Perspectives on the War on Trade in the 18th and 19th Centuries*, eds D. Starkey et al., Exeter, Univ. of Exeter Press, 1997

—, 'The Fortunes of War: Commercial Warfare and Maritime Risk in the War of 1812', *Northern Mariner*, 8 (4), 1998, pp. 1–16

—, *Prize and Prejudice: Privateering and Naval Prize in Atlantic Canada in the War of 1812*, Research in Maritime History 11, International Maritime Economic History Association, St John's, Newfoundland, 1997

Killick, J., 'The Atlantic Economy and Anglo-American Industrialization, 1783–1865', in *Liberal Capitalism: Political and Economic Aspects*, Milton Keynes, Open Univ. Press, 1997, pp. 87–102

Knight, R., 'The Introduction of Copper Sheathing into the Royal Navy, 1779–86', *Mariners' Mirror*, 59, 1973, pp. 209–309

—, Review in *Journal of Imperial and Commonwealth History*, 32 (3), 2004, pp. 132–3

—, 'The Royal Dockyards in England at the Time of the American War of Independence', PhD thesis, London, 1972

Lambert, A., 'Introduction', in *The Naval War of 1812*, ed. R. Gardiner, London, Caxton Editions/NMM, 2001

—, *War at Sea in the Age of Sail 1650–1850*, London, Cassel & Co, 2000

Langford, P., *Modern British Foreign Policy: The Eighteenth Century 1688–1815*, London, A & C Black, 1976

Latimer, J., *1812: War with America*, Cambridge MA, and London, Belknap Press/Harvard Univ. Press, 2007

Lavery, B., *Nelson's Navy: The Ships, Men and Organisation 1793–1815*, London, Conway Maritime Press/Brassey's, 1989

Lipscomb, A. and Bergh, A., eds, *Thomas Jefferson's Writings*, 20 vols, New York, 1903

Lipsey, R., 'U.S. Trade and Balance of Payments 1800–1913', in *The Cambridge Economic History of the United States, vol. II, The Long Nineteenth Century*, eds S. Engerman and R. Gallman, 3 vols, Cambridge Univ. Press, 2000

Lloyd, C., 'Armed Forces and the Art of War: Navies', in *The New Cambridge Modern History, Volume IX: War and Peace in an Age of Upheaval 1793–1830*, ed. C. Crawley, Cambridge, Cambridge Univ. Press, 1974, pp. 76–90

Lohnes, B., 'British Naval Problems at Halifax During the War of 1812', *Mariners' Mirror*, 59, 1973, pp. 328–35

—, 'A New Look at the Invasion of Eastern Maine, 1814', *Maine Historical Society Quarterly* 15, 1975, pp. 8–9

Lyons, D., *The Sailing Navy List*, London, Conway Maritime Press, 1993

McCusker, J., *How Much is That in Real Money? A historical price index for use as a deflator of money values in the economy of the United States*, Worcester MA, American Antiquarian Society, 1992; 2nd edn, Providence RI, Oak Knoll Press, 2001

— and Morgan, K., eds, *The Early Modern Atlantic Economy*, Cambridge, Cambridge Univ. Press, 2002

Mackesy, P., *The War for America 1775–1783*, London, Longman, 1964

McMaster, J., *A History of the People of the United States*, 7 vols, New York, D. Appleton & Co, 1902

Mahan, A., *The Influence of Sea Power upon the French Revolution and Empire*, 2 vols, London, Sampson Low, Marston & Co, 1893

—, *Sea Power in its Relation to the War of 1812*, 2 vols, Boston MA and London, Little Brown/Sampson, Marston Low and Company, 1905

Mahon, J., *The War of 1812*, Gainesville FL, Univ. of Florida Press, 1972, republ. De Capo Press, 1991

Markham, C., ed., *Selections from the Correspondence of Admiral John Markham During the Years 1801–4 and 1806–7*, London, Navy Records Society 28, 1904

Marsden, M., ed., *The Law and Custom of the Sea*, 2 vols, London, Navy Records Society, 1915–16

Marvin, W., *The American Merchant Marine*, New York, Charles Scribner's Sons, 1902

—, *Registered & Enrolled Tonnage 1800–1901*, US Bureau of Navigation, New York, Charles Scribner's Sons, 1902

Mayo, B., ed., *Instructions to British Ministers to the United States 1791-1812*, 3 vols, Washington DC, Annual Report to the American History Association, 1936, vol. III

Merriman, R., ed., *Queen Anne's Navy: Documents concerning the Administration of the Navy of Queen Anne, 1702-14*, London, Navy Records Society publications 103, 1961

Michell, J., 'Vexing your Neighbours for a Little Muck, British Prize-taking during the Seven Years War, 1756-63', Staff Seminar Lecture, NMM, London, 16 May 2007

Minor, D., *World Canals 1810-1819*, New York, Facts on File, 1986

Mitchell, B. and Deane, P., *Abstract of British Historical Statistics*, Cambridge, Cambridge Univ. Press, 1962

Morison, S., *The Life and Letters of Harrison Gray Otis, Federalist, 1765-1848*, 2 vols, Boston MA, Houghton Mifflin Co, 1913

Morriss, R., *Cockburn and the British Navy in Transition: Admiral Sir George Cockburn 1772-1853*, Exeter, Univ. of Exeter Press, 1997

—, *Guide to British Naval Papers in North America*, London and New York, NMM/Mansell, 1994

Murphy, B., *A History of the British Economy 1086-1970*, London, Longman, 1973

Nettels, C., *The Emergence of a National Economy 1775-1815, The Economic History of the United States vol. II*, New York and London, Harper & Row, 1969

North, D., *The Economic Growth of the United States 1790-1860*, New York, Prentice Hall Inc., 1961; repr. New York, W. Norton & Co, 1966

—, 'United States Balance of Payments 1790-1860', in *Trends in the American Economy in the Nineteenth Century*, Studies in Income and Wealth 24, National Bureau of Economic Research, Princeton, Princeton Univ. Press, 1960; repr. New York, Arno Press, 1975, pp. 573-628

— and Thomas, R., eds, *The Growth of the American Economy to 1860: Documentary History of the United States*, New York, Harper & Row, 1968

O'Brien, P., 'The Impact of the Revolutionary and Napoleonic Wars on the Long-run Growth of the British Economy', *Fernand Braudel Centre Review*, 12, 1989

—, *War and Economic Progress in Britain and America*, Milton Keynes, Open Univ. Press, 1997

O'Connell, D., *The Influence of Law on Sea Power*, Manchester, Manchester Univ. Press, 1975

Oddie, G., 'The Circulation of Silver, 1697-1817', Lecture to London Numismatic Club, Warburg Institute, 6 July 2004

Osborne, E., *Britain's Economic Blockade of Germany 1914-1919*, London, Frank Cass, 2004

The Oxford Dictionary of National Biography, Oxford, Oxford Univ. Press, 2004

Pack, J., *The Man who Burned the White House: Admiral Sir George Cockburn, 1772-1853*, Emsworth, Kenneth Mason, 1987

Padfield, P., *Broke and The Shannon*, London, Hodder & Stoughton, 1968

Pares, R., *Colonial Blockade and Neutral Rights 1739-1763*, Oxford, Clarendon Press, 1938

Perkins, B., *Castlereagh and Adams: England and the United States 1812-23*, Berkeley CA, Univ. of California Press, 1964

—, *Prologue to War: England & the United States 1805-12*, Berkeley CA, Univ. of California, 1961

Perkins, E., *American Public Finance and Public Services 1700-1815*, Columbus OH, Ohio State Univ. Press, 1994

Plumb, J., *England in the Eighteenth Century 1714–1815*, Harmondsworth, Pelican, 1950

Prados, L., ed., *Exceptionalim & Industrialisation: Britain and its European Rivals 1688–1815*, Cambridge, Cambridge Univ. Press, 2004

Richardson, J., *A Compilation of Messages and Papers of Presidents of the United States*, 10 vols, Washington DC, Govt. Printing Office, 1896–99

Richmond, H., *Statesmen and Seapower*, Oxford, Clarendon Press, 1946

Rockoff, H., 'Banking and Finance 1789–1914', in *The Cambridge Economic History of the United States, vol. II: The Long Nineteenth Century*, eds S. Engerman and R. Gallman, Cambridge, Cambridge Univ. Press, 2000

Rodger, N., *The Command of the Ocean: A Naval History of Britain 1649–1815*, London, Allen Lane/Penguin/NMM, 2004

Roosevelt, T., 'The Naval War of 1812', in *The Royal Navy: A History from the Earliest Times to the Present*, W. Clowes, 7 vols, London, Sampson Low, Marston & Co, 1897–1903, vol. VI, 1901,

Roskill, S., *The Strategy of Sea Power: Its Development and Application*, first publ. London, Collins, 1962; republ. Aylesbury, John Goodchild, 1986

Sainty, J., *Admiralty Officials 1660–1870*, London, Athelone Press, 1975

Schroeder, P., *Oxford History of Modern Europe: The Transformation of European Politics 1763–1848*, Oxford, Clarendon Press, 1994

Schumpeter, E., 'English Prices and Public Finance 1660–1822', *Review of Economic Statistics*, 20 (1), 1938, 21–37

Scott, K., *British Aliens in the United States during the War of 1812*, Baltimore MD, Genealogical Publishing, 1979

Silberling, N., 'The financial and monetary policy of Great Britain during the Napoleonic Wars', *Quarterly Journal of Economics*, 38, 1924, pp. 215–27

Skaggs, D. and Altoff, G., *Signal Victory: The Lake Erie Campaign 1812–13*, Annapolis MD, Naval Institute Press, 1997

Stacey, C., 'Another Look at the Battle of Lake Erie', *Canadian Historical Review*, 39, 1958, pp. 41–51

Stagg, J., *Mr Madison's War: Politics, Diplomacy and Warfare in the Early American Republic 1783–1830*, Princeton, Princeton Univ. Press, 1983

Stephen, J. and Piggott, F., ed., *War in Disguise: or the frauds of neutral flags reprinted for this edition*, London, Univ. of London Press, 1917

Syrett, D., *The Royal Navy in American Waters, 1775–1783*, Aldershot, Scolar, 1989

Taylor, G., *Economic History of US*, New York, 1951

Thistlethwaite, F., *America and the Atlantic Community: Anglo-American Aspects, 1790–1850*, Philadelphia, Univ. of Pennsylvania Press, 1959

—, 'The United States and the Old World, 1794–1828', in *The New Cambridge Modern History Volume IX War and Peace in the Age of Upheaval 1793–1830*, C. W. Crawley ed., Cambridge, Cambridge Univ. Press, 1974, pp. 591–611

Thompson, N., *Earl Bathurst and the British Empire*, Barnsley, Leo Cooper, 1999

Toll, I., *Six Frigates: How Piracy, War and British Supremacy at Sea gave Birth to the World's Most Powerful Navy*, London, Penguin/Michael Joseph, 2006

Townley, L., 'Sir William Scott, Lord Stowell, and the Development of the Prize Law in the High Courts of Admiralty, 1798–1828, with Particular Reference to the Rights of Belligerents', unpublished thesis, University of Birmingham, 1994

Tracy, N., *Attack on Maritime Trade*, Toronto, Univ. of Toronto Press, 1991

—, ed., *The Naval Chronicle: The Contemporary Record of the Royal Navy at War*, consolidated edn, 5 vols, London, Chatham Publishing, 1999

Tucker, S. P. and Reuter, F. T., *Injured Honor: The Chesapeake–Leopard Affair, June 22,*

1807, Annapolis MD, Naval Institute Press, 1996

Updyke, F., *The Diplomacy of the War of 1812: The Albert Shaw Lectures on Diplomatic History 1914*, Baltimore MD, John Hopkins Univ. Press, 1915

US Bureau of the Census, *Historical Statistics of the United States from Colonial Times to 1970*, Washington DC, 1975, and Supplement, to 1st edn, 1960, 1957

US War Department, *Instructions for American Servicemen in Britain*, Washington, 1942, republ. Oxford, Bodleian Library, Univ. of Oxford, 2004

US Works Progress Administration, *Boston Looks Seaward*, Boston MA, 1941, republ. London, MacDonald and Jane's, 1974

Vane, C., *Memoirs and Correspondence of Viscount Castlereagh*, 12 vols, London, H. Colburn, 1848–53

Walters, R., *Albert Gallatin: Jeffersonian Financier and Diplomat*, New York, Macmillan, 1957

Warren, G. and Pearson, F., *Wholesale Prices for 213 Years, 1720 to 1932, Part 1, Wholesale Prices in the United States for 135 Years from 1797 to 1932*, Ithaca NY, Cornell Univ., Agricultural Experimental Station, 1932

Watson, G., 'The United States and the Peninsula War, 1802–12', *Historical Journal*, 19, 1976, pp. 870–79

Webster, C., *The Foreign Policy of Castlereagh, vol. 1, 1812–15, Britain and the Reconstruction of Europe*, London, Bell & Sons, 1950

Wright, C., *Economic History of the United States*, 2nd edn, New York, McGraw-Hill, 1949

Yonge, C., *The Life and Administration of Robert Banks Jenkinson 2nd Earl of Liverpool*, 3 vols, London, Macmillan and Co, 1868

Zevin, R., *The Growth of Manufacturing in Early Nineteenth Century New England*, New York, Arno, 1975

INDEX

Note: People are listed surname first, with *vessels* and *newspapers* named in italics.